SQL SERVER DEVELOPER'S GUIDE TO OLAP WITH ANALYSIS SERVICES

SQL SERVER™ DEVELOPER'S GUIDE TO OLAP WITH ANALYSIS SERVICES

Mike Gunderloy
Tim Sneath

SYBEX®

San Francisco • Paris • Düsseldorf • Soest • London

Associate Publisher: Richard Mills
Contracts and Licensing Manager: Kristine O'Callaghan
Acquisitions and Developmental Editor: Denise Santoro Lincoln
Editor: Susan Berge
Production Editor: Mae Lum
Technical Editor: Dianne Siebold
Book Designer: Robin Kibby
Graphic Illustrator: Tony Jonick
Electronic Publishing Specialist: Kris Warrenburg
Proofreaders: Nanette Duffy, Nelson Kim, Mae Lum, Laurie
O'Connell, Nancy Riddiough
Indexer: Nancy Guenther
CD Coordinator: Christine Harris
CD Technician: Kevin Ly
Cover Designer: Design Site
Cover Illustrator/Photographer: Jack D. Myers

Library of Congress Card Number: 2001089818
ISBN: 0-7821-2957-9

Manufactured in the United States of America
10 9 8 7 6 5 4 3 2 1

This one's for Adam, who helped type some of it.
M.G.

To my wife, Louise, with my enduring love.
T.S.

ACKNOWLEDGMENTS

We'd like to thank the publishing and editorial teams that saw this project from original outline to published book: Richard Mills, Denise Santoro Lincoln, Mae Lum, Susan Berge, and Dianne Siebold. Thanks also to Dan Mummert, who helped us keep track of software for the CD, and Kris Warrenburg, who got everything into its final form.

Thanks to Angie Mogenson from ProClarity, Tanya Pobuda and Melissa Beresford from Cognos, and Keith Cauthen from Hungry Dog Software for arranging for copies of software. Dave Stearns from Microsoft deserves the credit for getting Mike into the OLAP field in the first place and introducing him to the wonderful world of MDX.

Thanks to Tim's friends and colleagues at Microsoft for their support and encouragement: John, Steve, Jenny, Lillie, Dave, Matt, Paul, and Debs. You guys are great! Also to his family, who have always supported him through thick and thin. Finished at last!

Mike's partners at MCW Technologies were always available for phone calls, whether to discuss technical information or just to chat while ignoring deadlines.

Of course, none of these people are responsible for the errors that we hope are not present in this book.

And as always, Mike wants to express his deepest thanks to Dana Jones for helping cook dinner, feed chickens, run errands, change diapers, carry firewood, weed the garden, and do everything else around the farm. Books are much easier to write when life is good.

CONTENTS AT A GLANCE

CONTENTS

INTRODUCTION

In 1996, Microsoft acquired the technology and development resources of a little company named Panorama Software Systems, and a new project, code-named Microsoft Plato, was born. That was the origin of Microsoft's entry into the Online Analytical Processing, or OLAP, field. Several years later Plato saw the light of day as Microsoft OLAP Services, a component of Microsoft SQL Server 7.0. Renamed Microsoft Analysis Services in its most recent incarnation, this software is the subject of this book.

Analysis Services is devoted to a single task: helping you make sense of large amounts of data. For example, Analysis Services can help you find the patterns in many gigabytes of data. A typical candidate for investigation with Analysis Services would be detailed store sales receipts for an entire supermarket chain over a period of years. Faced with such an overwhelming mass of detail, how do you find the trends? Which products sold best in which regions? Do some products sell better in the evening than in the morning? Answering such questions requires the dual ability to summarize data and to quickly drill into the summaries looking for patterns—tasks at which Analysis Services excels.

The amazing thing about Panorama and Microsoft is that they saw five years ago that this was going to be a commodity market, instead of a highly specialized (and expensive) one. OLAP software was already in production in 1996, but for the most part it had five-figure or higher price tags and required intensive training to use. Microsoft put OLAP within the reach of nearly anyone with business data to analyze, by including it in the Microsoft SQL Server box.

This was a smart move. In 1996, if you had a new computer, you might have had a 1-gigabyte hard drive. Now, new computers routinely have 50 gigabytes or more of storage, and it's not unusual for a database server to have hundreds of gigabytes, or even a terabyte or more, of storage. And all of that space is rapidly filling with data. Without tools for finding patterns, that data will never become useful information.

In this book, we're going to help you understand and use Microsoft SQL Server Analysis Services. We'll cover the basic concepts of OLAP and data mining, and show you how you can use Analysis Services through its graphical user interface. Then we'll dig into some of the programmatic ways to connect Analysis Services data to your own applications. By the end of the book, you should be well prepared to tackle a data analysis project of your own.

Chapter Walkthrough

The book contains twelve chapters and four appendices. You'll find all of the sample code from the chapters on the companion CD. For more information on the CD contents, see the last page of the book or the file readme.htm in the root directory of the CD itself.

The first three chapters give you an overview of Analysis Services. Chapter 1, "OLAP and Data Mining Concepts," sets the stage by giving you the terminology you need to understand OLAP. Chapter 2, "Analysis Services Architecture," builds on this to show you the major components of Microsoft's implementation of OLAP. In Chapter 3, "Analysis Services Lifecycle," we discuss how you can fit the pieces together to develop and maintain OLAP applications using Analysis Services.

The next two chapters discuss the user interface that Analysis Services presents through its Analysis Manager application. Chapter 4, "Using Analysis Services," covers the basics of building and analyzing OLAP cubes with Analysis Services and takes a brief look at third-party tools as well. Chapter 5, "Advanced Analysis Services," discusses more advanced topics such as write-enabled cubes, real-time cubes, drillthrough, and custom actions. When you've finished these chapters, you'll be prepared to harness the power of Analysis Services in exploring your own data.

Chapter 6, "Querying Analysis Services with MDX," introduces the Multidimensional Expression (MDX) querying language. This language, an extension of the standardized SQL language, is essential for retrieving data from OLAP cubes. You'll see how to understand MDX queries and construct your own queries.

The next two chapters dig into ADO/MD, the multidimensional extension to Microsoft's ActiveX Data Objects software. Chapter 7, "Building Analysis Services Applications with ADO/MD Part I: Cube Schema Objects," discusses the use of ADO/MD objects to retrieve the structure of an OLAP cube and its components, while Chapter 8, "Building Analysis Services Applications with ADO/MD Part II: Query Retrieval Objects," shows how you can use ADO/MD in conjunction with MDX to make data from Analysis Services available in your own applications.

Two other programmatic interfaces to Analysis Services are useful for more advanced purposes. Chapter 9, "Advanced Usage of the PivotTable Service," is devoted to the client-side analog of Analysis Services, which can be used for a substantial subset of OLAP operations without a dedicated Analysis Services server. Chapter 10, "Managing an Analysis Services Environment Using DSO," discusses the object model that is used by Analysis Manager itself to create and edit Analysis Services objects. You'll see how you can use DSO to create new OLAP cubes from your own code.

The last two chapters discuss extensions to the core OLAP functionality of Analysis Services. Chapter 11, "Building Data Mining Solutions with Analysis Services," discusses the data mining extensions that were added to Analysis Services in its SQL Server 2000 release. Chapter 12, "Supporting Natural Language Queries with English Query," discusses the integration of Analysis Services with Microsoft English Query, an application for allowing your users to ask for information without having to learn MDX.

Finally, the four appendices provide reference information on the MDX query language and on the various object models that make up the programmatic interface for Analysis Services.

Keeping Up to Date

This book was written in late 2000 and early 2001 using the then-current versions of the software it discusses:

- SQL Server 2000 Analysis Services

- Visual Basic 6.0 with Service Pack 4

- Windows 2000 with Service Pack 1

We've chosen to provide sample code in Visual Basic because it's a widely used language that can be used with all of the programming interfaces that Analysis Services supports. You can, of course, use many other languages to communicate with an Analysis Services server.

Inevitably, the software we've written about will be updated. Sharp-eyed readers will let us know when they find bugs. If we have any major changes to the samples, we'll make copies available on the Sybex web site, www.sybex.com.

If you do find any problems with the samples or have any other questions or suggestions, we're happy to get e-mail from our readers. You can reach us at our addresses of MikeG1@larkfarm.com and tim@sneath.org. Of course, we can't guarantee an answer to every question, but we'll do our best.

About the CD

The companion CD contains the following:

- All of the sample code and applications from the book, including the complete OLAP Workbench application from Chapter 8

- The data for the sample SQL Server databases used in the book examples, together with instructions for loading this data to your own SQL Server

- Instructions for creating the CallsCube OLAP cube used in the examples for Chapter 6

- Internet links to OLAP tool vendors and other useful web sites

- An evaluation version of ProClarity Corporation's ProClarity
- "The Cognos-Microsoft Solution," a white paper from Cognos
- An evaluation version of Hungry Dog Software's IntelliBrowser

To use the CD content, just insert it into your CD-ROM drive. The CD's installation program should launch automatically. If you've turned off AutoPlay, you can open the file readme.htm in the root directory of the CD to get started.

CHAPTER 1

OLAP and Data Mining Concepts

- Turning Data into Information

- Traditional Database Systems

- Data Analysis with OLAP

- Applying OLAP in Your Organization

- Limitations of OLAP

In this chapter, we'll take a look at what online analytical processing (usually referred to simply as OLAP) means and how it can help you in your own projects. We'll discuss some of the business problems that many organizations face relating to information management and explain how OLAP helps solve such problems. We'll then proceed to describe the basic database concepts that underpin "analytical" or multidimensional databases, and how OLAP can help your organization get the most out of the information it stores. This chapter will help you answer these questions:

- What does OLAP mean?

- What relevance does it have to my organization?

- What are the differences between relational and multidimensional databases?

- What are the differences between "data warehouse," "data mart," and "data mining"?

If you're already familiar with the general concepts behind data analysis, you might want to either skim this chapter or go directly to the next chapter, where we'll discuss the features and capabilities of Analysis Services, part of Microsoft SQL Server 2000.

NOTE   SQL Server 7.0 introduced OLAP capabilities in a component named OLAP Services. In SQL Server 2000, this component has been renamed Analysis Services, to reflect its extension beyond simple OLAP into the realm of data mining. We'll briefly discuss data mining in Chapter 11, "Building Data Mining Solutions with Analysis Services."

Turning Data into Information

We live in a data-rich world. Organizations across the globe have vast database systems containing all kinds of data related to their business operations.

Make a mental estimate of the number of different IDs, account numbers, and other references you have been allocated by the various institutions you regularly deal with: it's likely that an awful lot of companies have your details on file. Now multiply that number by the number of customers each of those organizations has worldwide, and you just begin to get a sense of the sheer quantity of customer-specific data that's available to these organizations. But how do they manage that data? In particular, how does such an organization bracket their customers for marketing purposes?

The problem with data is that, by itself, it doesn't mean anything. For example, a single field in a database might contain the value "345". Without knowing whether that's a customer ID, a price, or an item number, you can't extract any information from the data. Data itself, without interpretation, is largely meaningless. Data plus interpretation and analysis adds up to information, a much more valuable commodity than raw data. Sometimes information is distributed across multiple pieces of data. For example, no single entry in a sales database will identify frequent buyers of a particular product. The information as to which customers are frequent buyers is spread across multiple pieces of data. Extracting this sort of information from a mass of data is one of the most challenging aspects of database analysis.

Most organizations these days rely on database systems to keep their businesses running. From payroll to stock control, from the help desk to the sales executive, databases keep track of the operations of an organization. With the recent Y2K issues just behind us, companies are freshly aware of the importance that their IT systems have in keeping businesses alive. The new "Internet economy" is increasing still further the need for organizations to have information resources that enable them both to handle customers more effectively and to identify changing trends and new market opportunities.

The key to companies understanding their business is, therefore, better analysis of the information they possess on their customers, operations, staff, and processes. Without knowing their own strengths and weaknesses, a company can do little in the face of a rapidly changing marketplace.

As an example of the problem, imagine that you are a store manager for a nationwide chain of retail supermarkets. Suppose for a moment that you are given a large box containing all the paper cash register receipts for the last week's transactions. It'll no doubt be a big box containing thousands of receipts and tens of thousands of individual sale items. Now your boss calls you, wanting to know some information about the performance of your store over this time period:

- What was the most popular item your store sold over the last week?
- What was the *least* popular item?
- Which department took the most money for sale items?
- Which checkout operator was the most efficient, and which was the least efficient?
- What was the overall average value of a customer's shopping basket?

Well, you've got all the information at your fingertips: every sale is recorded on a receipt, and all the data necessary to answer each of the above questions is at hand. But how do you go about getting the answers when you've got to sort through all those receipts manually? Answering these kinds of questions would be an almost impossible challenge using purely paper-based means. Yet not only are the questions relevant; in fact, the answers are absolutely central knowledge for the business to understand how it is operating, where it can improve its efficiency, and how to maximize profits and revenue.

If you had enough time to analyze all the receipts, there's no reason why it would not be possible to answer the questions. You'd have to sort through the receipts one by one, tallying up the individual product sales until you got to a total figure, then sorting those figures by department and checkout operator, as well as calculating averages to enable you to answer the last question asked. But it would be a very repetitive task. Of course, repetitive tasks are *exactly* the kinds of things computers are well suited for.

The sad thing is that even with the incredible amount of computing power that most organizations possess, answering these kinds of questions is still tough for a lot of companies. Many business managers are still frustrated by the lack of access they have to the information they need. Getting management reports in some organizations still takes weeks or even months—if the desired information is even available at all.

Fortunately, there is an answer to this problem. What's needed is a different type of database system than the traditional relational database. Such a system needs to be able to take extracts of data from an operational system, to summarize the data into working totals, and to present that data to the end users of the system intuitively. This is the realm of OLAP, or *online analytical processing*.

Traditional Database Systems

Although much data is stored in databases, those databases are rarely optimized for the kinds of analysis discussed in the previous section. Most database information is stored in OLTP systems. OLTP stands for *online transaction processing* and describes a distributed or centralized system that is typically designed to handle a large number of concurrent database connections, with each either inserting, updating, or querying a small number of records. Examples of the kinds of transactions that might involve an OLTP system include the following:

- Insert a record into the sales database for customer 325903, showing a purchase of a number of items.

- Show all purchases made by customer 583472 that have not yet been invoiced.

- Update the details for supplier 1032 to show a change of company address.

These transactions share a couple of attributes in common:

- They operate on a very small number of discrete rows of data at a particular time.

- The context of each operation requires that the data is as up-to-date as possible with the real-world environment to which the data maps.

- They need an almost instantaneous response if the users of the system are to be satisfied with the performance of the application.

The above examples are not unusual. Other systems that share these characteristics include stock control systems, billing systems, customer management systems, and help desk systems, among many others. Generally, OLTP applications allow their users to manipulate individual (or at least a small quantity of) data records at any one time.

To achieve this, modern database systems are usually *relational* and *highly normalized*. A relational database holds its information in several individual linked tables. Each table contains data on a particular entity (for example, customers, sales, products, stores, etc.). Where there is a semantic link between two tables, those tables are joined together by means of a relationship. Relationships are created by one field in a table acting as a pointer to matching records in another table. For example, a table of orders will often contain a field that holds a customer number that matches the customer number in a table of customers.

The secret to a database system being optimized for OLTP usage is *normalization*. Normalization is a process of removing redundancy from database structures. Wherever a table contains information duplicated across multiple rows for an individual entity, that information can be split off into a separate table.

As an example, consider a database that might handle payroll information for a company. This database will likely need to store information concerning individual employees and their job positions. Table 1.1 is an example of the type of information that could be stored in this environment.

TABLE 1.1: Sample Payroll Table

Surname	Forename	Payroll #	Job Position	Grade
Smith	Harry	384192	Developer	F
O'Connell	Julia	349283	Senior Developer	G
Ahmed	Aleena	321458	Senior Developer	G
Matthews	Gloria	358299	Project Manager	H

Note the duplication of Job Position and Grade data in the second and third rows of the table. In a normalized relational database, we want to have a table containing information on individual employees, as well as a separate table that stores information on positions within the company. By giving each position a unique reference (or ID), we can connect the *Employees* table to the *Positions* table. Tables 1.2 and 1.3 demonstrate how this relationship might be implemented in the database.

TABLE 1.2: Sample Employees Table

Surname	Forename	Payroll #	Position ID
Smith	Harry	384192	1
O'Connell	Julia	349283	2
Ahmed	Aleena	321458	2
Matthews	Gloria	358299	3

TABLE 1.3: Sample Positions Table

Position ID	Job Position	Grade
1	Developer	F
2	Senior Developer	G
3	Project Manager	H

A relational structure works well for OLTP databases. Columns within tables can be indexed to ensure that individual records can be quickly retrieved or filtered. Normalizing data removes (or at least greatly reduces) data redundancy, ensuring that changes to data get reflected across all affected rows and minimizing the chances of inconsistencies across the database.

Unfortunately, the structures that work so well for day-to-day operational use of such a database do not work as well for answering the kinds of questions we asked our beleaguered store manager earlier. OLTP systems are designed for very high levels of data throughput; they may well contain many millions of rows of data per table, but since the operations they handle typically involve just a few specific rows at a time, they deliver great performance levels.

OLTP databases are almost always *transactional* as well. A transactional database is one that helps ensure that updates to multiple tables are performed consistently. Transactional features add overhead to a database, but they're essential for a database where data is changed frequently.

TIP   For a more detailed introduction to normalization and transactions, see Mike Gunderloy and Joseph L. Jorden's book, *Mastering SQL Server 2000* (Sybex, 2000).

Now take a very real business-oriented question such as, "Which product has lost the largest percentage of market share over time?" Ask those same database systems to categorize and summarize those millions of rows of data to answer such an analytical query, and they choke.

Data Analysis with OLAP

Fundamentally, the analytical or querying tasks that we want to use for a large amount of data require a very different kind of database design, tuned for handling more general, exploratory queries. Such a design is often classified as an *OLAP database*. An OLAP database, as distinct from a relational database, is designed primarily for handling exploratory queries rather than updates. By storing the data in a structure that is optimized for analytical purposes, OLAP solutions provide faster and more intuitive analysis capabilities than traditional environments. In addition, OLAP databases dispense with some of the features of OLTP databases (such as transactional processing), because they typically contain data that is never edited, only added to.

OLAP databases are focused specifically on the problem of data analysis. They give rapid responses to complex queries involving large amounts of data because of two distinct attributes:

- Rather than storing data in a purely relational database format, OLAP databases are normally stored in a "multidimensional" data structure. (In fact, this is a slightly simplistic statement compared to the real world, as we shall see in later chapters, but it is at least true that the optimum structure for the information we are storing is multidimensional.)

- They perform some of the summary calculations before the user requests them. By providing general information on the structure of the underlying data, an OLAP environment can precalculate totals and averages that enable the system to respond quickly to a user, even if their query requires analysis of thousands or millions of rows of data to answer.

These two concepts are crucial to the performance of OLAP and, more important, in terms of its underlying architecture.

NOTE   Several (more or less) synonymous terms are used within the computing industry to describe "analytical" databases as discussed within this book. In particular, you will sometimes hear the term "decision support" used in place of OLAP. The older term "executive information system (EIS)" has fallen out of fashion.

Comparing OLTP and OLAP Databases

The design of OLAP systems is fundamentally different from the design of OLTP systems. Many of the overriding principles of traditional, relational database designs are even the opposite of the best practices in OLAP multidimensional database designs.

For example, relational database designers strive to minimize or eliminate data redundancy within their schemas. Instead of having information duplicated across multiple rows of data, relational databases use normalization techniques to store pointers to duplicated information.

So a database containing books and their authors would separate book information from author information into tables to ensure that if, for example, an author changed their address details, the change would only need to be made in one location (specifically, the Authors table). Conversely, in an OLAP database design, redundancy is not only acceptable, it is positively encouraged! By reducing normalization and keeping multiple copies of information, the query processor can go to a single part of the database to obtain all relevant information, thus improving performance. Of course, there are tradeoffs for this performance improvement. In particular, storing redundant data increases the size of an OLAP database compared to the corresponding OLTP database.

Table 1.4 compares and contrasts the requirements of each of the different forms of database design, based on the nature of tasks each performs.

TABLE 1.4: OLTP and OLAP Database Design Requirements

Transactional Database (OLTP)	Analytical Database (OLAP)
Deals with *specific* items.	Interested in *general* trends.
High throughput (often millions of transactions per day).	Low throughput (tens or hundreds of transactions per day).
Operations make changes.	Operations answer questions.
Queries typically involve a few records only.	Queries often span the whole database.
Many operations update the source data.	Operations are generally read-only in nature.
Supports transactions.	Does not support transactions.
Needs to be completely up-to-date.	Often updated on a batch basis (e.g., at night or on weekends).
Reflects new data immediately.	Reflects new data eventually.

Let's look at a practical example of the differences between relational and multidimensional databases in a real-world situation. Imagine a sales manager who wishes to explore a product sales database to identify trends in marketing activities. The sales manager might be interested in viewing sales categorized by product, by time period, by sales executive, by region, by customer.

Now let's think about how we might store such information in a relational database format. The most obvious solution is to create a table for each major entity within the database. Figure 1.1 shows an example relationship diagram that implements this arrangement.

FIGURE 1.1:

Sales relationship diagram

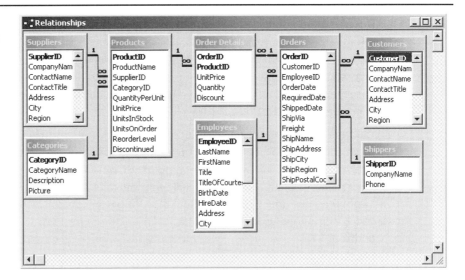

NOTE   The database used to generate this relationship diagram is the Northwind product database, which ships as a sample database for several Microsoft applications, including SQL Server 2000, Access, and Visual Studio.

This structure is optimized for data storage and manipulation: it minimizes redundancy by splitting each entity into a separate table. Making a change to a supplier's address only needs to be done once (in the Suppliers table), rather than amending the Products table for each item supplied by the company. However, it is hard to perform complex queries against this table structure.

Suppose we want to see the year-by-year changes in the sales of beverages made by particular suppliers. It's certainly true that all the data needed to answer this question is stored within the database. However, such a query would not be easy to write: we'd need to join five tables (Suppliers, Categories, Products, Order Details, and Orders), filter the data by category (Beverages), and then perform a SELECT operation on the suppliers, showing the total sales for each year together with the percentage difference between each.

Such a query is certainly beyond the capabilities of a novice or intermediate system user, yet queries just like this are commonly asked by anyone who wants to get an overview of the information held within their organization. By creating an OLAP database that stores this information in a multidimensional format, you can use a client tool to drag and drop the required information onto your desktop. The OLAP engine automatically joins the required tables and returns data in the relevant format without your having to specify this information yourself.

Let's examine a couple further examples of the kinds of queries people might ask and how OLAP-based solutions can help. Most organizations have accounting applications that store information on every aspect of their financial affairs. Once again, those organizations can use OLAP software to identify trends within their data that may improve their financial efficiency. They may want to view invoices by customer, department, date invoiced, payment period, payment type. "Slicing and dicing" the resultant data according to a range of criteria is the kind of problem that OLAP is ideal at tackling.

For another example that isn't specific to a particular industry, imagine a time sheet application that allows employees to record their working activities over a weekly period. Their managers will want to compare different employees' work patterns by project, client, week, and activity type. Similarly, the finance staff will want to know which clients are the most (or least) profitable, this time viewing income or profit by client, project manager, time period, and service type. Once again, OLAP solutions provide an effective mechanism for users to browse through this information, without necessarily understanding the underlying systems or the SQL syntax they would need to interrogate the database manually.

We've focused here on the structures and mechanisms of OLAP; later we'll explain what software you can use to analyze the information once it is stored in an OLAP environment.

Data Warehouses and Data Marts

The terms *data warehouse* and *data mart* are often used to describe corporate stores for data gleaned from production systems. There are almost as many definitions of these two terms as there are people talking about them! By and large, the difference is a matter of scale, with data warehouses being centralized systems containing all relevant data across the business processes of the whole organization and data marts being departmental-based subsets of the entire organization's data.

When building OLAP solutions, you might start by extracting data directly from a production system. This does not require the use of a data warehouse or data mart.

An alternative approach is to build a data mart or data warehouse containing extracts from one or more production systems. The data can then be cleaned up (cleansed) in this intermediate environment before you take it into the OLAP environment. This latter approach is often suitable when you wish to first restructure the data or add additional information from other databases (such as a market research database).

We'll talk about the use of data extraction and transformation tools in Chapter 3, "Analysis Services Lifecycle."

Applying OLAP in Your Organization

There are almost certainly hundreds of potential applications for OLAP solutions within your own organization: wherever you have a reasonable quantity of related data, you can probably get some benefit from applying OLAP techniques and technologies for reporting and summary purposes.

Until fairly recently, OLAP was a horribly expensive technology for companies to adopt. The software available for use typically cost a four-figure sum *per desktop*, which meant that you had to get very significant business benefits out of its use to make it financially viable. This limited the use of such technology to the high-end, typically financial or marketing applications.

In particular, many people have had bad experiences with data warehouse systems falling short on the promises they originally made. By attempting to act as the central repository for all data analysis, data warehousing projects have often failed due to issues such as poor data reconciliation, errors in the original data, and slow updates.

One reason for the failure of many data warehousing projects has been an attempt to solve all an organization's data storage and reconciliation issues at one time. Some multimillion-dollar projects never achieve any business benefits as a result. One benefit of using a product such as Analysis Services within SQL Server 2000 is that you can start with a cheap and easily implemented solution that works on a small part of the problem, then evolve the implementation to take on larger quantities of data and business analysis activity as the success of the initial solution is demonstrated.

Such a "bottom up" design approach allows analytical databases to be built in a modular fashion across a distributed environment and later joined as necessary without drastically impacting the performance of the end solution.

The good news, however, is that OLAP is now a mass-market technology that can deliver real bottom-line benefits for everyone. Most important, the price point has changed dramatically since the launch of SQL Server 7.0, the first version of Microsoft SQL Server with OLAP capabilities. SQL Server Analysis Services is included at no extra licensing costs as part of SQL Server, meaning that any database system based on SQL Server can add analytical functionality for no additional licensing cost beyond that of the original database system.

Limitations of OLAP Solutions

Although OLAP solutions can be helpful in the business environment for reporting and analysis purposes, they are *not* a replacement for the traditional relational and flat-file database models. The idea behind OLAP is to supplement existing databases and allow for resource-intensive queries to be offloaded to a secondary machine. The transactional updates and queries that are always required in a production database remain in the existing environment.

OLAP is largely a read-only solution, rather than a read-write solution. Since we're dealing with a snapshot of a live environment, writing back to that snapshot would not impact the original database anyway, even if there were a good reason for doing so. On the other hand, there is a case for doing "what if" types of analysis (for example, "What would happen if production costs were raised by 10 percent?"). Analysis Services therefore provides a limited set of facilities for writing back such values to a separate partition within the OLAP database. However, if you are doing such activities on a regular basis, you might want to take some OLAP data back into a traditional relational database for easier updating.

The release of Analysis Services extends the scalability of OLAP solutions on the Microsoft platform considerably. The analysis of multiple terabytes of data is well within the capabilities of Analysis Services. With sufficient processing power, memory, and hard disk capacity, Analysis Services can handle the majority of business requirements.

Conclusion

In this chapter, you've seen that OLAP solutions provide a valuable and necessary addition to the armory of tools that should be available to any database designer. Relational databases are great for many tasks, but reporting and analysis activities can be both complex and resource intensive as the number of related tables and the quantity of data stored increase.

In the next chapter, we'll look further at the terminology and architecture of OLAP solutions, as well as examine in greater depth the facilities provided in SQL Server 2000 for data analysis.

CHAPTER 2

Analysis Services Architecture

- Key Concepts

- OLAP Storage Choices

- Microsoft SQL Server 2000

- Using Analysis Services with Non-Microsoft Databases

In the last chapter, we described the difference between transactional, relational (OLTP) databases and analytical, multidimensional (OLAP) databases. We looked at the kinds of tasks that might be put to OLTP systems (specific tasks such as "update invoice #33864 to include product #138204") and contrasted them with the kinds of queries that might be asked of OLAP systems (general purpose queries such as "how many insurance policies were sold last year?").

In this chapter, we'll develop this further by covering some of the central concepts and terms used in Microsoft SQL Server 2000 Analysis Services. We'll define terms such as cubes, dimensions, and measures and give examples of how those elements are applied to real-world situations. The chapter will then go on to describe SQL Server 2000 and the key features within the product, before concluding with a discussion of Microsoft's Data Warehousing Framework and a brief description of some third-party products that support the use of Analysis Services for decision support systems.

If you're unfamiliar with the terminology used in the OLAP world or have no direct experience with Microsoft Analysis Services, this chapter is worth careful reading. The concepts we define here are going to crop up regularly in later chapters. Even if you've worked with another OLAP product, the chapter is worth carefully reading to understand how Microsoft uses the key terms in its product.

Key Concepts

The human brain is an amazing organ. Our brains are designed to assimilate and store huge quantities of information for long periods of time. Our brains are more powerful than any computer, with greater storage than the most impressive database system, and we can but hope to duplicate in software the feats that our brains can already perform.

We're still a long way from fully understanding the workings of the brain, and we certainly know that it operates in a very different manner from the computer. So we can only get glimpses of its operation by understanding the way we do things. We do know that human beings have always categorized and ordered the world around us. By sorting the information we have in such a way, we can more readily remember facts and put new memories into a context. Psychologists believe that one of the most important purposes of dreaming is to "reshuffle" our brains, arranging different pieces of information accordingly to better facilitate recollection at a future date.

To come back to the subject matter of the book, one of the best ways to quickly comprehend a large body of information (particularly computer-based data) is to organize it in such a way that we can identify broad trends and anomalies. This process is a specialist task, which we shall spend time looking at over the forthcoming chapters; for now, we'll identify a couple of concepts that will help us in our discussion.

Analyzing Sales with Analysis Services

Let's go back to the example we discussed at the beginning of Chapter 1, that of our beleaguered store manager in a chain of retail supermarkets. If we were to ask what types of information they found difficult to access, they might say something along the lines of "I want to know *what* we're selling, *when*, and *for how much*." We'll develop this picture a little further by generalizing it to the overall operations of a supermarket, thinking about the kinds of information a supermarket receives and suggesting ways in which it could be used.

First, the supermarket has *products*. Each product comes from a manufacturer and is typically stored in a warehouse before being displayed on the shelves. As the supermarket receives new products at its warehouse, they will enter a record for each product SKU onto the warehouse computer. At a minimum, this record will contain information on the product, its type, its location in the warehouse, its receipt date, and its sell-by date.

TIP   SKU stands for Stock Keeping Unit. A SKU is an alphanumeric value that uniquely identifies a particular product in a salable quantity and type (e.g., Brand X Diet Cola 6 × 12 ounce cans).

Meanwhile, each individual supermarket itself stocks the products as individual items on its shelves. It has its own stock records, containing information on how many products of each type are left on the shelves. Some of the most critical tasks for the store manager to perform are predicting the demand for each product over a period of time and ensuring that they have sufficient quantities either in their store or ordered from the warehouse. To do that, they need a clear understanding of sale trends.

NOTE   This is not as simple a process as it might at first appear. Fixed calendar events such as Easter and Christmas as well as sporting events will cause a surge in demand for certain products and a drop for others. People may be more likely to buy certain products on weekends; a sudden change of weather will have a significant impact. Special offers or deals will increase the popularity of one product while diminishing others. Add to the above the powerful effect of TV commercials and recommendations (one UK store had a rush for wild boar steak after it was featured in a cooking show!), and the underlying patterns can be very difficult to extract.

Assuming that the store has the right products in the right places at the right time, it will then also want to track purchases at the other end of the chain: the checkout. A large retail store uses a barcode scanner to identify products purchased, and the data scanned is generally saved to a central database of sales. The database contains information on the name of the product as displayed on the cash register receipt, together with its price and any special offers on the product. Having scanned all the products, the store produces a receipt and saves the sales data back to the database, so that the supermarket can track stock levels.

It becomes more interesting if the store offers a loyalty reward program. In such a case, the supermarket chain may already have information on you from the loyalty program application form; this probably includes the area you live in, the size of your family, your age, your salary bracket and/or occupation, and perhaps even your interests.

Match this personal information with your purchasing history, and the store has a marketing database of immense potential, *if* it can successfully analyze and use that information in an intelligent way. Here are a couple of examples:

- The store has information on products that other people similar to you are buying (based on age, family size, etc.). By knowing the kinds of product you are likely to buy, it can entice you to make purchases from the store that you were perhaps making elsewhere.

- If you switch stores for some or all purchases, the change in purchasing profile can be identified. Perhaps you weren't happy with something in the store: the supermarket might send a customer satisfaction survey, together with some coupons to encourage you to come back.

- Perhaps you've started (or stopped) buying something significant that gives away a change in your lifestyle. If you're suddenly buying diapers for the first time, chances are you've had a baby! The supermarket will no doubt then want to send information on special offers relating to other baby products.

Since the supermarket concept is such an easy one to relate to, we'll be using it throughout the book. In fact, Microsoft includes a sample database that is based on exactly this business context as part of Analysis Services. We'll be extensively using this database, *FoodMart 2000*, among others, in the remainder of this book to demonstrate specific examples of how to use Analysis Services to its fullest, along with a couple of other examples that we'll develop along the way.

NOTE   It's important to make clear that while FoodMart 2000 is a good sample for demonstrating concepts, it is based on fictional data in a fictional supermarket. The best way to see how this operates in practice is to take a sample of your own data and modify the included samples to work in your own business context. In this way, you can start getting real benefits immediately from this technology.

To turn these real-world scenarios into a structure that can be used, we need to build some structure into the information we have to make it easier to store and analyze.

In Microsoft Analysis Services, pretty much all data can be classified into one of three types: *measures*, *dimensions*, and *cubes*. These terms will be used throughout the book, so take careful heed of the information here if you are not already familiar with this terminology.

Measures

In any database, we are ultimately storing some kind of information about the entities within that database. Usually the pieces of data that are most likely to be summarized are stored as values of some description, either as a currency, as integers, or as floating point numbers. A database of a company's business customers may hold information on the number of employees in their target customer, their annual turnover and profit, the number of products purchased, the discount level applied, and the total revenue returned from that customer. These values form the *measures* used within an Analysis Services database.

Back to our supermarket example and the marketing information they have stored on product sales: they will have data on the number of products sold, the cost of those products (to the supermarket), the price of those products (in terms of the cost to the customer), and so on. We call the values that are of interest to us as parts of aggregates or summaries measures.

If we wanted to get an idea of the success (or otherwise) of a particular store, we could check all of the individual cash register receipts to see how often the product was sold and in what quantities. Alternatively, we could add up this information once and store a figure for each product to identify the performance of that product.

WARNING If we want to choose how we view these measures at a later stage rather than producing static tables, we need to store these measures against the lowest practical element of information within our database. We might choose to either make this an individual sale item or a cash register receipt as a whole. We'll discuss the general choice in design terms later on.

A measure is a numeric piece of information we are interested in analyzing. Some pieces of data that are likely to be measures include the following:

- Quantity
- Cost
- Profit
- Score
- Value

Note that when we aggregate a measure across a number of dimensions (e.g., showing a value for electrical products in the northern region in 2000), the value may not necessarily be a total produced by summing. The revenue across the dimensions above will certainly be calculated by adding up the revenue for individual sales of all matching products; however, what about the profit on all such products? We might calculate this by taking the cost to the store of a product, subtracted from its sale price; in other words,

```
Profit = Sales Price - Cost to Store
```

Alternatively, we might even calculate the profit margin, thus,

```
Profit Margin = (Sales Price - Cost to Store) / Cost to Store
```

Profit and *profit margin* are examples of *calculated measures*.

We can use multiple columns of source data to derive a calculated measure. For that reason, we can classify the source values into two types:

Additive   Values that can be summed together to give a meaningful result in aggregation (e.g., price).

Non-additive   Values that, when summed together, make no meaningful sense (e.g., account numbers).

Non-additive values are themselves not suitable as measures, but they can be combined with other data to produce a calculated measure. We'll discuss calculated measures in more detail over the next few chapters.

Dimensions

Being able to produce a single value representing the total quantity of sales across all stores is not spectacularly useful in its own right. Most people want to see the information broken down in categories, rather than the absolute top-line figure or the individual cell-level data.

Within the supermarket sales scenario, it might be relevant to see sales figures broken down by store, by time period, by department, by product, by customer age, and by customer gender. In OLAP terminology, each of these different categories represents a single *dimension*.

For instance, Table 2.1 isn't necessarily helpful for understanding sales patterns because it simply shows the overall sales figure without any breakdown of how that number is reached by product.

TABLE 2.1: Total Aggregate Sales

Sales Price	All Time Periods
All products	$151,482,232.48

On the other hand, although Table 2.2 shows detailed information on each item, it is *too* detailed to be valuable for establishing overall business trends. Here we can see the individual line items, but we have no concept of which category each product fits into.

TABLE 2.2: Individual Item Sales

Product SKU	Store Cost	Sales Price	Quantity	Customer ID
48312KS	$2.87	$4.99	2	19238490
14839TT	$14.53	$20.00	8	19238490
49231FX	$0.37	$0.70	20	19548392

Table 2.3 offers far more useful management information than either of the previous two tables, because it breaks down the overall sales figure to intermediate categories from the time and product dimensions. Here we can immediately see how sales vary by product and time. For example, we can see that 1998 was a generally weak year for sales of non-electrical products.

TABLE 2.3: Sales Aggregated by Time and Product Category

	YTD 1997	**YTD 1998**	**YTD 1999**	**YTD 2000**
Kitchenware	$1,385,482.88	$1,281,110.38	$1,493,104.20	$804,319.22
Clothing	$4,239,145.67	$3,850,139.68	$4,280,254.72	$2,691,582.44
Foods	$3,001,403.13	$2,789,104.58	$3,505,937.43	$1,864,302.68
Electrical	$5,194,493.93	$6,231,454.99	$5,739,002.42	$3,132,394.13

Each way of breaking down the overall figure (or aggregating the individual pieces of data) constitutes a different dimension. Common types of dimension include the following:

- Products
- Organizational structures
- Time
- Geography
- Customers
- Promotions
- Discount ratios
- Channels of sale (e.g., direct, reseller, Internet, etc.)

For a different example, let's imagine a busy customer call center or help desk. Here the measures might be number of calls taken, number of calls resolved, satisfaction level of caller, length of call, and so on. We might be interested in breaking this information down by time, by call center representative, by problem type, by caller, by training pattern, and so on. These categories would then be the dimensions.

In general, if you can describe your problem in terms of, "I need to see *x*, *y*, and *z* pieces of information broken down by *a*, by *b*, by *c*...," the x, y, and z will represent measures and the a, b, and c will represent dimensions.

Levels

Dimensions alone aren't always sufficient to break down the information to a manageable or interesting form. A large supermarket may have as many as 100,000 product lines available at any one time. It would be frustrating if we could only see measures for all products or individual ones. We therefore usually break down our dimensions into a hierarchical structure. Each member of the hierarchy is called a *level*.

Looking at products, for example, we might break them down as shown in Figure 2.1.

FIGURE 2.1:

Dividing a product's dimension into multiple levels

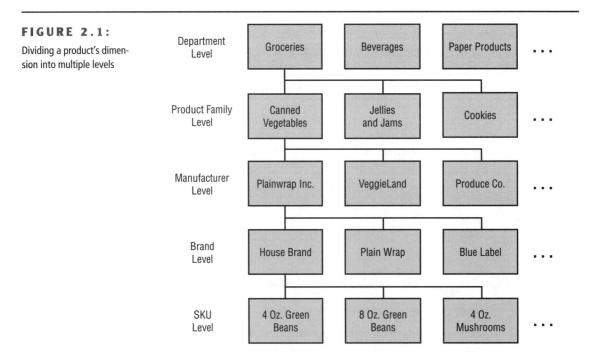

The "product" dimension in this case would therefore have five levels; an OLAP tool should allow us to navigate through each of these levels, showing the measures against each of the level information.

Cubes

In OLAP terms, the basic unit of analysis is the cube. A *cube* represents a particular domain of inquiry, such as "sales data" or "help desk statistics." A cube is a storage unit that combines a number of dimensions and the measures they contain into one whole.

We've used the term "dimension" to indicate a category by which the data will be analyzed. If we only wished to store measures indexed by two dimensions (sales by product by time), we could have a two-dimensional table, as shown, for example, in Table 2.3. Now let's imagine that we want to add a third dimension: that is, to analyze sales by product by time by region. To draw a picture of all this information, we would need a three-dimensional cube, as shown in Figure 2.2.

FIGURE 2.2:

A three-dimensional cube

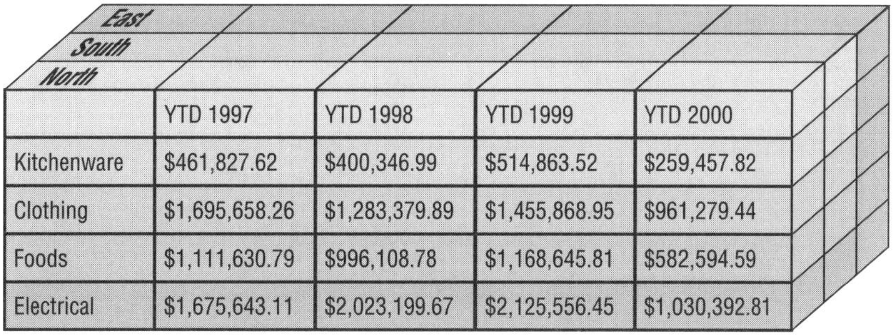

	YTD 1997	YTD 1998	YTD 1999	YTD 2000
Kitchenware	$461,827.62	$400,346.99	$514,863.52	$259,457.82
Clothing	$1,695,658.26	$1,283,379.89	$1,455,868.95	$961,279.44
Foods	$1,111,630.79	$996,108.78	$1,168,645.81	$582,594.59
Electrical	$1,675,643.11	$2,023,199.67	$2,125,556.45	$1,030,392.81

If we added a fourth dimension (perhaps to represent sales by product by time by region by customer age), it becomes extremely difficult to represent such a structure graphically within this book! Regardless of how many dimensions are actually contained, however, we still term the storage unit a "cube." Although a literal cube would only store three dimensions of information, the same term is metaphorically used to represent n dimensions of data.

NOTE The term "cube" can sometimes be confusing, as it implies both a number of dimensions and, worse, an underlying structure for the data storage. As described above, cubes can contain three dimensions but can also contain more. However, in the absence of a more general term and given the widespread usage of the word "cube" within Analysis Services, the term will continue to be used within this book.

The process we describe in this book is therefore one of *multidimensional data analysis*; in other words, extracting useful knowledge from an n-dimensional structure and representing it in such a form as to be easily understood.

TIP   We'll describe exactly *how* an *n*-dimensional structure is stored physically within the system in Chapter 5, "Advanced Analysis Services."

Figure 2.3 shows an actual cube from the FoodMart 2000 sample application (which is installed when you install Analysis Services). In this example,

- Product and Education are dimensions.
- Product Family, Product Department, and Product Category are levels.
- The sales for each combination (in the unshaded cells) are a measure.
- All of these together make up one view of a cube.

FIGURE 2.3:

Cubes, dimensions, levels, and measures

			Education Level		
- Product Family	- Product Department	+ Product Category	All Education Level	Bachelors Degree	Graduate Degree
All Products	All Products Total		266,773.00	68,839.00	15,570.00
	Drink Total		24,597.00	6,423.00	1,325.00
	+ Alcoholic Beverages	Alcoholic Beverages Total	6,838.00	1,763.00	352.00
		Beverages Total	13,573.00	3,591.00	730.00
- Drink		+ Carbonated Beverages	3,407.00	917.00	188.00
	- Beverages	+ Drinks	2,469.00	631.00	141.00
		+ Hot Beverages	4,301.00	1,090.00	256.00
		+ Pure Juice Beverages	3,396.00	953.00	145.00
	+ Dairy	Dairy Total	4,186.00	1,069.00	243.00
+ Food	Food Total		191,940.00	49,365.00	11,255.00
+ Non-Consumable	Non-Consumable Total		50,236.00	13,051.00	2,990.00

OLAP Storage Choices

Once we've worked out what kinds of information we want to access, designed our cube, and chosen the relevant dimensions and measures, we need to go ahead and physically create the structure. In the last chapter we described the benefits that Analysis Services provides by storing data in a multidimensional structure. In fact, it's *slightly* more complicated than that: as an OLAP designer, you have several choices as to how the data, coupled with the aggregations, is stored. Analysis Services can store data in two locations:

- In the relational database that contains the source data
- In a special repository optimized for cube storage

Certain elements of information are always stored by Analysis Services in its own repository format regardless of the storage design chosen. Examples of this include dimensional metadata, processing instructions, and data transformation options. Other parts can either be stored in multidimensional format or as part of the source tables. To understand the different choices for storing data, let's consider the problem of precalculated aggregations.

Aggregations and Exponential Growth

It would be perfect if we could store ahead of time all the measures against each level of every combination of dimensions. That way, anytime a query was put to Analysis Services, it could get the value directly using these previously calculated *aggregations*, without having to sum up any source data while the user waits.

Unfortunately, this is just not possible in practice. To explain why, let's imagine the number of aggregations one would need for cubes of various sizes. In a simple cube with three dimensions (products, regions, and time) and just one level, you would need to simply store three aggregations. As you increase the number of dimensions, and particularly the number of levels per dimension, the number of aggregations rises exponentially as

$$a = l^d$$

where d is the number of dimensions and l is the number of levels. Table 2.4 will give you some sense of how quickly the number of aggregations can grow.

TABLE 2.4: Number of Aggregations by Dimensions and Levels

		Levels			
		2	**3**	**4**	**5**
Dimensions	**2**	4	9	16	25
	3	8	27	64	125
	4	16	81	256	625
	5	32	243	1,024	3,125
	6	64	729	4,096	15,625
	7	128	2,187	16,384	78,125
	8	256	6,561	65,536	390,625

Many real-world cubes may have twenty or more dimensions, perhaps with an average of three levels per dimension. That would leave us requiring 3,486,784,401 aggregations! Although in theory we could precalculate 3 billion aggregations, in practice this would take an immense amount of time and storage space. In fact, it makes little sense to calculate many of the lower-level aggregations, since they are often only summing up a few rows of source data.

For that reason, the pragmatic solution to the problem of "exploding aggregations" is to precalculate those aggregations that either a) will be frequently accessed or b) involve many thousands of rows of the source data.

This means that OLAP databases must store (or have access to) two kinds of data:

- Source data, i.e., the individual rows of data that are used to build aggregations

- Aggregations themselves, i.e., the measures combined across a dimensional level

As we mentioned above, both types of information can be stored either in a multidimensional structure or in a relational database. The storage choices are abbreviated MOLAP, ROLAP, and HOLAP.

MOLAP   The *M* in MOLAP stands for Multidimensional. In MOLAP, *both* the source data *and* the aggregations are stored in a multidimensional format. MOLAP is almost always the fastest option for data retrieval; however, it often requires the most disk space.

ROLAP   In the ROLAP (or Relational OLAP) approach, all data, including aggregations, is stored within the source relational database structure. ROLAP is always the slowest option for data retrieval. Whether an aggregation exists or not, a ROLAP database must access the database itself.

HOLAP   HOLAP (or Hybrid OLAP) is an attempt to get the best of both worlds. A HOLAP database stores the aggregations that exist within a multidimensional structure, leaving the cell-level data itself in a relational form. Where the data is preaggregated, HOLAP offers the performance of MOLAP; where the data must be fetched from tables, HOLAP is as slow as ROLAP.

We'll go into the various choices in more detail in Chapter 4, "Using Analysis Services." Figure 2.4 shows the differences between these choices schematically.

FIGURE 2.4:

MOLAP, ROLAP, and HOLAP

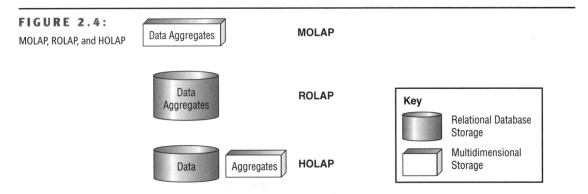

Microsoft SQL Server 2000

Microsoft SQL Server 2000 is a large and complex piece of software. At its heart resides a powerful relational database engine, but a broad range of associated services, tools, and development technologies are also available for installation. We will be using many of these features throughout the course of this book to build our OLAP solutions. In this section we'll take a look at what SQL Server provides for data mart developers. Figure 2.5 shows the major SQL Server components that we'll be discussing, together with their relationships.

FIGURE 2.5:

SQL Server database architecture

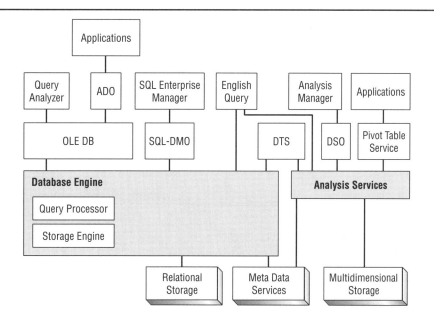

SQL Server Database Engine

SQL Server 2000 would be nothing without the core database engine. The new database engine provided in SQL Server 7.0 and later is a world away from the rather slow and dated engine in previous versions. Many of the new features, such as row-level locking, multiple instances (new in SQL Server 2000), automated consistency checks, and transactional replication, make it feasible to now use SQL Server for highly intensive transactional environments, where the database provides mission-critical services to an organization.

NOTE   The SQL Server database engine comes in several versions, including desktop and enterprise versions, as well as a version called MSDE (Microsoft Database Engine) that is bundled with other products such as Microsoft Office 2000.

The SQL Server database engine itself contains two major components: the *query processor* and the *storage engine*. The query processor takes SQL statements and breaks them down into a number of constituent atomic steps that can be processed sequentially or in parallel. It then selects an execution plan from a range of choices, choosing to use indexes as appropriate. The storage engine itself is responsible for performing those operations against the physical database itself: it manages the database file structure and handles all tasks that directly interact with the data on disk.

A Brief History of SQL Server

SQL Server has had a checkered history: it originally began life as a Sybase database for a range of operating systems including VAX/VMS and UNIX. Microsoft co-licensed Sybase's product, originally for LAN Manager on OS/2 and then for Windows NT. Microsoft needed a database platform to support their own strategic direction, and Sybase was more than happy to see their database product extended to different operating platforms. Eventually Microsoft and Sybase went their separate ways, leading to Microsoft SQL Server 6.0 as the first release produced entirely by Microsoft without coding from Sybase.

Microsoft SQL Server 6.0 (and the 6.5 update) still greatly reflected its origins, however. The original code base from Sybase was designed to be portable across various operating systems. Although Microsoft had updated significant portions of the code, much of the architecture remained from the original releases.

Since all serious commercial database systems are written to protect the integrity of their underlying data files at all costs (including operating system crashes), most systems effectively reimplement significant portions of the underlying operating system, including locking and caching mechanisms, file storage, and write access. While this insulates the database from changes between different platforms, it also adds significant performance and administrative overhead. In SQL Server 6.x, this was visible in several ways, including the use of "devices" as files on which databases could be stored. Even though Microsoft was supporting only one operating system, this portable code was still present in its database system. Added to this, other parts of the architecture were starting to become obsolete or inconsistent with the rest of the product, and vendors were publicly humiliating Microsoft for its lack of support for features that were by then considered essential by most relational database administrators (for example, row-level locking).

In early January 1999, Microsoft released SQL Server 7.0, a major revision of the product. SQL Server 7.0 introduced a new engine that for the first time was fully integrated into the operating system, as well as a redesigned query processor and administrative facilities. In addition, SQL Server 7.0 added some important new features, including support for OLAP Services and Data Transformation Services. SQL Server 7.0 was a major step forward, yet in many ways it was almost like version 1.0 of a new product. OLAP Services provided a great set of features and yet somehow omitted several crucial features, including a robust security model.

SQL Server 2000 builds further on the architecture introduced with SQL Server 7.0. It adds some much-needed features in both the core database engine and the supporting products (including an updated version of OLAP Services, now with a change of name to Analysis Services) and is a worthwhile upgrade. The marketplace continues to evolve, however, and other vendors themselves offer increasingly competitive features integrating the core database platform with comparatively new applications such as Enterprise Resource Planning (ERP) and Customer Relationship Management (CRM). Time will tell whether Microsoft can continue to evolve its product at a sufficient pace to stay competitive.

TIP   The SQL Server query processor is a *cost-based* rather than *syntax-based* processor. Syntax-based processors simply look at the SQL statement itself, picking an execution plan based purely on the various keywords of the statement itself. Cost-based processors also take into account the size of the tables that are used within the expression, any indexes, and other factors calculating a "cost" for each element of the execution plan. This takes account of the fact that what works well for a ten-row table may work very poorly for a million-row table.

The two components of the database engine are accessed from other applications by using an interface called OLE DB. OLE DB is a database-independent communication layer (much like the older Open Database Connectivity, or ODBC standard) that allows SQL statements to execute against any compliant database. The advantage of this is that you can link different databases into SQL Server (see "Linked Servers" in the SQL Server Books Online), allowing one SQL statement or query to operate against multiple databases at once.

Most people access a SQL Server database using an application rather than writing queries directly against the database itself. These days, such access is typically provided through ActiveX Data Objects (ADO). ADO provides an object-oriented interface atop OLE DB. Alternatively, you can use the SQL Server Query Analyzer, a tool that allows you to enter and execute SQL statements. Query Analyzer is particularly useful when you want to see how a SQL statement will be executed. You can ask it to show the execution plan for a query that has been or will be executed, and Query Analyzer displays graphically the different steps it will take, along with the time and processor cost for each part of the operation.

SQL Server is typically administered through a Microsoft Management Console (MMC) snap-in, called the SQL Enterprise Manager (SQL/EM). This provides the ability to create and modify databases, tables, indexes, replication, triggers, etc., as well as set security and run other tools and wizards. SQL/EM does not interact directly with the database engine: instead, it communicates with a compiled COM library called SQL Distributed Management Objects (SQL-DMO). The DMO interface is well documented, making it possible to write management applications that do any or all of what the Enterprise Manager does, coupled with custom actions.

Data Transformation Services

Data Transformation Services (DTS) comes in really useful for shifting data around. It effectively acts like a pump: it sucks in data from one or more data sources and puts that data back into another database. But it's more than just a kind of bulk copier:

- DTS supports *any* OLE DB or ODBC data source or destination, neither of which needs to be SQL Server (or for that matter, even a Microsoft product). That means you can use it, for example, to transfer data from Oracle to DB2.

- DTS provides a rich script-based programming interface to allow you to manipulate the data on the way through the pump. You can write VBScript or JavaScript code to "cleanse" your data, split or merge different fields between source and destination, and even create new fields by performing calculations or string operations on existing fields. If scripting languages don't deliver sufficient power, you can go still further and call out to external COM components to deliver the functionality you need. We'll show you how to do this in Chapter 10, "Managing an Analysis Services Environment using DSO."

- DTS includes a workflow editor that allows you to string together several steps into a single process. Perhaps you want to transfer some data from one location to another, then run a stored procedure on the target, and finally e-mail the database administrator to let them know when the tasks are complete and if any errors occurred. You can even build in "success/failure" paths so that you can trigger remedial action if one task fails, or only continue with further tasks if the previous one succeeds.

DTS is fast: on an old Pentium II/450MHz with 256MB RAM and Windows 2000, it copies multiple tables with a sustained rate of well over 50,000 rows of data per minute. You can also use it in combination with the SQL Server Agent to automate the transfer of data (for example, as a batched, nightly process).

SQL Server 2000 increases the significance of DTS for OLAP applications. One of the major new features is that DTS is now directly integrated with the Analysis Services tasks, meaning that you can load some data from multiple separate source databases, cleansing that data as it is loaded. On the successful completion of that task, you can automatically start processing an OLAP cube based on those databases to produce a cube with refreshed data.

TIP   Some fairly large commercial organizations have bought a copy of SQL Server for no other purpose than because DTS is better than anything available separately. They effectively "throw away" the SQL database engine and simply use DTS itself for their own data integration/migration needs across other database systems!

Analysis Services

The software that became SQL Server OLAP Services was originally available as part of a software suite from Panorama, a small Israeli software firm specializing in data analysis software. Microsoft bought the rights from Panorama and developed it further to fit better into the SQL Server 7.0 architecture and to add supporting features. Now renamed Analysis

Services, the product can exist independently of SQL Server on a machine. It provides a fully functional OLAP environment: that is, it contains the following:

- A multidimensional database engine that can store and access data through read-only and read-write interfaces using Multidimensional Expressions (MDX), a query language similar to SQL

- An extensible management tool, *Analysis Manager*, which provides an MMC-based user interface for carrying out administrative functions, including creating and editing cubes, dimensions, and measures

- A COM library called Decision Support Objects (DSO, for short), which provides programmatic access to the administrative layers exposed in the user interface (and slightly more beyond)

- A PivotTable service that allows other applications supporting OLE DB for OLAP to store and access locally cached copies of an OLAP cube

Analysis Services is not a unique product: other offerings are available as part of database suites from Oracle and IBM, for example, as well as dedicated OLAP or decision support packages from companies such as Cognos, Business Objects, and Hyperion. Each has its strengths and weaknesses. Some of the major strengths of Microsoft SQL Server Analysis Services are the following:

- Price per seat: any client machine with a SQL Server Client Access License (CAL) can freely use Analysis Services. This compares with other OLAP software suites, some of which can cost upward of $1000 per seat.

- Automatic dimension design/usage-based optimization: Analysis Services can automatically assess which aggregations will offer the most significant performance improvement and create those, rather than a database administrator having to manually design aggregations for each dimension. It then logs the *actual* usage profile, to identify whether this affects the optimal arrangement of aggregations, and can modify the processing accordingly.

- OLE DB for OLAP architecture: Analysis Services integrates well with a range of third-party analytical tools, including Cognos PowerPlay, ProClarity, and Hungry Dog Software's IntelliBrowser, allowing freedom of choice in terms of the client front-end tools. Analysis Services also supports Excel PivotTables to allow dimensional analysis from within a spreadsheet environment.

In SQL Server 2000, Analysis Services adds several new features that were sorely lacking in the original version, including parent-child dimensions, ragged dimensions, and cell-level security. We'll discuss the new features as we develop our own examples throughout the course of this book.

But probably the biggest new feature in Analysis Services, which reflects the name change from the previous OLAP Services, is the introduction of data mining capabilities within the core product. Data mining provides a way to understand the cause-and-effect relationships between the dimensions within a cube and the resulting values within the measures. Data mining technologies allow you to predict outcomes for new data based on historical data and to discover patterns within the data in your cube.

We'll cover data mining in more depth in Chapter 11, "Building Data Mining Solutions with Analysis Services."

English Query

One of the frustrating things about database systems is that seemingly simple English questions can turn into spaghetti SQL code when translated into the database's native language. A query phrased in English, such as "Show me all products sold by John Bradley," may require the use of several tables, with corresponding database joins and filters, to give a correct set of answers. In addition, such a question masks much underlying contextual information. For example, who is John Bradley? Is he a salesperson, a customer, or a supplier? And for that matter, how do we know that John Bradley is a person in the first place?

These difficulties occur even before we address the issue that human languages are by nature vague and flexible. One of the key differences between machine-based languages (such as SQL) and human languages (such as English) is how specific the languages are. A SQL statement will always mean exactly the same thing, no matter how often it is executed or by which computer. English phrases are, by contrast, highly subjective and can be misinterpreted (or at least, differently interpreted) by different listeners.

Microsoft English Query, first shipped with SQL Server 6.5 Enterprise Edition, is an attempt to try to bridge these difficulties by providing a machine-based interpreter for database queries phrased in English rather than SQL. It uses two different elements to understand and break down a query:

- First, it has a natural language interpreter that parses English sentences, removing redundant words that play no part in giving the sentence meaning and identifying words as grammatical elements within a sentence.

- Second, English Query draws on stored contextual information about the various database entities. For example, it knows that "salespeople sell products" and that "sold by" is an English construct drawn from the verb "to sell." Using this information, it can map words onto the underlying databases, even if a synonym is used rather than the specific word chosen by the database designer for an entity.

Using the information provided, English Query can continue to produce a SQL statement that (hopefully) matches the intent of the original English question or statement. If necessary, English Query can prompt for further clarification, if there is not sufficient information within the question for the parser to link the relevant database entities together.

English Query has shown increasing promise but, until SQL Server 2000, was only able to query against the central database engine itself using SQL. Given that the vast majority of uses for English Query reside within the analytical domain, it has been a notable omission that the product provided no support for queries against Analysis Services in the native language, MDX. SQL Server 2000 fulfills that promise by allowing English queries to be parsed into MDX. Thus English Query can now be used to perform queries directly against cubes stored by Analysis Services. Among other new features in SQL Server 2000, English Query now uses Visual Studio as its development environment and provides a graphical designer for building the contextual information around the database, as well as providing a usable client for entering and displaying queries written in English.

We'll discuss English Query later in Chapter 12, "Supporting Natural Language Queries with English Query," when we'll describe how to create English Query applications based on Analysis Services data.

Meta Data Services

Microsoft Meta Data Services is one of the hardest aspects of the product to fully describe. The purpose of Meta Data Services is basically to provide an "information store" for developers to put almost anything they want. For example, Meta Data Services can be used as a library for shared COM components, so that developers can build up a toolbox that contains groups of COM components together with their source code and documentation. The structure and presentation of the store is up to you: what you get out of the box is the Meta Data Services engine itself and a series of COM interfaces that expose the functionality of the engine.

TIP   Meta Data Services is a new name for Microsoft Repository, which shipped with SQL Server 7.0 and Visual Studio 6.0. It is a direct upgrade for the previous version, containing all the old features as well as several new ones.

The product is often used as a repository for *metadata*; that is, data *about* data. While a traditional database is good at storing structured information itself, it is often less good at holding information about the nature of the data, such as its origin, the underlying meaning of the data, and the purpose of the data.

TIP Visual Basic includes a version of the original Repository engine as part of its Enterprise Edition. The Repository comes with add-ins for Visual Basic that allow you to store and manage COM components. In fact, the VB6 version includes a sample component library that can be used as a starting point for your own component-based projects.

Within the OLAP context, Meta Data Services is frequently used to store information on *data lineage*; that is, where the data has come from originally. This is particularly helpful when working with multiple source databases because it can otherwise be hard to keep track of which data comes from each source.

Meta Data Services is also used by Analysis Services in SQL Server 2000 to store much of the cube and database metadata, including the data sources, structure and properties of cubes, and so on. In Analysis Services, the metadata can be stored either separately in an Access database called msmdrep.mdb or within a SQL Server database itself. For more details, see the SQL Server Books Online documentation.

Data Access Components 2000

Since this book is dedicated to writing OLAP-based solutions using Visual Basic as the development language, we'll be spending much of our time accessing the Analysis Services engine programmatically. Fortunately, Microsoft has provided a fairly rich architecture (shown in Figure 2.6) that makes it easy for developers to access directly into the database structure itself and get at the various components necessary to do their work.

FIGURE 2.6:

Tiers of the Microsoft data access component architecture related to OLAP

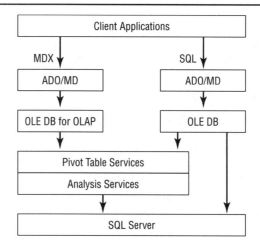

Read on for a brief overview of the role each of these architectural layers plays in promoting connectivity to OLAP cubes.

SQL

SQL, of course, stands for Structured Query Language. This is a standard, implemented by a wide variety of products, for retrieving information from a database. The problem with SQL, from our point of view, is that it is optimized for non-aggregated individual rows of data (found in relational databases). Although the dialect of SQL implemented by Microsoft SQL Server contains some multidimensional features (such as support for the CUBE and ROLLUP operators), it does not have any easy way to refer to the structure of a cube.

MDX

MDX stands for Multidimensional Expressions. MDX is a language, based on SQL, that is designed specifically for retrieving multidimensional information. Thus, it's optimized to gather the sort of information that one might like to retrieve from an Analysis Services cube. We'll discuss MDX extensively in Chapter 6, "Querying Analysis Services with MDX."

MDX is at the heart of programmatic access to Analysis Services. Using MDX, you can produce pretty much any view of a cube, showing aggregations, comparisons between measures within a dimension, calculated measures, and so on. You can change the structure of a cube in terms of its presentation and even write back updated values into the cube or dimension you are viewing. SQL Server 2000 includes MDX Builder, a graphical tool that allows you to drag and drop dimensions to build up an MDX statement (in a similar manner to Excel PivotTables).

ADO

ADO stands for ActiveX Data Objects. This is Microsoft's core technology for providing object-oriented access to data of all sorts. The basic ADO library is optimized for executing traditional SQL statements against relational databases, but with extensions it can be used for everything from retrieving e-mail messages from an Exchange mailbox to updating the design of a table in an Access database.

TIP   For more information on ADO and ADO/MD, see *Visual Basic Developer's Guide to ADO* by Mike Gunderloy (Sybex, 1999).

ADO/MD

ADO/MD is a set of extensions to ADO that allows COM-based applications to operate against a multidimensional source via the OLE DB for OLAP interfaces. ADO/MD uses some of the existing ADO objects and collections but extends them with some additional new objects that you can use to query specific elements of the multidimensional structures.

Here's an example:

```
Dim cnn As New ADODB.Connection
Dim cat As New ADOMD.Catalog
Dim cub As ADOMD.CubeDef
Dim dmn As ADOMD.Dimension

cnn.Open "Provider=MSOLAP;Data Source=localhost;" & _
    "Initial Catalog=FoodMart 2000"
Set cat.ActiveConnection = cnn
Set cub = cat.CubeDefs("Sales")

For Each dmn In cub.Dimensions
    Debug.Print dmn.Name
Next dmn
```

NOTE To run this code, you'll need to set references to the Microsoft ActiveX Data Objects 2.6 Library and the Microsoft ActiveX Data Objects (MultiDimensional) 2.5 Library within your Visual Basic project. The sample also assumes that you're running Visual Basic on the computer that also runs Analysis Services. If that's not the case, you'll need to change the name of the data source in the Open statement from "localhost" to the actual name of the computer that runs Analysis Services. This sample, like all the other code in the book, is available on the companion CD-ROM.

In this example, the code makes a connection to the Analysis Services database using an ADO connection object. Once the connection is activated, we can drill down into the cubes and dimensions using the relevant ADO/MD objects. In this example, we simply print the names of each dimension, but we could do much more, as you'll see in the course of the book.

Of course, you can also use ADO/MD to execute MDX statements against Analysis Services. Rather than using an ADO recordset object, the ADO/MD cellset object provides much better access to the potentially n-dimensional structure that could be returned as the result of a query. Here's an example:

```
Dim cst As New ADOMD.Cellset
Dim axs As ADOMD.Axis
Dim intI As Integer

With cst
    .ActiveConnection = "Provider=MSOLAP;" & _
     "Data Source=localhost;" & _
     "Initial Catalog=FoodMart 2000"
    .Source = "SELECT " & _
```

```
        "{[Measures].[Units Shipped]} ON COLUMNS," & _
        "NON EMPTY {[Store].[Store Name].MEMBERS} ON ROWS " & _
        "FROM Warehouse"
      .Open
  End With

  Set axs = cst.Axes(1)
  For intI = 0 To axs.Positions.Count - 1
     Debug.Print axs.Positions(intI).Members(0).Caption & _
        " " & vbTab & cst(0, intI).Value
  Next
```

This example opens a cellset that includes the total units shipped for each store in a cube named Warehouse. It then prints the results by iterating through the cellset. We'll discuss ADO/MD in greater depth in Chapter 7, "Building Analysis Services Applications with ADO/MD Part I: Cube Schema Objects," and Chapter 8, "Building OLAP Services Applications with ADO/MD Part II: Query Retrieval Objects."

OLE DB

OLE DB is a set of COM interfaces that sits underneath ADO. ADO translates the object-oriented syntax that it presents to client applications into procedural calls to the OLE DB interfaces. By using different software drivers, OLE DB can use identical interfaces for a wide variety of database and other data storage systems. When you're writing code in Visual Basic, you won't be working directly with OLE DB, but it's always there, translating your code so that it works with the ultimate data source.

OLE DB for OLAP

OLE DB for OLAP provides the extensions to OLE DB that are necessary for client applications to use the Analysis Services engine. OLE DB for OLAP provides a series of COM interfaces that can be utilized from within a separate component or application. While it is possible to write applications that directly implement the OLE DB for OLAP interfaces, this interface is too low-level for any but the most sophisticated uses. Unless you're an ISV (Independent Software Vendor) writing a complex data mining tool that transfers large quantities of data in and out of the Analysis Services engine, you're better off using the object-oriented view of the data provided by ADO/MD.

OLAP Support for SQL/ADO

Despite the fact that MDX, coupled with the multidimensional extensions to ADO, provides a querying language optimized for OLAP-based activities, it is still possible to use "traditional" techniques based around ADO. That's why Figure 2.6 shows a connection directly from OLE DB to the PivotTable service. In most cases, you'll be better off using ADO/MD and MDX instead of ADO and SQL when working with multidimensional data, but you may occasionally want to use an ADO recordset to retrieve a single-dimensional view of OLAP data.

Using Analysis Services with Non-Microsoft Databases

Despite Microsoft's own aspirations, the vast majority of corporate data is not stored in SQL Server. There is a general perception within many companies (although this attitude is changing) that SQL Server is not capable of storing the volumes of data or handling the high levels of transaction throughput required. In the longer term, and as a result of recent substantive improvements to the engine and administrative tools, SQL Server may gain greater acceptance within the corporate world, but here and now data is stored on a broad mix of environments and databases.

Much of the data you might want to use as source material for your own OLAP solution may therefore reside in a completely different environment. Does that mean that the OLAP capabilities built into SQL Server are not sufficient for your OLAP tasks? By no means!

First, Analysis Services does not require SQL Server as its host database: it can also use Microsoft Access or Oracle (7.3.3 or later) to store multidimensional data. In fact, the demonstration database, FoodMart 2000, included with Analysis Services is stored in the Access format.

Second, it's rare to see a tool such as Analysis Services used directly against a production database system, even if the data is held in a separate database. More common is to create a separate environment for Analysis Services purposes and transfer the data from the production environment using a data extraction/transformation tool such as DTS. An obvious candidate database for this would be SQL Server since buying a license for Analysis Services entitles you to also use the parent database engine. So it's possible to transfer your heterogeneous data to a single SQL Server database before analyzing it.

Finally, SQL Server 2000 itself includes connectivity to other databases. By using linked servers, you can cause data in other database systems to appear as native SQL Server data to other tools such as Analysis Services. So using the combination of SQL Server and Analysis Services allows you to build multidimensional cubes based on heterogeneous data.

Either way, Analysis Services operates well in a heterogeneous environment and is suitable for any environment where Windows client software can be used.

Conclusion

In this chapter, we've concentrated on describing the key concepts that prevail in Analysis Services:

- Measures, the values we want to be able to "slice and dice"
- Dimensions, the categories under which we wish to view our measures
- Levels, the hierarchy for an individual dimension
- Cubes, the domain of interest for a particular set of analysis

Additionally, we've learned about the various storage options that exist, including MOLAP, ROLAP, and HOLAP.

This chapter also introduced the basic building blocks of OLAP solutions in SQL Server 2000, including the various services and drivers that we'll use in the rest of the book.

In the next chapter, we'll discuss how an OLAP solution is built up and look at some further examples of how OLAP can be used in real-world business scenarios.

CHAPTER 3

Analysis Services Lifecycle

- Applications of OLAP Technologies

- Design and Implementation Process

- Building a Scaleable OLAP Architecture

- Multidimensional Database Designs

Up until this point, we've discussed the basic mechanics of OLAP, describing the key concepts behind multidimensional data analysis and looking at what Microsoft SQL Server 2000 provides to aid us with building decision-support applications. This chapter concludes our introductory section by describing some practical examples of how OLAP can be used in real-world situations, focusing on several different industry sectors that can benefit from using this technology.

In addition, we describe some of the practical steps necessary to implement a decision-support solution, and we look at a basic development process that can be applied for building such applications.

Applications of OLAP Technologies

As we have mentioned earlier, you can apply the technologies described in this book to almost any situation where a database is used for reporting purposes. This section presents a few real-world examples of how Analysis Services can be (and has already been) used.

Much of the focus on data warehousing over the last few years has been specifically targeted at the retail sector. That's because retail offers a combination of large volumes of data from past sales to be analyzed, together with a strong incentive to understand buying patterns in order to sell more merchandise in the future. Indeed, the results of successfully implemented solutions in that sector have been impressive. Consider, for example, the front page of the Amazon.com web site. If you have registered there, you'll find that the site makes recommendations of things you might like to buy based on what you've purchased in the past. Without knowing any of the details of Amazon's system, it's clear that they are making generalizations based on the vast history of purchasing behavior in their database—and doing an excellent job of it as well.

Now that the cost of implementation has been scaled down, business intelligence solutions can be effectively applied to a much broader range of situations and market sectors. The following sections describe briefly some of the opportunities that exist for the exploitation of business intelligence obtained from decision-support systems such as data warehouses in other situations.

Insurance

Insurance companies can apply business intelligence solutions to help them understand their enterprise in two major areas: transactions relating to the formulation and issue of policies, and those relating to claims.

The process of offering and issuing policies relies heavily on understanding the risks involved in that policy. Identifying the most and least profitable coverage types is key to making a service offering; as policies are issued, it is important to be able to track revenue against cost for geographic location, demographic profile, coverage type, previous risk, and many other attributes. Achieving accurate, timely, and flexible visualization of this information is impossible without effective business intelligence tools.

The claims process, too, can greatly benefit from better information analysis capabilities. From the insurance company's perspective, reducing costs and improving efficiency offers clear financial benefits. Improvements to the claim handling process also greatly affect customers' perceptions of the service they receive. Giving companies the ability to "drill down" into production data while not affecting the operational service allows them to understand what happens over the lifetime of a claim and thus positively influence future such claims.

Financial and Banking Services

Although not traditionally the heaviest users of business intelligence solutions, banks and financial service companies are increasingly taking advantage of OLAP and data mining services to improve their understanding of their customers. This is particularly relevant with the surge of Internet services offered by rival financial institutions, new and old players alike.

Most banks offer a broad range of financial and other services to their clients, including current and deposit accounts, credit cards, mortgages, loans, share dealing, and travel services. A major goal of such institutions should be to capitalize on their existing loyal customer base by capturing additional service business (for instance, offering a credit card to a current account holder).

Improving the effectiveness of such marketing activities is vital if the institution is not to offend their customers by flooding them with irrelevant mail; in addition, it reduces the cost of sales and increases take-up rates.

Creating a multidimensional data repository that accurately models a bank's activities without adversely affecting existing services is not a simple process. The quantity of data precludes a simple design, and maintaining data security is a critical requirement. Keeping a clear solution focus and a manageable scope allows business intelligence solutions to succeed where data warehousing projects have underachieved.

Utility and Energy Sectors

The highly competitive nature of gas and electricity markets, combined with deregulation in many parts of the world, requires companies to understand their customers better than ever before. High levels of customer satisfaction are paramount if utility companies are to win and retain new supply accounts. Better awareness of the reasons why customers switch suppliers, make late payments, or change payment methods can also help utility companies offer a better and more profitable service.

The key to all this is the customer database. A business with fifteen million customers has a huge amount of data on their operations; the usage of that information can have a significant and tangible effect on the way the company aligns its services.

The design of a business intelligence system for such an environment is less complex than it is in other market sectors. In this situation the judicious use of data transformation and visualization tools, together with a scalable back-end database system, are key to a successful implementation. The architecture proposed here offers one of the best performance/value combinations in the database world and can therefore manage the high data throughput necessary to meet the requirements placed upon it.

Healthcare and Pharmaceutical

The healthcare sector has a mammoth task on its hands. The sheer quantity of medical information, coupled with its distribution across tens of thousands of hospitals, surgeries, health centers, and so on, makes data reconciliation issues almost impossible. While data warehousing solutions could have a huge impact on the healthcare system, the scope for implementation is limited by the difficulties in accumulating the relevant data, as well as serious concerns about patient privacy and confidentiality.

The picture is not completely bleak, however. Within individual hospitals it is often possible to start to integrate this information. Even if patient data is stored across multiple platforms, the use of data extraction and transformation tools such as Data Transformation Services (DTS) can assist in bringing a snapshot of the data into one place. Dimensional analysis tools can then be used to reveal interesting statistics such as the following:

- Rates of recovery for standard procedures between doctors (this could highlight the need for additional training)

- Success and failure rates for the efficacy of different medications in treating a particular disease

- Utilization efficiency of different wards or departments within a hospital (allowing resources to be directed to situations of greatest need)

Internal Operations

The benefits of OLAP solutions internally within an organization should not be underestimated. Most businesses are constantly on the lookout for new ways to shave their internal costs and become more efficient; the concept of an "internal market" in many larger corporations is driven by the desire to focus resources wisely and expose the costs of running noncustomer-facing departments. Many of the reasons for improving business intelligence therefore apply as much here as elsewhere within an organization.

Furthermore, OLAP and data mining solutions can often replace or at least supplement existing reporting solutions, saving the time and resources needed to create a custom solution while offering a higher quality of information back to the user. Here are a few ideas for places to implement business intelligence solutions internally:

Time sheet reporting   Many organizations require their employees to fill out time sheets, corporate diaries, work logs, etc.; whatever the name given, the purpose of recording this information is to understand where time is being spent within a company and to spot productive and profitable (or non-productive and non-profitable!) activities. Yet the reporting applications applied to this kind of database are usually limited to project-by-project breakdowns of time spent. By moving the generated data out of a relational database and into a multidimensional environment, it becomes far easier to see the broader picture and to compare individuals or projects across a far bigger perspective.

Financial analysis   Every finance director wants to keep a close eye on their company's ledgers and balance of accounts, but this information is often difficult to keep up-to-date with the steady stream of financial transactions within an organization, as supplies are bought and sales made. As a company introduces OLAP solutions elsewhere, however, it comes far easier to integrate budgeting capabilities to the overall picture. A "chart of accounts" cube can be built up by adding existing dimensions (such as time or products) to new dimensions and fact tables. This adds to the value of the overall database by centralizing knowledge management facilities into a single repository.

Web site analysis   Perhaps one of the most interesting applications of dimensional tools is that of "clickstream analysis": in other words, tracking visitors to a web site, particularly when that web site offers e-commerce facilities. Analyzing web site activity gives a clear picture of how well the facilities offered match the requirements of the users. Starting with a raw set of data, traditional tools usually produce basic logs showing (for example) users by location, by time, and by page route. Immediately you should see several potential dimensions for a "web" cube. Once again, adding existing product-based information from a Sales cube substantially fills out the picture and builds in much more powerful analysis capabilities.

Although each of the examples above are obvious candidates for OLAP and data mining tools, until very recently the proprietary nature of existing solutions put them way beyond the reach of administrative departments; the potential bottom-line benefits were vastly outweighed by the costs of the solutions themselves.

Although a cost will always be associated with the design and implementation of such solutions, the ease of use and open architecture promoted by Analysis Services goes a long way in dispelling the arguments against such an implementation. If a company stores their expense claim data in SQL Server, for example, they have already paid for all the server software they need to build an OLAP cube; by adding the PivotTable capabilities of Excel 2000, they have a full analysis solution for almost no extra software cost.

Design and Implementation Process

By this stage, you've seen how multidimensional OLAP and data mining tools such as Analysis Services can be of use wherever there is a large quantity of data to analyze and, in particular, where that data can be broken down into subtotals.

Turning this concept into reality inevitably involves more than just running a Wizard to magically produce all the reports you could ever want, despite what Microsoft might wish you to believe! Theoretically, at least, you could connect Analysis Services directly to your production database and start using it for multidimensional analysis. In practice, however, it makes a lot more sense to create an intermediate data staging area (often described as a *data mart*) that can be used to transform or manipulate the raw data into something more workable from Analysis Services' point of view. This methodology also helps protect your production databases from any potential performance impact of performing the multidimensional analysis.

The architecture behind many small- to medium-scale Analysis Services solutions is shown in Figure 3.1. The process necessary to turn a raw production database into an OLAP cube used for multidimensional analysis can be divided into three stages:

1.   Data extraction and transformation

2.   Designing and processing an OLAP cube

3.   Performing multidimensional analysis

FIGURE 3.1:

The three tiers of multi-dimensional analysis

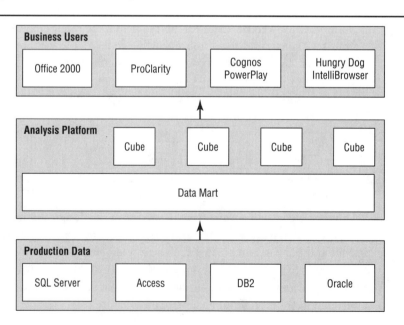

Let's take a look at each of these stages in a little more detail.

Data Extraction and Transformation

First, note that the source for all data to be analyzed remains as one or more relational databases or other data sources accessible through OLE DB. It would be politically unacceptable, as well as unnecessary, for data analysis to require a change in the central production systems that run the company's business. Instead, you will typically use some data extraction tool to take a snapshot of the data at a regular interval (often nightly or weekly) as the data source for your cubes. This is usually run as a batch process at around the same time as the database is backed up. The purpose here is to extract the data quickly and efficiently from the original source.

As the data is extracted from the source database, you may simultaneously perform one or more transformations on that data to restructure it in a form better suited for analysis purposes. Rather than keeping the data in a highly normalized form, it is generally better to break the tables up in such a way that each table corresponds to one dimension in the eventual OLAP cube. Such a structure is known as a *star schema*, and we'll be discussing this in much more detail later in the chapter.

While you're extracting the data and performing the necessary transformations on it to produce this intermediate staging area (or data mart), it's also a great time to do any cleaning up of the data. This *data cleansing* process is absolutely critical to the quality of the analysis results: it's another case of "garbage in, garbage out." Here are some different activities that might go on in the data cleansing process:

- Some of the data in the production database may be missing certain key fields that you can fill in automatically based on the data in other fields (for example, an address may be missing the zip or postal code). You could use an external postal code database to fill in these missing values in this instance. In certain cases, the missing data will be so important that it would be better to remove these rows from the data mart than to include a partial version of them. It is always better to fix incomplete data in the original database, rather than at this stage, but this may be impossible for other, nontechnical reasons.

- Some rows in the production database may be control markers or test data; any such instances will need to be removed before we analyze the remainder. Depending on the quality of the original data, there may also be instances where single rows of data hopelessly skew the overall results (for example, a date that is mistakenly entered as 1900 rather than 2000). This kind of error is often missed within the relational database but will be quickly apparent when the OLAP cube is viewed using analysis tools.

- Now is also a good time to merge any columns that will be more meaningful to the end user as a single entity. For example, most databases store names as at least two fields: "firstname" and "lastname." This makes it easier to manage the data, but for someone compiling a report, it will usually make sense for these columns to be concatenated into a "display name" field. This sort of data cleansing can also increase the performance of the analysis server by performing some calculations in advance.

- In the opposite way, other fields in the production database may be broken up into multiple columns in the target data mart or simply modified to conform to a format better suited for analysis. For example, a field containing date of birth could be turned into an "age" or "age range" column in the target table. Normally, you'd avoid this approach at all costs (because the age of a person changes over time), but because the data is updated from a snapshot on a regular basis, the age field can be calculated each time. The end result is that it's easier to show a breakdown of product sales by age range (under 18, 18 to 25, etc.) than by date of birth. Again, there's a potential performance improvement by precalculating such results.

- Last, some fields may be codes that mean little to the end user but are nevertheless efficient for storage purposes in the source database. For example, some organizations break products stored in a warehouse into "A list," "B list," and "C list" items, depending on whether the stock is held within a regional warehouse, ordered from a central facility, or on special order direct from the manufacturer. From the perspective of the end user of the data, it would be better if this information were stored with a slightly more intuitive naming convention, even though this might result in an increased quantity of data stored.

As you can see, the data extraction and transformation process is critical to the overall quality of the information available in the OLAP cube, as well as to the ease of manipulating that information. A wide range of tools on the marketplace provides these capabilities. For the majority of purposes, the DTS component included as part of SQL Server 2000 offers much power and flexibility.

As shown in Figure 3.2, DTS works in some ways like a sausage machine: it sucks in the sausage mixture (raw data) and reforms it to the size and shape of your choice (the transformation and cleansing process). As the sausage is processed, you can add any extra ingredients such as spices (in the case of DTS, you can build in information from other databases). The end result in both cases is hopefully something far more palatable to the consumer than the input!

In its simplest form, DTS allows you to copy selected columns from multiple tables between a source and a destination database. During the copy process, you can use any ActiveX scripting language (such as VBScript or JavaScript) to apply a custom transformation to achieve any of the purposes described above. In addition, multiple tasks can be chained together in a DTS package, using several different databases if necessary, to build a complex set of tasks that can be performed immediately or at a scheduled time. DTS can also be used to trigger other tasks, such as processing an OLAP cube, executing a remote application, or sending an e-mail message. Figure 3.3, for example, shows a DTS package that creates four tables and then extracts data from an Access database to populate those tables. Although this package was designed graphically using the tools built into SQL Server 2000 Enterprise Manager, a complete object model for DTS is also available. This enables the creation and execution of DTS packages on a programmatic basis.

FIGURE 3.2:

DTS is like a sausage machine.

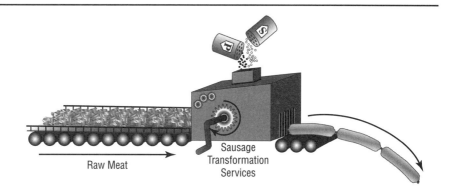

FIGURE 3.3:

DTS in SQL Server 2000

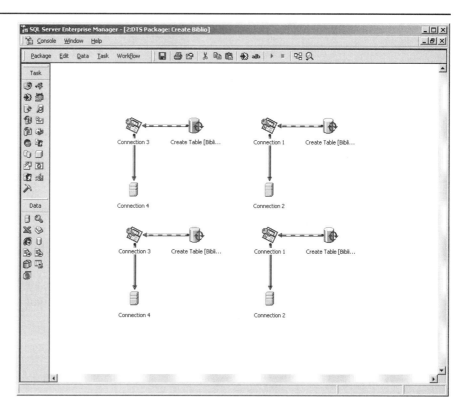

Whichever tool you use to extract, transform, and cleanse the raw data within your production environment, the output of this will be a relational database that contains a relevant subset of data in a schema that will facilitate the creation of the OLAP cube later on. This intermediary database is quite useful in its own right as a repository for other reporting and analysis tools as well as Analysis Services and is often described as a data mart or data warehouse, depending on the size of the database and the number of input sources.

TIP   Keep in the back of your mind that, as the data mart grows, it may increasingly become a central store for the analysis of data from multiple different origins. When designing your data mart, you should keep in mind the possible requirement to accommodate more data sources in the future, and to provide reconciliation between various data sets. This is by no means a simple process, however, so the best advice is to start by keeping the problem domain small and gradually increasing the system by adding additional databases in a modular way, rather than by attempting to solve the entire problem at one time.

TIP   For more information on the use of DTS from Visual Basic, see Dianne Siebold's *Visual Basic Developer's Guide to SQL Server 2000* (Sybex, 2000).

Designing and Processing an OLAP Cube

When you've completed the data transformation process, you should be left with a data mart containing reliable data ready for use with any analytical environment. You could stop the process here and use a relational data reporting tool such as Crystal Reports or a spreadsheet such as Excel to build your own view based on the data.

Indeed, for many purposes, this would be an entirely suitable approach. Simply moving the query analysis off the production database avoids the worries of performance impacts on the source data, and the data cleansing and transformation process provides you with a better quality of data for analysis.

But for reasons such as those described in previous chapters, an OLAP cube is capable of allowing still faster and more effective analysis. Although the data transformation process cleans up the data, it doesn't really give any context to the columns of data within each table. For example, take the database table shown in Table 3.1, which might be a portion of a larger table in an actual data mart.

TABLE 3.1: Geography Sample Table

GeogID	Country	StateProvince	Locality
306	United States	Washington	Seattle
307	United States	Alabama	Birmingham
308	United States	Texas	Austin
309	United States	Texas	Houston
422	United Kingdom	London	Westminster
423	United Kingdom	West Midlands	Birmingham
457	Germany	Baden-Württemberg	Stuttgart

Although this table contains useful information for identifying localities within a parent country and state/province, nothing formally identifies that relationship here. Without knowledge of world geography, the computer has no way of identifying that localities are contained within states. After all, both the StateProvince and Locality columns contain six distinct items in the extract shown here. Neither does the locality field alone above distinguish between the two cities named Birmingham. For example, consider this query:

```
SELECT DISTINCT Geography.Locality
    FROM Geography
    INNER JOIN Orders ON Geography.GeogID = Orders.GeogID
    WHERE Orders.FreightCost > 10
```

Using the locality field alone would make no allowance for the fact that both places named Birmingham are entirely different.

NOTE   Despite these limitations, Table 3.1 is still easier to query against as a result of being transformed. In a fully normalized database, this table would probably be broken down into three tables, one for each of the country, state, and locality columns.

By creating an OLAP cube, you can provide this additional information. This will help enhance performance and make it easier for an end user to query the database effectively. When you turn Table 3.1 into a dimension within an OLAP cube, an end user will see the structure as shown in Figure 3.4, which represents this dimension in the Cube Browser.

FIGURE 3.4:

Geography sample
dimension

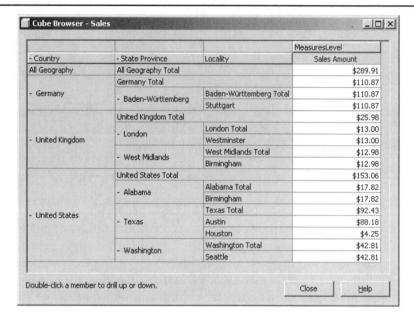

Building an OLAP cube in Analysis Services requires the following steps:

1. Definition of a data source for the cube. This involves creating an ODBC or OLE DB connection to the data mart built earlier and setting any security or connection properties.

2. Defining dimensions for each table in the schema. A dimension defines a single way of breaking down the headline total that corresponds to all items in the database. Examples of dimensions in a typical sales/ordering system include time, product, promotion, employee, customer, and order.

3. Creating one or more cubes out of several dimensions. Once the dimensions have been defined, you can create a cube that combines the dimensions to allow analysis by "slicing and dicing" the data. Each cube usually contains information on a different aspect of a company's operations (for example, Sales, Finance, Logistics, Human Resources), although cubes may be subdivided themselves for various reasons we'll discuss later.

4. Designing storage for a cube. Having defined the metadata that defines a cube and its dimensions, we can decide how we will aggregate the data within a cube for the best trade-off between processing time, disk space, and query performance. Here we choose between MOLAP, ROLAP, and HOLAP storage options and decide which of the many ways of preaggregating the data will have the biggest effect on the system performance.

5. Processing the cube. Finally, the cube itself is processed on a scheduled basis using the data stored in a star schema within the data mart we created earlier. As the data is updated, the cube needs to be reprocessed to update the aggregations with new totals.

We'll go through this process in great detail in Chapter 4, "Using Analysis Services."

Performing Multidimensional Analysis

To actually do something with the data you've so painstakingly manipulated and processed, you need to query the OLAP cube using a client of some description. One of the strengths of Analysis Services, as described in the previous chapter, is the definition of a fairly open standard called OLE DB for OLAP that can be used to query the database.

OLE DB for OLAP is built on the underlying OLE DB technology and provides an interface into the data mart database that can be used for the execution of queries and retrieval of result sets in multidimensional format. Since the release of the first OLE DB for OLAP–compliant server product, OLAP Services 1.0, some impressive third-party clients have been created that provide a wide variety of options for visualizing the data in a cube. Examples include ProClarity (shown in Figure 3.5), Cognos PowerPlay (shown in Figure 3.6), Hungry Dog IntelliBrowser (shown in Figure 3.7), not to forget Microsoft Excel 2000 (shown in Figure 3.8). There is a varying degree of support for the standard, which leaves some clients better equipped for detailed analysis than others.

FIGURE 3.5:

ProClarity

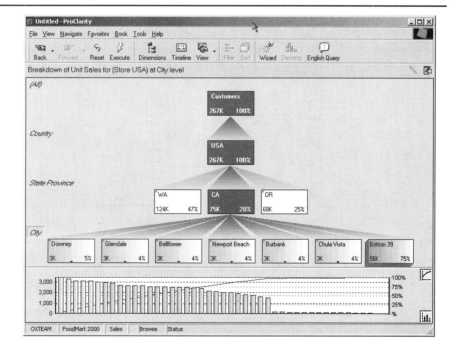

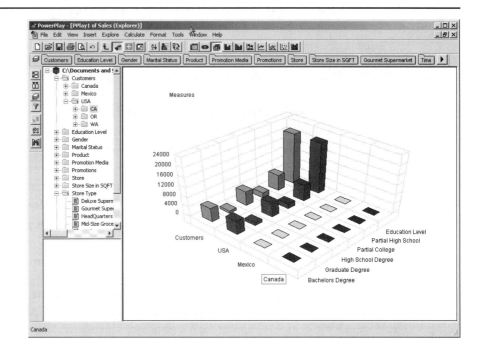

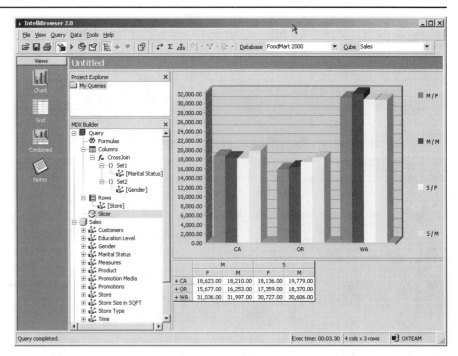

FIGURE 3.8:

Microsoft Excel 2000

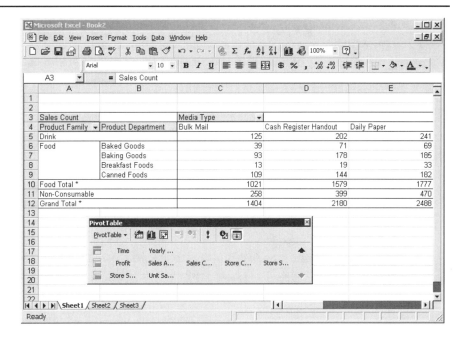

Although many people choose to purchase a shrink-wrapped application for detailed analysis, it's also quite possible to write your own dedicated client software using a language such as Visual Basic. In the same way as ADO provides a high-level interface into OLE DB, Microsoft also provides the ADO/MD extension library, which provides the same facilities for OLE DB for OLAP. There's also a multidimensional query language, MDX, which is not dissimilar to SQL but provides better capabilities for accessing cube structures.

In later chapters, we'll show you how you can build your own query analyzer tool using MDX and ADO/MD.

Building a Scaleable OLAP Architecture

The process of extracting and transforming data using DTS, turning it into OLAP cubes with Analysis Services, and then analyzing the results with a shrinkwrapped or homegrown client application is fairly typical for a source database of up to about 10GB (although the actual figure will vary depending on the type of data and number of dimensions in your cube). As the database starts to grow beyond that size, some additional considerations come into play.

First, the data extraction and transformation process takes an increasingly long time to run. You can obviously add additional processors and memory to the data mart system to improve its capacity for moving data between locations, but even this strategy will become insufficient as the complexity of the transformations and the sheer quantity of data being extracted increases. When designing for this kind of scenario, additional abstraction may be required between the source database and the data marts. One option is to do a bulk extract of the data from the host system to a staging area and then perform the transformation and cleansing processes at a later stage. In the largest situations, a data warehouse is utilized as the central point for all extracted data, with data marts storing subsets of the data for further analysis and cube building.

A similar set of problems arises with cube processing as the quantity of data increases. At first, cube processing may take a matter of minutes, but as this increases to hours, the window of opportunity becomes increasingly difficult. Two solutions to this problem exist. One option is to simply reduce the number of aggregations processed. This is only a temporary fix, though—the less data that is preaggregated, the harder the Analysis Services engine has to work to answer queries, because fewer will be able to be answered without reference to the data source. The longer-term solution to this issue is to move from processing the entire cube to performing incremental updates. To do this, you can create a separate *partition* of the OLAP database that contains the relevant subset of updated information. This partition can be processed independently and later merged with the original database.

Third, as the number of members in each dimension increases, so it gets harder to store the dimension in the optimum MOLAP structure. This is where hybrid solutions become more relevant. Analysis Services now provides an option to store individual dimensions outside of the MOLAP structure, providing the highest performance for the majority of dimensions while keeping large dimensions from exhausting available memory and resources.

Last, as the size of a single cube increases, it can become impossible to keep everything running on a single machine environment. Fortunately, Analysis Services gives you several choices for the way any solution is distributed. The data mart and the Analysis Services engine can be separated, and cubes stored on other machines can be linked. Subsets of the data can be partitioned and aggregations designed independently for each partition to enable finer-grained control of the storage usage.

Multidimensional Database Designs

Let's finish this chapter by going right back to the beginning of the process again and looking at the most appropriate data structure within the data mart to facilitate the building of OLAP cubes within Analysis Services.

With very few exceptions, the best structure for a database that will be used in conjunction with Analysis Services is a *star schema*. In this model, a single central table contains all the *measures* used in the OLAP cube, and several outlying tables each contain the necessary data for one or more of the *dimensions* that can be accessed. Figure 3.9 shows a simple star schema. Here the Sales table contains the measures and the other tables contain the dimensions for the analysis.

FIGURE 3.9:

Star schema

In practice, such a schema is not a million miles away from the database model you may be using already in your existing relational database systems.

The biggest difference between the star schema and the relational model is the focus on one central table in the schema known as a *fact table*. This table contains a row for every single transaction or item that is being analyzed. In a Sales cube, this table might contain a row for every individual sale that was made; in a cube containing time sheet information, the fact table might contain a row for every entry made in the log.

WARNING The level of detail for which information is stored into a fact table is directly responsible for the granularity of the resultant cube. For example, a Sales cube could measure individual product SKUs as they are sold for the highest degree of granularity, or alternatively, it could measure shopping baskets as a whole. If the latter option is chosen, though, it will be impossible to dig deeper into the data and show sales by product. Think carefully about the intended use of that cube, therefore, when you are determining the level of detail you plan to include in your cube.

Fact tables usually contain two different types of fields. First, a fact table must obviously contain a column for every measure you wish to include in the cube. In our Sales cube example, this might include quantity of items sold, net price, and item cost to the store. In a cube for analyzing calls made to a call center, the measures might include length of call, customer satisfaction level, and whether the query was resolved.

Measures, as we see, are usually numeric measures, whether integers or decimals. Occasionally they might be Boolean values, but even in this case it is easier to store them as integers; this allows you to add the values together to result in an aggregated total, which is the aim in the first place.

As well as measures, fact tables contain several foreign keys, which point to the tables at the points of the star schema. These tables are called *dimension tables* and contain the various levels of the dimensional hierarchy. Each distinct dimension should have a separate table, and each of these tables is linked back via a primary key/foreign key relationship to the fact table.

Dimension tables in a star schema contain one column for each level. Table 3.1 (shown previously) is a good example of a dimension table: it contains a primary key and a column for each of three levels. The hierarchy in which the columns are placed is defined later within the Analysis Services management environment.

One other thing to note here is that the ratio of rows between fact tables and dimension tables is huge. A large fact table could contain hundreds of thousands or even millions of rows of data. On the other hand, many dimension tables will contain no more than a few hundred rows. The implication of this is that you should generally avoid adding dimensional data into the fact table. Instead, keep it in a separate table and refer to it via a foreign key.

An exception to this rule is dimensional data that has almost as many different values as there are rows in the fact table. Generally, datetime fields such as OrderDate or ShipTime fall into this category. As you'll see in Chapter 4, special logic is built into Analysis Services to consolidate such fields into useful groupings.

Taking the time to transform an existing relational database structure into a star schema is a worthwhile investment. Sometimes, however, practical considerations mean that a single dimension is spread over two or more related tables. Such a structure is known in the industry as a *snowflake schema*. Figure 3.10 shows a possible snowflake schema for our hypothetical Sales cube. The Sales table remains the single fact table, but dimensional information is spread out over multiple tables for each dimension.

FIGURE 3.10:

Snowflake schema

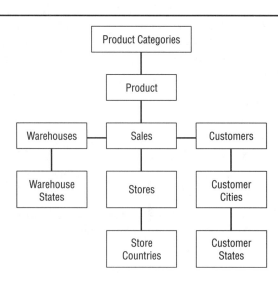

It's possible to mix and match: you can store some dimensions in a star schema, and others in a snowflake schema. Note, though, that a star schema offers better performance than a snowflake schema and is easier to manage. Where practical, therefore, dimension tables should always be directly linked to the central fact table, and you should avoid separate tables for levels within the dimension.

Creating a Data Mart from Northwind Traders

The Northwind sample database, which ships with Microsoft Access, SQL Server 2000, and Visual Basic, is a good example of a database in relational structure. Looking at the database in the Relationships window from Microsoft Access, as shown in Figure 3.11, you may notice that there is no clearly visible fact table/dimension table structure. If we want to do some dimensional analysis on this database, we'll therefore need to convert it into a star schema.

If we think about the granularity of the data we might want to analyze using a cube built on this database, we have two basic options. We can analyze either by order or by line item. For most purposes, analyzing by line item will give us the most useful information, so the fact table will therefore contain one row for each instance of a line item order. Figure 3.12 shows one way of building the data mart.

FIGURE 3.11:

Northwind relational schema

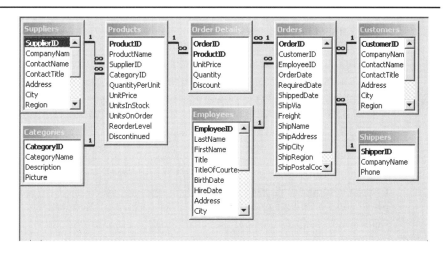

FIGURE 3.12:

Northwind as a data mart

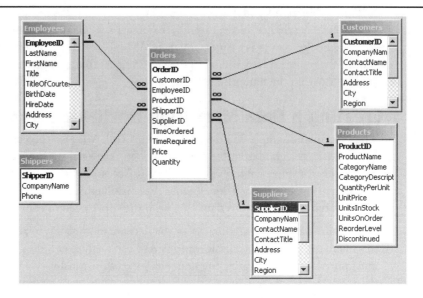

In this case, we've got the option of creating up to seven dimensions from original source data. These would be Customer, Shipper, Employee, Product, Supplier, TimeOrdered, and TimeRequired. We've cheated here slightly, as you'll notice that there are only five dimensional tables. In fact, we've put the two time dimensions in the fact table. This is a little bit naughty; as we mentioned earlier, it's not usually a good move to store dimensional information in the fact table. You can sometimes get away with this for time-based dimensions, though, because it only adds one additional field per dimension, and nearly every time stamp will be different anyway. The purist approach would probably be to break the time field up into different columns (year, month, day, etc.), in the same way as for other dimensions.

You'll notice that two measures are visible from this diagram: Price and Quantity. These are both *additive* measures; in other words, they can be added together when totaling a number of rows in the fact table. Some measures are aggregated in other ways; for example, an "average price" field would be aggregated by averaging each of the rows together. (We'll also see later that certain measures are only semi-additive or even non-additive.)

To turn the relational structure into a star schema, we created a fact table; we then copied the Price, Quantity, time, and various ID fields that are foreign keys into other tables from the OrderDetails and Orders table into the fact table (also named Orders in this example). This results in a certain amount of redundancy, but don't forget that redundancy is never an issue in dimensional data structures: we're not updating this information, so it doesn't matter that certain pieces of data are duplicated.

The last stage was to ensure that every entity that became a dimension was connected directly to the fact table, rather than being connected through another intermediary table. We created an

ID field for each dimension and then linked it to the fact table using a primary/foreign key relationship.

This is a fairly simple example, but hopefully it gives you a better flavor of the issues involved in translating a production database schema into one suitable for analytical purposes. Don't be constrained by your source database tables when designing a star schema; if you're struggling to visualize the resultant schema, start again with a blank canvas and design the data mart model from scratch. Then identify which fields in the existing database can be transformed to produce the schema you're looking for.

Sample Databases

Throughout this book, we've tried to incorporate a range of different OLAP databases in examples to demonstrate usage of OLAP in different business scenarios. For consistency, however, the FoodMart 2000 database will be used in many places to demonstrate key concepts. This Access database ships in a ready-made state with SQL Server 2000 and is preinstalled in Analysis Services via a system DSN called FoodMart2000. It provides sales and inventory information for a small supermarket selling over 2,000 product lines. The source database for FoodMart 2000 contains several separate fact tables covering different time periods for sales and inventory information.

The following diagram shows the schema for the data that combines to form the *Sales* cube in the FoodMart 2000 sample database.

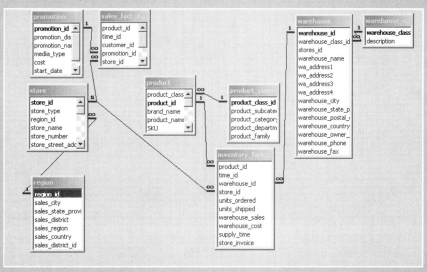

Additional sample databases are on the CD included with this book; refer to the readme file there for further information.

Conclusion

You've seen in this chapter that OLAP solutions can be used in almost any business scenario where there's a large quantity of data to deal with. Creating an OLAP cube involves some design work up front, just as with any other database environment, but once complete, the cube can be used repeatedly for queries even the original designers hadn't anticipated.

You also learned about a basic three-tiered design process for building analysis solutions and saw the differences between star and snowflake schemas.

In the next chapter, we'll start building an OLAP database example using Analysis Manager. We'll look at all the options available in Analysis Services for building dimensions and cubes and take a look at designing storage options for an existing cube structure.

CHAPTER 4

Using Analysis Services

- Creating and Connecting a Database

- Creating a Cube

- Browsing a Cube

- Partitioned Cubes, Linked Cubes, and Virtual Cubes

- Updating a Cube

Now that you've had the 30,000-foot view of Analysis Services and have probably started thinking about how to use it in your own organization, it's time to come down to earth. In this chapter, we'll open up the Analysis Services interface and see how to build a new cube and how to view the results. When you finish this chapter, you'll be prepared to build your own cubes and start performing multidimensional analysis. You'll also have seen the first of many ways in which Visual Basic can interact with Analysis Services. If you already know the basic mechanics of Analysis Services, you might want to skim this chapter and move to the more advanced material later in the book.

Creating and Connecting a Database

The first step in using Analysis Services is to launch the Analysis Manager (Start ≻ Programs ≻ Microsoft SQL Server ≻ Analysis Services ≻ Analysis Manager). Analysis Manager is a Microsoft Management Console (MMC) snap-in, just like SQL Server Enterprise Manager. Figure 4.1 shows the default Analysis Manager interface, with the treeview on the left expanded to show some of the objects that Analysis Services installs as sample data.

The next step is to create an Analysis Manager database and tell Analysis Services where the data in that database should come from. Don't confuse an Analysis Services database with a SQL Server database. Even if the data you want to analyze is stored in SQL Server, you still need to create a separate Analysis Services database to hold the metadata and aggregations that are specific to Analysis Services.

NOTE   For the examples in the first part of this chapter, we'll be using some sample web site traffic log data rather than the FoodMart 2000 data that ships with Analysis Services. That's because FoodMart 2000 is already installed, and we want to show you the full process. The traffic log data is included on the companion CD, together with instructions on loading it to your own SQL Server if you'd like to follow the examples in this chapter.

To create a new Analysis Services database, follow these steps:

1. Launch Analysis Manager and expand the treeview to show the server where you want the database to reside.

2. Right-click the server node and choose New Database. You'll be prompted for a database name and (optional) database description. We'll call our database for this chapter BookSamples.

3. Click OK. Analysis Services will create the new database.

FIGURE 4.1:

Analysis Manager

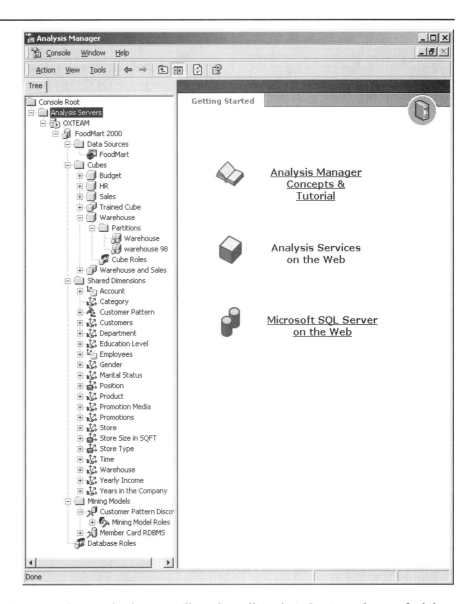

After you've created a new database, you'll need to tell Analysis Services where to find the data for that database. To do that, follow these steps:

1. Expand the BookSamples database in the Analysis Manager treeview to show its child nodes.

2. Right-click the Data Sources folder and choose New Data Source. This will open the Data Link Properties dialog box.

3. Select an appropriate OLE DB provider and fill in the required data. For our sample SQL Server database, we've used the Microsoft OLE DB Provider for SQL Server. For the sample data, you'll need to enter the server name, BookSamples as the database name, and your username and password if you're not using Windows Integrated authentication.

4. Click OK to use the specified database as the data source for this Analysis Services database.

If you expand the Data Sources folder in Analysis Manager, you can click the data source and see the metadata information that Analysis Services has stored for the server, as shown in Figure 4.2 (here OXTEAM is the name of our test server).

FIGURE 4.2:

Data Sources in Analysis Manager

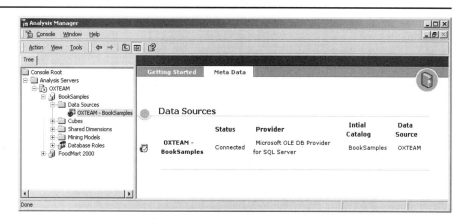

> **TIP**
>
> You can add multiple data sources to a single Analysis Services database. However, a single cube can only have one data source. The exception is a cube that's split over multiple partitions. In that case, each partition can have a different data source, as long as each data source contains fact and dimension tables with the same structure. You'll learn more about partitions in Chapter 5, "Advanced Analysis Services."

Although the Data Link Properties dialog box will show you all of the OLE DB drivers on your computer, Analysis Services is limited to using only a few source database types:

- SQL Server 6.5 or later
- Microsoft Access 97 or later
- Oracle 7.3 or 8.0

If you try to use another OLE DB provider, Analysis Services will let you link to the data, but it will give you an error message when you try to actually build a cube. To use a different data source, you should use Data Transformation Services to first migrate the data into a SQL Server Data Mart, as we discussed in Chapter 3, "Analysis Services Lifecycle."

Creating a Cube

Once you've created your Analysis Services database and connected it to a data source, you're ready to begin creating cubes. In this section, we'll demonstrate the Cube Wizard, which walks you through the cube creation process step-by-step. There's also a Cube Editor, which allows you to build cubes without using the Wizard and to modify existing cubes. You'll learn about the Cube Editor in Chapter 5.

Figure 4.3 shows the schema of the tables that we'll be using in this section. As you can see, this database is set up with a relatively small star schema. There is a single fact table (tblWeblog) and three dimension tables (tblClientIP, tblUserAgent, and tblURL).

FIGURE 4.3:

The Weblog tables in the sample database

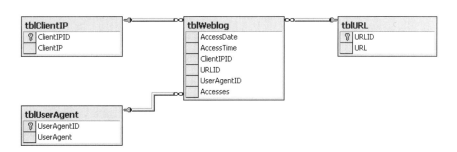

To begin the process of creating a cube with the Wizard, right-click the Cubes folder in the Analysis Services database and choose New Cube ➤ Wizard. This will launch the Cube

Wizard, shown in Figure 4.4. Like most Wizards, the Cube Wizard starts with a panel that explains the purpose of the Wizard, together with a check box to suppress this panel in the future.

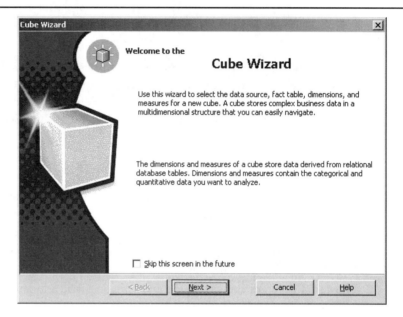

Click Next on this panel to proceed with creating measures for your cube.

Creating Measures

Creating measures for a cube is a two-step process:

1. Selecting the fact table for the cube

2. Selecting the columns that define the measures

This process is broken up into two panels in the Cube Wizard. The first of these panels lets you select a fact table. This panel shows you all of the data sources in your database, together with the tables in each data source. When you select a table, you can see the columns within that table. You can also create a new data source from this panel, or browse the data in a table. Browsing the data will show you up to 1000 rows from the table so you can determine whether it's an appropriate table to use as a fact table.

In our sample cube, we want to use tblWeblog as the fact table. It's easy to see this from the database diagram in Figure 4.3; the fact table is nearly always the central table in a star schema.

After you select a table and click Next, the Cube Wizard presents a panel to allow you to choose the measures in your cube. This panel shows you all of the numeric columns in the selected fact table and lets you choose one or more of them to be measures. In our sample data, the Accesses column is the only appropriate measure. The other numeric columns are foreign keys to the other tables in the database schema.

TIP   Measures created with the Cube Wizard are always simple additive measures. To create more complex calculated measures, you'll need to use the Cube Editor.

After choosing measures for your cube, click Next to proceed with creating dimensions for the cube.

Creating Dimensions and Levels

Analysis Services dimensions can be either private to a cube or shared between cubes. The Select Dimensions panel in the Cube Wizard thus opens with a list of shared dimensions within the current Analysis Services database. You can select any or all of these to be dimensions in the new cube that you're creating.

Of course, the first time you create a cube in a particular database, there won't be any shared dimensions for you to choose. In this case, your only option is to click New Dimension to launch the Dimension Wizard.

The Dimension Wizard includes these panels:

Introductory panel   This panel explains the use of the Wizard. You can choose to suppress this panel on subsequent uses of the Wizard.

Dimension Type panel   In this chapter, we'll limit our cube to using star schema dimensions. There are four other choices (Snowflake Schema, Parent-Child, Virtual Dimension, and Mining Model). We'll discuss the first three of those in Chapter 5. You'll learn about Mining Models in Chapter 11, "Building Data Mining Solutions with Analysis Services."

Select Dimension Table panel   If you've chosen a star schema dimension, you must choose exactly one table here. For example, in the sample database we'll select the tblClientIP table. When you select a table, the Wizard shows you the columns in this table. You can also browse up to a thousand rows of data in each table from this panel.

Select Levels panel   In the case of the tblClientIP table, there's only a single level, represented in the ClientIP column. In some cases, you'll want to choose multiple levels here. For example, a denormalized Address table might contain columns for Country, Region, and Postal Code, which would lead to a hierarchy of three levels on this panel.

Specify Member Key Column panel   In most cases, you can leave the columns you selected as levels to be the member keys. However, if the data in those columns is not unique, you'll need to provide an alternate key column on this panel.

Select Advanced Options panel   We'll discuss these options in the next chapter. For now, you can just leave them untouched.

Finish Panel   This panel, shown in Figure 4.5, lets you assign a name to the dimension, preview the data in the dimension, and decide whether the dimension should be shared with other cubes.

FIGURE 4.5:

Finish panel of the Dimension Wizard

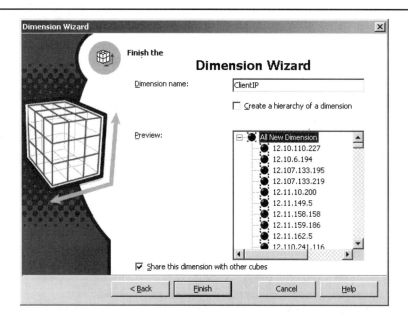

When you've clicked Finish in the Dimension Wizard, you'll be returned to the Cube Wizard. Here you can create more dimensions or proceed. For our example, we'll start by creating three dimensions, one for each of the dimension tables in the star schema:

- ClientIP, from tblClientIP
- URL, from tblURL
- UserAgent, from tblUserAgent

You might think that exhausts the possibilities for dimensions in this case, because we've used up all of the dimension tables. However, if you look back at Figure 4.3, you'll see that the fact table itself contains two fields that are useful as dimensions: AccessDate and AccessTime. It's not unusual to find dimensions, particularly date and time dimensions, stored in the fact table. This is often the case when there are not many duplicate values in the dimension, as typically happens with time columns. In such a case there's nothing to be gained from splitting the dimension off to a separate table.

Having a dimension stored in the fact table is not a problem for Analysis Services. Simply create a new dimension and select the fact table as the dimension table. If you do this with tblWeblog in the sample database, you'll find that you get an extra panel in the Wizard after choosing the dimension table. Figure 4.6 shows the Select Dimension Type panel. The Wizard will present this panel whenever it detects any date or time columns in the selected dimension table.

FIGURE 4.6:

Select Dimension Type panel of the Dimension Wizard

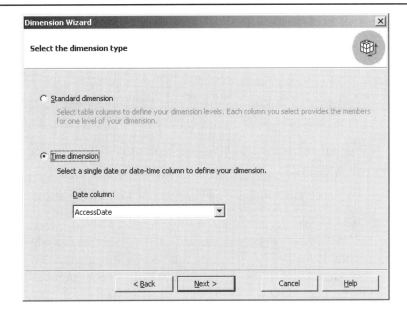

If you select a datetime field as a dimension, the next panel you see will be the Create Time Dimension Levels panel, shown in Figure 4.7. Often what you'll want to do with a datetime column is sort records into groups based on natural units of time (weeks, months, years, and so on). Analysis Services is smart enough to do this sorting for you, as long as you decide what levels you want to use for grouping.

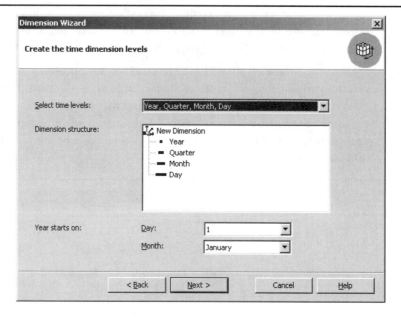

For our sample cube, we'll create two time dimensions:

- AccessDate, grouped by Year, Quarter, Month, Day
- AccessTime, grouped by Year, Month, Day, Hour, Minute

When you're done creating dimensions, click Next to move to the Finish panel of the Cube Wizard. Analysis Manager will offer to count the fact table rows at this point; you can skip this if you'd rather postpone that potentially time-consuming step until the cube is processed. Assign a name to the cube (we named our sample Weblog) and click Finish to exit the Cube Wizard.

WARNING   If you do skip the row-counting step, you need to open the cube in the Cube Editor and resave it before processing. Otherwise, you'll get an error telling you that the object structure is not valid when you attempt to process the cube.

Setting Storage Options

When you exit the Cube Wizard, Analysis Services will automatically load your new cube into the Cube Editor. This allows you to fine-tune any of the choices you made in the Cube Wizard. For now, you might just like to note that the fact and dimension tables are automatically joined according to the relationships that were present in the source database. You'll learn about the Cube Editor in Chapter 5.

To proceed with this initial cube, close the Cube Editor (either with the Close button or with the File ➤ Exit menu item). This will bring up a dialog box with the prompt, "You must design storage options and process the cube to query it. Do you want to set the data storage options now?" You can postpone setting data storage options, but you must do this before you can use the cube. So generally, it's a good idea to answer Yes to this prompt, which will open the Storage Design Wizard.

After the introductory panel, the Storage Design Wizard will prompt you to select the type of data storage. We discussed the possible choices in Chapter 3. Here's a brief review:

- MOLAP stores both the data and the aggregations in the multidimensional Analysis Services database. This choice takes the most disk space but will also give the best performance for browsing the cube.

- ROLAP stores the data and the aggregations in the relational database that is the source of the cube. ROLAP takes less space than MOLAP but may result in performance degradation. If you're using a SQL Server 2000 data source, you can also enable real-time updates for a ROLAP cube, which allows the cube to present up-to-date information without reprocessing.

- HOLAP stores the data in the relational database and the aggregations in the multidimensional database. HOLAP represents a compromise between MOLAP and ROLAP for both storage space and performance.

After you select a storage type (we chose MOLAP storage for the sample, because there is so little data that disk space really isn't a consideration here), the Storage Design Wizard will move to the Aggregation Options panel, shown in Figure 4.8. As you can see in the figure, the Next button on this panel is initially disabled. That's because you must tell the Wizard what aggregation options to use before proceeding.

Choosing aggregation options offers you another tradeoff between storage space and processing speed. Suppose you have a cube that includes several dimensions. If Analysis Services were to calculate the totals for every combination of those dimensions when you created the cube, then it could answer any query almost instantly. On the other hand, the storage space to store all those precalculated aggregations might be immense. So the goal is to figure out how many aggregations to calculate in advance to be able to answer queries quickly without taking up too much storage space.

FIGURE 4.8:

Setting aggregation
options in the Storage
Design Wizard

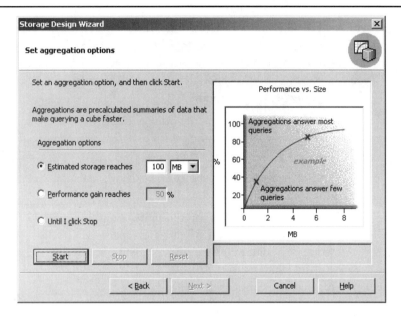

Rather than making you make decisions about individual aggregations, Analysis Services offers three ways for you to tell it when to stop calculating:

- You can select a maximum amount of storage to use for the aggregations.

- You can specify the percentage of performance improvement that you want the aggregations to provide.

- You can watch the graph on this page and click the Stop button when you're satisfied with the combination of storage space and performance improvement that it shows.

When you've selected one of these options, click the Start button. When the Storage Design Wizard is done determining which aggregations it should create, you'll be able to click the Next button to move to the final panel of the Storage Design Wizard.

Processing the Cube

The final step in creating a cube is to process the cube. Processing is the time that Analysis Services uses to create the precalculated aggregations. Because this can take a long while to finish, the final panel of the Storage Design Wizard offers you the choice between processing the new cube immediately and saving it to process later.

TIP   If you choose to save a cube without processing it, you can process it later by right-clicking the cube in the Analysis Manager interface and choosing Process.

When Analysis Services processes a cube, it will continually update a dialog box showing its progress. Figure 4.9 shows this dialog box for our sample Weblog cube.

FIGURE 4.9:

Processing a cube

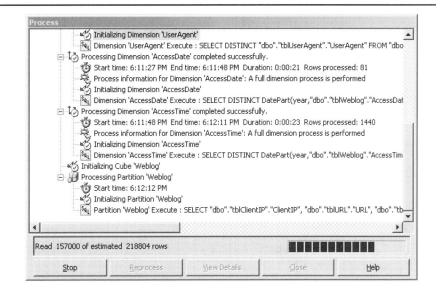

Browsing a Cube

After you've created a cube, you can use its data. In upcoming chapters you'll see a variety of ways to interact programmatically with Analysis Services. For now, though, we'd like to show you a few ways to manually view data from an Analysis Services cube:

- Using the Cube Browser
- Using Excel
- Using Visual Basic
- Using a web browser
- Using ProClarity
- Using Hungry Dog IntelliBrowser
- Using Cognos PowerPlay

In this section, we'll use the FoodMart 2000 sample data to demonstrate the various browsing alternatives. That way, you can follow along even if you didn't create the new Weblog cube from the first part of this chapter.

PowerPlay, ProClarity, and IntelliBrowser are examples of third-party OLAP clients. Because the Analysis Services API is well-documented, it's possible for anyone to write an application that displays Analysis Services data. We've chosen these three applications as a representative sample of the many that are on the market. You'll find more information, and some trial versions of third-party software, on the companion CD.

Using the Cube Browser

Analysis Services ships with a component called the Cube Browser. If you're working at a computer that has Analysis Services installed, you can load a cube into the Cube Browser in two ways:

- You can click the cube name in the Analysis Manager treeview and select the Data tab of the taskpad that appears in the main MMC panel to host the Cube Browser directly in the Analysis Manager.

- You can right-click the cube name in the Analysis Manager treeview and select Browse Data to open the Cube Browser in a separate window.

Figure 4.10 shows the default view of the Sales cube from the FoodMart 2000 sample database in a stand-alone Cube Browser window.

FIGURE 4.10:

The Cube Browser

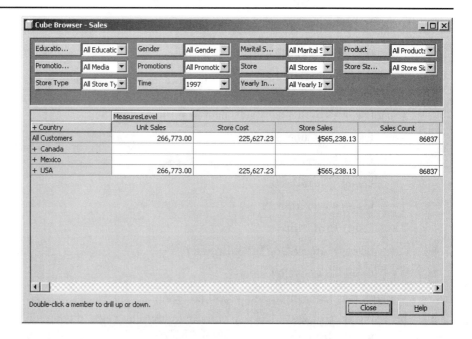

The Cube Browser interface displays quite a bit of information. That's because a cube is a complex structure. Microsoft's designers have done an excellent job of allowing the user to manipulate a cube within the constraints of a two-dimensional interface.

Turn your attention first to the grid in the lower part of the Cube Browser. This is where you can see dimensions and measures that you are actively working with. In the default view of the Sales cube shown in Figure 4.10, only one dimension is displayed: the Country dimension, which occupies the leftmost column of the grid. The other columns of the grid are taken up with the measures in this cube: Unit Sales, Store Cost, and so on. The result is a grid that shows all of the measures broken down by the top level in the Country dimension. For example, the Store Sales for all records from stores in the USA totals $565,238.13.

You can expand and contract the levels within a dimension by double-clicking. For example, you can expand the Country dimension to the StateProvince level for all measures and then suppress the StateProvince breakdown for Mexico by following these two steps:

1. Double-click the + Country label to expand all of the countries to show the StateProvince column.

2. Double-click the – Mexico cell to collapse the StateProvince detail for Mexico to a single Mexico Total row.

Figure 4.11 shows the results of these actions. The Cube Browser still shows all the measures broken down by various elements in the Country dimension.

FIGURE 4.11:

Modifying the display of a dimension in the Cube Browser

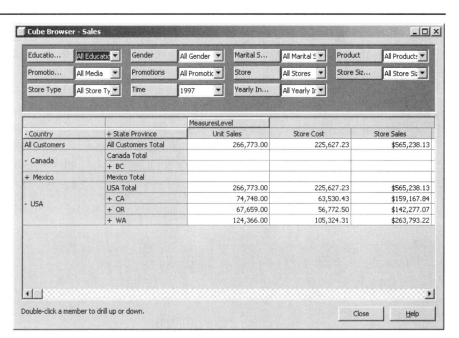

The Sales cube in the FoodMart 2000 sample database has a dozen dimensions: the eleven dimensions that are displayed above the grid, plus the Customers dimension, which supplies the grid rows. The Cube Browser wouldn't be very useful if you could only view the data broken down by a single dimension. Fortunately, the Cube Browser allows you to choose dimensions in a flexible manner. It's easy to add a new dimension to the grid, or to replace an existing dimension with a new one.

For example, to see a count of sales broken down by education, gender, and marital status, follow these steps (starting with the Cube Browser as shown in Figure 4.11):

1. Drag the button (not the combo box) for the Education dimension from the upper part of the Cube Browser to the lower part and drop it directly on top of the `- Country` button to replace the Country dimension with the Education dimension. You'll know you're in the right place to drop the dimension when the cursor shows a picture containing a two-headed arrow.

2. Drag the button (not the combo box) for the Gender dimension from the upper part of the Cube Browser to the lower part and drop it directly on top of the `MeasuresLevel` button to replace the Measures with the Gender dimension.

3. Drag the button (not the combo box) for the Marital Status dimension from the upper part of the Cube Browser to the lower part and drop it beside the `Gender` button. You'll know you're in the right place when the cursor does not show a two-headed arrow.

4. Select Sales Count in the Measures combo box in the upper part of the Cube Browser.

The result of following these steps is shown in Figure 4.12. Note that we've used the horizontal scroll bar to move sideways in the grid. The rows of the grid show the various education levels in the data; the columns are broken down first by gender and then by marital status; and the numbers in the white portion of the grid are the Sales Count measure values. For example, single females with a bachelor's degree were responsible for 5418 sales.

The activities we've performed on the Sales cube thus far in this section (choosing different combinations of dimensions and measures) are sometimes referred to as "slicing," because each combination represents a different slice through the n-dimensional data in the cube. You can also use the Cube Browser to perform "dicing," that is, selecting a filtered subset of the data.

FIGURE 4.12:

The Sales cube sliced by a different set of dimensions

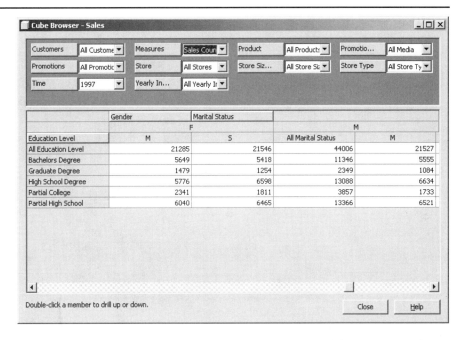

Suppose, for example, you want to see what the buying patterns look like only in the data for California. To filter the existing Cube Browser view to show only the totals for California, follow these steps:

1. Click the drop-down arrow for the Store dimension in the upper part of the Cube Browser.

2. Click the + sign next to All Stores to expand the list of countries.

3. Click the + sign next to USA to expand the list of states.

4. Click CA to filter the records to include only records for California.

Figure 4.13 shows the process of choosing to filter data in the Cube Browser. When you complete the operation, the combo box for Store will show CA, the value that's being used for filtering.

Finally, if a cube supports drillthrough, you can use the Cube Browser to view the original source data behind an aggregation. *Drillthrough* is a process in which Analysis Services retrieves the source data that was used to produce an aggregation from the cube's data source. The data is joined according to the joins in the cube's schema and presented as a simple recordset. To drillthrough in the Cube Browser, right-click any white cell and choose Drillthrough. Figure 4.14 shows some drillthrough data from the Sales cube.

FIGURE 4.13:

Filtering records in the
Cube Browser

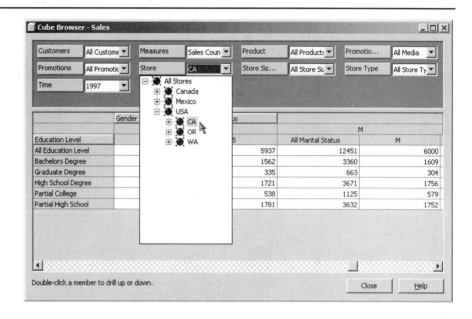

NOTE   You'll learn how to enable drillthrough for a cube in Chapter 5.

FIGURE 4.14:

Cube with drillthrough data

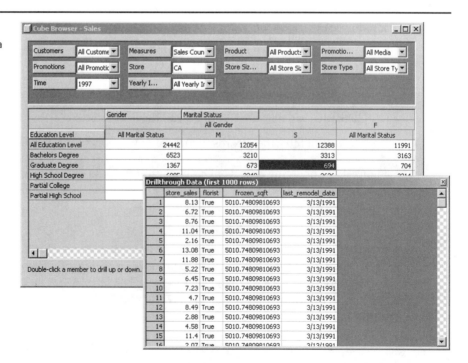

Using Excel

Of course, the Cube Browser is not the only application that can display data from an Analysis Services cube. (That's a good thing, because the Cube Browser only works on computers where you've installed Analysis Services.) Perhaps the easiest client in widespread use is Microsoft Excel. You can connect Excel 2000 directly to cube data by using an Excel PivotTable.

To display the FoodMart 2000 Sales cube as an Excel PivotTable, follow these steps:

1. Launch Excel 2000 and open a new worksheet.

2. Select Data ➢ PivotTable and PivotChart Report from the Excel menus.

3. In the first step of the PivotTable and PivotChart Wizard, choose External Data Source as the source of your data, and PivotTable as the type of report that you wish to create. Click Next.

4. In the second step of the PivotTable and PivotChart Wizard, click Get Data. This will open the Choose Data Source dialog box.

5. Click the OLAP Cubes tab of the Choose Data Source dialog box. Select <New Data Source> and click OK.

6. In the Create New Data Source dialog box, enter a name for your data source and choose Microsoft OLE DB Provider for Olap Services 8.0 as the OLAP provider to use. Click the Connect button. Depending on the software that's installed on your computer, you may also see a driver for an older version of the Olap OLE DB provider.

7. In the Multidimensional Connection dialog box, select Analysis Server as the location of the data source and enter the name of the computer where Analysis Services is running. Click Next.

8. Select the FoodMart 2000 database. Click Finish.

9. In the Create New Data Source dialog box, select the Sales cube. Click OK.

10. In the Choose Data Source dialog box, select the data source that you just created (the one that you named in step 6). Click OK.

11. In the PivotTable and PivotChart Wizard, click Next.

12. In the third step of the PivotTable and PivotChart Wizard, choose whether you would like the PivotTable in a new worksheet or an existing worksheet, and click Finish.

Figure 4.15 shows the results of following these steps: a blank PivotTable. Although this doesn't look like much, you've now made all the connections necessary to work with the Sales cube data from within Excel.

FIGURE 4.15:

Blank Excel 2000 Pivot-
Table connected to an
Analysis Services cube

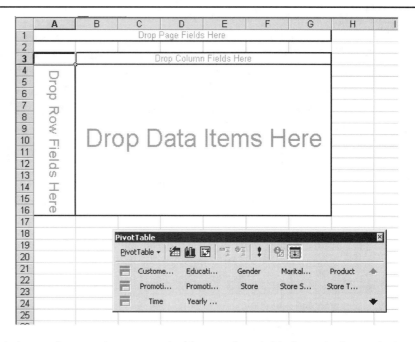

To fill in the skeleton of an Excel 2000 PivotTable, you drag fields from the list at the bottom of the PivotTable toolbar (this area is sometimes called "the well") and drop them at the indicated spots in the skeleton of the PivotTable. Although the terminology is different from that of the Cube Browser, the idea is the same:

- Dimensions can be dragged to the Drop Row Fields Here and Drop Column Fields Here areas. These become the basis for the slice of the cube to be displayed.

- Dimensions can also be dragged to the Drop Page Fields Here area. Dimensions in this area provide a drop-down interface to filter the displayed data.

- Measures can be dragged to the Drop Data Items Here area. If you're in doubt as to whether something is a dimension or a measure, you can look at the little icon to the left side of the well. It will show you the areas where you can drop this field.

Excel will let you drag fields back and forth and rearrange them, so you get the same sort of interactive analysis that you can achieve with the Cube Browser. You can also right-click the PivotTable and choose PivotChart to create a bar graph from the data. Figure 4.16 shows a PivotChart of Store Cost and Profit, sliced by education, gender, and marital status, for stores in California.

FIGURE 4.16:

An Excel PivotChart based on an Analysis Services cube

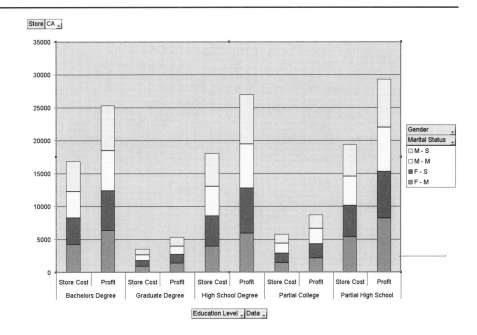

Excel PivotCharts and PivotTables can display data from multiple measures at the same time even when you're slicing by more than one dimension, unlike the Cube Browser.

Using Visual Basic

Visual Basic 6.0 does not display the same tight integration with Analysis Services that Excel 2000 displays. That's because Visual Basic 6.0 came out well before SQL Server 2000 did. Nevertheless, if you just want a quick look at Analysis Services data on a Visual Basic form, it's pretty easy. Follow these steps for an example:

1. Launch Visual Basic and create a new standard EXE project.

2. Use Ctrl+T to open the Components dialog box and add Microsoft ADO Data Control 6.0 and Microsoft DataGrid Control 6.0 to the project.

3. Add an ADO Data Control and a DataGrid Control to the default form in the project.

4. Set the ADO Data Control's ConnectionString property to

    ```
    Provider=MSOLAP;Integrated Security=SSPI;
    ➡Data Source=localhost;Initial Catalog=FoodMart 2000
    ```

If your Analysis Server is on a different computer from the one where you're running the Visual Basic project, change localhost to the name of that computer.

5. Set the ADO Data Control's RecordSource property to

```
SELECT
[Education Level].MEMBERS ON ROWS,
{[Measures].[Unit Sales]} ON COLUMNS
FROM Sales
```

6. Set the DataGrid control's DataSource property to the name of the ADO Data Control (by default, Adodc1).

7. Run the project.

Figure 4.17 shows the result of running this simple Visual Basic project.

FIGURE 4.17:

Analysis Services data in
Visual Basic

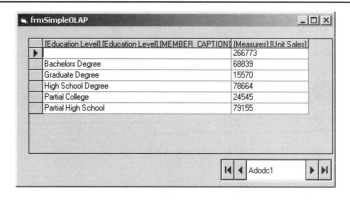

The RecordSource property that you entered in step 4 is an example of a Multidimensional Expression (MDX), Analysis Server's extension to SQL to allow access to multidimensional data. You'll learn about MDX in detail in Chapter 6, "Querying Analysis Services with MDX."

NOTE   This example shows how easy it is to establish a connection between Visual Basic and Analysis Services. You'll see a variety of more sophisticated ways to manipulate and communicate with Analysis Services from Visual Basic in later chapters. You may also want to investigate the SimpleOLAP sample that installs as part of Analysis Services. You'll find it in the Program Files\Microsoft Analysis Services\Samples\VbAdoSimple folder on your hard drive.

Using a Web Browser

Of course, these days the user interface of choice for many organizations is the web browser. You can display Analysis Services data directly in a web browser if you choose. The main problem is that there's no good cross-browser way to do this. However, if you're working in a Microsoft-centric organization, the Office Web Components offer a PivotTable control that can display data from an Analysis Services cube. As you'll see, this control is reminiscent of the Excel PivotTable, although there are some differences.

We'll demonstrate the creation of a web page using the PivotTable control with Microsoft FrontPage 2000. To display Analysis Services data in your web browser, follow these steps:

1. Open FrontPage and create a new web page.

2. Select Insert ➢ Component ➢ Office PivotTable from the FrontPage menus. This will place a blank PivotTable on your web page.

3. Click once within the PivotTable to activate it. The control will get a crosshatched border when it's activated.

4. Click the Property Toolbox button on the PivotTable toolbar.

5. Click the expand icon for the Data Source section in the Property Toolbox.

6. Set the control to get data using a connection. Click the Connection Editor button to open the Data Link Properties dialog box.

7. On the Provider tab of the Data Link Properties dialog box, choose Microsoft OLE DB Provider for OLAP Services.

8. On the Connection tab of the Data Link Properties dialog box, enter the name of your Analysis Server as the Location of the data, and enter appropriate security information. Select FoodMart 2000 as the initial catalog to use. Click OK to dismiss the Data Link Properties dialog box.

9. Select Sales as the Data Member in the PivotTable Property Toolbox.

10. Click the Field List toolbar button in the PivotTable control. This will open a list of all the measures and dimensions in the Sales cube. Figure 4.18 shows this stage in the design process.

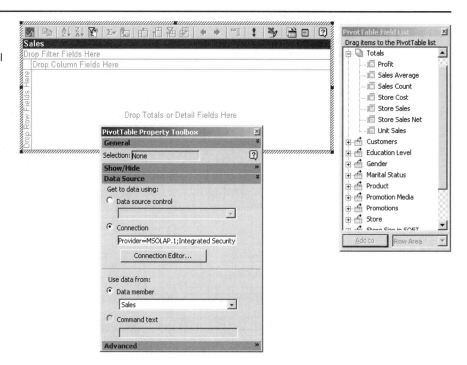

11. You can drag and drop fields from the PivotTable Field List to the PivotTable control, just as you can drag and drop fields from the well to the PivotTable in Excel. Drag the Sales Count field to the data area.

12. Drag the Education Level dimension to the Row Fields area.

13. Drag the Gender dimension to the Column Fields area.

14. Drag the Product dimension to the Filter Fields area.

15. Save the web page and open it in a web browser.

Figure 4.19 shows the completed page open in Internet Explorer. Note that the web page is interactive. Internet Explorer automatically displays the Field List, and the user can drag and drop, rearrange fields, and filter the data just as they could in Excel 2000.

FIGURE 4.19:

Data from Analysis Services
in a web browser

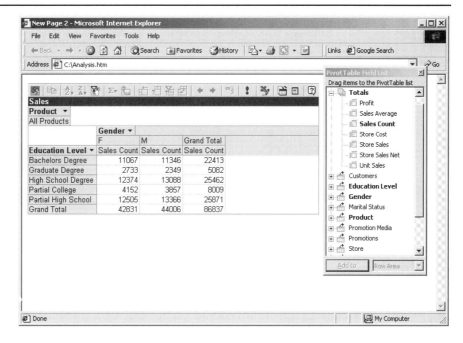

Although the completed web page is flexible and easy to use for anyone with Excel experience, this is probably only a solution for users on an intranet, rather than on the wider Internet. There are two problems with using the Office Web Controls to display data. The first is that they won't work in all browsers, so if you're not in control of the browser version, you can't guarantee that the viewer of the page will actually see the data. The second problem is licensing. To use the Office Web Controls, you must have a valid Office 2000 license on the viewing computer. There is currently no supported, legal way to redistribute these controls.

Using ProClarity

ProClarity 3.0 is an OLAP client from ProClarity. It offers a browser-like interface, extensive integration with Microsoft Office, and VBA customization. You'll find an evaluation version of ProClarity on the companion CD.

ProClarity offers several innovative ways to view data from Analysis Services, including pie charts and other graphs, grids, and scatter plots. These views can be combined into briefing books that allow you to capture a set of views of interest for later inspection.

One of the most innovative ways to view data in ProClarity is on a decomposition tree. To view the Sales data from FoodMart 2000 in a decomposition tree, follow these steps:

1. Install the sample ProClarity client from the companion CD.

2. Launch ProClarity.

3. Choose Open a Cube for Browsing from the Welcome dialog box.

4. Select the server containing your Analysis Services data and click OK.

5. Select the Sales cube from the FoodMart 2000 database and click OK.

6. Click Decomposition Tree to launch the Decomposition Tree Wizard. Click Next to dismiss the introductory panel of the Wizard.

7. Select the Sales Count value and the Customers item. Click Finish. This will open the decomposition tree. You'll see a single box in the workspace labeled "Customers – 87K – 100%." This indicates that you're looking at information from about 87,000 customers, which represents 100 percent of the source data.

8. Click the Customers box to expand the Country level of the data.

9. Click the USA box, then the WA box, then the Puyallup box to expand three levels further in the data along the Customers dimension.

10. At this point the lowest level of data shown is for an individual customer. You can see the contribution of each customer to the overall data and how those contributions fit together into the next level of aggregation. If you hover the cursor over any particular customer, you'll get details of that customer. Figure 4.20 shows the decomposition tree at this point.

ProClarity also offers impressive export capabilities. Once you've created a view of the data that you find useful, you can have it available as a fully interactive page within Microsoft Outlook or even in a PowerPoint presentation. All in all, ProClarity is a great tool for data analysis by any moderately sophisticated Windows user.

NOTE   In discussing third-party software, we're not trying to show you the complete feature set. We're just trying to give you some idea of the breadth of OLAP clients available. Refer to the companion CD for additional information and web links to explore further.

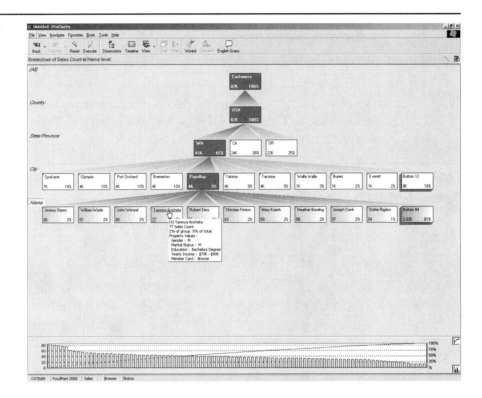

Using Hungry Dog IntelliBrowser

IntelliBrowser 2.0 is an OLAP client from Hungry Dog Software. It concentrates on presenting data in a combined graph and grid view, with easy drilldown and the ability to use
MDX functions. In this section we'll show you how to use the IntelliBrowser interface to
investigate the data in a cube. You can read about the product's support for MDX functions
in its help file. There's an evaluation copy of IntelliBrowser available on the companion CD.

1. Install the IntelliBrowser sample from the companion CD.

2. Launch IntelliBrowser.

3. Select the server where your Analysis Services database is located, click Connect, then
    select the FoodMart 2000 database and the Sales cube and click OK.

4. In the MDX Builder section of the screen, expand the Measures dimension until you
    can see the individual measures. Drag the Unit Sales and Profit measures up and drop
    them on the Columns node under the Query node in the MDX Builder treeview.

5. Drag the Product dimension up and drop it on the Rows node under the Query node in the MDX Builder treeview.

6. Select Query ➢ Execute from the menus. This will display the top-level data in bar graph and grid format.

7. Double-click All Products and then Food to drill down to the Food level of the Products dimension. The grid and chart will update in tandem. Figure 4.21 shows the Intelli-Browser interface at this point.

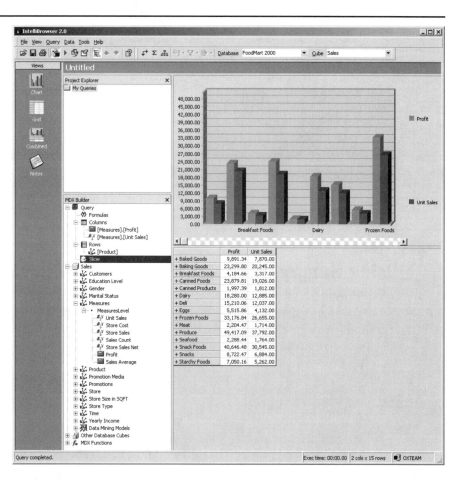

One excellent use of IntelliBrowser is as a tool for understanding MDX query syntax. Once you've drilled down to the level of data you're interested in, you can choose Query ➢ Edit Query to see the exact MDX statement that was used to retrieve the currently displayed data.

IntelliBrowser can also save MDX queries or open MDX queries that were saved with other software.

Another area in which IntelliBrowser excels is access to MDX functions. The MDX Functions node of the MDX Builder offers complete access to the MDX function library. You can drag and drop these functions to the Query node, and then use drag and drop to fill in their arguments.

Using Cognos PowerPlay

Unlike the other tools mentioned in this section, Cognos PowerPlay is part of a complete OLAP solution. Cognos offers its own OLAP server as well as a variety of connectivity and analysis tools that span the spectrum of business intelligence needs, from creating cubes to publishing data on the web. In this section, we'll show you how you can use the Cognos software with an existing Analysis Services cube.

1. Launch PowerPlay Connect. This is the Cognos tool for linking data from other servers to their own software.

2. Select MS SSOS ODBO as the database type and localhost as the server. Enter the provider string `MSOLAP;CATALOG=FoodMart 2000;CUBE=Sales` to describe the cube to PowerPlay.

3. Use the Test button on the toolbar to make sure that the connection is set up properly, then save the connection as Sales.mdc.

4. Close PowerPlay Connect.

5. Launch PowerPlay.

6. Choose Create a New Report from the opening prompt.

7. Select Sales.mdc as the local cube to use and click Open. Note that PowerPlay can also use CUB files saved by the Microsoft PivotTable Service directly.

8. Click the Customers folder and select USA to drill into the USA data.

9. Drag the Product folder and drop it next to the Customers list to break the numbers down by Customer and then Product.

10. Click the 3D Chart button on the toolbar to see the data in a 3D bar chart. Note that PowerPlay presents both the totals and the drilled-down data in the chart.

11. Right-click any bar on the chart and select Explain to see the details that go into that bar. Figure 4.22 shows the PowerPlay interface at this point.

FIGURE 4.22:

Exploring data with Cognos PowerPlay

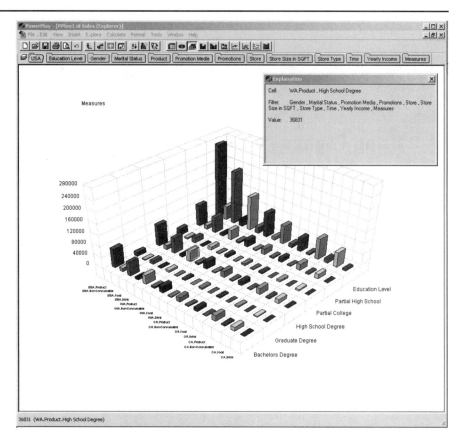

In addition to making graphical interactive exploration of cube data easy, Cognos Power-Play makes it easy to share the data with others in your organization. You can publish a PowerPlay report as HTML and control whether other users can interact with it, including which filters and options they can choose. You can also publish briefing books containing multiple views of the data.

PowerPlay is more expensive than the other options we've looked at in this chapter. But if you are looking for an OLAP analysis package that's designed specifically for business needs and that offers a wide variety of useful analyses, it's an excellent choice.

Partitioned Cubes, Linked Cubes, and Virtual Cubes

So far, we've only used what are sometimes called regular cubes. Analysis Services supports other varieties of cubes. In particular, you should be familiar with these three types of cubes:

Partitioned cubes   Use different storage modes for subsets of data within a single cube.

Linked cubes   Are cubes based on data stored on a different Analysis Services server.

Virtual cubes   Are combinations of regular cubes in a larger logical cube.

In this section, you'll learn the basics of creating and working with these types of cubes.

NOTE   In addition to regular, partitioned, linked, and virtual cubes, you'll also run across references to local cubes, real-time cubes, and write-enabled cubes. Local cubes are disk files created and maintained by Microsoft Excel that can be used as the basis for PivotTables; you'll learn more about local cubes in Chapter 9, "Advanced Usage of the PivotTable Service." Real-time cubes and write-enabled cubes are discussed in Chapter 5.

Partitioned Cubes

Cubes are stored by Analysis Services in units called *partitions*. When you create a new cube, Analysis Services automatically creates a default partition for the cube and stores the data for the cube in this partition. You can see the partition structure of any cube by expanding that cube in the Analysis Manager treeview and inspecting the contents of its Partitions folder.

If you're running the Enterprise Edition of Analysis Services, you can distribute the data in a single cube over multiple partitions. Multiple partitions give you finer control over the storage of the cube's data than a single partition allows. For example,

- You can store part of the data on the same Analysis Server that stores the cube (a *local partition*) or on another Analysis Server (a *remote partition*).

- You can choose among MOLAP, ROLAP, and HOLAP storage on a partition-by-partition basis.

- You can devote more or less space to aggregations on a partition-by-partition basis.

All of these decisions are completely transparent to the end user who is browsing the data stored in a cube. The cube always appears as one large dataset no matter how many partitions it uses.

The sample Sales cube that ships as part of the FoodMart 2000 database contains only sales data for 1997. If you open the underlying Access 2000 database, you'll discover that the database also includes data for 1998 sales. This data is in a second fact table that has the same structure as the 1997 fact table.

Suppose you were responsible for this cube and had just gotten the 1998 data to update the cube. You might want to add the 1998 data, while at the same time minimizing the space occupied by the 1997 data. To do this, you can adjust the storage options for the 1997 data and then add the 1998 data as an additional partition. To perform these tasks, follow these steps:

WARNING   You can only follow this entire sequence of steps if you've got the Enterprise Edition of Analysis Services installed.

1. Expand the treeview of the Sales cube until you can see the default Sales partition. This is where the 1997 data is stored.

2. Right-click the Sales partition and choose Design Storage. This will open the Storage Design Wizard. Click Next to skip past the introductory panel if it's displayed.

3. Inspect the aggregations that already exist for this partition, select Replace the Existing Aggregations, and click Next.

4. Select HOLAP as the data storage type and click Next.

5. Select Performance Gain Reaches 10% and click Start. Click Next when the Wizard has finished designing aggregations.

6. Choose to process the aggregations and click Finish to exit the Storage Design Wizard. When Analysis Services has finished processing the partition, click Close to dismiss the dialog box.

7. Right-click the Partitions folder and select New Partition to launch the Partition Wizard.

8. Click Next to skip the introductory panel of the Partition Wizard.

9. The Specify Data Source and Fact Table will default to showing the data source and fact table that are used by the default partition of the cube. We'll use a different fact table from the same data source for the second partition of the cube. Click Change and select sales_fact_1998 as the fact table for this partition. Click Next.

10. You can optionally select to store just part of a cube on a partition. We're going to store all of the dimensions on the new partition, so just click Next to move on.

11. The next panel will give you the choice of creating a local or remote partition. If you have a second Analysis Services server on your network, you can choose to create a remote partition here. Whether the partition is local or remote will not affect the behavior of the cube. Click Next after you've made your selection.

12. Name the new partition `Sales 1998`, choose to design the partitions now, and click Finish. This will launch the Storage Design Wizard. Click Next to skip the introductory panel for the Storage Design Wizard if it's displayed.

13. Select MOLAP as the type of the new partition.

14. Choose to create aggregations until the performance gain reaches 50 percent. Click Start to create the aggregations. Note that these aggregations will take much more space than those you created for the existing partition.

15. Click Next, choose to process the cube immediately, and click Finish.

Figure 4.23 shows the resulting partition information within Analysis Manager. The green color for the Sales partition indicates that it is the default partition for this cube. If you browse the data for the full Sales cube, you'll find that it's impossible to tell from the user interface which partition is responsible for a particular aggregation.

FIGURE 4.23:

Partition information for the Sales cube

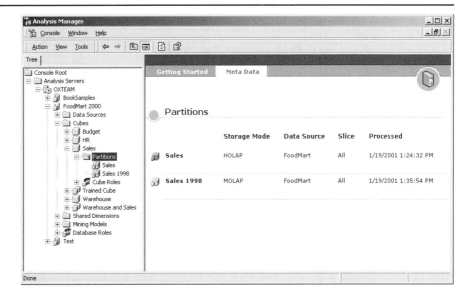

Linked Cubes

It's possible for a cube to get all of its data from a cube stored on a different Analysis Server. This is referred to as a *linked cube*. In other words, the cube named Sales on Server1 might actually be stored as a cube named SalesCurrent on Server2.

NOTE   Linked cubes are only available in the Enterprise Edition of Analysis Services.

Why might you want to create a linked cube? Here are some reasons:

- The cube can be more easily available to users who log on to different servers, without the overhead of storing the data on all the servers.

- Security can be implemented so that the source data of the cube is protected but the aggregations are available more widely.

- A cube can be maintained and updated by a single group in your company and made widely available to users who can't modify it, even by accident.

If you happen to have multiple installations of Analysis Server available, creating linked cubes is simple. Follow these steps:

1. In Analysis Manager, navigate to the Cubes folder of the database where you wish to create the linked cube. This is the database where the new linked cube will be available, not the database containing the existing cube.

2. Right-click the Cubes folder and select New Linked Cube.

3. In the Linked Cube dialog box, click New Data Source.

4. In the Multidimensional Data Source dialog box, enter the name of the server that contains the source cube, and select the source database. Click OK.

5. In the Linked Cube dialog box, select the source cube and assign a name for the linked cube. Figure 4.24 shows the creation of a linked cube named Remote Sales based on the Sales cube in the FoodMart 2000 database on a server named STALLION.

6. Click OK to create the linked cube.

7. In the Analysis Manager treeview, right-click the new linked cube and select Process.

8. In the Process a Cube dialog box, select Full Process and click OK.

9. Close the Process dialog box when Analysis Services has finished processing the cube.

You'll find that you can now browse the data in the linked cube just as if it were located on the server where you created the link.

FIGURE 4.24:

Creating a linked cube

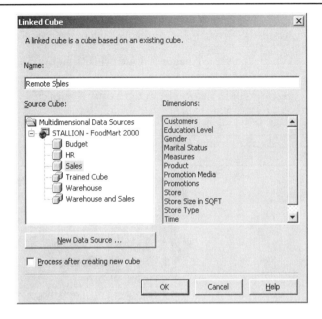

Virtual Cubes

A virtual cube is a cube consisting of one or more measures and one or more dimensions from one or more regular or linked cubes. There are generally two reasons why you might want to create a virtual cube. The first is to combine the data from several cubes into a set of data that can be browsed all at once. For example, if you had separate cubes for 1997 sales, 1998 sales, and 1999 sales, you could use a virtual cube to represent all of the data on sales from 1997 through 1999. Second, a virtual cube can hide excess detail from some users. For example, you might have a cube with eight dimensions of which only three interest the bulk of your users. You could create a virtual cube that uses only those three dimensions.

Virtual cubes do not store their own data, so there is very little overhead to creating a virtual cube compared to creating another regular cube to display the same data. To create a virtual cube in the FoodMart 2000 database, follow these steps:

1. Right-click the Cubes folder and select New Virtual Cube.

2. Read the introductory panel and click Next.

3. Select the Sales cube from the list of available cubes and move it to the list of cubes that the virtual cube will include. Click Next.

4. Select the Store Sales measure and click Next.

5. Select the Store, Product, and Store Size in SQFT dimensions and click Next.

6. Name the virtual cube MiniSales. Select Process Now and click Finish.

7. When Analysis Manager is done processing the cube, close the Process dialog box. Processing the cube should be very fast because Analysis Manager can extract all of the necessary information from the existing Sales cube.

Figure 4.25 shows the MiniSales cube in the Cube Browser. Note how much less confusing this virtual cube is compared to the full Sales cube.

FIGURE 4.25:

Browsing a virtual cube

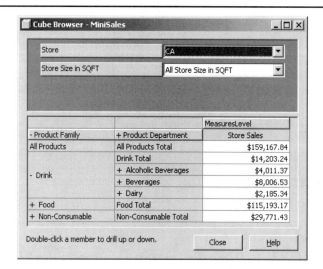

Updating a Cube

One of the problems that any Analysis Services administrator faces is that of keeping cubes up-to-date when their source data changes. From the user interface, it's as simple as right-clicking the cube, choosing Process, and selecting the type of processing to do:

- The *Incremental Update* option adds any new data from the data source to the cube and recalculates the affected aggregations.

- The *Refresh Data* option clears and reloads all of the data in the cube and then recalculates the aggregations.

- The *Full Process* option completely rebuilds the entire cube, just as if you had deleted and recreated it from scratch.

Manually processing a cube, though, is not an attractive option for routine use. More typically an administrator will want to reprocess a cube on a regular basis as a scheduled job. You can use SQL Server 2000 Data Transformation Services (DTS) to accomplish this.

To create a DTS job to process an Analysis Services cube, follow these steps:

1. Launch SQL Server 2000 Enterprise Manager.

2. Navigate to the Data Transformation Services folder of the server that hosts your Analysis Server.

3. Right-click the Data Transformation Services folder and select New Package.

4. From the DTS Package menu, choose Task ➤ Analysis Services Processing Task.

5. Expand the treeview to show the cube you wish to process.

6. Select the type of processing to perform. Figure 4.26 shows the Sales cube being selected for Refresh Data processing.

FIGURE 4.26:

Creating a DTS task to process an Analysis Services cube

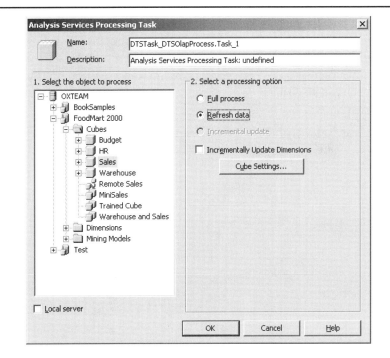

7. Assign a name and description to the task and click OK to add it to the DTS package.

8. Save the DTS package to the local SQL Server.

9. Close the DTS package and navigate to the Local Packages node of the SQL Server Enterprise Manager treeview.

10. Right-click the DTS package and choose Schedule Package. This will open the SQL Server recurring job schedule dialog box, which offers flexible options for executing the package on a regular basis.

In most cases you would create the Analysis Services Processing Task as part of a larger DTS package that actually collects new source data. For example, a DTS package might use a Transform Data task to move data from an OLTP database to a data warehouse, followed by one or more Analysis Services Processing Tasks to update the cubes that depend on that data.

Conclusion

In this chapter, you've learned the basic skills that you'll need to deal with Analysis Services from the Analysis Manager user interface. You now know how to create cubes and how to browse cubes with a variety of software. We also discussed some varieties of cubes other than regular cubes and showed how you can use Data Transformation Services to keep a cube up-to-date.

In the next chapter, we'll dig into the Analysis Manager interface in more depth. You'll see that SQL Server 2000 Analysis Services offers several advanced options that bring increased flexibility to your OLAP processes.

CHAPTER **5**

Advanced Analysis Services

- Dimension Types

- The Cube Editor

- Drillthrough and custom actions

- Write-enabled cubes

- Real-time cubes

- Security

- Configuring Analysis Services

Now that you understand the basics of SQL Server 2000 Analysis Services, we'd like to introduce some of the more advanced capabilities of this software. In this chapter you'll learn about ways to gain more control over your cubes and the data that they contain. Many of the features we'll be covering here are new in this version of Analysis Services, so you should at least skim this chapter even if you're already familiar with the SQL Server 7.0 release.

Dimension Types

In Chapter 4, "Using Analysis Services," you saw how to use the Dimension Wizard to create a new star schema dimension. A star schema, you'll recall, is one in which all of the dimension tables are related directly to the fact table. As you can see in Figure 5.1, the Dimension Wizard can actually create five different types of dimension:

- Star schema
- Snowflake schema
- Parent-child
- Virtual dimension
- Mining model

FIGURE 5.1:

Choosing a dimension type
in the Dimension Wizard

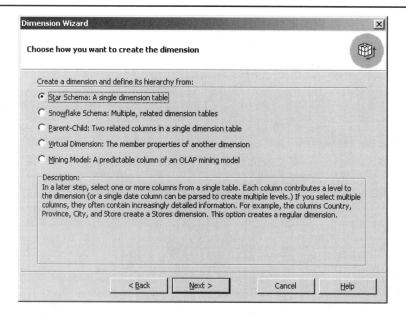

We discussed the star schema dimension in Chapter 4. You'll learn about data mining models in Chapter 11, "Building Data Mining Solutions with Analysis Services." In this section, we'll discuss the other three types of dimensions and look at the advanced options offered by the Dimension Wizard.

Snowflake Schemas

As we discussed earlier in the book, a star schema, in which every dimension table is directly related to the fact table in a cube, is often the most efficient way to organize the source data for a cube. Sometimes, however, you don't have the luxury of a star schema. In a normalized relational database, it's not unusual for the information for a single dimension to be spread across several tables. For example, a ProductID field in the fact table may be related directly to a Products table, which in turn is related to a Suppliers table. If the Suppliers table has no direct link to the fact table, then information from that table cannot be included in a star schema.

That's where the *snowflake schema* comes in. A snowflake schema allows you to select a set of tables that together contain the information for a single dimension. For example, in Chapter 4 we included as one dimension of the Weblog cube a table, tblURL, that contained the URLs that were retrieved from a web server. But there's a more relational way to store this data: as separate tables of pages and paths, as shown in Figure 5.2. To combine the information from tblPath and tblURL2 into a dimension, you need to create a snowflake schema dimension.

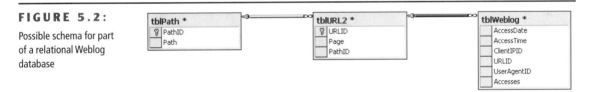

FIGURE 5.2:

Possible schema for part of a relational Weblog database

To create a snowflake schema dimension in the BookSamples database, follow these steps:

1. Launch the Dimension Wizard. You can do this from within the Cube Wizard, as you saw in Chapter 4, or by right-clicking the Shared Dimension folder within an Analysis Services database in Analysis Manager and selecting New Dimension ➢ Wizard.

2. If the Wizard presents the introductory panel, click Next.

3. Select Snowflake Schema as the type of dimension and click Next.

4. Select tblURL2 and tblPath as the dimension tables and click Next.

5. In this case, the Dimension Wizard will automatically create the proper join between the tables. You can use the Create and Edit Joins panel, which appears next, to adjust joins if necessary. Click Next when the dimension tables are properly joined.

6. Select Page and Path as the levels for the dimension. Ordinarily you should select parent levels before child levels. The Dimension Wizard counts the number of members in each level, and if you select them in the wrong order it will offer to reverse the order of levels for you in a Move Level dialog box. If you see this dialog box, click Yes to reorder the levels. Click Next when you've selected both levels.

7. Select the PathID column as the key for the Path level and the URLID as the key for the Page level from the combo boxes in the Member Key Column column. This ensures that two pages with the same name but different paths are not confused. Click Next.

8. Leave the Advanced Options unchecked and click Next.

9. Name the dimension PagePaths and click Finish.

10. Close the Dimension Editor to save the new dimension.

Figure 5.3 shows a cube that uses the new PagePaths dimension, opened in the Cube Browser. Note that nothing here indicates that the dimension is a snowflake schema dimension; the cube browser displays it just the same as it would were the dimension a star schema dimension.

FIGURE 5.3:

Snowflake schema dimension in the Cube Browser

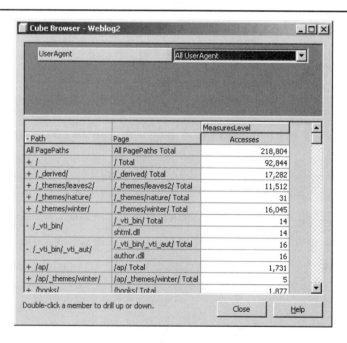

Parent-Child Dimensions

Many dimensions are naturally organized into hierarchies. Some examples:

- Employee dimensions can be placed on the hierarchy of an organization chart.

- Part dimensions can be mapped to a hierarchical bill of materials.

- Person dimensions can sometimes be mapped to a family tree.

These three examples share the property that they can be represented in a relational database by a *self-join*. That is, each record has a parent, the parent record has the same fields as the child record, and both records are stored in the same table. A table of employees, for example, might include a field for the employee ID of the employee's boss, which would relate back to a different record in the same employees table.

Analysis Services includes *parent-child dimensions* to capture this sort of information. Figure 5.4 shows another way that the Weblog database could be organized. In this schema, instead of storing each path separately, the paths are stored in a hierarchy.

FIGURE 5.4:

Possible schema for part of a Weblog database

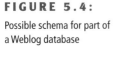
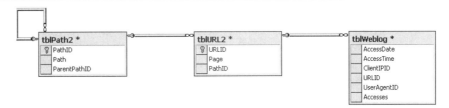

To create a parent-child dimension, follow these steps:

1. Launch the Dimension Wizard. You can do this from within the Cube Wizard, as you saw in Chapter 4, or by right-clicking the Shared Dimension folder within an Analysis Services database in Analysis Manager and selecting New Dimension ➤ Wizard.

2. If the Wizard presents the introductory panel, click Next.

3. Select Parent-Child as the type of dimension and click Next.

4. Select tblPath2 as the dimension table and click Next.

5. Select PathID as the member key, ParentPathID as the parent key, and Path as the member name. Click Next.

6. Leave the Advanced Options unchecked and click Next.

7. Name the dimension PathHierarchy and click Finish.

8. Close the Dimension Editor to save the new dimension.

Virtual Dimensions

A *virtual dimension* is a dimension that's based on a member property in a shared dimension. So, before we show you how to create a virtual dimension, we need to explain member properties.

A *member property* is a value stored in a dimension table that is not a natural part of the hierarchy of the dimension. For example, consider the tblWeblog table in the BookSamples database that we provided. As you recall from Chapter 4, we based the AccessDate dimension on this table. The table also contains a column named Weekday. This column holds values from 1 through 7 indicating the day of the week that each row of data was collected. Weekday is not a natural part of the date hierarchy in the AccessDate dimension. That is, there's nowhere in the sequence year, month, day, hour, minute, second where "day of the week" naturally fits. But each row of the table has a unique value for Weekday. This makes it a natural candidate for a member property: something you can use to split the data into categories but that doesn't participate in the dimension hierarchy.

To create a member property, you need to open the dimension that will contain the member property in the Dimension Editor. To do this, select the dimension in the database's Shared Dimension folder (the AccessDate dimension in this case), right-click, and choose Edit.

To create a member property beneath the Day level of the AccessDate dimension, expand the level in the Dimension Editor to show its Member Properties folder. Then right-click the folder and choose New Member Property. This will show you all the columns in the dimension's table that can be member properties. In the case of our sample dimension, choose the Weekday column and click OK. Figure 5.5 shows the process of choosing a member property in the Dimension Editor.

After creating the member property, click the Save button on the Dimension Editor's toolbar and close the Dimension Editor. You're now ready to create a virtual dimension based on this member property. To do so, follow these steps:

1.   Launch the Dimension Wizard. You can do this from within the Cube Wizard, as you saw in Chapter 4, or by right-clicking the Shared Dimension folder within an Analysis Services database in Analysis Manager and selecting New Dimension ➢ Wizard.

2.   If the Wizard presents the introductory panel, click Next.

3.   Select Virtual Dimension as the type of dimension and click Next.

4.   Select the AccessDate dimension as the dimension with member properties, and click Next. Note that by default the available dimensions list will only show you dimensions that have member properties. You can also base a virtual dimension on a level in an existing dimension. To do this, check the Display Member Keys and Names check box on this panel.

FIGURE 5.5:

Creating a member property

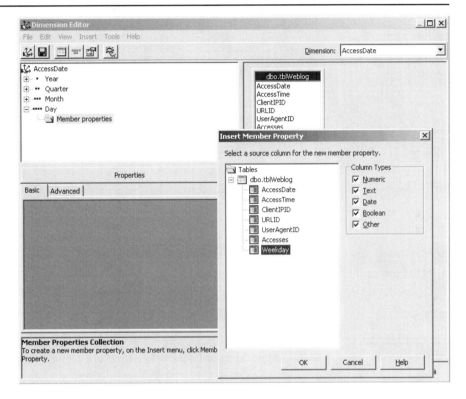

5. Select Weekday as the single virtual level for this dimension. Click Next.

6. Leave the Advanced Options unchecked and click Next.

7. Name the dimension DayOfWeek and click Finish.

8. Close the Dimension Editor to save the new dimension.

Figure 5.6 shows a cube using the finished DayOfWeek dimension. As with other types of special dimensions, a virtual dimension cannot be distinguished from a regular dimension when you're browsing the cube.

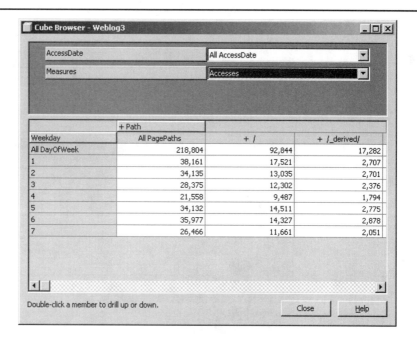

	+ Path		
Weekday	All PagePaths	+ /	+ /_derived/
All DayOfWeek	218,804	92,844	17,282
1	38,161	17,521	2,707
2	34,135	13,035	2,701
3	28,375	12,302	2,376
4	21,558	9,487	1,794
5	34,132	14,511	2,775
6	35,977	14,327	2,878
7	26,466	11,661	2,051

NOTE   Adding a virtual dimension to a cube does not increase the size of the cube. That's because Analysis Services always calculates the aggregations associated with a virtual dimension on-the-fly as the dimension is displayed. This can have the side effect of making cubes containing virtual dimensions slower than those containing only regular dimensions.

Advanced Dimension Options

If you've been following along with the examples, you'll have seen a variety of advanced options that are available within the Dimension Wizard. In this section we'll briefly explain the use of these options. The available options are as follows:

- Changing dimension
- Ordering and uniqueness of members
- Storage mode and member groups
- Custom rollups
- Members with data
- Writeback

A *changing dimension* is optimized by Analysis Services for frequent changes. In particular, you can make changes to the underlying data that add, move, rename, or delete levels within the dimension, other than the top level and the bottom level, without forcing the cube to be reprocessed. Because reprocessing the cube disconnects users who are browsing that cube, marking a dimension as a changing dimension can help increase the availability of the cube (at the cost of some overhead in the initial cube processing and data retrieval). Generally, you'll only want to make a dimension a changing dimension if changes to the database must be available in a cube immediately. Otherwise, changes will be picked up when you reprocess the dimension. Virtual dimensions, parent-child dimensions, and dimensions using ROLAP storage are always changing dimensions.

The *ordering and uniqueness of members* choice in the Dimension Wizard lets you set several properties. For each level within the dimension, you can choose whether to sort by the data itself, by the unique key for the data, or by the contents of another column in the table. You can also specify whether keys and names are unique in the dimension, among level members only, or among siblings (children of the same parent level). Choosing a wider scope of uniqueness can result in less overhead within the cube.

The *storage mode and member groups* option in the Dimension Wizard lets you adjust the physical storage of the dimension. This option was added to help Analysis Services accommodate extremely large dimensions (ones with millions of members at a particular level). Ordinarily dimensions are stored in MOLAP format: that is, the metadata that describes the dimension is stored in the special Analysis Services database. If a dimension has 10 million members or more, though, it cannot be stored in MOLAP format. In this case, you can choose to store the dimension in ROLAP format instead, keeping it in the underlying relational database. For very large dimensions, you can also choose to create *member groups*. Ordinarily, a dimension does not support more than 64,000 children for a parent in a dimension. Member groups solve this problem by creating arbitrary intermediate groupings, producing an extra level in the hierarchy to ensure that no parent has more than 64,000 children.

NOTE   You can only store dimensions in ROLAP format if you are using the Enterprise Edition of Analysis Services.

If you're designing a parent-child dimension, the Dimension Wizard will offer you the option of *custom rollups*. Custom rollups are included for one very specific situation: when the parent-child dimension represents a chart of accounts for a business. If you're familiar with basic accounting, you'll know that some accounts are added to their parent accounts while others are subtracted from their parent accounts. Custom rollup operators allow you to specify, for each member of a level in a parent-child dimension, how the value of that level should be aggregated into the parent value.

Members with data is another option that applies only to parent-child dimensions. Suppose you are creating a parent-child dimension in which all the levels contain a value. For example, an organizational hierarchy might contain a salary value for all employees, whether they have employees of their own or not. If you set the Members with Data option, then the salary value will be taken from the original data, rather than rolled up from the salaries of the child nodes.

Finally, the *writeback* option is also specific to parent-child dimensions. If you tell Analysis Services to enable the writeback option for a dimension, then end users can (assuming they are using client software with the right capabilities) write data back to the original dimension table. For example, in a parent-child dimension that represents a bill of materials, a writeback dimension would allow moving parts or subassemblies to different assemblies. This would enable the end user to investigate the effect of such changes on the other data stored in the cube (perhaps the breakdown of costs by department, or labor hours by assembly).

The Cube Editor

So far, we've used the Cube Wizard to build all the cubes that we've used in this book. For many users of Analysis Services, the Cube Wizard will do a perfectly fine job—it's very flexible compared to most other wizards and does a good job of building cubes. Sometimes, though, developers want more control over cube options than the Cube Wizard can deliver (or they don't want to stoop to using a Wizard). That's when the Cube Editor comes into play.

TIP   You may find that the easiest way to create a customized cube is to build the cube with the Cube Wizard and then fine-tune the results with the Cube Editor. As you saw in Chapter 4, cubes created with the Cube Wizard are automatically loaded into the Cube Editor when you close the Cube Wizard.

The Cube Editor can do everything that the Cube Wizard can do, and then some. The Cube Editor offers complete control over all of the properties that define a cube.

NOTE   We won't describe all of the capabilities of the Cube Editor in this section. For full documentation of the Cube Editor, see the Analysis Services Books Online.

Creating a Cube

To launch the Cube Editor, right-click the Cubes folder in an Analysis Services database and choose New Cube ➢ Editor. The Cube Editor will prompt you to choose a fact table for the new cube and then offer to count the rows of the fact table. After you've done this, the Cube Editor will open, displaying that fact table, as shown in Figure 5.7.

FIGURE 5.7:

Cube Editor displaying a
fact table

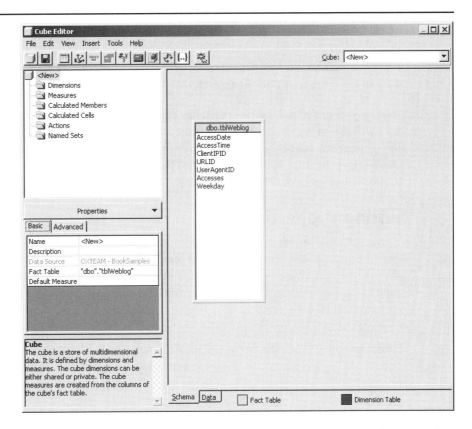

After the Cube Editor launches, you'll probably want to choose the dimensions for your cube. You can use the Insert Dimension toolbar button to open a Dimension Manager dialog box that looks like the Choose Dimension panel from the Cube Wizard and works the same way. Alternatively, you can choose Insert ➤ Dimension ➤ Existing to open the Dimension Manager dialog box, or Insert ➤ Dimension ➤ New to launch the Dimension Wizard directly. As you choose dimensions, the Cube Editor will display them in the Dimensions folder in the treeview of the cube at the upper left and add the appropriate tables to the schema view of the cube at the right of the editor.

The Cube Editor will automatically choose what it considers to be appropriate joins between the fact table and the dimension tables. If you disagree with its choices, you can click a join line and press Delete to remove a join, or drag and drop columns between tables to create a new join.

You'll also need to define measures for the cube. You can do this three ways:

- Choose Insert ➤ Measure from the Cube Editor menus.
- Right-click the Measures folder in the treeview and select New Measure.
- Right-click a field in the fact table and select Insert As Measure.

Once you've defined the fact table, dimensions, and measures, you can click the Data tab for the right-hand panel of the Cube Editor. After a moment, the Cube Editor will show you the structure of your cube as it currently exists. The data in this view, however, is not the real data in the cube. Instead, it is sample data that the Cube Editor generates to give you a sense of the way the pieces of the cube fit together.

Setting Properties

The Property Sheet (displayed at the lower left of the Cube Editor) allows you to set the properties of all the parts of the cube in detail. Each component of the cube has its own property sheet, divided into basic and advanced properties. As you click different components of the cube in the treeview, the Cube Editor updates the property sheet to show the properties of the currently selected component.

Table 5.1 shows the available properties for the cube itself. Of these properties, you'll certainly want to set the cube name. Some of the properties (such as the Data Source and the Fact Table Size) are displayed for information only; you can't set them from the Cube Editor.

TABLE 5.1: Properties of a Cube in the Cube Editor

Property	Basic/Advanced	Explanation
Name	B	Name of the cube.
Description	B	Description of the cube.
Data Source	B	Analysis Services data source for the cube.
Fact Table	B	Fact table for the cube.
Default Measure	B	Measure to use when a client application queries the cube without specifying a measure.
Fact Table Size	A	Number of rows in the fact table. You can click the build button in this cell to tell the Cube Editor to recount the rows in the fact table.
Aggregation Prefix	A	Prefix to use when naming aggregations for this cube.
Visible	A	True to display the cube when end users browse a list of cubes. Hidden cubes can still be opened by name.
Source Table Filter	A	SQL WHERE clause to apply to the fact table when choosing which rows to include in a cube. By default, all rows are included.

Continued on next page

TABLE 5.1 CONTINUED: Properties of a Cube in the Cube Editor

Property	Basic/Advanced	Explanation
Processing Optimization	A	Regular to calculate all aggregations before allowing the cube to be browsed; Lazy Aggregations to allow browsing as soon as the raw data is loaded. Applies to MOLAP cubes only.
Stop Processing on Key Errors	A	Yes to stop processing when the key error limit is hit. A key error occurs when the fact table has a foreign key that should refer to a value in a dimension table, but the dimension table has no corresponding row.
Key Error Limit	A	Maximum number of key errors to tolerate before halting processing of the cube.
Key Error Log File	A	Disk file to track any key errors.

Table 5.2 shows the available properties for a measure in a cube. Note that, as with the cube itself, some of these properties cannot be set within the Cube Wizard.

TABLE 5.2: Properties of a Measure in the Cube Editor

Property	Basic/Advanced	Explanation
Name	B	Name of the measure.
Description	B	Description of the measure.
Source Column	B	Column in the fact table that contains this measure.
Aggregate Function	B	Function to use when aggregating the measure. The Cube Wizard always chooses Sum as the Aggregate Function. Other choices include Min, Max, Count, and Distinct Count.
Data Type	A	OLE DB type of the measure.
Display Format	A	Format string used to display the measure.
Visible	A	Controls whether the measure is visible in the cube. You might use an invisible measure as the basis for a calculated measure.

Table 5.3 shows the available properties for a dimension in the Cube Editor. As you might guess, given the variety of options in the Dimension Wizard, there are many properties for dimensions.

If a dimension is a shared dimension, most of its properties cannot be edited in the Cube Editor. You can edit these dimensions in the Dimension Editor, which is available by right-clicking the dimension in Analysis Manager and choosing Edit. The Dimension Editor is a subset of the Cube Editor that deals only with dimensions.

TABLE 5.3:   Properties of a Dimension in the Cube Editor

Property	Basic/Advanced	Explanation
Name	B	Name of the dimension.
Description	B	Description of the dimension.
Data source	B	Analysis Services data source containing the dimension's data.
All Level	A	Indicates whether an "All" Level should be created for this dimension containing a sum total of all the values in the level.
All Caption	A	The caption to use for the All Level, if one exists.
Type	A	Type of the dimension. Can be either "Standard" or "Time."
Default Member	A	The member of the dimension to use to slice the data if no member is specified for this dimension when querying the cube.
Depends on Dimension	A	Underlying dimension if this is a virtual dimension.
Changing	A	Indicates whether this is a changing dimension.
Write-Enabled	A	Indicates whether this is a write-enabled dimension.
Member Keys Unique	A	Indicates whether member keys are unique throughout this entire dimension.
Member Names Unique	A	Indicates whether member names are unique throughout this entire dimension.
Allow Duplicate Names	A	Indicates whether children of the same parent can have identical names in this dimension.
Source Table Filter	A	SQL WHERE clause that limits which rows of the underlying table are used when determining the values in this dimension.
Storage Mode	A	MOLAP or ROLAP.
Enable Real-Time Updates	A	Indicates whether this dimension supports real-time updates when the underlying data is changed.
Virtual	A	Indicates whether this is a virtual dimension.
All Member Formula	A	Custom MDX expression to calculate the value of the All Level.
Aggregation Usage	A	Indicates which levels of the dimension should be used when calculating aggregates.
Enable All Level Aggregation	A	Indicates whether the All Level should be considered when optimizing aggregations.
Visible	A	Indicates whether this dimension should be visible to end users when they browse the cube.

If you click a dimension in the Cube Editor, it will expand in the treeview to show the levels in the dimension. Table 5.4 lists the properties that you can set for a level in the Cube Editor. Note that the level properties tell you where the data in a dimension originates; a dimension itself has no properties that refer to particular database columns.

TABLE 5.4: Properties of a Level in the Cube Editor

Property	Basic/Advanced	Explanation
Name	B	Name of the level.
Description	B	Description of the level.
Member Key Column	B	Table column that contains keys for this level.
Member Name Column	B	Table column that contains names for this level.
Member Count	A	Estimated count of members of this level.
Member Keys Unique	A	Indicates whether keys are unique across this entire level.
Member Names Unique	A	Indicates whether names are unique across this entire level.
Disabled	A	Indicates whether the level is available in the cube. You may wish to disable levels for which there is no detail information in the fact table.
Level Type	A	Type of the level.
Key Data Size	A	Bytes allocated to hold one value from the key column.
Key Data Type	A	Data type used to store the key.
Enable Aggregations	A	Controls whether this level should be considered when optimizing aggregations.
Hide Member If	A	Includes a variety of cases where you may wish to hide this level. For example, in a parent-child dimension, you'll probably want to hide a level that has the same value as its parent.
Visible	A	Indicates whether this level should be available in the cube.
Order By	A	Property that controls the ordering of members within this level.
Custom Rollup Formula	A	Custom formula used for calculating aggregations at this level.
Custom Members	A	True if custom formulas can be created for individual members of the level.
Custom Member Options	A	True if calculation options can be defined for individual members of this level.
Grouping	A	True if members of this level are grouped.
Unary Operators	A	True if members of this level are associated with operators that indicate how each member should be aggregated.

Calculated Members

One capability that the Cube Editor adds, over and above the functionality provided by the Cube Wizard, is that of calculated members. A *calculated member* is a measure or a dimension level that is derived from one or more columns in the source data, rather than being a column of source data itself.

As an example, consider the Warehouse cube that ships as part of the FoodMart 2000 sample database. Two of the measures in this cube are Warehouse Sales and Units Shipped. By using these two measures together, you could calculate the average sale for any warehouse. What a calculated measure can do is make this calculation for you automatically.

To add the Average Sale calculated measure to the Inventory cube, follow these steps:

1. Right-click the Warehouse cube in the FoodMart 2000 sample database, and select Edit.

2. In the Cube Editor, right-click the Calculated Members folder and select New Calculated Member. This will open the Calculated Member Builder.

3. Enter Average Sale as the member name.

4. In the Data list, expand Measures and then MeasuresLevel to see the existing measures within the cube.

5. Drag the Warehouse Sales measure from the data list to the Value Expression box above it.

6. Type "/" (without the quotes) in the Value Expression box after the Warehouse Sales measure.

7. Drag the Units Shipped measure from the data list to the Value Expression box. If you want to be sure you didn't make a mistake, use the Check button to check the syntax of the value expression. Figure 5.8 shows the Calculated Member Builder after defining the value expression.

8. Click OK to save the calculated member and return to the Cube Editor.

9. Select the Average Sale calculated member in the treeview. On the Advanced tab of the property sheet, set the Format String property to "Currency."

10. Select File ➢ Save to save the cube and then close the Cube Editor.

11. Right-click the cube and choose Browse Data.

FIGURE 5.8:

The Calculated Member
Builder

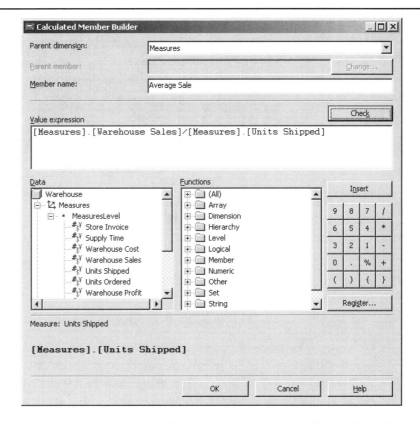

You'll note that you don't have to process the cube to make the new calculated member available. That's because calculated members are calculated on the fly as client applications ask for the data; they are not stored in advance. This is true whether the calculated member is a measure or part of a dimension. Figure 5.9 shows the new calculated member within the Cube Browser interface.

FIGURE 5.9:

Browsing a cube with a calculated member

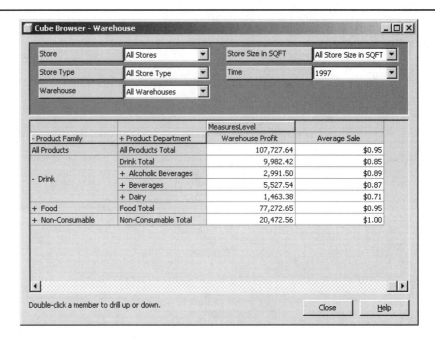

The syntax for calculated members is much more complex than this simple example might indicate. In fact, you can use any MDX expression in a calculated member. You can also use VBA functions in a calculated member and (if Excel is installed on the computer with Analysis Services) Microsoft Excel functions as well. In fact, you can even write and register your own library of custom functions if you require something that's not covered in the standard libraries.

TIP   We'll cover the syntax of MDX functions in Chapter 6, "Querying Analysis Services with MDX."

For an example of a calculated member in a dimension, consider the portion of the Sales cube from the FoodMart 2000 sample database shown in Figure 5.10. Note that the Drink product family is broken down into Alcoholic Beverages, Beverages, and Dairy. Suppose you want to see a total for Non-Alcoholic Beverages that includes Beverages and Dairy. You can do this by creating a Non-Alcoholic Beverages calculated member.

Browsing drink data in the
Sales cube

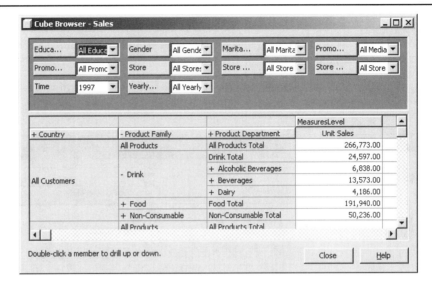

To create the Non-Alcoholic Beverages calculated member, follow these steps:

1. Right-click the Sales cube in the FoodMart 2000 sample database and select Edit.

2. In the Cube Editor, right-click the Calculated Members folder and select New Calculated Member. This will open the Calculated Member Builder.

3. Select Product as the parent dimension for the member.

4. Click the Change button next to the Parent Member box, and navigate to the Drink member of the hierarchy and click OK. This will be the parent of the new calculated member.

5. Enter Non-Alcoholic Beverages as the member name.

6. In the Functions list, expand the Numeric folder and then drag the Aggregate function to the Value Expression box. This will initialize the Value Expression to

    ```
    Aggregate(«Set»[, «Numeric Expression»])
    ```

7. The Aggregate function is used to aggregate multiple data items into a single total. By default it uses addition to perform the aggregation, so we won't need the optional Numeric Expression parameter. Also, sets are always enclosed in curly brackets. Using the keyboard, edit the Value Expression to

    ```
    Aggregate({})
    ```

8. In the Data list, expand Product, then Product Family, then Drink.

9. Drag the Beverages node from beneath the Drink node to the Value Expression box and drop it between the curly brackets. Type a comma after the expression that this produces, then drag the Dairy node from beneath the Drink node to the Value Expression box and drop it after the comma.

10. Use the Check button to check the syntax of the completed expression. Figure 5.11 shows the Calculated Member Builder after the expression is completed.

FIGURE 5.11:

Building a calculated member for a dimension

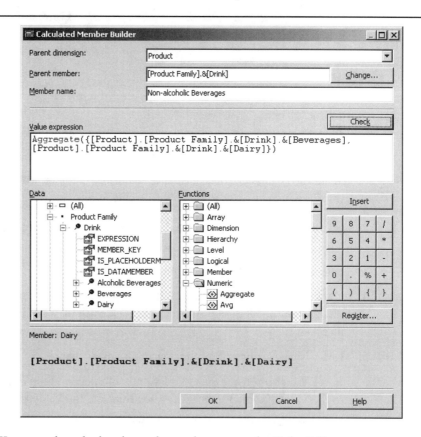

11. Click OK to save the calculated member and return to the Cube Editor.

12. Select File ➢ Save to save the cube and then close the Cube Editor.

13. Right-click the cube and choose Browse Data.

Figure 5.12 shows the cube with the new calculated member open in the Cube Browser. Note that the calculated member is shown at the same level as the members that it aggregates, and that Analysis Services is smart enough to not double-count when coming up with overall totals for the Drink level.

FIGURE 5.12:

Browsing a cube with a calculated member in a dimension

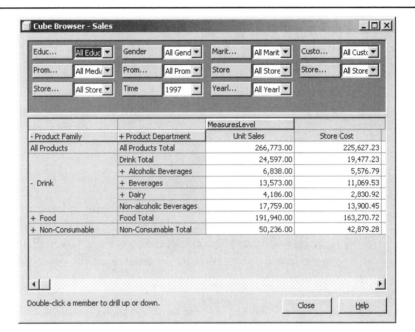

Drillthrough and Custom Actions

In SQL Server 7.0 OLAP Services, once you displayed the data for a cube, that was it. SQL Server 2000 Analysis Services adds two important pieces of interactivity to the data displayed in cube cells:

- Drillthrough lets the end user retrieve the raw data that was used to calculate the value displayed in the cell.

- Custom actions let the cube developer associate shortcut menu items with the cells of a cube.

In this section, we'll show you how to enable drillthrough for your cubes and how to create custom actions.

Drillthrough

By default, cubes do not allow drillthrough operations. That's because drillthrough can be a resource-intensive process, perhaps trying to retrieve millions of rows of source data if the user tries to drillthrough on a highly aggregated cell. To enable drillthrough, you must use the Cube Editor.

TIP   You can use Analysis Services security, discussed later in this chapter, to limit drillthrough capabilities to only certain users within your organization.

For example, let's add drillthrough to the Weblog cube that we created as an example in Chapter 4. To enable and configure drillthrough for this cube, follow these steps:

1. Right-click the Weblog cube in the BookSamples database and select Edit.

2. Select Tools ➤ Drillthrough Options.

3. Check the Enable Drillthrough box.

4. Select the columns that should be shown to the end user when they use drillthrough. Note that all of the columns within the cube's database are available here. For our example, we'll choose AccessDate, AccessTime, ClientIP, and UserAgent. Note that you can also specify a WHERE clause to filter the data if you like.

5. Click OK to save the drillthrough options and return to the Cube Editor.

6. Select File ➤ Save to save the cube and then close the Cube Editor.

7. Right-click the cube and choose Browse Data.

Figure 5.13 shows the Weblog cube in the Cube Browser, with drillthrough data displayed for one cell. In the Cube Browser, you can drillthrough by right-clicking the cell and choosing Drill Through, or by double-clicking the cell.

NOTE   The Cube Browser will display up to 1000 rows of drillthrough data for a single cell. Other client tools may display more. If you're retrieving information programmatically, you can get the entire result set for any drillthrough operation.

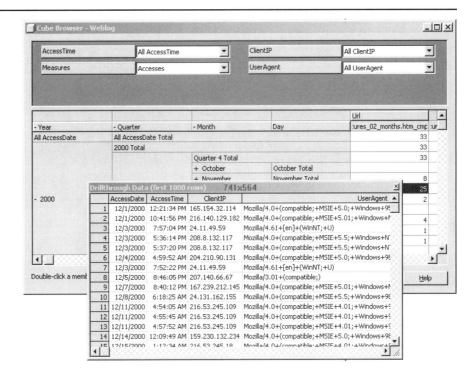

Custom Actions

Custom actions add interactivity to a cube. By adding a custom action to a cube, the designer can make it possible for the user to launch a web site, query a database, or perform nearly any other action from shortcut menus attached to cells, dimensions, or even the cube itself.

To create a custom action, you need to use the Cube Editor. For example, you can follow these steps to add a custom action to the Weblog cube that we created in Chapter 4:

1. Right-click the Weblog cube in the BookSamples database and select Edit.

2. Right-click the Actions folder and select New Action. This will launch the Action Wizard.

3. Read the introductory panel and click Next.

4. The Select Target panel allows you to define where the action will be attached to the cube. For this example, select "A dimension in this cube" as the target, select the URL dimension, and define the target as "Members of the selected dimension." Click Next to proceed.

5. Select URL as the action type. Table 5.5 shows the available action types and what they do. Click Next.

6. Define the action syntax to add a fixed prefix to the URL stored in the cube with this syntax:

```
"http://www.larkfarm.com" +
➥[URL].CurrentMember.Name
```

7. Click Next and name the action Open URL.

8. Click Finish to create the action.

9. Select File ➤ Save to save the cube and then close the Cube Editor.

10. Right-click the cube and choose Browse Data.

11. Move the URL dimension to the cube.

12. Right-click any member of the URL dimension and choose Open URL to display the corresponding web page.

TABLE 5.5: Types of Custom Actions

Action Type	Use
Command Line	Executes a command at the Windows command prompt
Statement	Executes an MDX statement that does not return a dataset
HTML	Assembles an HTML string and displays the results using the user's default web browser
URL	Assembles a URL and uses the user's default web browser to navigate to that URL
Dataset	Executes an MDX statement that returns a dataset
Rowset	Executes a SQL statement that returns a rowset
Proprietary	Executes a statement from a proprietary add-in library

Write-Enabled Cubes

You might think that the data displayed in an Analysis Services cube is automatically read-only. After all, it doesn't make sense, in the relational database way of thinking about things, to allow changes to aggregate data. And you'd be almost right about that. But Analysis Services introduces the concept of *write-enabled cubes*.

A write-enabled cube is very nearly sleight of hand. Changes can be written to the cube's data—but the original fact table is never modified. Rather, the changes are stored in a separate table defined by the cube's developer. When the cube is displayed, the data from the original fact table and from the writeback table is combined to produce the results. What's the point of this scheme? Write-enabled cubes allow the user to perform "what-if" analyses, changing values at the atomic level in the cube (the level beneath which the cube cannot be sliced or diced any further), to see the results of those changes on the cube's aggregations.

To explore write-enabled cubes, we'll create a very simple cube in the BookSamples database. By now you may want to try creating this cube without step-by-step instructions, following these specifications:

- Measure: InventoryAmount from the tblShirtInventory table

- Dimensions: Size and Color

- Cube Name: Writeback Inventory

- Storage Mode: MOLAP

If you have trouble, here are the step-by-step instructions:

1.   In the BookSamples database, right-click the Cubes folder and choose New Cube ➢ Wizard.

2.   If the introductory panel is displayed, click Next to proceed.

3.   Choose tblShirtInventory as the fact table and click Next.

4.   Select InventoryAmount as the measure and click Next.

5.   Click New Dimension to launch the Dimension Wizard.

6.   If the introductory panel is displayed, click Next to proceed.

7.   Select Star Schema and click Next.

8.   Select tblColor as the dimension table and click Next.

9.   Select Color as the only level and click Next.

10.   Leave the Member Key column alone and click Next.

11.   Leave the Advanced Options unchecked and click Next.

12.   Name the new dimension Color and click Finish.

13.   Click New Dimension to launch the Dimension Wizard.

14.   If the introductory panel is displayed, click Next to proceed.

15.   Select Star Schema and click Next.

16. Select tblSize as the dimension table and click Next.

17. Select Size as the only level and click Next.

18. Leave the Member Key column alone and click Next.

19. Leave the Advanced Options unchecked and click Next.

20. Name the new dimension Size and click Finish.

21. Click Next and tell the Cube Wizard that it's OK to count the fact tables.

22. You'll get a warning message about joins (because the linking fields have different names in the different tables). Click OK.

23. Name the cube Writeback Inventory and click Finish.

24. In the Cube Editor, drag the ColorID column from dbo.tblColor and drop it on the InventoryColor column in dbo.tblShirtInventory to join the two tables.

25. In the Cube Editor, drag the SizeID column from dbo.tblSize and drop it on the InventorySize column in dbo.tblShirtInventory to join the two tables.

26. Save the cube and close the Cube Editor.

27. Select Yes in the next screen to open the Storage Design Wizard.

28. If the introductory panel in the Storage Design Wizard is displayed, click Next to proceed.

29. Choose to store the cube in MOLAP mode and click Next.

30. Click Start to design aggregations, and then click Next.

31. Select Process Now and click Finish.

32. Click Close when Analysis Services is done processing the cube.

Once you've created the cube, follow these steps to write-enable it:

1. Right-click the cube and choose Write-Enable. This will open the Write-Enable dialog box shown in Figure 5.14.

2. Accept the default table name.

3. Click OK to write-enable the cube.

FIGURE 5.14:

Write-enabling a cube

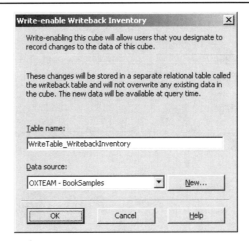

Write-enabling a cube appears to break any drillthrough options set on the cube.

Now that you've created and write-enabled the cube, your first thought may be to browse and edit it in the Cube Browser. That was our first thought as well. Unfortunately, if you try this, you'll discover that you can browse the cube—but you can't edit it. That's because the Cube Browser does not include writeback functionality.

In fact, if you want to actually see writeback in action, you need to use the programmatic interface to Analysis Services via ADOMD. We've provided the Chapter5.vpb sample program on the companion CD to demonstrate the writeback process. This program, shown in Figure 5.15, uses an MDX query to retrieve data from the Writeback Inventory cube, and ADOMD objects to change the data. We'll cover MDX in Chapter 6 and ADOMD in Chapter 8, "Building OLAP Services Applications with ADO/MD Part II: Query Retrieval Objects." You might like to browse the code in the Chapter5.vbp sample for a preview, but we won't analyze it here.

FIGURE 5.15:

Changing data in a writeback cube

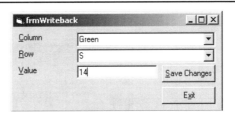

About Connection Strings in the Samples

The Visual Basic sample code supplied with this book uses connection strings to connect to Analysis Services. As shipped, these samples assume that you're running the sample on the same computer where Analysis Services is installed, and that you're using Windows integrated security to connect. If those assumptions aren't true, you'll need to modify the connection strings.

If Analysis Services is installed on a different computer from the one where you're installing the code, replace `localhost` in the connection string with the name of the computer where Analysis Services is installed.

If you need to supply a username and password to connect to your Analysis Services installation, replace `Integrated Security=SSPI` in the connection string with `User ID=user name;Password=password;Persist Security Info=True`.

Try running the sample program to change values in several of the cube's cells, and then browse the data in the cube using the Cube Browser. You'll see the edited data, rather than the original data, and the aggregated cells will be based on the edited data as well.

TIP   You'll discover that the sample program will only let you edit *atomic* cells—those that cannot be drilled into. For example, you can change the inventory value for small green shirts, but not for small shirts of all colors. This is generally true of writeback operations. If you want to allow writeback to non-atomic cells, your application code will have to determine how to split the changed values across all of the affected cells.

Analysis Services lets you see the exact writeback operations that have been performed on a cube. In the Analysis Manager treeview, right-click the cube and select Writeback Options ➤ Browse Writeback Data. You'll get a table similar to that shown in Figure 5.16. Analysis Services tracks the user, time, affected cells, and changes made. Note that the changes are stored as a value to be added to the original value. When displaying the cube, Analysis Services combines any changed values with the original value to come up with the value to display.

FIGURE 5.16:

Browsing writeback data

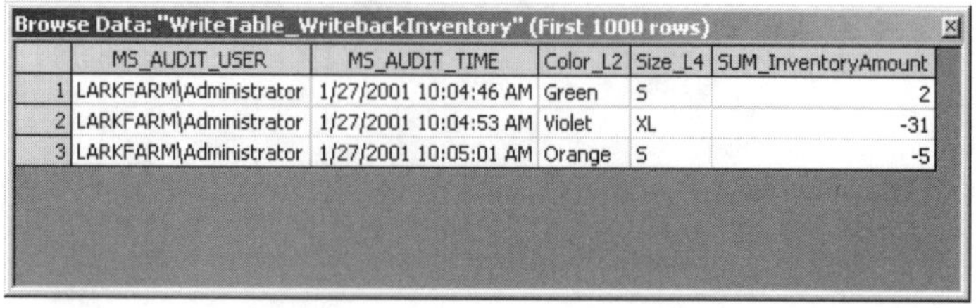

Browse Data: "WriteTable_WritebackInventory" (First 1000 rows)

	MS_AUDIT_USER	MS_AUDIT_TIME	Color_L2	Size_L4	SUM_InventoryAmount
1	LARKFARM\Administrator	1/27/2001 10:04:46 AM	Green	S	2
2	LARKFARM\Administrator	1/27/2001 10:04:53 AM	Violet	XL	-31
3	LARKFARM\Administrator	1/27/2001 10:05:01 AM	Orange	S	-5

You can do two things with writeback data after it accumulates. If you no longer need the writeback data, you can discard it by right-clicking the cube and choosing Writeback Options ➤ Disable Writeback. This will discard all the existing writeback data and return the cube to its original state. If you want to allow more writeback operations in the future, of course, you will need to re-enable writeback on the cube.

Alternatively, you can choose to save the writeback data in a more permanent format, making it a legitimate part of the cube. To do this, right-click the cube and select Writeback Options ➤ Convert to Partition. This will save the writeback data as a new partition for the cube. It will also disable writeback as a side effect. Once again, you can re-enable writeback on the cube if you so choose.

Real-Time Cubes

For the most part, Analysis Services is a "real-enough time" application. At any time when you require current data, you can reprocess a cube and have it reflect the most current information in the fact table and dimension tables. But sometimes, real-enough time isn't good enough. Suppose you have a cube that's being used to help purchasing agents decide what needs to be ordered, and the underlying inventory is rapidly changing. In such situations, it would be nice if the cube actually reflected the current state of the fact tables without reprocessing.

SQL Server 2000 Analysis Services adds just this capability by supporting *real-time cubes*. A real-time cube uses ROLAP storage, and whenever the data in the underlying relational database changes, the aggregates are updated without forcing the cube to be placed offline for processing. Thus a real-time cube can show current data while still allowing users to stay connected to the cube at all times.

You can choose to make a cube real-time when you are designing the storage for the cube. In the Storage Design Wizard, you must choose ROLAP storage and check the Enable Real-Time Updates box as shown in Figure 5.17. Then, on the aggregation options, choose to allocate zero space to aggregations. This will force the cube to be created without aggregations, which is the other requirement for a real-time cube.

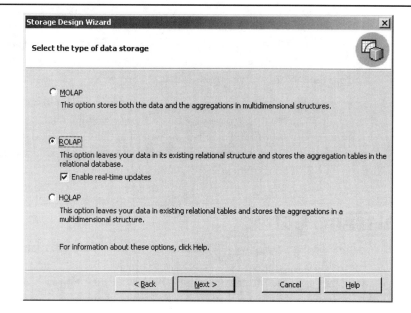

Real-time cubes can only be created with data that is stored in SQL Server 2000 databases. Analysis Services will retain a permanent connection to the database and poll it for changes in the data as well. You should be aware of this overhead if you choose to create a real-time cube.

> **WARNING**   The Analysis Services Books Online claims that you can use aggregations in a real-time cube if they are based on SQL Server 2000 indexed views. We have been unable to make this actually work.

Security

Analysis Services includes a full security model to control who can administer cubes, view data, and (in the case of write-enabled cubes) modify data. In fact, the security model is full enough that it can be confusing. You can set security at many different levels and in different places in the interface.

Generally speaking, you should set the most wide-reaching security first, and then fine-tune on increasingly small objects. In this section we'll cover the Analysis Services security model at four levels:

- Administrator security
- Database roles

- Cube roles
- Dimension and cell security

There are other security features that relate only to data mining. We'll cover data mining security in Chapter 11.

Administrator Security

The most sweeping level of Analysis Services security is not set within Analysis Services itself. When you install Analysis Services, it creates an OLAP Administrators group on the local computer and adds the logged-on user to this group. Members of the OLAP Administrators group have complete access to all functionality within Analysis Services and Analysis Manager.

TIP If the computer where Analysis Services is installed is a Windows 2000 domain controller, the OLAP Administrators group is created as a domain group within Active Directory.

Certain functionality within Analysis Services is limited to members of the OLAP Administrators group:

- Only members of this group can execute the Analysis Manager application.
- Only members of this group can perform administrative functions via Decision Support Objects (DSO). You'll learn about DSO in Chapter 10, "Managing an Analysis Services Environment Using DSO."

Membership in the OLAP Administrators group overrides any restrictions set within Analysis Manager. You can control the membership of this group with the User Manager application in Windows NT, or the Computer Management or Active Directory Users and Computers MMC snap-in in Windows 2000.

Database Roles

Within Analysis Manager, the first level of security is the database role. A database role is a collection of Windows users and groups that are allowed to access the database. When you connect to an Analysis Services database from a client application, Analysis Services checks the database roles within that database for your name. You must be included in at least one of the database roles for the connection to succeed.

To create a new database role, expand a database within Analysis Manager and then right-click the Database Roles folder and select Manage Roles. This will open the Database Role

Manager, which will initially have no roles (remember, you're using Administrative Security to access Analysis Services when you open Analysis Manager). To create a new role, click the New button to open the Create a Database Role dialog box, shown in Figure 5.18.

FIGURE 5.18:

Create a Database Role
dialog box

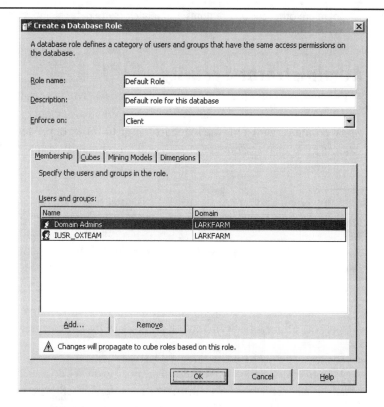

To define the role, supply the information that the Create a Database Role dialog box calls for:

- Assign a name to the role.

- Optionally provide a description for the role.

- Choose whether to enforce the role on the client or the server. Client-side security is faster but less secure than server-side security.

- On the Membership tab, click Add and choose the Windows users and groups that will participate in this role.

- On the Cubes tab, click the cubes that members of this role will be able to use.

Click OK to create the role in the database. When you're done defining database roles, close the Database Role Manager.

TIP   A user who is included in a database role can view the names of all the cubes contained in that database. However, they can only access data from the cubes that are checked on the Cubes tab of the role.

Cube Roles

The next layer of Analysis Services security is the cube role. A *cube role*, as you might guess, controls access to the details in an individual cube. You'll find the cube roles in the Cube Roles folder beneath each cube in the Analysis Manager treeview.

When you create a database role and assign that role permission to access a cube, Analysis Manager creates a cube role for that cube with the same name as the database role. By modifying the cube role, you can change the defaults from the database role and control cube-specific security.

To modify a cube role, right-click the Cube Roles folder for the cube and select Manage Roles. This will open the Cube Role Manager, which looks very much like the Database Role Manager. If you select an automatically created role here and click Edit, you'll discover a new set of properties that you can set on the cube level.

Some of the actions you can perform when editing a cube role include the following:

- Change the membership of the role. Any membership changes are automatically propagated back to the matching database role.

- Set dimension and cell security (we'll talk about dimension and cell security in a moment).

- Choose whether to allow drillthrough on this cube. Drillthrough must be defined using the Cube Editor, as we discussed earlier in the chapter. The option within the Cube Role Editor merely controls who can use this capability after it's been defined.

- Choose whether linked cubes on other servers can use this cube as a data source.

- Choose whether SQL querying by users in this role is allowed against the data in this cube.

Dimension and Cell Security

If security on a cube-by-cube level is not adequate for your needs, you can control security on the dimension and cell levels. You might use this sort of control if, for example, a cube contained payroll information that should only be available to certain users. Users who are in other roles can be denied access to the payroll dimension.

Dimension security is set on the Dimensions tab when editing a role. At the database level, you can set security for shared dimensions within the database. At the cube level, you can set security for shared dimensions that are used in that particular cube, as well as for private dimensions used only in the cube. Restrictions set at the cube level override restrictions set at the database level.

For the Measures dimension, the default security is Unrestricted, which provides read access to all measures. You can also select Custom security, which lets you control exactly which measures members of the role should be able to access. For other dimensions, the default security is Restricted. You can also select Fully Restricted, which hides the dimension completely from members of the role, or Custom. Figure 5.19 shows the Custom Dimensions Security dialog box. As you can see, you have fine-grained control over the levels that are available to users. You can choose to only allow viewing levels between specified top and bottom levels, or even to allow or deny access to particular members within the level.

FIGURE 5.19:

Setting custom dimension security

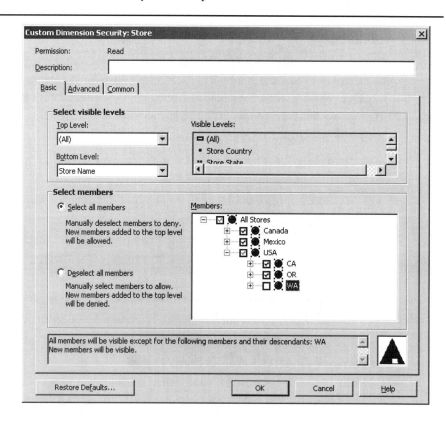

Cell security is set on the Cells tab when editing a role. Cell security can be set only at the cube level. The basic cell security choices are Unrestricted Read, which allows access to all cells in the cube (assuming that they are not in a dimension that is unavailable to the user) and Advanced, which lets you set security on individual cells. If you choose Advanced, you can specify which cells should carry Read, Read Contingent, and Read/Write privileges. Read privileges allow reading a cell. Read Contingent privileges allow reading a cell only if all the cells that it contains can be read. Read/Write privileges are necessary to use writeback to modify the contents of a cell.

You can set each of these three levels of privilege to Unrestricted (allowed for the entire cube), Fully Restricted (denied for the entire cube), or Custom. If you choose Custom, you can supply an MDX expression that specifies exactly the range of cells to which the selected privileges will be applied.

Configuring Analysis Services

Although Analysis Services is ready to use as soon as you finish installing it, you should know about a few things if you're responsible for administering an Analysis Services installation. In this section, we'll cover the most important of these tasks:

- Fine-tuning server properties
- Migrating the Repository to SQL Server 2000
- Archiving and restoring Analysis Services databases

Server Properties

To fine-tune the properties of an Analysis Services server, launch Analysis Manager, right-click the server name, and choose Properties. You'll be presented with the six-tab Server Properties dialog box shown in Figure 5.20.

The General tab of the Server Properties dialog box lets you set three user-interface options that apply to all databases stored on the server:

- Enable Dimension Level Counting sets the Dimension Wizard to warn the user if they attempt to add a level beneath a level with more members.
- Show Process Warning causes Analysis Services to prompt the user to process new and saved cubes.
- Show Database Password Warning displays a warning when a password is saved with a database.

In addition, you can set the data and temporary folders used by Analysis Services on this tab.

FIGURE 5.20:

Properties dialog box for
Analysis Services server

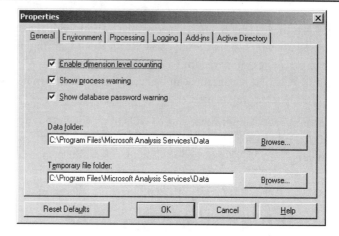

> **WARNING**   If you change the data folder, Analysis Services will be unable to access existing data.

The Environment tab of the Server Properties dialog box lets you set performance and memory settings:

- Maximum Number of Threads lets you control the number of threads that Analysis Services will launch. You probably won't need to change this number.

- Large Level Defined lets you choose how many members a level must have to be considered large. Levels with fewer than this many members will be sent to clients for caching even if not all of the members have been requested.

- Minimum and Maximum Allocated Memory control the use of memory by Analysis Services. If you're using Analysis Services on a computer that is also running other software, you may wish to decrease the minimum memory allocated to Analysis Services.

The Processing tab of the Server Properties dialog box controls some of the optimization settings for Analysis Services. The only one of these settings that you might wish to change is the server timeout. By default, Analysis Services waits forever for data to come back from a data source. You can set a server timeout in seconds here to cause cube operations to fail with an error if data is unavailable for a long time.

The Logging tab of the Server Properties dialog box controls the use of the Analysis Services log. By default, Analysis Services saves a log of all queries that it performs. This log can be used to help optimize server operations.

The Add-Ins tab of the Server Properties dialog box lets you start Analysis Services add-ins at the same time as the server, and control their loading priority. However, as Analysis Services itself does not ship with any add-ins, you are unlikely to use this tab.

The Active Directory tab lets you register your Analysis Services servers with Windows 2000 Active Directory. By default, Analysis Services servers are not registered in Active Directory. If your organization uses an Active Directory search tool, you will probably want to enable this option.

Migrating the Repository

Analysis Services stores metadata (information about the schema of cubes, dimensions, and other Analysis Services objects) in a database called the Repository. By default, the Analysis Services Repository is stored in a Microsoft Access database named msmdrep.mdb.

While storing the Repository as an Access database is convenient for installing Analysis Services (because the installation process can create a new Repository just by copying the file), it's not a good plan for serious production work. The information in the Repository is critical to the proper functioning of your Analysis Services server. If this information is stored in an Access database, it does not have the automatic protection (such as scheduled backups and transaction logging) that is provided by SQL Server.

Fortunately, there's an easy process to migrate your Analysis Services Repository from Access format to a SQL Server database. Just follow these steps:

1. Right-click the server name in Analysis Manager and choose Migrate Repository to launch the Migrate Repository Wizard.

2. Select the format for the new Repository database. If you're moving the Repository to a SQL Server 7.0 server, select the SQL Server 7.0 OLAP Services format. If you're moving the repository to a SQL Server 2000 server, select the Meta Data Services repository format. Click Next.

3. Enter the name of the target SQL Server and click Next.

4. Enter authentication information for the SQL Server and click Next.

5. Select a database to hold the Repository. Generally, you should select the msdb database. Click Finish.

WARNING After you've migrated the Repository to SQL Server, you can run the Migrate Repository Wizard again to change it from SQL Server 7.0 OLAP Services format to Meta Data Services format or vice versa. However, there is no way to go back to using an Access database.

After migrating the Repository, you should use the SQL Server 2000 Maintenance Plan Wizard to set up a backup and maintenance schedule for the database that contains the Repository, if one does not already exist.

Archiving and Restoring Databases

Analysis Services includes facilities for archiving and restoring databases. To archive an Analysis Services database, right-click the database in Analysis Manager and select Archive Database. This will open the Archive Database dialog box shown in Figure 5.21.

FIGURE 5.21:

Archiving an Analysis Services database

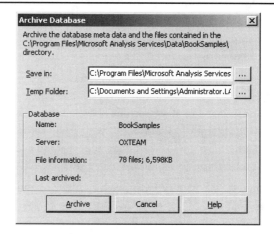

Archiving a database makes a copy of all the disk files for that database, and the metadata from the Repository for that database, as a CAB file in the directory that you specify. Keep in mind, however, some important caveats about the Analysis Services archive facility:

- Archive files contain potentially confidential information. You should use Windows security to protect these files from unauthorized access.
- Writeback data is not archived.
- Source data and aggregations stored in ROLAP partitions are not archived.
- Data in remote partitions is not archived.

To restore an archived database, right-click the Analysis Server in Analysis Manager and choose Restore Database. This will let you browse for a CAB file to restore.

If the original source data for the cube is unavailable when an Analysis Services database is restored, the effect depends on the type of storage:

- Restored MOLAP partitions remain usable even if the source data is lost, but they cannot be updated.

- Restored HOLAP and ROLAP partitions are unusable if the source data is lost.

TIP   Analysis Services also includes a command-line utility named msmdarch that can archive and restore Analysis Services databases. This utility is useful for batch processes. For example, you might call it as a command-line step in a SQL Server job. For syntax details for msmdarch, refer to Analysis Services Books Online.

Conclusion

In this chapter you learned about some of the advanced capabilities of Analysis Services. We discussed the available dimension types and the use of the Cube Editor. You also learned how to use drillthrough, custom actions, write-enabled cubes, and real-time cubes. Finally, we covered the administrative tasks of setting security and configuring Analysis Services.

So far, everything we've done with Analysis Services has involved the Analysis Manager user interface. In the rest of the book, you'll learn how to work with Analysis Services data programmatically. As a first step, the next chapter covers the MDX query language, which is essential for retrieving data from Analysis Services.

CHAPTER 6

Querying Analysis Services with MDX

- An Introduction to MDX

- MDX Functions

- Calculated Members

- Advanced MDX

- Write-Enabled Dimensions

- Creating Actions with MDX

- Custom Functions

Up to this point, we've spent much of our time working with a graphical user interface to create and work with cubes using Analysis Services. But this is a programming book, so it's about time we got down to doing some coding! In this chapter we'll look at MDX (Multi-dimensional Expressions), the query language provided for supporting queries against any Analysis Services database. In later chapters, we'll be using MDX extensively in conjunction with ADO/MD to build OLAP-aware applications using Visual Basic.

MDX is very similar to SQL in syntax, although a fair bit simpler in some ways. Whereas most implementations of SQL include a large number of different operations (such as SELECT, UPDATE, INSERT, and DELETE), MDX itself fundamentally supports just a few operations. As a result, MDX in its own right offers little in the way of update capabilities. Despite the apparent simplicity of MDX, the large number of functions and parameters available within the MDX SELECT operation makes it worthy of detailed consideration here.

NOTE   Despite the lack of support for making changes to data within MDX itself, write-enabled cubes can be updated using a combination of MDX and ADO/MD. For further information on this, see Chapter 10, "Managing an Analysis Services Environment Using DSO."

We start this chapter with a brief introduction to basic MDX queries, before looking at some of the most common functions within the MDX library. We then look briefly at calculated members and examine some issues commonly faced in a business environment. Last, this chapter discusses how to use external function libraries (for example, the mathematical libraries provided with Microsoft Excel) and shows you how to extend MDX with your own custom functions written in Visual Basic.

An Introduction to MDX

The core of the MDX language is the SELECT statement. An MDX SELECT statement allows you to choose just about any view of an Analysis Services cube that you want to see. You can specify dimensions and measures, slice the data, or apply a variety of functions to the source data to produce the SELECT output. In this section, we'll discuss the basics of the SELECT statement and show you how it works on some sample cube data.

Comparisons with SQL

Let's start with a simple question: why use MDX and not SQL? After all, SQL is an established standard for querying databases, and its syntax is well understood and supported by a range of applications.

In answer to this question, we've seen already how the major differences between an Analysis Services database and a SQL Server database lie in the way that the data is structured. In an Analysis Services application, we are frequently trying to represent one or more values (measures) broken down by a range of categories (dimensions). When we query such a database, we often want to see the values broken down and sorted in very specific ways, often using three or more dimensions at a time to produce a result set.

If we were trying to produce a result set such as that shown in Figure 6.1, the SQL query would be extremely complex, with intricate JOIN statements linking the various source tables. In fact, this query would require joining four tables (one for each dimension, plus the fact table) three times (once for each column of data) and executing a UNION query to come up with the final results. As we added more axes, the number of database joins would increase exponentially, thereby making the query required increasingly hard both to write and understand. The multiple joins would also make the query very slow to process. Although we could retrieve the results shown in Figure 6.1 with SQL, it would be far better if we had something designed for the task of addressing large numbers of tables that are all joined in exactly the same way.

FIGURE 6.1:

Example result set

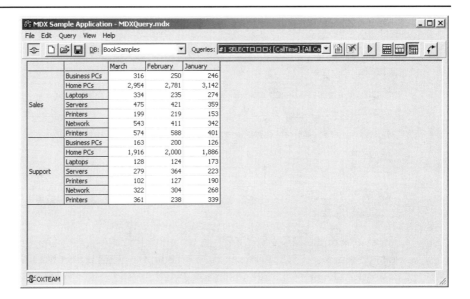

In Analysis Services, the answer is MDX, a language that offers a syntax similar to SQL, but with far better capabilities for handling multidimensional data. With MDX you can reference dimensions and axes, dynamically create new calculated members, and return three or more dimensions in the result set. MDX is currently proprietary to Analysis Services, but as an integral part of the OLE DB for OLAP specification, it could be supported by any other provider that matched the same architecture.

NOTE   Despite the expanded range of facilities MDX offers for OLAP database analysis, it is not as far removed from SQL as one might think. When querying a ROLAP database, Analysis Services "translates" the source MDX statements into the equivalent SQL before executing them on the target server, using a series of internal macros to expand the queries. In fact, the OLE DB for OLAP driver supports both MDX and SQL as query languages, although its support for SQL is rather limited and the published documentation is generally rather thin on the ground in this regard.

Anatomy of an MDX Statement

By far the most common task you will do using MDX is that of querying an OLAP database that has already been created. The tool for doing this is the SELECT statement. At the simplest level every MDX query follows a similar structure:

```
SELECT <axis> [, <axis>,...]
FROM <cube>
WHERE <slicer>
```

The three clauses shown above describe the scope and nature of a query. They include the following:

- One or more axis clauses specifying what information should be returned and how it should be displayed.

- A FROM clause, specifying which cube contains the required data.

- A WHERE clause, specifying the subset of data that is relevant (how the data should be *sliced*).

The syntax of the MDX SELECT statement is, of course, very similar to the equivalent statement in SQL. However, several marked differences reflect both the nature of the source database (relational or multidimensional) and the returned structure (recordset or cellset, respectively).

In SQL, the results of a simple SELECT query are usually provided in the form of a two-dimensional grid, with each column describing a different field of data returned, and the rows themselves containing an entry for each record in the result set. Implicit within this is the knowledge that *rows and columns each have a distinct purpose* and cannot be simply interchanged.

Conversely, in MDX a query can return any number of dimensions (up to the total number of dimensions in the source cube) and *rows and columns have no semantic meaning of their own*. When we execute an MDX query, the resulting cellset represents a subset of the queried multidimensional database. We could, therefore, choose to return a one-dimensional view, as shown in Figure 6.2, a three-dimensional view, as shown in Figure 6.3, or any number up to a maximum limit of 128 dimensions (including a measure dimension)! Of course, whether the application you are using to execute the MDX query can display that number of dimensions is another matter altogether.

FIGURE 6.2:

One-dimensional cellset

CallType	Sales	Service
Calls	55607	36811

FIGURE 6.3:

Three-dimensional cellset

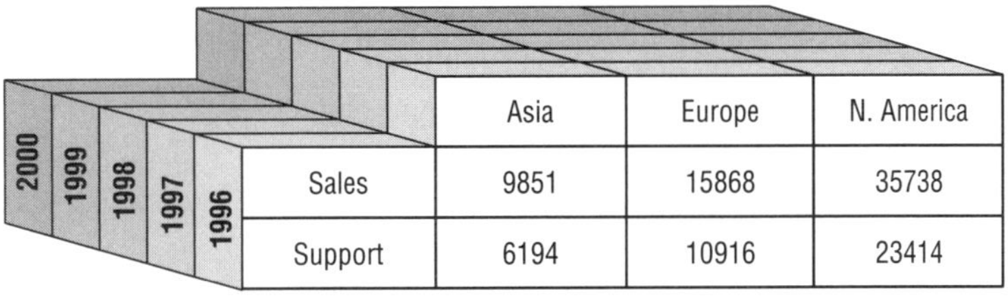

2000 1999 1998 1997 1996		Asia	Europe	N. America
	Sales	9851	15868	35738
	Support	6194	10916	23414

> **NOTE**   In theory at least, MDX is a database-neutral language that can support any OLE DB for OLAP provider. For example, the OLE DB for OLAP documentation (part of the MDAC SDK available from www.microsoft.com/data) describes the use of MDX in a provider-neutral language. In reality, however, this boils down at present to a single choice of the Microsoft OLE DB Provider for OLAP Services, although this may change in the future. This chapter presumes the use of this provider and describes provider-specific features and settings.

Simple MDX Queries

To demonstrate the concepts behind MDX, we're going to use a cube that represents inbound calls taken by a fictitious computer hardware manufacturer. This cube contains two measures and five dimensions, as shown in Table 6.1.

TABLE 6.1: Structure of the Calls Sample Cube

Name	Type	Comments
CallCount	Measure	Count of the number of calls received
CallDuration	Measure	Total duration of calls received
CallType	Dimension	Information as to the nature and issue of the call
CallLeadSource	Dimension	Origin of sales-related calls
CallProduct	Dimension	Breakdown of information about the product that generated the need for a call
CallRegion	Dimension	Geographical information about the caller
CallTime	Dimension	Time and date the customer called

TIP
The cube structure and the sample data used in this chapter are available on the companion CD. The readme file on the CD includes full instructions for installing the data and building the cube.

Let's start with a relatively simple MDX query:

```
SELECT
[CallTime].[1996].Children ON COLUMNS,
[CallProduct].[PCs].Children ON ROWS
FROM [Calls]
WHERE [Measures].[CallCount]
```

TIP
If you're following the examples on your computer, you'll need an OLAP query tool that supports MDX. The MDX Sample Application provided with Analysis Services will fit the bill, and we'll use it to display the results of most of the queries in this chapter. Other alternatives include the third-party tools on the companion CD, or OLAP Workbench, a sample program that is developed later in this book (also on the companion CD).

NOTE
If you're looking for an MDX query analyzer with similar capabilities to the SQL Query Analyzer as an integral component of Analysis Services, you're going to be disappointed. Analysis Services includes MDX Sample Application, an application that executes MDX queries and shows the end result, but it is nowhere near as powerful or user-friendly as the equivalent SQL tool. While you can use it for testing basic queries, don't expect it to provide such niceties as color-coded keywords, multiple query windows, or even support for the more esoteric parts of the MDX syntax. On the plus side, it is a Visual Basic application with source code provided, which you can use as a reference to the syntax and usage of ADO/MD.

This query produces the result shown in Figure 6.4.

FIGURE 6.4:

Basic MDX query

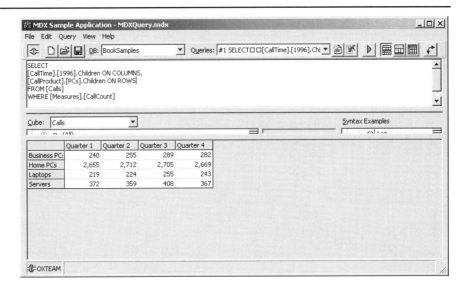

The query above has two axes: columns and rows. In the columns axis, it displays an entry for each quarter in the year 1996; in the rows axis, it displays an entry for each type of PC that generated a support request. In each cell of the result set, we display the number of calls received (CallCount).

> **TIP**
>
> MDX allows keywords (such as "columns" or "where") to appear in any case. In this chapter, we've used the SQL convention of showing keywords entirely in uppercase.

It is relatively easy to correlate this back to the original MDX query. In the query, we used the clause [CallTime].[1996].Children to describe the columns axis. The [CallTime] portion represents the CallTime dimension, with [1996].Children as a set function returning the child members (i.e., quarters) in 1996.

You can use a similar syntax to view any individual member of a dimension. For example, to specify the month of March 1996 alone, you can use the clause [CallTime].[1996].[Quarter 1].[March]. If you're interested in viewing selected members together, you can group them with curly braces ({ and }) to specify a set, as in the following example:

```
SELECT
{[CallTime].[1996].[Quarter 1].[January],
[CallTime].[1996].[Quarter 3].[July],
[CallTime].[1996].[Quarter 4].[December]} ON COLUMNS,
{[CallRegion].[Europe].[UK],
[CallRegion].[Europe].[Germany],
[CallRegion].[North America].[Canada]} ON ROWS
FROM [Calls]
WHERE [Measures].[CallCount]
```

This query produces the results shown in Figure 6.5.

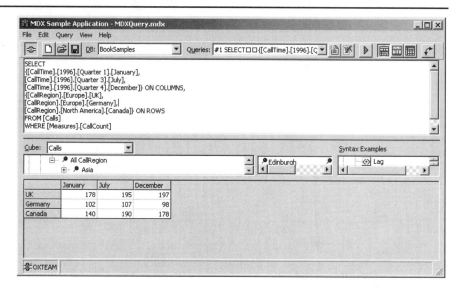

The FROM clause of an MDX SELECT statement is quite simple: it specifies the cube(s) that contain the data we are searching for. If the name of the cube contains a space, then we must enclose it in square brackets, just as in SQL.

NOTE   Transact-SQL allows the use of quotation marks as well as square brackets to delimit identifiers in certain circumstances. MDX only allows square brackets as a delimiter. Square brackets are sometimes required (as in the case of an object name with spaces) but never forbidden, so we follow the convention of most MDX tools and use square brackets around every identifier, whether required or not.

Last, the WHERE clause is used to "slice" the data into a subset. In the above examples, [Measures].[CallCount] is used to limit the result set to only contain one measure (CallCount). As with the axis specification, we can use more than one clause to limit the returned set still further, as in the following example:

```
SELECT
[CallTime].[1996].Children ON COLUMNS,
[CallRegion].[Continent].Members ON ROWS
FROM [Calls]
```

```
WHERE ([Measures].[CallCount],
       [CallType].[All CallType].[Sales],
       [CallLeadSource].[All CallLeadSource].[Show],
       [CallProduct].[All CallProduct])
```

The slicer dimensions (i.e., any dimension listed in the WHERE clause) can be any or all of the dimensions or measures within the cube, except for those that are used within the axis specification. So in the above example, it would not be acceptable to use the CallRegion dimension in the WHERE clause, since the dimension has already been used in specifying the ROWS axis.

Where a dimension is not explicitly specified within the SELECT statement as a whole, the default member is implicit within the WHERE clause. For a dimension x, the default member is typically equivalent to [x].[All x] but may not necessarily be so if a different member has been defined as such. Thus in the above example the specification of [CallProduct].[All CallProduct] is unnecessary unless a different default member has been defined within the cube.

This SELECT statement also introduces a new set function: Members. This function returns a complete set of each of the underlying members for that level, dimension, or hierarchy. For example,

```
[CallType].[CallType].Members
```

returns

```
{[CallType].[Sales], [CallType].[Support]}
```

(in other words, all the members of the Call Type level in the CallType dimension), whereas

```
[CallType].Members
```

returns

```
{[CallType].[All CallType], [CallType].[Sales],
[CallType].[Sales].[Evaluation Request],
[CallType].[Sales].[Literature Request],
[CallType].[Sales].[Order],
[CallType].[Sales].[Post Sales Info],
[CallType].[Sales].[Price Quote],
[CallType].[Support],
[CallType].[Support].[Configuration],
[CallType].[Support].[Installation],
[CallType].[Support].[No Trouble Found],
[CallType].[Support].[Return]}
```

(that is, all members of the CallType dimension for every level).

Using the Members and Children Keywords

There's often confusion at first as to when the Children keyword should be used and when the Members keyword should be used to represent the underlying set of members. A simple rule to remember is that levels have members, and members have children (which are themselves members).

Don't forget that a level is a generic description of a particular point in the dimension hierarchy (for example, year, country, or store). Conversely, a member is one value from that level (e.g., 1999, Germany, or Store 35, respectively). So `[Time].[2000].Children` is valid, as is `[Time].[Year].Members`, but `[Time].[Year].Children` and `[Time].[2000].Members` are semantically incorrect. If you are getting the error message, "Formula error: invalid bind request: in a <level> base object," chances are you've got the two keywords switched around.

You can also use both Members and Children keywords at the dimension level, with different results from each. Here, Members returns *all* descendant members, whereas Children returns just the direct child members of a dimension. Thus in the FoodMart 2000 database, `[Products].Children` returns the top-level members (i.e., Drink, Food, and Non-Consumable), whereas `[Products].Members` returns all 1500+ descendant members (including the `[All Product]` member that represents the grand total of all products). So be careful which you choose!

Designing an MDX Query

As will be seen throughout this chapter, MDX is probably the most powerful way of interrogating an OLAP database. While its syntax takes a little while to learn, the rewards are worthwhile. Although you can use a tool such as the Excel PivotTable Service to query an OLAP database by simply dragging and dropping dimensions and measures to a table, you lose the fine level of control that is available with MDX.

Furthermore, by using MDX, you can also use one of over a hundred internal functions to manipulate the data before it is presented. We'll take a look at some of the most common functions over the next few pages; in addition, a full function reference is provided in Appendix A, "MDX Reference."

Before we get too carried away, however, let's just take a moment to consider the design process for an MDX query. Here's a step-by-step guide to building an MDX query:

- First, consider what information you are trying to show. Will your result set contain measures that already exist within the database? Or will the cells contain the results of a calculation or formula based on other values?

- Then think about the dimensions by which you want to break down the result set. How many different ways will the data be broken down? How many levels deep do you want to include in the result set? If you will be writing the client yourself, consider whether you should retrieve more levels than you actually need at once or whether you will issue further queries for more information. Do you need to display all the members at a particular level or only selected members?

- Now consider how the information should be handled within the cellset. Which dimensions will you place on each axis? If you are returning three or more dimensions, do you want to return an axis for each dimension, or will you present several dimensions on one axis? (Note that many OLAP clients can only display two axes at any time.)

While it is entirely possible to put together a one-off query without "designing" it, if your query will be hard-coded or parameterized into a client application, some extra thought at the authoring stage can pay dividends in the long run.

Unique Names in MDX

As a language, MDX tries to be relatively forgiving in the structure of the queries it receives. It allows arbitrary quantities of whitespace and/or carriage returns throughout the query and allows you to leave out unnecessary detail in specifying cube members. For instance, the following query is valid:

```
SELECT
    {[PCs], [Peripherals]} ON COLUMNS,
    {[No Trouble Found], [Return]} ON ROWS
    FROM [Calls]
```

Since there is only one member within the cube for each of the names referenced above within the cube, the query above has no ambiguity in its meaning. Another equivalent (albeit long-winded) way of writing the same query would be as follows:

```
SELECT
    {[CallProduct].[All CallProduct].[PCs],
     [CallProduct].[All CallProduct].[Peripherals]} ON COLUMNS,
    {[CallType].[All CallType].[Support].[No Trouble Found],
     [CallType].[All CallType].[Support].[Return]} ON ROWS
    FROM [Calls]
```

This time, all the parent levels for each member are fully described. A member name containing all its ancestor members is known as a *qualified* name. In SQL Server 2000 Analysis Services, qualified names can be used to avoid ambiguity wherever a member reference is required. Like square brackets, qualified names are always allowed—so the simple rule is to always qualify the name if you have any doubt.

Continued on next page

Be aware that in some cases, a member will need to be at least partially qualified. For example, if the Time dimension for a particular cube contains Year and Month levels, the reference [January] is likely to be ambiguous because there will be more than one member with the name (unless the cube contains data for only a single year). In such a case, the member will need to be more fully described, as in [2000].[January]. Members that exist in multiple hierarchies will also require such treatment. For example, if both the CustomerLocation and SupplierLocation dimensions contain cities, a reference to [New York] will need to be qualified as [CustomerLocation].[New York].

In passing, it is worth noting that members have two name properties that can be retrieved, either from within MDX or by using an object model such as ADO/MD (see Chapter 8, "Building OLAP Services Applications with ADO/MD Part II: Query Retrieval Objects"): *Name* and *UniqueName*. The Name property always contains the name of the member itself (e.g., PCs); the UniqueName property contains a unique reference to the member—in SQL Server 2000 Analysis Services, this is the qualified name itself.

Axes and Dimensions

Up to this point, the examples we've chosen have all involved information taken from two dimensions displayed in a grid structure. This is a common scenario, but often it will be necessary in real-world applications to query against three or more dimensions at once.

MDX will happily return an *n*-dimensional cellset in response to such a query and includes several keywords to support this. We've used the terms COLUMNS and ROWS to support two dimensions thus far, but the keywords PAGES, CHAPTERS, and SECTIONS can be used additionally to represent the third, fourth, and fifth axis, respectively. Thus the following statement

```
SELECT
    {[1996].[Quarter 1].[January],
     [1996].[Quarter 1].[February],
     [1996].[Quarter 1].[March]} ON COLUMNS,
    {[CallProduct].[Product].Members} ON ROWS,
    {[CallType].[Call Type].Members} ON PAGES
FROM [Calls]
WHERE ([Measures].[CallCount])
```

returns the results shown in Figure 6.6. This figure was composed with Hungry Dog Software's IntelliBrowser (the evaluation version is included on the accompanying CD), which uses the PAGES dimension as a second set of columns.

WARNING You can't open this query in the MDX Sample Application that ships with Analysis Services, because that sample supports only two axes in a single query.

FIGURE 6.6:

Cellset containing three dimensions

		+ March	+ February	+ January
+ Sales	+ Business PCs	316	250	246
	+ Home PCs	2,954	2,781	3,142
	+ Laptops	334	235	274
	+ Servers	475	421	359
	+ Network	543	411	342
	+ Printers	773	807	554
+ Support	+ Business PCs	163	200	126
	+ Home PCs	1,916	2,000	1,886
	+ Laptops	128	124	173
	+ Servers	279	364	223
	+ Network	322	304	268
	+ Printers	463	365	529

As mentioned at the beginning of this chapter, MDX can return up to 127 dimensions; indeed, each of these can be on a separate axis if necessary. Although there are only keywords for the first five axes, you can also specify an arbitrary number of axes by using AXIS(*x*), where *x* represents an index number for the axis starting from 0. Table 6.2 summarizes the relationships between the keywords and number of axes.

TABLE 6.2: Keywords for Representing Axes

Dimension	Keyword	Synonym
1	COLUMNS	AXIS(0)
2	ROWS	AXIS(1)
3	PAGES	AXIS(2)
4	SECTIONS	AXIS(3)
5	CHAPTERS	AXIS(4)
6	N/A	AXIS(5)
...	...	...
127	N/A	AXIS(126)

WARNING Be selective in your use of a large number of axes: although perfectly valid MDX syntax, some OLAP clients that support MDX are limited to displaying a maximum of two axes at any one time. Hopefully, future data-visualization client tools will improve to better support multi-dimensional analysis. Of course, if you are building your own OLAP client, you can include support for as many axes as you wish.

Conversely, it is entirely possible to create a one- or even zero-dimensional result set. Consider the following:

```
SELECT [CallProduct].[PCs].Children ON AXIS(0)
FROM [Calls]
WHERE (Measures.Callcount)
```

which will result in the cellset shown in Figure 6.7.

FIGURE 6.7:

One-dimensional
MDX query

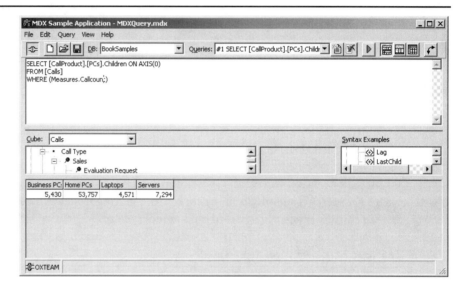

Or even consider the simplest possible query, as follows:

```
SELECT FROM [Calls]
```

which will return the total value across all dimensions for the default member, in this case, 92,418.

WARNING   Once again, be warned that some third-party Analysis Services clients do not fully conform to the MDX specification for queries with fewer than two dimensions. The sample application developed in Chapter 9, "Advanced Usage of the PivotTable Service," supports both zero- and one-dimensional MDX queries.

The one thing to remember is that you must never leave gaps in the axis definitions. The axes within a particular query must be a continuous set starting at AXIS(0) or COLUMNS, although they can appear in any order within the query. Thus, the following query is invalid and will return an error:

```
- This query is invalid...
SELECT [1996].Children ON AXIS(1),
[CallProduct].[PCs].Children ON AXIS(2)
FROM [Calls] WHERE (Measures.CallCount)
```

In this case the command will fail because axes must be numbered from 0 upward. This query uses ROWS (the second axis) and PAGES (the third axis) without using COLUMNS (the first axis) and will therefore be rejected by the query processor.

Collapsing Multiple Dimensions onto an Axis

Perhaps a more pragmatic way of retrieving a cellset containing three or more dimensions is to collapse them into a smaller number of axes. In the preceding examples, we have often specified the positions on an axis in terms of individual members, as in the following:

```
{[USA], [Canada], [Mexico]}
```

An axis specified in the above terms would contain three positions: USA, Canada, and Mexico. However, we can join two or more members from different dimensions to form a *tuple*, as in the following example:

```
{([USA], [Sales]), ([USA], [Support]),
 ([Canada], [Sales]), ([Canada], [Support]),
 ([Mexico], [Sales]), ([Mexico], [Support])}
```

Such an axis would contain six positions, one for each tuple: USA/Sales, USA/Support, Canada/Sales, Canada/Support, Mexico/Sales, and Mexico/Support. Each position would contain the relevant calls received in a particular region, so USA/Sales would include all Sales calls within the USA. Thus the following MDX query

```
SELECT
    {([USA], [Sales]), ([USA], [Support]),
     ([Canada], [Sales]), ([Canada], [Support]),
     ([Mexico], [Sales]), ([Mexico], [Support])} ON COLUMNS,
    [1996].Children ON ROWS
FROM [Calls]
WHERE [Measures].[CallCount]
```

produces the result shown in Figure 6.8.

A simpler way of writing the same query is to use the CROSSJOIN function, which combines two sets to produce a set of tuples containing every possible permutation containing one member from each set. The function CROSSJOIN takes two sets and can be expressed in the following terms:

```
CROSSJOIN({a, b, c}, {x, y} =
    {(a, x), (a, y), (b, x), (b, y), (c, x), (c, y)}
```

FIGURE 6.8:

Defining columns
with tuples

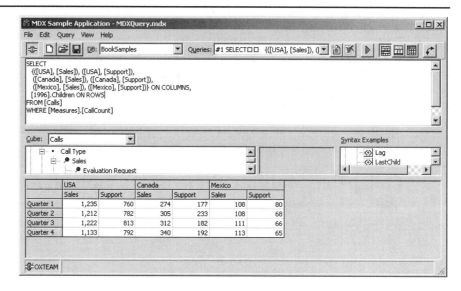

Thus the last example above could alternatively (and equivalently) be written as the following:

```
SELECT
CROSSJOIN ({[USA], [Canada], [Mexico]}, {[Sales], [Support]}) ON COLUMNS,
[1996].Children ON ROWS
FROM [Calls]
WHERE [Measures].[CallCount]
```

Whether you use the CROSSJOIN function or explicitly provide each position on an axis yourself, you can combine as many dimensions or *levels within a dimension* as you wish. Thus the following is valid:

```
SELECT
  {PCs, Network, Printers} ON COLUMNS,
  CROSSJOIN(CROSSJOIN({Sales.[Order], Support}, {UK, USA}),
  {[1996].[Quarter 1].January,
   [1996].[Quarter 4].December}) ON ROWS
FROM [Calls]
WHERE [Measures].[Callcount]
```

and results in the cellset shown in Figure 6.9.

TIP The CROSSJOIN function will combine only two sets at any one time; to combine three or more sets, simply nest several CROSSJOIN statements as in the above example.

FIGURE 6.9:

Using nested CROSSJOIN functions

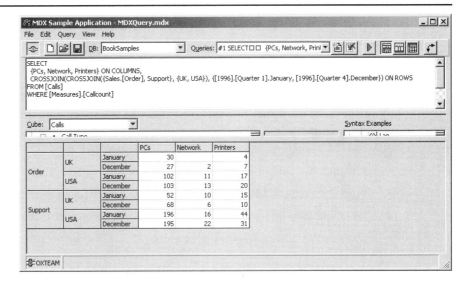

Notes on Query Syntax

We've mentioned some of the syntactical issues surrounding MDX SELECT statements earlier in this chapter. Now we'd like to formally explain the rules for a few things:

- Case and whitespace
- Comments
- Delimiters

Case of Expressions and Comments

We have already mentioned that MDX is a case-insensitive language. This applies to both the keywords and the clauses themselves. In practice, common convention is to capitalize keywords (such as SELECT) for the sake of clarity, and to enter other elements of MDX syntax in their original case. Whitespace is also ignored; you can therefore use tabs, space characters, or carriage returns to format MDX queries for ease of readability.

You can, of course, include comments that describe a query within MDX. You can use one or more of the following styles to comment your query:

Double hyphens (i.e., --)   Any characters after the end of a double hyphen up until the end of a line are ignored.

C++-style comments (i.e., //)   Any characters after the end of a double slash up until the end of a line are ignored.

C-style comments (i.e., /* ... */) Any characters contained within the opening comment marker (/*) and closing comment marker (*/) are treated as comments. C-style comments can span multiple lines.

Token Delimiters

In the previous example (demonstrating usage of nested CROSSJOIN statements), we dropped some of the square brackets around various set members. Although you will often see MDX examples with brackets around every token, they are only *required* in the following cases to avoid ambiguity:

- The member contains a space, as in Call Center.

- The member is an MDX reserved word or keyword, as in Order.

- The member contains non-alphanumeric characters, such as the (All) default member.

- The member's name begins with a number.

Usage is optional in all other cases. You may simply wish to enclose all member tokens in square brackets to avoid any risk of a conflict, particularly if you generate MDX programmatically. If square brackets are used, each individual item should be delimited to avoid ambiguity. In other words, you should use `[Product].[Small Ticket].[Ornaments]` rather than `[Product.Small Ticket.Ornaments]`.

MDX Functions

You've seen how you can use MDX to query an Analysis Services cube and return a subset of that cube, by specifying members to be displayed across several axes with measures returned in the body of the cellset. However, MDX goes somewhat further than this; in particular, it includes well over a hundred intrinsic functions that operate on various elements of a query component.

The functions available fall into nine categories:

- Set functions, such as the CROSSJOIN() function described previously, that operate on one or more sets and return a set.

- Member functions that return an individual member based on input parameters.

- Dimension, hierarchy, and level functions that return information about a member's ancestors.

- Tuple functions that return a tuple from a set, based on user-defined criteria.

- Numeric functions that calculate a value based on a series of measures.

- Logical functions that return a Boolean value based on the output of an expression.

- Array functions that manipulate a tuple or set and return an array.

- String functions that manipulate a tuple or set and return a string.

This chapter does not attempt to provide an exhaustive reference to the use of every single function in the MDX library, but instead, it covers the most regularly used functions based on real-world requirements. Appendix A provides a full list of the functions and their usage.

TIP   For more details about MDX functions, you can also use the MDX Function Reference in Analysis Services Books Online.

Returning Top and Bottom Elements

Perhaps the most important question a sales manager needs to have answered from a company's sales database is the following:

> "What are my top 10 (or bottom 10) selling products?"

or alternatively, perhaps the following:

> "Which are my best 10 (or worst 10) customers in terms of profitability?"

In practice, it's usually comparatively simple questions that are most often asked. It's rare that someone wants to retrieve four dimensions of information drilled down to five levels: if nothing else, such a query generates far too much data to be easily assimilated at one time.

MDX provides several functions to help in answering such questions. TOPCOUNT and TOPPERCENT return respectively the top n and top n% of items that otherwise match the criteria specified in the query. Thus the statement,

```
SELECT
  {Measures.CallCount} ON COLUMNS,
  {TOPCOUNT([Item Name].Members, 10, Measures.CallCount)} ON ROWS
FROM [Calls]
```

returns the results shown in Figure 6.10.

FIGURE 6.10:

Using the TOPCOUNT()
function

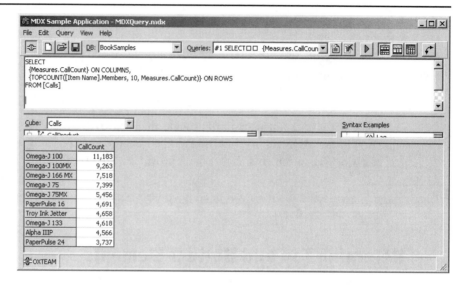

Both TOPCOUNT and TOPPERCENT have similar syntax:

```
TOPCOUNT(<set>, <count>[, <numeric_value_expression>])
TOPPERCENT(<set>, <percentage>[, <numeric_value_expression>])
```

Both TOPCOUNT() and TOPPERCENT() take three parameters:

- The <set> parameter represents the set of members that you wish to be returned. In the example above, TOPCOUNT() returns the members of the [Item Name] level as the first column of the cellset.

- The <count> or <percentage> parameter specifies the number (for TOPCOUNT) or percent of the total number (for TOPPERCENT) of items to return in the set.

- The <numeric_value_expression> parameter specifies how the items should be ordered when choosing which ones to return. The expression can be either simply a measure, or alternatively, a result based on a calculation combining one or more measures with numeric functions.

The functions select the top items according to the specified criteria and place them in descending order. Any hierarchical structure in the input set will be eliminated, and if there is a tie for the last item to be returned, one will be arbitrarily discarded so as to return the exact number requested.

The TOPSUM function can also be useful in this regard. Here's a sample query using TOPSUM:

```
SELECT
    {Measures.CallCount} ON COLUMNS,
    {TOPSUM(City.Members, 20000, Measures.CallCount)} ON ROWS
FROM [Calls]
WHERE [1996]
```

An English translation of this query might be, "Show me the top 20,000 calls, grouped by city, for the year 1996." Figure 6.11 shows the result.

FIGURE 6.11:

Using the TOPSUM function

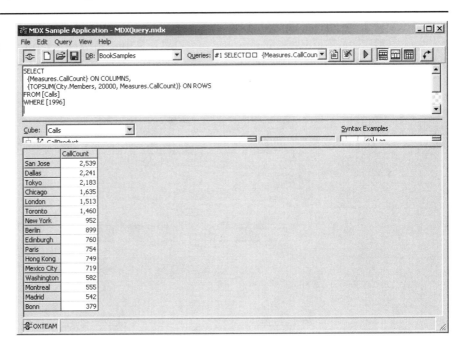

Ordering Results

Often it is useful to specify the order for a query, without selecting only the top or bottom elements (as TOPCOUNT or BOTTOMCOUNT would allow). You could use a TOP-PERCENT function, specifying 100% of the items, but a better choice is the ORDER function. The syntax for this function is as follows:

```
ORDER(<set>, {<string_value_expression> | <numeric_value_expression>}
➥ [, ASC | DESC | BASC | BDESC])
```

This function can be used to sort any set in ascending or descending order, either keeping or breaking the hierarchy of the original set depending on which sort order is chosen. For example, look at the following query:

```
SELECT
{[1996].[Quarter 3].August,
 [1996].[Quarter 3].September,
 [1996].[Quarter 4].October}  ON COLUMNS,
NON EMPTY {ORDER({[Home PCs].Children, Printers.Children},
  ([1996].[Quarter 4].October, Measures.CallCount), BDESC)} ON ROWS
FROM [Calls]
WHERE (Measures.CallCount, [CallType].Support)
```

In this query, the members displayed on the row axis are all the members of {[Home PCs].Children, Printers.Children}. The ORDER function is used to sort the cellset in descending order by the number of calls received in October. Figure 6.12 shows the results. Note that the printers and PCs are intermixed in the list.

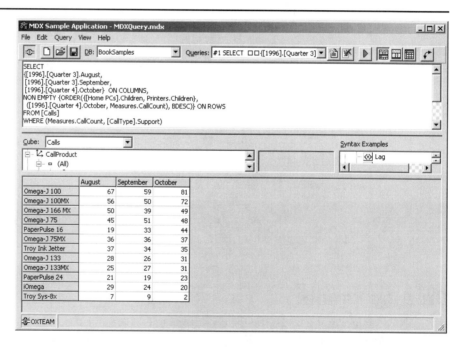

FIGURE 6.12:

Returning an ordered cellset

The keyword NON EMPTY eliminates any members that contain no data from the axis specified. For example, had there been no calls at all for the PaperPulse 24, it would have been deleted from the result set.

The ORDER function can either keep or eliminate the imposed hierarchy on the result set. The BASC and BDESC keywords sort the results in ascending or descending order while eliminating any hierarchy in the sorted axis. By contrast, the ASC and DESC keywords perform the sort within each hierarchy in the set. Making the change of BDESC to simply DESC in the query above results in the cellset shown in Figure 6.13.

FIGURE 6.13:

Using DESC to return an ordered cellset with hierarchy

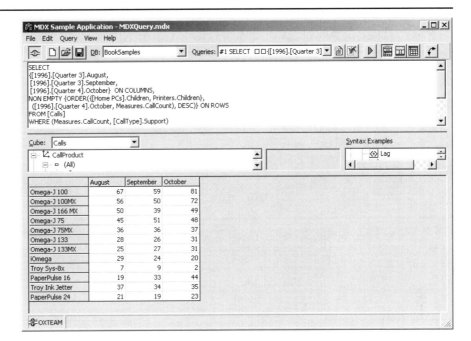

Note that now all the PCs are sorted first, followed by the Printers, without the two lists being intermingled.

Filtering Results

You've seen how the WHERE clause and the axis specification clauses can be used to limit the returned dataset by dimension or member. Sometimes you'll want to limit the returned set based on a more complex set of criteria (for example, only showing members where the measure is within a certain range). These kinds of filtering operations can be achieved relatively simply by using the FILTER function.

The syntax for this function is as follows:

```
FILTER(<set>, <search_operation>)
```

To filter a set, simply specify the criteria against which each member in the set should be tested; for instance,

```
FILTER([Item Name].Members, (Measures.CallCount > 2000))
```

The above operation returns just the members for which the total call count is greater than 2000. Within the <search_operation> clause, the standard mathematical operators can be used, including +, -, <, and >.

Thus the following query,

```
SELECT
{[1996].[Quarter 1].January,
 [1996].[Quarter 2].April} ON COLUMNS,
{FILTER([Item Name].Members,
 (([1996].[Quarter 1].January, Measures.CallCount) <
  ([1996].[Quarter 2].April, Measures.CallCount)))} ON ROWS
FROM [Calls]
WHERE (Measures.CallCount)
```

returns only those products where the number of support calls have increased in April compared to January, as shown in Figure 6.14.

FIGURE 6.14:

Filtering a cellset by comparing members

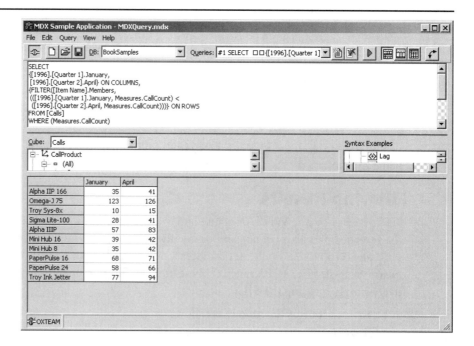

WARNING The way MDX handles filters is rather different from SQL, which uses expressions within the WHERE clause to limit the returned data. Although MDX contains a WHERE clause, it is purely used for identifying the subset of the cube's dimensions that are used to return a query. Instead, use the FILTER function on an axis to limit the returned rows within the subset of dimensions and levels requested.

Calculated Members

Calculated members are an extremely important concept in extending Analysis Services to answer more complex queries and support detailed analyses of a database. They can be used within Analysis Services to achieve almost any task, given sufficient processing time. In essence, a calculated member is an expression that derives a value from one or more constituent members (dimensions, levels, or measures) of a cube.

Up until now, all the queries that we've specified against the Calls cube have only displayed one measure in the returned cellset, CallCount. Many cubes will, of course, have more than one measure, but even when the cube only has one measure included, you can calculate new values as part of the execution of the query. This is achieved by adding a new WITH clause to the front of the SELECT query, as follows:

```
WITH MEMBER <member> AS <expression>
    [MEMBER <member> AS <expression> ...]
SELECT <axis> [, <axis>,...]
FROM <cube>
WHERE <slicer>
```

Once you have defined one or more calculated members, you can use them throughout the rest of the query. Calculated members are usually used for generating new measures; however, this is not always the case, and it is entirely possible to provide a calculated member based on part of a dimensional hierarchy.

Let's look at a simple, practical example of the use of calculated measures:

```
WITH MEMBER Measures.[Average Call]
AS 'Measures.[CallDuration] / Measures.[CallCount]'
SELECT
[CallProduct].Members ON ROWS,
{Measures.[CallDuration], Measures.[CallCount],
 Measures.[Average Call]} ON COLUMNS
FROM Calls
WHERE (CallTime.[1997])
```

In this example, a new measure [Average Call] is set to be equal to [CallDuration] divided by [CallCount]. This new measure is then used, along with the other measures, to provide values for the column axis of the resulting set. Figure 6.15 shows the result.

FIGURE 6.15:

Simple use of a calculated member

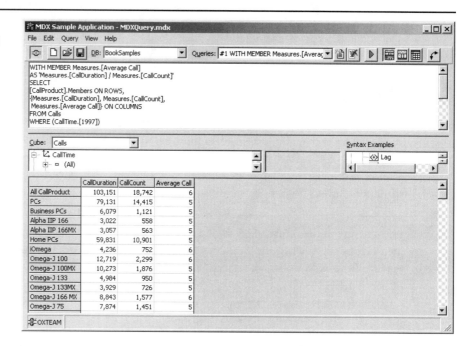

In this example, we used a simple mathematical expression to calculate the [Average Call] measure. You can also use the full range of intrinsic MDX functions to produce a result. Some of the functions that you might use to build a calculated member to use as a measure include the following:

- Time-based functions, such as YTD, PrevPeriod, and NextPeriod
- Arithmetical functions such as LinReg, Avg, and Sum
- Standard arithmetical operators such as +, -, *, and /

Indeed, many of the functions supplied within the MDX library have little use outside of a calculated member.

You can also go beyond the bounds of what is possible in MDX itself by using external registered function libraries supporting the COM specification for MDX. These include the mathematical function add-ins that are provided by Microsoft Excel or other scientific packages, or even one or more functions developed by yourself using Visual Basic or another COM-supporting development language. We'll describe how to do this at the end of the chapter.

One important point to note is that calculated members defined within a query have a lifetime of that query alone. That means, of course, that if you wish to reuse the calculated member in a second query, the calculated member needs to be defined afresh.

Sums, Counts, and Averages

Perhaps the most common uses of functions within calculated members are to sum or average a set of underlying values. Two functions, SUM and AVG, provide the mechanism to support each of these activities. The syntax for the functions is as follows:

```
SUM(<Set>[, <Numeric Expression>])
AVG(<Set>[, <Numeric Expression>])
```

To use each function, you pass it the set of members or tuples for which you wish to calculate the sum or average and, optionally, an expression that will be calculated to provide each component of the sum. Typically, the expression will simply be the name of a measure; if no expression is supplied, then the default measure is used (e.g., for the Calls cube, the CallCount measure).

As an example, the following statement shows the average number of calls received per month for each product type in the Calls cube:

```
WITH MEMBER [CallTime].[Average Calls Per Month] AS
    'AVG(DESCENDANTS([CallTime].[All CallTime], [CallTime].[Month]))'
SELECT {[CallTime].[Average Calls Per Month]}
    ON COLUMNS,
[CallProduct].[Product].MEMBERS ON ROWS
FROM [Calls]
WHERE (Measures.[CallCount])
```

In addition to the AVG function, you'll note the use of the DESCENDANTS function in this statement. DESCENDANTS returns a set of values reflecting all of the descendants of a particular member at a particular value. Thus, DESCENDANTS([CallTime].[All CallTime], [CallTime].[Month]) returns a set of all the values at the Month level beneath the top-level [All CallTime] member. By enclosing this in the AVG function, we retrieve the average call count per month.

Figure 6.16 shows the results of this query.

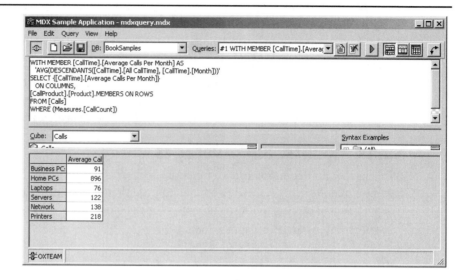

> **TIP**   The MIN and MAX functions use the same syntax as the SUM and AVG functions.

In a similar vein, you can use the COUNT function to count the number of elements within a set. The syntax for the COUNT function is as follows:

```
Count(<Set>[, ExcludeEmpty | IncludeEmpty])
```

By default the COUNT function excludes empty cells, but you can optionally include them with the second parameter of the statement. An alternative syntax for the COUNT function also exists, which can be used directly on the set, as follows:

```
<Set>.Count
```

With this syntax, empty cells are always excluded.

As an example of COUNT, here's a query to retrieve the number of products in each product group, whose results are shown in Figure 6.17:

```
WITH MEMBER Measures.[NumProducts] AS
    'COUNT(DESCENDANTS([CallProduct].CURRENTMEMBER, [CallProduct].[Item Name]))'
SELECT {Measures.[NumProducts]}
    ON COLUMNS,
[CallProduct].[Product].Members ON ROWS
FROM [Calls]
```

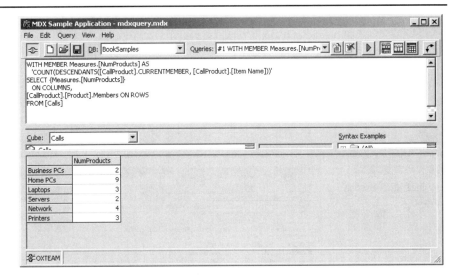

Note the use of the CURRENTMEMBER function inside the COUNT. This tells Analysis Services to execute the COUNT operation on whatever value in the CallProduct dimension is current as it goes to fill in each cell in the cellset.

Navigating through a Dimension Hierarchy

You will often want to operate with values at various levels in a dimension as part of an MDX query. MDX provides several functions that support such navigation through the hierarchy. We have seen several of these already: MEMBERS, CHILDREN, DESCENDANTS, and CURRENTMEMBER. Several other similar functions can also be very useful within a calculated member.

One classic example of the use of such functions is showing how a total value for a parent is broken down into its constituent child portions. A good example within the Calls cube is the question, "What percentage of each product group's calls is made for each product?" To answer this question, we can use the PARENT function, which simply returns the parent member for any member within the cube. The syntax for this function is as follows:

```
<Member>.PARENT
```

and the result returned is a member itself.

This allows us to write the above query in the following way:

```
WITH MEMBER Measures.PercentageCalls AS
    '([CallProduct].CURRENTMEMBER, Measures.[CallCount]) /
    ([CallProduct].CURRENTMEMBER.PARENT, Measures.[CallCount])',
```

```
        FORMAT_STRING = '#.00%'
MEMBER Measures.[CurrentGroup] AS
  '[CallProduct].CURRENTMEMBER.PARENT.NAME'
SELECT {Measures.[CallCount], Measures.PercentageCalls,
Measures.[CurrentGroup]} ON COLUMNS,
[CallProduct].[Item Name].MEMBERS ON ROWS
FROM [Calls]
```

Figure 6.18 shows the results of the query. You can see, for example, that the iOmega model accounts for 6.87% of all calls in the Home PCs product group.

FIGURE 6.18:

Using the PARENT function in a query

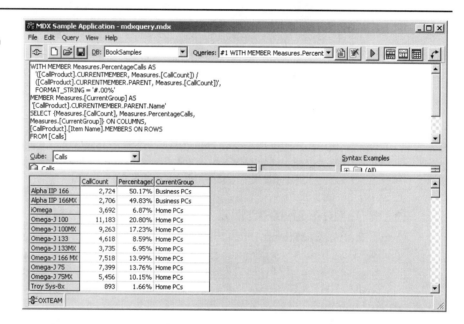

In addition to the PARENT function, this query demonstrates two other pieces of syntax that we haven't seen before. First, the FORMAT_STRING parameter in the WITH MEMBER clause simply allows you to specify the format that should be used to display the results of a calculation. Second, the NAME function returns the name displayed by a dimension or level.

TIP
     For details on the FORMAT_STRING parameter, refer to Books Online. It is very similar to the VB Format() function. We'll discuss the most common format strings later in this chapter.

The PARENT function can be used on itself to return the "grandparent" ancestor, as shown below:

```
<Member>.PARENT.PARENT
```

This syntax can get tedious rather quickly; as a result, it is often easier to use two generalized functions in place of the PARENT/CHILDREN functions. First, the ANCESTOR function returns the ancestor of a member at any parent level within the hierarchy. This allows you to quickly reference two or three levels up the dimension and is also more readable than the alternative discussed above. Second, as you already saw, the DESCENDANTS function returns child members at an arbitrary number of dimensions deep within the tree. The usage pattern for each of these functions is as follows:

```
ANCESTOR(<Member>, <Level>)
DESCENDANTS(<Member>,<Level>,<[Desc_flags]>)
```

The optional Desc_flags argument allows for easy specification of some particular sets of descendants. For example, you can set this argument to the value AFTER to return the descendants on the level immediately after the level specified in the function. You can find the other values for this argument in Books Online.

NOTE   ANCESTOR returns a single member while DESCENDANTS returns a set of members. There is also an ANCESTORS function with the same syntax as ANCESTOR. The only difference is that ANCESTORS returns a set instead of a member. Of course, since a member only has one ancestor at a particular level, the ANCESTORS function always returns a set with only one member.

Session Calculated Members

Rather than redefining a calculated member every time you plan to use it, you can set it to have *session-wide scope*; in other words, to be available for the length of your current connection to the Analysis Server. You can do this with a CREATE MEMBER statement, in the following manner:

```
CREATE MEMBER Sales.Measures.[Average Unit Profit] AS
    '([Store Sales] - [Store Cost]) / [Unit Sales]',
    FORMAT_STRING = '$0.00;($0.00);$0.00;\N\U\L\L'
```

One important thing to notice with this statement is that you must specify the cube into which you wish to insert the member. A SELECT statement contains a FROM clause that describes the source cube for an operation; in the absence of this, CREATE MEMBER statements must prefix the cube name to the remainder of the member.

WARNING   If you execute this statement in the MDX Sample Application (or most other OLAP clients, for that matter), the application will not return any response to indicate successful execution. Many applications erroneously assume that any executed statement will return a result set. You have been warned!

When you have finished with the calculated member for that session, you can drop it using a statement such as the following:

```
DROP MEMBER Sales.Measures.[Average Unit Profit]
```

Permanent Calculated Members

If you instead want to create a permanent calculated member, you can do so by updating the parent cube itself, in one of three ways:

- Use the Calculated Member Builder interface within Analysis Manager to define a new formula. You can launch this builder from within the Cube Editor, as we discussed in Chapter 5, "Advanced Analysis Services."

- Write code that calls the equivalent functions in the Decision Support Objects COM library to create a calculated member within the cube. You'll see an example of this technique in Chapter 10.

- Use the dimension write-back facilities in MDX to modify the dimension to support the relevant function, as in the following example:

```
ALTER CUBE CallCenter
CREATE MEMBER Measures.CallsYTD
    AS 'YTD(CallCount)'
```

Once the calculated member has been created, it can then be accessed in the same way as for any other existing measure.

Advanced MDX

In this section we look at some of the more advanced functions that are available in MDX, and we show you how to handle some of the most common business issues using Analysis Services:

- Retrieving member properties
- Formatting results
- Comparing different time periods

Retrieving Member Properties

In Chapter 5 we saw how individual data members can have properties associated with them to store additional information. For example, an Employees parent-child dimension would likely use the employee's name as the member name, but you could choose to store additional information (such as salary, grade, or hire date) in the properties for each member.

In the FoodMart 2000 sample database provided with SQL Server 2000, the member properties facility is used extensively to store additional information. For instance, the Store dimension includes information at the Store Name level that describes the size and type of the store as well the manager's name.

Figure 6.19 shows a view of the Employee member properties from the FoodMart 2000 sample database, using the Analysis Manager Dimension Editor.

FIGURE 6.19:

Member properties

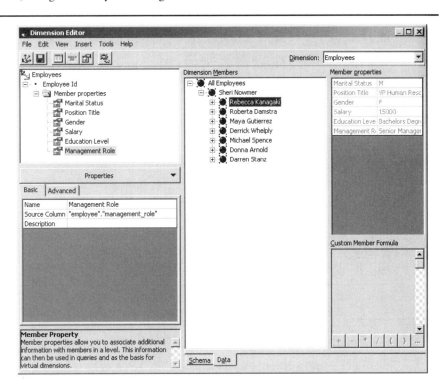

TIP

The Dimension Editor is a subset of the Cube Editor that only shows information relating to a dimension. To open the Dimension Editor, right-click a dimension in the Analysis Manager treeview and select Edit.

Once you have member property information stored in your cube, you can retrieve it with a query such as the following (this one against the FoodMart 2000 sample database):

```
SELECT
    {[Measures].[Unit Sales]} ON COLUMNS,
```

```
NON EMPTY
    ORDER([Store Name].Members, [Unit Sales], BDESC)
        DIMENSION PROPERTIES [Store Name].[Store Manager], [Store Name].
➡ [Store Type] ON ROWS
FROM Sales
```

This query returns the information shown in Table 6.3.

TABLE 6.3: Returning Member Properties

Store Name	Store Manager	Store Type	Unit Sales
Store 13	Inmon	Deluxe supermarket	41,580.00
Store 17	Mays	Deluxe supermarket	35,257.00
Store 11	Erickson	Supermarket	26,079.00
Store 7	White	Supermarket	25,663.00
Store 24	Byrd	Supermarket	25,635.00
Store 15	Ollom	Supermarket	25,011.00
Store 3	Davis	Supermarket	24,576.00
Store 16	Mantle	Supermarket	23,591.00
Store 6	Maris	Gourmet supermarket	21,333.00
Store 23	Johnson	Mid-size grocery	11,491.00
Store 2	Smith	Small grocery	2,237.00
Store 22	Byrg	Small grocery	2,203.00
Store 14	Strehlo	Small grocery	2,117.00

NOTE The dimension properties are not, strictly speaking, part of the cellset returned by the query. Some MDX clients (such as the MDX Sample Application shipped with Analysis Services itself) will not automatically display these properties. You may have to double-click the row header or perform some other operation to display this information. For further information, check the vendor-supplied documentation.

You can have any number of member properties returned within an MDX query, but they must of course be included as part of the same axis as the member itself. Thus the following query will fail:

```
- This is an invalid query...
SELECT NON EMPTY
    {[Store].[All Stores].[Mexico].
        [Zacatecas].[Hidalgo].Children} ON COLUMNS,
    {[Time].[1998].Q1:Q3}
        DIMENSION PROPERTIES [Employees].[Employee Name]
        ON ROWS
FROM HR
```

Formatting Results

Up to this point, we've taken the simple approach of performing a query and presenting the results to the user in the raw form they arrive from the server. MDX, however, provides a range of options that allow you to format the numeric results so they are more presentable on the screen. You can do this by specifying options within the calculated member string, as in the following example in the FoodMart 2000 database, which formats a calculated Markup member as a percentage:

```
WITH MEMBER Measures.Markup AS
    '([Store Sales] - [Store Cost]) / [Store Cost]',
    FORMAT_STRING = '#.0%'
SELECT NON EMPTY
{ORDER (DESCENDANTS(Product, [Brand Name]), Markup, BDESC)} ON ROWS,
{Measures.[Store Sales], Measures.[Store Cost], Measures.Markup} ON COLUMNS
FROM Sales
```

It is up to the OLAP client as to how this information is actually displayed. The OLAP provider returns two values for each item in the cellset: the raw data and the formatted string, and the OLAP client chooses which of the two to use in a particular context. The OLAP Workbench application described in Chapters 8 and 9 supports the use of formatted string sets.

The contents of the FORMAT_STRING property operate in the same manner as the Format( ) function in Visual Basic: the characters contained in the string are used to format the raw data into its output form. The property can be used for string, numeric, and date/time values, and the potential values vary accordingly. Most commonly, it's used for numeric values, since most queries return numbers rather than strings or dates. Table 6.4 shows the most commonly used formatting characters for numeric data.

TABLE 6.4: FORMAT_STRING Numeric Values

Character	Description
#	Digit placeholder. If a digit appears in that position within the string, that digit is displayed; otherwise nothing is displayed. If additional numbers are to the left of the placeholder, they are displayed without further formatting.
0	Digit placeholder. If a digit appears in that position within the string, that digit is displayed; otherwise the digit 0 is displayed. Useful for fixed-point decimal expressions, e.g., #.000 applied to the number 5.1 yields 5.100.
.	Decimal placeholder. The locale-specific decimal point is displayed. If only # digit placeholders exist to the left of the decimal placeholder, and the value is −1 < x < 1, then no digits will be displayed to the left of the decimal point. (For instance, the format expression #.# applied to the number 0.5 yields a result of .5, whereas expression 0.0 applied to the number 0.5 yields 0.5.)

Continued on next page

TABLE 6.4 CONTINUED: FORMAT_STRING Numeric Values

Character	Description
,	Thousands placeholder. The locale-specific thousands separator is displayed in the equivalent position in the formatted string.
%	When used at the end of a formatting string, denotes that the figure represents a percentage. The number is automatically multiplied by 100; thus #.0% applied to the figure 0.358 yields 35.8%.
\	Used to denote that a character should be represented literally in the output text, rather than used as a formatting placeholder. Note that the characters -, +, $, (, and) are automatically treated as literals.

For numeric values, you can optionally include up to four different formatting strings, each separated by a semicolon. The first format is used for positive values, the second is used for negative values, the third for the number zero, and the fourth for the NULL value. Thus the following is valid:

```
WITH MEMBER Measures.[Average Unit Profit] AS
   '([Store Sales] - [Store Cost]) / [Unit Sales]',
   FORMAT_STRING = '$0.00;($0.00);$0.00;\N\U\L\L'
SELECT
ORDER(DESCENDANTS(Product, [Product Name]), Measures.[Average Unit Profit],
➥ BDESC) ON ROWS,
{Measures.[Unit Sales], Measures.[Average Unit Profit]} ON COLUMNS
FROM Sales
```

WARNING There is no locale-sensitive currency placeholder: if you wish to show an amount in a currency other than dollars, you have to specify it as a literal string. To display a currency value in euros, for example, the format string \€0.00 should be used. This is deliberate: if currencies were displayed in locale-appropriate fashion, a U.S. system would display all currency values in dollars, regardless of what actual currency was represented!

The options that are available for text and date/time formatting are identical to those available for the creation of custom text and date/time formats within Visual Basic; refer to Books Online for more information.

In addition to setting a format for the results themselves, you can also make adjustments to the display characteristics of those results using the FONT_NAME, FONT_SIZE, and FORE_COLOR properties. These can be set in the same way as for the FORMAT_STRING property and are passed on to the client application; once again, it is up to the client as to whether these properties are evaluated and displayed. Table 6.5 provides further information on these properties.

TABLE 6.5: Additional Formatting Properties

Property Name	Usage
FONT_NAME	String value representing the name of the OpenType or TrueType font family used to display the cell values.
FONT_SIZE	Integer value representing the size of the font in points.
FORE_COLOR	Four-byte integer representing the text color in which the cell should be displayed. The standard RGB encoding from Windows and Visual Basic is used.

The underlying OLE DB for OLAP provider also supports an ALIGNMENT property, but this is not used by Analysis Services in the current release.

Comparative Time Functions

As we've seen earlier in this book, time-based dimensions are treated somewhat differently from other dimensions. For starters, most source databases contain a single date/time field within the fact table that by its nature contains all the levels within the dimension in one field. Second, all time dimensions share a common concept of their hierarchy (i.e., year, quarter, month, etc.). Although different implementations may include a different number of levels (for instance, excluding Hour and Minute or including Quarterly as well as Monthly), they each share a common notion of a *period-based hierarchy*, with the descendants of a given member in a level being the same as those of their peers. Figure 6.20 shows how this works in practice. Note that each year has a [Quarter 1] member, each [Quarter 1] has a January member, and so on.

This common structure makes for easy comparisons between different members within the dimension. For instance, MDX provides several functions that allow you to compare members with the same name that exist in different parts of the hierarchy (for example, [Time].[1998].Q1 and [Time].[1999].Q1), or consecutive members within a period (for example, [Time].[1999].March and [Time].[1999].April).

FIGURE 6.20:

A time hierarchy

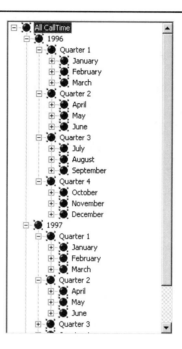

Table 6.6 lists the main time-based functions that are included within the core MDX library:

TABLE 6.6: MDX Time-Based Functions

Function	Description
LastPeriods(<index>, <member>)	Returns a set containing the last <index> periods before the member specified.
PeriodstoDate(<level>, <member>)	Returns a set of members that contain the periods to the date specified in member.
YTD(<member>) QTD(<member>) MTD(<member>) WTD(<member>)	Returns the period to date for a year, quarter, month, or week. Equivalent (and identical) to `PeriodstoDate(Year|Quarter|Month|Week, <member>)`.
OpeningPeriod(<level>, <member>)	Returns the member that commences the period defined in <member> at level <level>. Thus `OpeningPeriod(Quarter, [1998])` returns `[1998].[Q1]`.

Continued on next page

TABLE 6.6 CONTINUED: MDX Time-Based Functions

Function	Description
ClosingPeriod(<level>, <member>)	Similar to OpeningPeriod, this function returns the member that ends the period defined in <member> at level <level>. Thus `ClosingPeriod(Month, [1999])` returns `[1999].[December]`.
ParallelPeriod(<level>, <index>, <member>)	Returns the cousin period <index> prior to the current period specified by <level> and <member>. Thus `ParallelPeriod(Quarter, 1, [1999].[August])` returns `[1998].[August]`.

NOTE Although these functions are designed to be used against time-based dimensions, they do not require that to be the case. They can be used in other dimensions, so long as the same members exist at each cousin level within the hierarchy.

These functions are typically used as part of a calculated member. For instance, consider this query:

```
WITH MEMBER Measures.[Call Volume Change] AS
'(Measures.[CallCount], CallTime.CURRENTMEMBER) -
    (Measures.[CallCount], PARALLELPERIOD([CallTime].[Year]))'
SELECT {Measures.[CallCount], Measures.[Call Volume Change]} ON COLUMNS,
{DESCENDANTS([CallTime].[1997], [Month])} ON ROWS
FROM [Calls]
```

As you can see in Figure 6.21, the cellset produced by this query shows the number of calls for each month in 1997, together with the change in number of calls in that month in 1997 as compared to 1996 (the parallel period one year before).

To see the call volume change from the corresponding month in the previous quarter simply requires changing the argument to the PARALLELPERIOD function:

```
WITH MEMBER Measures.[Call Volume Change] AS
'(Measures.[CallCount], CallTime.CURRENTMEMBER) -
    (Measures.[CallCount], PARALLELPERIOD([CallTime].[Quarter]))'
SELECT {Measures.[CallCount], Measures.[Call Volume Change]} ON COLUMNS,
{DESCENDANTS([CallTime].[1997], [Month])} ON ROWS
FROM [Calls]
```

FIGURE 6.21:

Using PARALLELPERIOD in a query

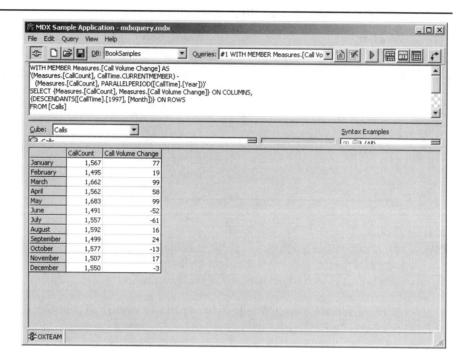

Write-Enabled Dimensions

As mentioned in Chapter 5, Analysis Services includes the ability to create write-enabled cubes. This capability allows a user to test possible "what-if" scenarios by making some changes to a copy of the underlying data and seeing the net effect on the overall picture. Write-enabled cubes are useful for forecasting the potential effects of a change to a company's operating environment, such as an increase in the cost of supply for a particular product. However, this facility only operates on the data contained within a cube, rather than the structure of the cube itself.

NOTE The use of write-enabled cubes is discussed in more detail in Chapter 10.

With SQL Server 2000, Analysis Services introduces the concept of *write-enabled dimensions.* Setting a dimension as write-enabled makes it possible to make changes to the structure of that dimension in a live setting. For example, you could add or delete new members, or move members from one position in a tree to another. Unlike the data in a write-enabled cube, changes to a write-enabled dimension are actually made to the underlying data from which the dimension is derived. Note that only parent-child dimensions may be enabled for write-back in SQL Server 2000.

TIP   The OLE DB for OLAP 2.6 specification describes the use of dimension write-back with non–parent-child dimensions. While this is a valid part of the OLE DB for OLAP specification, it is not supported by Analysis Services itself. For details on other areas where the Analysis Services implementation differs from the OLE DB for OLAP specification, search for the topic "OLE DB for OLAP Compliance" within the Analysis Services documentation.

The following operations can be performed on a write-enabled dimension:

- Creating a new member under any node within the dimension hierarchy
- Deleting a dimension member or even an entire subtree of members
- Updating the member properties for a specified member within a dimension
- Moving a dimension member or an entire subtree from one position to another within the hierarchy

Imagine that you have a dimension called Employees that contains details on all the employees within your organization. Such a dimension would be most effective if created as a parent-child dimension, with an arbitrary number of levels to match the hierarchical structure of your organization. Figure 6.22 shows an example of an organization chart for a fictional company.

FIGURE 6.22:

Employees organization chart

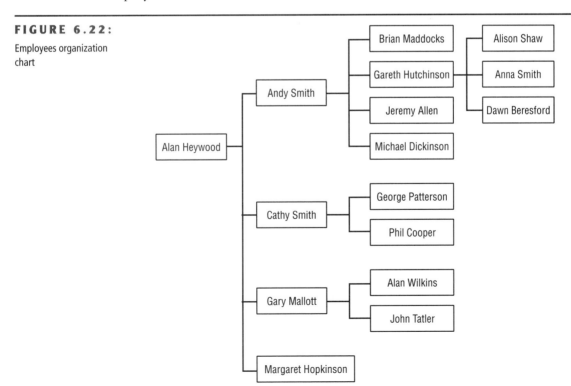

Table 6.7 shows an Employees table that matches the organization chart in structure. Note the empManagerID field, which makes this table suitable for use in a parent-child dimension.

TABLE 6.7: Employees Source Data Table

empID	empFullname	empPayrollNo	empManagerID
1	Alan Heywood	3483	1
2	Gary Mallott	3589	1
3	Cathy Smith	3942	1
4	John Tatler	3841	2
5	Alan Wilkins	3194	2
6	Brian Maddocks	3084	9
7	Gareth Hutchinson	3018	9
8	Michael Dickinson	3992	9
9	Andy Smith	3821	1
11	Alison Shaw	3154	7
19	Margaret Hopkinson	3101	1
20	Anna Smith	3347	7
22	Phil Cooper	3977	3
25	George Patterson	3685	3
35	Dawn Beresford	3011	7
45	Jeremy Allen	3087	9

To enable a dimension for write-back, select the write-back option during the creation of the dimension. When the cube is processed, write-back will be enabled on that dimension and you can make changes to the structure of the dimension.

WARNING   Be aware that, unlike updates to a write-enabled cube, which are stored in a separate write-back table, changes to write-enabled dimensions are recorded directly in the original dimensional table. This is not something you can control at present. Since these commands have a great deal of power, much caution should be taken with security settings before implementing dimension write-back in any production environment.

The general syntax for modifying a write-enabled dimension is as follows:

```
ALTER CUBE <cube_name>
{CREATE|DROP|UPDATE|MOVE} DIMENSION MEMBER <member>
[WITH DESCENDANTS] [UNDER <new_member>]
```

We'll look at the specific syntax for each example below.

NOTE   To modify a write-back dimension, you must use it in a cube. The companion CD contains the data for the Timesheet cube used in these examples.

Adding New Members to a Dimension

To add a new member to a dimension, use the ALTER CUBE statement, as in the following statement:

```
ALTER CUBE Timesheet
CREATE DIMENSION MEMBER
[Employees].[Alan Heywood].[John Armitage],
KEY='55',
[emp Payroll No]='3484'
```

The above statement adds a new member to the Employees dimension named "John Armitage." This member is inserted as a direct descendant of the member named "Alan Heywood."

To add a new member successfully, you must either specify a unique reference (key) for that member or edit the dimension within the Dimension Editor to no longer require unique keys for each member. We don't recommend the latter approach: without a unique key, it will be impossible to definitively reference the member at a later stage if, for example, its display name is modified.

Entering such a query from the MDX Sample Application will not show any results or information messages if the query is successful; you will only see a response (in the form of an error message) if the query fails for some reason.

You must also define any non-nullable columns in the source table for the dimension to be member properties of the dimension and supply values for those member properties as part of the ALTER CUBE statement. Here, the empPayrollNo column in the original table has been mapped to the [emp Payroll No] member property of the Employees dimension.

Deleting Members from a Dimension

You can delete a member from a dimension using the following syntax:

```
ALTER CUBE Timesheet
DROP DIMENSION MEMBER
[Employees].[John Armitage]
```

The above command removes the member John Armitage from the dimension Employees in the Timesheet cube.

What happens to the children of a member when you delete it with the DROP DIMENSION MEMBER command? It's up to you. By default, the command will delete the specified member from the database and attach its child members (if any) to the parent of the deleted member.

You can instead delete both the member itself and all child members with the following command:

```
ALTER CUBE Timesheet
DROP DIMENSION MEMBER
[Employees].[John Armitage]
WITH DESCENDANTS
```

WARNING   Be *very careful* when you use the DROP DIMENSION MEMBER command in this way: not only can you delete a large number of members from your dimension, but you also delete them from the data source specified within the OLAP Manager for that dimension. If your data source is not a stand-alone database, based on a batch extract from a live database, we highly recommend that you either disable dimension write-back altogether or apply severe security restrictions on this command to avoid accidental data loss.

Updating Dimension Members

Making changes to dimension members is also supported in Analysis Services 2000. You can amend either the name of a member or its associated properties. Thus you can use the syntax here to, for instance, raise an employee's salary or set an employee's married name.

The following statement changes employee Cathy Smith's name to Cathy Brown:

```
ALTER CUBE Timesheet
UPDATE DIMENSION MEMBER
[Employees].[Cathy Smith], Name = 'Cathy Brown'
```

What happens to the source data when a dimension member is updated? We already know that dimension changes are reflected down to the base level. As a result, when you make any changes to the dimension structure or members, those changes *are made to the underlying source data*. This may well not be what the user intended: if you are writing an application that allows this type of change, you should warn the user of the global impact of such changes.

For database administrators, the implication is clear: if you plan to allow write-back access to dimensions, make sure that the source for the database is not a live production environment. Ensure that the data aggregation and loading stages for your cube are done from snapshots of the data, rather than the original data itself.

Moving Members

Use the following syntax to move a member from one part of a dimension to another:

```
ALTER CUBE Timesheet
MOVE DIMENSION MEMBER [Employees].[George Patterson]
UNDER [Employees].[Alan Heywood]
```

The above statement effectively deletes member [George Patterson] and all its child members from the tree in its current location and recreates those same members (with the same structure) in the new location. No other members are affected and the effects of this change are written back to the original database. In practice, this usually culminates in a single change to a foreign key on the source Employees table (in this instance).

Creating Actions with MDX

In Chapter 5, you saw how to use the Action Wizard to create a custom action in the context of an Analysis Services cube. The MDX language supports a CREATE ACTION statement that can also create a custom action. Here's a sample CREATE ACTION statement:

```
CREATE ACTION [weblog].[OpenURL2]
FOR [URL] MEMBERS AS
'"http://www.larkfarm.com" + [URL].CurrentMember.Name',
TYPE='URL'
```

This statement creates an action named OpenURL2 as a part of the Weblog cube. The action is attached to the members of the URL dimension. The action text concatenates some fixed text to the name of the current member of the dimension and supplies it as a URL to the user's default browser.

NOTE You're unlikely to need the CREATE ACTION statement unless you're writing some sort of automated tool to manage cubes. In most cases, you'll find it easier to use the Action Wizard from the Analysis Manager user interface to create actions.

Custom Functions

In all, the MDX library contains over a hundred intrinsic functions supporting a wide variety of requirements, from arithmetical expressions to complex statistical analytical tasks. Even when you combine these functions, however, at some point you will hit the limit of their capabilities. Perhaps your analysis requires a sophisticated scientific expression that MDX cannot handle, or perhaps your MDX query needs to reference some external source of information to generate the results required.

Fortunately, the Analysis Services architecture allows you to register external function libraries to extend the capabilities of MDX beyond the functions included within the product itself. You can register an external function library that has been written to support the Component Object Model (COM) specification, and you can then use the appropriate functions within an MDX query. You can also use external functions within the Analysis Services user interface; for example, to build a calculated member.

You can register a function library using the following statement:

```
USE LIBRARY <libname>[, <libname>...]
```

The parameter <libname> must represent a valid COM library and can be referenced either by its file location or by a ProgID (if the library has been already registered). Either way, the library name must be delimited by double quotes. The following statements are valid (and equivalent) examples of using a custom function library:

```
USE LIBRARY "MSOWCFLib.OCATP"
USE LIBRARY "C:\Program Files\Microsoft Office\Office\MSOWCF.DLL"
```

Once registered, a library lasts for as long as the current OLAP session.

To unload the libraries that are currently registered, pass the USE LIBRARY command an empty parameter, as in the following example:

```
USE LIBRARY
```

Any USE LIBRARY command must be the only command passed to the query processor; you cannot use the library until the command has been executed. Don't expect anything to be returned from the USE LIBRARY statement either, unless an error is in the command you enter (for example, the library doesn't exist).

External Function Libraries

Analysis Services installs and automatically registers the Visual Basic for Applications (VBA) function library when Analysis Services is installed. At the same time, it searches the computer where it is installed for the Microsoft Excel function library. If the Excel function library is present, Analysis Services registers that library as well.

To use a function from a registered library, specify it with the syntax Library!Function. For example, this is a valid MDX query using the VBA LCase function:

```
WITH MEMBER Measures.[LCName]
AS 'VBA!LCASE([CallProduct].CURRENTMEMBER.NAME) '
SELECT
[CallProduct].Members ON ROWS,
{Measures.[CallDuration], Measures.[CallCount],
 Measures.[LCName]} ON COLUMNS
FROM CALLS
WHERE (CallTime.[1997])
```

Figure 6.23 shows the results of running this query.

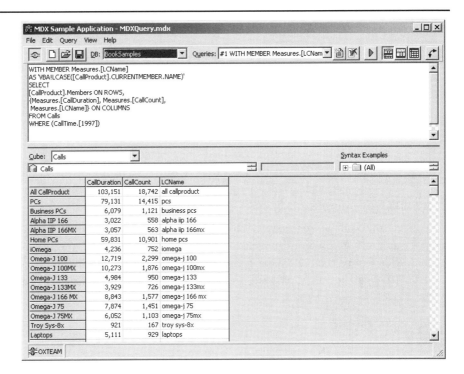

User-Defined Function Libraries

If you're satisfied with neither the intrinsic functions available within MDX nor the functions available from an external library, you have the ultimate flexibility: you can write your own library using Visual Basic. Once registered, the functions you write can be called in exactly the same way as those from any other external function library.

To create your own library, use an ActiveX DLL Visual Basic project. Your library must expose each function as a Public Function within the project. User-defined functions are subject to these limitations:

- Arguments to functions can only be string, numeric, or arrays of string or numeric data.

- The return value from a user-defined function must be a string, a number, or a variant containing a number.

- Analysis Services cannot use hidden or private functions from a user-defined library.

- User-defined functions can have optional arguments. However, because Analysis Services does not support named arguments, if you omit an argument, you must also omit all arguments that follow that argument in the function definition.

Conclusion

We've seen in this chapter how MDX provides a complete and comprehensive interface for querying Analysis Services cubes, supporting *n*-dimensional queries, calculated members, and complex JOIN capabilities. We've also looked at some of the common issues facing the Analysis Services user and examined some potential solutions for these problems. Last, we looked at extending the capabilities of MDX itself by importing external function libraries, both pre-packaged as DLLs with shrink-wrapped applications and written specifically for the purpose using Visual Basic.

Although we've unraveled many of the complexities of MDX here, so far we've not looked at how you can build your own applications that use MDX to retrieve and display information from a remote database. In the next four chapters, we'll look at using Analysis Services from custom client programs, using a variety of object libraries and services.

CHAPTER 7

Building Analysis Services Applications with ADO/MD Part I: Cube Schema Objects

- ADO and Analysis Services

- ADO/MD Object Model

- ADO/MD Schema Objects

- Developing the Dimension View Control

In the last chapter, we focused on MDX, the query language that allows you to interrogate multidimensional Analysis Services cubes in much the same way as SQL allows you for traditional relational databases. But how do you integrate MDX queries into your own applications? The answer is ADO/MD (ActiveX Data Objects/Multidimensional), an extension of the traditional ActiveX Data Objects (ADO) library that deals specifically with multidimensional queries.

ADO/MD is a powerful yet relatively simple object model that provides two functions:

- Read-only access to the schema hierarchy for a cube within an OLAP database

- Query processing and data retrieval capabilities, supporting the execution of MDX statements and analysis of the resulting dataset

In this chapter, we'll introduce ADO/MD and then concentrate on using the cube schema objects to retrieve information about Analysis Services cubes. In the next chapter, we'll look at the query retrieval objects that ADO/MD also provides.

ADO and Analysis Services

ADO was originally introduced into Visual Basic 5.0, back in 1996, as yet another object model for accessing data from inside applications. Since then it has grown significantly in popularity, largely because of Microsoft's continuing development of the object model and demotion of alternatives such as RDO and DAO. ADO was designed as a lightweight and flexible object model, supporting access to both relational and non-relational data stores.

Unlike its immediate predecessor, RDO, which accessed relational databases only through ODBC, ADO introduced a new architecture called OLE DB that makes it possible to write drivers (called "providers" in OLE DB terminology) for proprietary and non-relational data sources. It even included providers to access Microsoft Exchange and Index Server.

While the OLE DB provider for Analysis Services (provided as part of the PivotTable Service) supports certain SQL queries through the main ADO interface, ADO itself doesn't provide the full functionality of MDX. The problem is that the central ADO data structure, the *recordset*, is designed to hold relational, two-dimensional data. Recordsets largely assume that a command will be executed against a server that will return a tabular structure; they have no concept of central OLAP tenets such as dimensions and levels.

Rather than attempting to force the existing ADO objects to handle OLAP data, Microsoft instead designed a new model that represented each OLAP concept with a separate object. This model eventually became *ADO/MD*, the ADO Multidimensional library.

Comparing ADO/MD with DSO

ADO/MD isn't the only object model available for querying Analysis Services. Another option is DSO, or Decision Support Objects. DSO provides a management or administrative interface into Analysis Services, in the same way as DMO (the Distributed Management Objects library) does for the SQL Server engine. You can use DSO to manipulate OLAP and data mining schemas and to create new objects in Analysis Services.

A certain amount of overlap exists between DSO and ADO/MD: both object models can be used to get information on the cubes, dimensions, measures, and so on within Analysis Services. However, whereas ADO/MD is a generic multidimensional query language included as part of Microsoft's Data Access Components library, DSO is a proprietary object model that requires Windows NT or Windows 2000 to operate and is not generally redistributable.

For general-purpose client-side OLAP programming, then, ADO/MD should be the default choice, with DSO reserved for administrative tasks.

We'll look more at DSO in Chapter 10, "Managing an Analysis Services Environment Using DSO."

ADO/MD Object Model

ADO/MD (sometimes written as ADOMD or ADO MD) is a series of extensions to the traditional ADO object model to better support the multidimensional data model. ADO/MD can be used in conjunction with ADO itself: the two object models can share certain objects, including the Connection object, but ADO/MD also works quite happily in its own right without need for ADO.

The ADO/MD library is provided as part of the Microsoft Data Access Component suite, which is included as part of the SQL Server 2000 installation. The latest public release (usually marked as GA—Generally Available) can be obtained from Microsoft's Universal Data Access web site at `www.microsoft.com/data/download.htm`; bug fix releases occur quite frequently so it's worth checking regularly for updates.

NOTE   The installation of Microsoft's data access components has caused a lot of problems in the past, with setup routines often leaving a system with a mixture of versions partly installed. Many problems relating to crashes within these components can be traced to such version inconsistency. The introduction of a new update process for system components in Windows 2000 should hopefully reduce these issues from now on, but it's wise to keep track of the version numbers of the core system DLLs and check them against the release manifests posted to the web site. At the time of writing, a component checker tool was available from the web site to simplify this process, but even so it's still a bit of a mess.

To enable ADO/MD within a Visual Basic project, navigate to Project ➤ References, and select the check box for Microsoft ActiveX Data Objects (Multidimensional) 2.5 Library. Figure 7.1 shows the dialog box.

TIP   As of this writing, ADO 2.6 has been released. However, even in the ADO 2.6 release, ADO/MD is still version 2.5.

FIGURE 7.1:

The Project References
dialog box

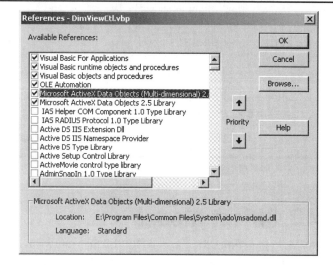

TIP   Although ADO/MD is described as an extension to ADO, you can use some of the objects and methods within ADO/MD without also loading the ADO library. However, some of the objects exposed by the ADO/MD library can only be accessed if both libraries are referenced (for example, the Properties collection).

Once ADO/MD is referenced within your project, several new data types, enumerations, and constants will become available. You can use the Object Browser (press F2 or choose View ➤ Object Browser) to see the supported facilities. All the functions within ADO/MD are provided through the ADO/MD library, as shown in Figure 7.2.

FIGURE 7.2:

Viewing the ADO/MD
library through the Object
Browser

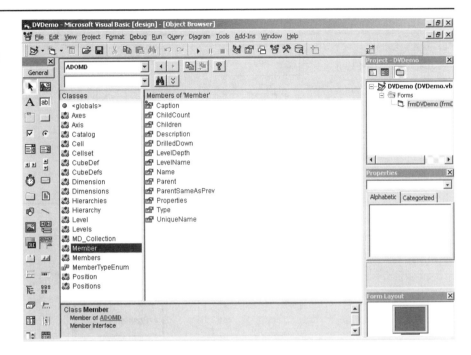

The ADO/MD object model can be neatly divided into two sections. One group of objects deals with the schema of the OLAP database, allowing a program to navigate through the dimensions, levels, members, calculated measures, and so forth. The second group of objects provides access to the data returned from a given MDX query, supporting a multidimensional return set and the formatting of individual cells.

If you look at the various objects shown on the left-hand pane of the Object Browser, you'll see that most of the keywords are present both in plural and singular form. The ADO/MD object model is neatly structured as a series of collections, with each collection containing several objects that in turn may point to another collection lower in the hierarchy. At first things can be rather baffling, but we'll demonstrate how it all fits together with some code examples in due course.

The diagram presented in Figure 7.3 represents the object model in a hierarchical form:

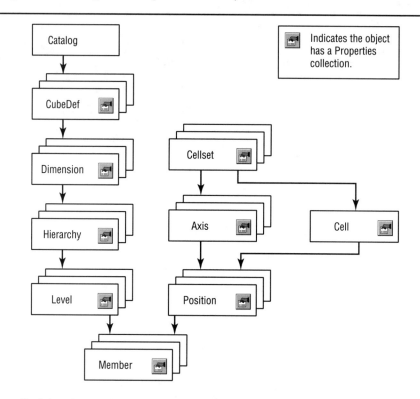

Table 7.1 lists all of the objects that are provided by the ADO/MD library. You'll see each of these objects in more detail as we dig into ADO/MD.

TABLE 7.1:   Overview of the ADO/MD Object Model

Object	Description
Catalog	This object represents an individual OLAP database connection and can be used to connect to a particular provider. The Catalog object is the highest-level object in the library and provides access to an underlying collection, CubeDefs. This object can be attached to a particular OLAP database by using an ADO Connection object.
CubeDefs	A collection of CubeDef objects.
CubeDef	Represents an individual OLAP cube and the properties associated with it. Both real and virtual cubes are supported. Each CubeDef object contains a Dimensions collection.
Dimensions	A collection of Dimension objects.
Dimension	Represents a single dimension within a cube. All dimension types are supported, including real-time dimensions, virtual dimensions, and parent-child dimensions. The measures within a cube are also included as a "special" dimension. Each Dimension object contains a Hierarchies collection.

Continued on next page

TABLE 7.1 CONTINUED: Overview of the ADO/MD Object Model

Object	Description
Hierarchies	A collection of Hierarchy objects.
Hierarchy	Represents a hierarchy within a cube. Hierarchies are used specifically within parent-child dimensions (new in SQL Server 2000) to present an arbitrary number of levels within a relationship. In other dimension types, there is only one Hierarchy within a Hierarchies collection. Each Hierarchy object contains a Levels collection.
Levels	A collection of Level objects.
Level	Represents a specific level within a dimension or hierarchy. Each Level object contains a Members collection.
Members	A collection of Member objects.
Member	Represents an individual point within the cube, which might be an aggregation of a number of underlying members or an individual row descriptor from the fact table itself. A member is the lowest denominator of information and contains no further collections.
Cellset	The multidimensional equivalent of an ADO Recordset, a Cellset contains a number of Cell objects stored across multiple axes. A Cellset can be used to retrieve the results of any MDX query.
Cell	Represents one discrete element of information (similar to the ADO Field object), together with properties including formatting information.
Axes	A collection of Axis objects.
Axis	Represents an individual axis within the returned cellset (such as columns or rows). There may be multiple dimensions or levels within one axis. Each Axis object contains a Positions collection.
Positions	A collection of Position objects.
Position	Represents a set of one or more members of different dimensions that define a particular point within a given axis.
MemberTypeEnum	An enumeration of different types of member (e.g., an entity, a measure or formula, or an aggregation).

We'll go into each of the above object types throughout this chapter as we develop a fully working sample application that uses much of the functionality exposed through the ADO/MD object library.

The PivotTable Service

There's often much confusion in the nomenclature of ADO/MD; in particular, in relation to the PivotTable Service used as the provider for Analysis Services. The story goes that around the same time as Microsoft was readying SQL Server 7.0, the Excel team was also working on an updated version of their product (later to become Excel 2000). One of the things they wanted to improve was the PivotTable functionality in Excel; in particular, its links to external databases.

Continued on next page

When the team got wind of OLAP Services (as the product was known then), they "borrowed" the code from the SQL team to use within Excel.

One of the positive side effects of this collaboration was a cut down version of Analysis Services that could be used for local analytical processing; this version is called the PivotTable Service (PTS). The PivotTable Service is included with both SQL Server and Excel and has replaced the old PivotTable engine that existed in versions of Excel previous to Office 2000.

In fact, the PivotTable Service acts both as an OLE DB Provider and an OLE DB Consumer. It runs on the client and provides access to Analysis Services databases using ADO/MD, operating itself as a consumer. In addition, because it has much of the Analysis Services functionality embedded, it can act far more intelligently than most data providers, internally caching data it has already retrieved and reusing the data to answer queries where possible.

Something that amazes many people when they first realize it is that the PivotTable Service can operate in complete isolation from Analysis Services itself. You can use it against relational databases directly or using a CUB file containing subsets of data from Analysis Services itself. This functionality allows Excel to provide basic multidimensional capabilities without requiring Microsoft's database server to be present, but you can equally well use it for yourself program-matically. We'll discuss how in Chapter 9, "Advanced Usage of the PivotTable Service."

You'll come across the term PivotTable Service a lot in Microsoft's documentation. You can think of PivotTable Service as the intelligent client layer for Analysis Services, with sufficient power to operate without requiring Analysis Services to be present.

ADO/MD Schema Objects

This section covers each of the ADO/MD objects relating to the cube schema. We describe here the object properties and methods, giving examples where appropriate of how to use the objects. At the end of this section is a longer example, as we develop an ActiveX control to view and access schema members. This control can, of course, be added to your own projects, either in its existing form or with your own enhancements.

The Connection Object

Before you can execute a query or use ADO/MD, it is first necessary to make a connection to the Analysis Services engine. You can do this several ways. You can use the Connection object that forms part of the ADO object library. Alternatively, you can implicitly create a connection from both the Catalog and Cellset objects. Either way, you need to build up an appropriate connection string.

It's important to realize that an ADO Connection object is created by ADO/MD even if you create the connection implicitly. It's just that you don't get to set the Connection object's properties explicitly if you let ADO/MD create it for you.

As you may remember from previous chapters, you can either connect to an online database or to an offline cube (CUB) file. Table 7.2 lists the values that you can set in an ADO/MD connection string.

TABLE 7.2: Connection String Values

Parameter	Value
Provider	The name of the OLE DB for OLAP provider you are using to connect to the OLAP engine. For solutions using Analysis Services, this value is always MSOLAP.2, the name of the Microsoft OLE DB Provider for OLAP Services 8.0.
Data Source	For an online database, this should contain the location of the local or remote server, expressed as a hostname. For an offline cube file, this should contain the location of the file to which you want to connect.
Initial Catalog	The name of the OLAP database to which you want to connect. This argument is required only for online databases.
Integrated Security	To use Windows integrated security, include the string `Integrated Security=SSPI` in your connection string.
User ID	Username to use when connecting to the server.
Password	Password to use when connecting to the server.
Auto Synch Period	Sets the period between synchronizing the data cache and security parameters stored for a client session with the server. At the interval specified, clients check that they have sufficient security privileges to access server facilities and synchronize their data cache with the server. The period is specified in milliseconds and is a minimum of 250. By default, this argument is set to 10,000.
Client Cache Size	Controls the amount of memory used by the client connection for caching data. If set to 0, the cache space is limited only to the available memory; if set between 1 and 99, the value represents the maximum percentage of memory that can be used; if set to 100 or greater, the value represents the maximum quantity of memory in KB. By default, this argument is set to 25 (percent).
Locale Identifier	Specifies the locale (region) that should be used for communicating with the PivotTable Service. The locale sets the sort order and case handling for result sets returned from the connection. When this parameter is set to NULL, the default locale is used (as set within Control Panel).

To connect to the Stores database on a server called ARMADILLO, for instance, you could use this connection string:

```
Provider=MSOLAP.2;Data Source=ARMADILLO;Initial Catalog=Stores;
```

TIP   With some OLE DB providers, such as the Microsoft SQL Server provider, you can make a connection to the local machine without specifying its name by setting Data Source=(local); however, this fails using the Analysis Services OLE DB Provider. Fortunately, you can use Data Source=localhost for exactly the same effect.

NOTE   You can also use Provider=MSOLAP instead of Provider=MSOLAP.2. However, in some cases this may prevent you from using new functionality introduced in the SQL Server 2000 version of Analysis Services.

Once you have constructed a connection string, you can use it to connect an ADO/MD Catalog object to a data source by setting the Catalog object's ActiveConnection property. You'll find this sample, and the other code from this chapter, in the Chapter9 sample project on the companion CD:

```
Private Sub cmdConnectCatalog_Click()
    'Connect a Catalog object directly
    Dim cat As ADOMD.Catalog
    Dim strConn As String

    On Error GoTo HandleErr

    strConn = "Provider=MSOLAP.2;Data Source=" & _
     "localhost;Initial Catalog=FoodMart 2000;"

    Set cat = New ADOMD.Catalog
    cat.ActiveConnection = strConn

    MsgBox "Connection Succeeded"

ExitHere:
    Exit Sub

HandleErr:
    MsgBox "Error " & Err.Number & ": " & _
     Err.Description, "cmdConnectCatalog"
    Resume ExitHere
    Resume
End Sub
```

NOTE   Just setting the ActiveConnection property opens a connection to the OLAP database. You don't need to call an Open method, as you do with an ADO Connection object.

The same approach can be used to initialize a Cellset object, which also has an Active-Connection property available.

TIP

If you get a "type mismatch" error when trying to connect a Catalog object in this fashion, double-check the names of the data source and the initial catalog.

If you need to do more advanced manipulation of the connection parameters or simply want to execute some commands against the OLAP Server without returning any results, you can use the ADO Connection object to create a reusable connection. This active ADO Connection can then be used to initialize a Catalog or Cellset object, as shown in the following example (this time using a local offline cube file as the data source):

```
Private Sub cmdConnect_Click()
    'Use a Connection object to connect
    Dim cnn As ADODB.Connection
    Dim cat As ADOMD.Catalog
    Dim strConn As String

    On Error GoTo HandleErr

    strConn = "Provider=MSOLAP.2;Data Source=" & _
     App.Path & "\CallsLocal.cub"

    Set cnn = New ADODB.Connection
    cnn.Open strConn

    Set cat = New ADOMD.Catalog
    Set cat.ActiveConnection = cnn

    MsgBox "Connection Succeeded"

    Set cat = Nothing
    cnn.Close
    Set cnn = Nothing

ExitHere:
    Exit Sub

HandleErr:
    MsgBox "Error " & Err.Number & ": " & _
     Err.Description, "cmdConnect"
    Resume ExitHere
    Resume
End Sub
```

WARNING Be careful not to leave out the Set keyword when assigning an active connection to a Catalog object. The default property of the Connection object is ConnectionString; if you leave out the Set keyword, a second Connection object will be implicitly created. Although the code will work, you will be left with an additional (and useless) instance of the Connection object in memory, which could adversely affect the performance of both the client and the database engine if you have a large number of concurrent users. The Set statement tells the Catalog object to use the connection already created.

There's no strong advantage to using either of the above approaches in terms of performance. If you're going to create several objects based on the same connection, then it makes sense to create the connection first independently. If you've made a connection by setting the ActiveConnection property of an object, you can always assign it back to an ADO Connection object to manipulate the connection further.

NOTE The PivotTable Service also allows a small number of connection string parameters that allow the creation of a local offline cube from within an ADO Connection object. These include CREATE_CUBE, INSERTINTO, and SOURCE_DSN. We'll look at these commands in detail in Chapter 9.

The Catalog Object

Once your code has made a valid connection to the Analysis Services engine, you can start delving into the various objects that expose query functionality within ADO/MD. At the top of the query objects hierarchy lies the Catalog object. The Catalog object is used to represent the concept of an OLAP database in its entirety, containing all the cubes and their underlying components.

NOTE It is important to remember that the ADO/MD library only provides access to data manipulation and querying capabilities, as well as basic data definition capabilities, for the objects in the library. The Decision Support Objects (DSO) library, described in Chapter 10, contains all the management functionality of Analysis Services, including the ability to create, view, and modify dimensions, calculated members, and security roles.

Table 7.3 details the functionality of the Catalog object.

NOTE In Table 7.3 and the tables following, the Type column indicates whether a particular item is a property (P), an object property (O), or a collection (C) of the parent object. The default member of the object has been highlighted in italics.

TABLE 7.3: Catalog Object Details

Name	Type	Explanation
ActiveConnection	P	The connection string used to retrieve this object
CubeDefs	*C*	*A collection containing a CubeDef object for each of the cubes contained within the OLAP database*
Name	P	The name of the catalog (i.e., the name of the OLAP database)

The Catalog object doesn't actually do very much at all, apart from providing the facility to make a direct connection. Its function is purely to connect to an Analysis Services database or offline cube file and provide access to the cubes contained within that store.

> **NOTE**   The Name property of a Catalog object is read-only from within ADO/MD: to rename a database, use the Decision Support Objects functions.

The CubeDef Object

The CubeDef object represents the definition of a particular OLAP cube and its underlying dimensions. It also provides information on the cube's history, such as the date and time that the last modification was made to the schema or the data within the cube. Table 7.4 details the various properties and collections available within the CubeDef object.

TABLE 7.4: CubeDef Object Details

Name	Type	Explanation
Description	P	Provides a brief description of the OLAP cube as set within OLAP Manager or DSO (read-only)
Dimensions	*C*	*A collection containing a Dimension object for every dimension within the cube (read-only)*
GetSchemaObject	M	Retrieves a Dimension, Hierarchy, Level, or Member object directly, without the need to navigate through the intervening levels of the object model
Name	P	Contains the name of the cube, as used for referencing purposes (read-only)
Properties	C	A collection containing an object for each property relating to the cube that has been exposed by the data provider (read-only)

As you can see from the table, the properties and collections exposed from the CubeDef object are all read-only. Once again, the only way to amend the name of a cube or its description or to manage any other aspects is to use the Decision Support Objects, either directly through programmatic means or indirectly through the OLAP Manager.

The Dimensions collection contains a Dimension object for every dimension, whether real or virtual, regular or parent-child. It also contains a special "dimension" called Measures, which contains all the measures and calculated members available within the cube.

The CubeDef name can be used as the index to the CubeDefs collection, to quickly refer to the OLAP cube required. The following code snippet shows how this can be achieved:

```
Private Sub cmdCubeDescription_Click()
    ' Retrieve the description of a Cube
    Dim cat As ADOMD.Catalog
    Dim cub As ADOMD.CubeDef

    On Error GoTo HandleErr

    Set cat = New ADOMD.Catalog

    cat.ActiveConnection = "Provider=MSOLAP;Data Source=" & _
      "localhost;Initial Catalog=FoodMart 2000"

    Set cub = cat.CubeDefs("Sales")

    MsgBox cub.Name & " cube successfully opened. " & _
      "Description (if set): " & cub.Description, vbInformation

    Set cub = Nothing
    Set cat = Nothing

ExitHere:
    Exit Sub

HandleErr:
    MsgBox "Error " & Err.Number & ": " & _
      Err.Description, "cmdCubeDescription"
    Resume ExitHere
    Resume
End Sub
```

The Properties collection of a CubeDef object is populated, not by ADO/MD, but by the underlying OLE DB provider. In theory this means that the contents of this collection might change. In practice, because you'll only be using the MSOLAP provider, you can expect a stable set of properties. Table 7.5 shows the properties available through the CubeDef Properties collection when the MSOLAP provider is used to access the cube.

TABLE 7.5: CubeDef Properties Collection

Name	Description
CATALOG_NAME	The name of the catalog (database) from which the cube is derived
SCHEMA_NAME	The name of the schema to which this cube belongs
CUBE_NAME	The name of the cube (this value is the same as CubeDef.Name)
CUBE_TYPE	The type of the cube
CUBE_GUID	128-bit unique identifier for the cube
CREATED_ON	Date/time the cube was originally created
LAST_SCHEMA_UPDATE	Time stamp for the last update to the cube schema
SCHEMA_UPDATED_BY	The user context under which the cube schema was last modified
LAST_DATA_UPDATE	Time stamp for the last update to the cube data/aggregations
DATA_UPDATED_BY	The user context under which the cube data/aggregations were last modified
DESCRIPTION	The description of the cube (this value is the same as CubeDef.Description)
IS_DRILLTHROUGH_ENABLED	Boolean value, specifying whether the cube has had drillthrough access enabled
IS_LINKABLE	Boolean value, specifying whether the cube can be linked to from a remote server
IS_WRITE_ENABLED	Boolean value, specifying whether the cube is write-enabled
IS_SQL_ENABLED	Boolean value, specifying whether the cube allows querying via SQL

The frmCubeInfo sample form in the Chapter7 sample project allows you to view the properties exposed by a cube through the ADODB.Properties object.

Listing 7.1 shows the code this form uses for retrieving cube properties and displaying them on the user interface.

Listing 7.1:   frmCubeInfo

```
Option Explicit

Private mcat As ADOMD.Catalog
Private mcub As ADOMD.CubeDef

Private Sub cmdClose_Click()
    Unload Me
End Sub

Private Sub cmdDimensionInfo_Click()
    Load frmDimensionInfo
    Set frmDimensionInfo.CubeDef = mcub
```

```
        frmDimensionInfo.Show
End Sub

Private Sub Form_Load()
    Dim cub As ADOMD.CubeDef

    On Error GoTo HandleErr

    Set mcat = New ADOMD.Catalog

    mcat.ActiveConnection = InputBox("Please enter an " & _
      "OLE DB connection string representing the OLAP " & _
      "database to which you wish to connect.", _
      "OLAP Database Info", _
      "Provider=MSOLAP.2;Data Source=localhost;" & _
      "Initial Catalog=FoodMart 2000")

    For Each cub In mcat.CubeDefs
        lstCubes.AddItem cub.Name
    Next cub

    With grdProperties
        .TextMatrix(0, 0) = "Name": .ColWidth(0) = 2560
        .TextMatrix(0, 1) = "Value": .ColWidth(1) = 2560
    End With

    lstCubes.ListIndex = 0

ExitHere:
    Exit Sub

HandleErr:
    MsgBox "Error " & Err.Number & ": " & _
     Err.Description, "Form_Load"
    Resume ExitHere
    Resume
End Sub

Private Sub lstCubes_Click()
    Dim prp As ADODB.Property

    On Error GoTo HandleErr

    Set mcub = mcat.CubeDefs(lstCubes. _
        List(lstCubes.ListIndex))

    With grdProperties
        .Redraw = False
        .Rows = 1: .FixedRows = 0
        For Each prp In mcub.Properties
            .Rows = .Rows + 1
            .TextMatrix(.Rows - 1, 0) = prp.Name
```

```
        .TextMatrix(.Rows - 1, 1) = _
        IIf(IsNull(prp.Value), "<NULL>", prp.Value)
    Next prp
    .FixedRows = 1
    .Redraw = True
End With

ExitHere:
    Exit Sub

HandleErr:
    MsgBox "Error " & Err.Number & ": " & _
     Err.Description, "lstCubes"
    Resume ExitHere
    Resume
End Sub
```

Figure 7.4 shows the sample form displaying the properties of the Sales cube from within the FoodMart 2000 sample database.

FIGURE 7.4:

Sales cube properties

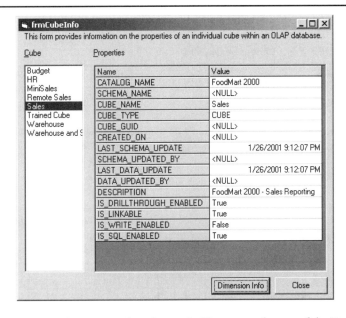

A couple of elements in Listing 7.1 are worthy of remark. First, note the use of the For…Each statement. This is a commonly used method of iterating through Visual Basic collections: since the ADO/MD library consists of a number of nested collections, this approach will be utilized throughout many of the code samples in this chapter. The variable prp is defined as an ADODB.Property; it can therefore be used in such a way. Note once again the close connection between the standard ADO library and the ADO/MD library. In this case you also need a reference to the standard ADO library in your VB project.

Second, note the use of an IIf() function to insert the property's value into the FlexGrid control. Many developers are unaware of this useful function. The syntax for the function is as follows:

```
IIf(expr, truepart, falsepart)
```

The IIf() function is often used on the right hand of an assignment operator, as in the listing example. In this instance, Visual Basic evaluates the expression IsNull(prp.Value). If the expression is true, then the second parameter in the function is used as the return value; otherwise, the third is used.

Many ADO/MD objects (including Dimension, Level, and Cell) have their own Properties collection; you can use similar code to that presented in Listing 7.1 to view the properties of each.

The Dimension Object

The Dimension object contains a complete set of information about an individual dimension within a cube. It allows you to view the properties of a particular dimension and extract the hierarchies, levels, and members as collections from within a dimension. Table 7.6 shows the properties and collections available within the Dimension object.

TABLE 7.6: Dimension Object Details

Name	Type	Explanation
Description	P	Provides a description of the dimension as set within OLAP Manager or DSO (read-only)
Hierarchies	C	*A collection containing a Hierarchy object for every hierarchy within the dimension (for dimensions not using hierarchies, this collection just contains a single hierarchy containing all the levels) (read-only)*
Name	P	Contains the name of the dimension, as used for referencing purposes (read-only)
Properties	C	A collection containing an object for each property relating to the dimension that has been exposed by the data provider (read-only)
UniqueName	P	A field containing the fully qualified name for a particular dimension, in the form [*dimension*] (read-only)

The dimension object, like those before it, contains a default member that is a collection of objects: in this case, Hierarchies. In a parent-child dimension, there is no real concept of levels. Instead, the dimension is broken down in a hierarchical chain of arbitrary length.

As mentioned in earlier chapters, one of the best examples of a parent-child dimension is an organizational structure, where a hierarchical relationship exists between an employee and their manager, and on to *their* manager, and so on until you reach a topmost employee who has no manager. The Hierarchies collection mirrors that chain of command, with one Hierarchy object for each level in the chain.

Traditional dimensions (as opposed to parent-child dimensions) can also contain multiple hierarchies with SQL Server 2000 Analysis Services but need not do so. In a dimension that does not utilize the hierarchy concept, just one Hierarchy object is in the collection, with an index number of 0. To identify whether a dimension contains hierarchies, we can simply count the number of hierarchies, as follows:

```
Private Function IsDimensionHierarchical (dmn As ADOMD.Dimension) As Boolean
    IsDimensionHierarchical = IIf(dmn.Hierarchies.Count = 1, False, True)
End Function
```

TIP

Because Analysis Services does not offer support for creating multiple hierarchies in a dimension through its user interface, you are unlikely to encounter multiple hierarchies in practice (except in parent-child dimensions, of course).

The Dimension object also contains several properties that can be accessed as a collection through the ADO Property object. Table 7.7 lists the properties available. Like the CubeDef's Properties collection, the Dimension's Properties collection is populated by the underlying OLE DB provider.

TABLE 7.7: Dimension Properties Collection

Name	Description
CATALOG_NAME	The name of the catalog from which the cube (and ultimately the dimension) is derived.
SCHEMA_NAME	The name of the schema to which this dimension belongs.
CUBE_NAME	The name of the cube to which this dimension belongs.
DIMENSION_NAME	The name of the dimension (this is the same as Dimension.Name).
DIMENSION_UNIQUE_NAME	*Fully qualified name for the dimension (this is the same as Dimension.UniqueName).
DIMENSION_GUID	128-bit unique identifier for the dimension.
DIMENSION_CAPTION	A label associated with the dimension.
DIMENSION_ORDINAL	The index number for the dimension within the Dimensions collection.
DIMENSION_TYPE	A value indicating what type the dimension is. There is a DimensionTypes enumeration that gives the possible values for this property.
DIMENSION_CARDINALITY	The total number of members contained within the dimension.
DEFAULT_HIERARCHY	The name of the default hierarchy within the dimension.
DESCRIPTION	A brief description of the dimension, if available.
IS_VIRTUAL	Boolean value indicating whether the dimension is a virtual dimension.

Continued on next page

TABLE 7.7 CONTINUED: Dimension Properties Collection

Name	Description
IS_READWRITE	Boolean value indicating whether the dimension itself has been enabled for write-back.
DIMENSION_UNIQUE_SETTINGS	Specifies how the unique name is derived at dimension level.
DIMENSION_MASTER_UNIQUE_NAME	If the dimension is virtual, contains the unique name of the dimension on which this dimension is based.
DIMENSION_IS_VISIBLE	Boolean value indicating whether the dimension is public or private in viewing scope.

The Hierarchy Object

The Hierarchy object contains information for any hierarchies that are stored within the dimension. In SQL Server 2000, hierarchies are used within the context of parent-child dimensions for handling the relationship between parent and child. They can also be used for normal dimensions to allow a single dimension to be broken down in several different ways.

Table 7.8 lists the properties and collections available within the hierarchy object.

TABLE 7.8: Hierarchy Object Details

Name	Type	Explanation
Description	P	Provides a description of the hierarchy as set within OLAP Manager or DSO (read-only)
Levels	*C*	*A collection containing a Level object for every level within the hierarchy (read-only)*
Name	P	Contains the name of the hierarchy, as used for referencing purposes (read-only)
Properties	C	A collection containing an object for each property relating to the hierarchy that has been exposed by the data provider (read-only)
UniqueName	P	A field containing the fully qualified name for a particular hierarchy, in the form [*dimension*].[*hierarchy*] (read-only)

For dimensions that do not contain hierarchies, this object is empty; it is, however, still used as part of the object model for the purpose of navigation. If you know that a dimension falls into this category, you can reference the levels simply as follows (where *cub* is a CubeDef object):

```
cub.Dimensions("Projects").Hierarchies(0).Levels
```

In the same way as for the Dimension and CubeDef objects, the Hierarchy object also has a Properties collection, which can be used to access additional information about the hierarchy. Table 7.9 provides a list of the provider-supplied properties available for the Hierarchy object and their usage.

TABLE 7.9: Hierarchy Properties Collection

Name	Description
CATALOG_NAME	The name of the catalog from which the cube (and ultimately the hierarchy) is derived
SCHEMA_NAME	The name of the schema to which this hierarchy belongs
CUBE_NAME	The name of the cube to which this hierarchy belongs
DIMENSION_UNIQUE_NAME	The unique name of the dimension to which this hierarchy belongs
HIERARCHY_NAME	The name of the current hierarchy object (same as Hierarchy.Name)
HIERARCHY_UNIQUE_NAME	The fully qualified name for the current hierarchy object (same as Hierarchy.UniqueName)
HIERARCHY_GUID	The globally unique 128-bit identifier for the current hierarchy object
HIERARCHY_CAPTION	A display name for the hierarchy, if available
DIMENSION_TYPE	A number indicating the kind of dimension (numbers are the same as with the Dimensions object)
HIERARCHY_CARDINALITY	The total number of members contained within this particular hierarchy
DEFAULT_MEMBER	The unique name of the default member within the hierarchy
ALL_MEMBER	The unique name for the level collection containing all the members
DESCRIPTION	A description for the hierarchy, if available (same as Hierarchy.Description)
STRUCTURE	A constant indicating whether the hierarchy is balanced, ragged, unbalanced, or a network
IS_VIRTUAL	Boolean value indicating whether the parent dimension is virtual
IS_READWRITE	Boolean value indicating whether the parent dimension has been enabled for write-back
DIMENSION_UNIQUE_SETTINGS	Same as for parent Dimension object
DIMENSION_MASTER_UNIQUE_NAME	Same as for parent Dimension object
DIMENSION_IS_VISIBLE	Same as for parent Dimension object
HIERARCHY_ORDINAL	The index number for the hierarchy within the Hierarchies collection
DIMENSION_IS_SHARED	Boolean value indicating whether the parent dimension is shared

The Level Object

While being able to break up a body of data by dimension is useful, it is even more important to be able to break up a dimension itself into underlying categories or values. For example, a computer software support help desk might break down statistics on its incoming calls based on the product in use. They may be interested in knowing about calls received based on the product manufacturer, the product category, the product name, and the product version. Each of these different levels of grouping is a level in OLAP terminology.

The Level object is provided as a collection, storing each one of the levels within a particular dimension. The object can be used to view the different levels, together with information on how many objects are contained within that level. Table 7.10 shows the properties and collections available for this object.

TABLE 7.10: Level Object Details

Name	Type	Explanation
Caption	P	A display name for the level (read-only)
Depth	P	A value indicating the depth of the level or the number of levels between the current level and the parent hierarchy (read-only)
Description	P	Provides a description of the level as set within OLAP Manager or DSO (read-only)
Members	*C*	*A collection containing a Member object for every member within the level (read-only)*
Name	P	Contains the name of the level, as used for referencing purposes (read-only)
Properties	C	A collection containing an object for each property relating to the level that has been exposed by the data provider (read-only)
UniqueName	P	A field containing the fully qualified name for a particular level, in the form [*dimension*].[*level*] (read-only)

Table 7.11 provides a list of the properties that are stored in the ADO Properties collection within the Level object and are supplied by the MSOLAP provider.

TABLE 7.11: Level Properties Collection

Name	Description
CATALOG_NAME	The name of the catalog from which the cube (and ultimately the level) is derived
SCHEMA_NAME	The name of the schema to which this level belongs
CUBE_NAME	The name of the cube to which this level belongs
DIMENSION_UNIQUE_NAME	The unique name of the dimension to which this level belongs
HIERARCHY_UNIQUE_NAME	The unique name of the current hierarchy object to which the level belongs

Continued on next page

TABLE 7.11 CONTINUED: Level Properties Collection

Name	Description
LEVEL_NAME	The name of the level itself, presented as a string
LEVEL_UNIQUE_NAME	The fully qualified level name, including the parents of the level as required
LEVEL_GUID	The globally unique 128-bit identifier for the current level object
LEVEL_CAPTION	A display name for the level, if available
LEVEL_NUMBER	A number indicating the level's position within the Levels collection stored in its parent Hierarchy object
LEVEL_CARDINALITY	The total number of members contained within this particular level
LEVEL_TYPE	An integer representing the category of level (a child level or the (All) levels type)
DESCRIPTION	A description for the level, if available (same as Level. Description)
CUSTOM_ROLLUP_SETTINGS	Shows the custom rollup expression used, if applicable
LEVEL_UNIQUE_SETTINGS	Constant indicating whether keys or names in the level are unique
LEVEL_IS_VISIBLE	Boolean value indicating whether the level can be viewed for query activity
LEVEL_ORDERING_PROPERTY	Indicates whether the level is ordered by name or key, or through a separate "ordering" field in the database
LEVEL_DBTYPE	Data type of the underlying database column
LEVEL_MASTER_UNIQUE_NAME	If the level is part of a virtual dimension, the unique name of the level
LEVEL_NAME_SQL_COLUMN_NAME	Column in the underlying database containing the names for the level
LEVEL_KEY_SQL_COLUMN_NAME	Column in the underlying database containing the keys for the level
LEVEL_UNIQUE_NAME_SQL_COLUMN_NAME	Column in the underlying database containing the unique names for the level

The Member Object

At last, we've reached the bottom of this chain of collections!

A member is the individual unit of information we're actually looking for. Members represent the actual content of a particular identifier within a level. For example, if the level within a Geography dimension contained Country, then you might expect to find a collection of members including United States, Canada, United Kingdom, and Germany.

The member object is used extensively within the ADO/MD object model. Referring back to the object model diagram (Figure 7.3), you can see that the Members collection is available as a property of both the Level and the Position object. We'll touch upon the Position object later in this chapter, when we discuss the use of ADO/MD for returning cellsets, and we'll return briefly to the Member object at that time.

Table 7.12 shows the properties and collections available for the Member object.

TABLE 7.12: Member Object Details

Name	Type	Explanation
Caption	P	A display name for the member (read-only).
ChildCount	P	Returns an estimate of the number of children below this member (read-only).
Children	C	A collection of the member's children containing a Member object for each child (read-only).
Description	P	Provides a description of the member if set within OLAP Manager or DSO (read-only).
DrilledDown	P	A Boolean value indicating whether there are any child members of this object. This is faster than using ChildCount to return a number of children (read-only).
LevelDepth	P	Returns the number of levels between the member and the root member (read-only).
LevelName	P	Returns the name of the level to which the member belongs (read-only).
Name	P	Contains the name of the member, as used for referencing purposes (read-only).
Parent	O	Contains the parent member, if one exists (read-only).
ParentSameAsPrev	P	A Boolean value indicating whether the parent of the member is the same as the member immediately before it (read-only).
Properties	C	A collection containing an object for each property relating to the member that has been exposed by the data provider (read-only).
Type	P	A value representing the type of member (regular, measure, formula, or container), as described in the MemberTypeEnum enumeration (read-only).
UniqueName	P	This field contains the fully qualified name for a particular member, in the form [dimension].[hierarchy].[level].[member] (read-only).

WARNING   Some of the properties and objects described in Table 7.12 are not available when accessing the Members object from a Level.Members collection.

The Member object, like those objects above it, contains a Properties collection. Table 7.13 lists the Member properties that are made available to this collection by the MSOLAP provider.

TABLE 7.13: Member Properties Collection

Name	Description
EXPRESSION	The source formula from which a calculated member is derived.
MEMBER_KEY	A value that can be used to uniquely identify this member within its parent collection.
IS_PLACEHOLDERMEMBER	Boolean value indicating whether this member is a placeholder for an empty position in a dimension hierarchy.
IS_DATAMEMBER	Boolean value indicating whether the member contains data.
<custom>	A custom property exists for each member property that has been defined within Analysis Services. The name of such a property corresponds with the name defined there.

The EXPRESSION property is used within calculated members to provide information on how the calculated member has been derived. For example, within the FoodMart 2000 Sales cube, the Profit measure contains the value `[Measures].[Store Sales]-[Measures].[Store Cost]` for this property.

The MEMBER_KEY property, new in the SQL Server 2000 release of Analysis Services, can be used to uniquely identify a particular member within a collection. This can be particularly useful when multiple members have the same name, such as within the time dimension. Open the Quarter level within any time dimension spanning multiple years, and you will see duplicate entries of Q1, Q2, etc. Although the entries are duplicated, they have distinguishing member keys that can be used to access each one individually. This property is generated automatically.

Developing the Dimension View Control

So far in our discussion of the ADO/MD object model, we've looked at the various objects that allow navigation through the OLAP schema. Before going any further, let's look at a longer example that brings the various threads together.

As is apparent from the depth of the object model presented in the previous section, quite a lot of work can be involved in using ADO/MD within your own applications. Once you become familiar with the objects exposed, however, ADO/MD presents a very powerful set of facilities you can use extensively within an application.

Visual Basic has always been designed to reduce complexity in favor of greater ease of use and flexibility. In fact, perhaps one of the greatest reasons for the popularity of Visual Basic is the way you can extend its functionality through the use of custom controls, or OCXs, now known as ActiveX controls. With the introduction of Visual Basic 5, for the first time it became possible to build one's own controls in VB itself, making it even easier to produce reusable code.

In the remainder of this chapter, we will develop an ActiveX control in Visual Basic that can be used from any language that supports COM components. The control will provide us with the ability to show the entire structure of an OLAP database in a hierarchical treeview. The control will allow access to any cube accessible over the network and will enable an end user to drill down from the cube to individual members. It can be used programmatically within the development environment, too, to retrieve a particular object from within the OLAP schema.

Figure 7.5 shows the ActiveX control in action.

FIGURE 7.5:

Dimension view control

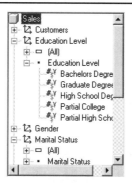

In later sections, we'll use this control ourselves to build a fully fledged application for viewing OLAP cubes. However, you can freely use the control (subject to the licensing agreement on the Sybex web site) within your own applications, giving you a starting point that can be adapted and extended to your own purposes.

NOTE   A fully working version of the control can be found on the companion CD for this book. To show this control and the related test harness, open the DimensionView.vbg project group.

Designing the Control

First, some words about the basic design for the control. Since we need to be able to view a hierarchical set of information, we need an appropriate display mechanism. We have two main choices:

- Start from first principles and create a hierarchical control from scratch

- Extend a preexisting control to handle OLAP dimensional functionality

In fact, Visual Basic already contains a great control for viewing hierarchical information: the TreeView control. This control allows us to store an arbitrary amount of information with a linear or hierarchical structure and allows us to include a graphical icon against each item (or node) of information. We'll go ahead and use this control within our own custom control.

WARNING   The TreeView control is a relatively complicated control, using several related objects to populate the structure. If you are not familiar with it, you may wish to take a look at the section entitled, "Using the TreeView Control," within the Visual Basic Concepts manual.

Our ActiveX control will also contain an ImageList object; this object will be used to contain an array of icons to represent each category of node (cube, dimension, hierarchy, level, etc.). We can populate this object at design time with suitable graphics.

The control will also support several properties, methods, and events. Table 7.14 provides a list of each of these.

TABLE 7.14: Dimension View Control Interface Details

Name	Type	Explanation
DataSource	P	This property can be set to an OLE DB connection string representing the database to which we want to connect. It must be a valid, well-formed connection string for the control to work properly.
Cube	P	The cube property is a string that should contain the name of a valid cube: this cube will be used for display purposes. This property can be changed at runtime; such a modification will reset the view control.
ViewStyle	P	This property sets the items that can be viewed from within the Dimension View control. It should be set to one of the following constants from the ViewStyles enumeration: **vsViewAl** Show both dimensions and measures. **vsViewDimensionsOnly** Show dimensions. **vsViewMeasuresOnly** Show measures.
SelectedItem	P	Available at runtime only, this property contains an ADO/MD object representing the currently selected item within the Dimension view control. The object can be identified using the TypeOf operator and will be one of the following: CubeDef, Dimension, Hierarchy, Level, or Member (read-only).

Continued on next page

TABLE 7.14 CONTINUED: Dimension View Control Interface Details

Name	Type	Explanation
Enabled	P	Enables/disables the custom control.
Font	P	Sets the font used to display the contents of the dimension view control.
Refresh	M	Refreshes the contents of the control.
ShowAboutBox	M	Displays an About box for the view control.
Click	E	Triggered when the control is clicked or gains focus.
DblClick	E	Triggered when the control is double-clicked with a mouse.
KeyDown	E	Triggered when a key goes down while the control has focus.
KeyPress	E	Triggered when a key is pressed while the control has focus.
KeyUp	E	Triggered when a key is released while the control has focus.
MouseDown	E	Triggered when a mouse button goes down while the control has focus.
MouseMove	E	Triggered when the mouse is moved while the control has focus.
MouseUp	E	Triggered when a mouse button is released while the control has focus.

Creating the Project

To create the project, select File ➤ New Project from the Visual Basic menu. Since we are creating a control, we select the option entitled ActiveX Control rather than the standard Visual Basic EXE. If the TreeView control is not loaded by default on your system, you can select Project ➤ Components and select Microsoft Windows Common Controls 6.0 to add the appropriate references to your project. This library also contains the ImageList control we are using to store the icons that are used within the TreeView control. You'll also need to add references to the ADO and ADO/MD libraries through Project ➤ References.

Add a TreeView control to the design pane, and name it tvwDimensions. Also add an ImageList control to the pane called imlIcons. Last, we need to name the custom control itself; we chose the name DimensionView.

You can now proceed to set properties for the control. To do this most easily, select Add-Ins ➤ ActiveX Control Interface Wizard. The Wizard provides a front-end for adding in default and custom properties, methods, and events. It then generates the appropriate code to map any properties. When running, the Wizard allows you to add any of several standard interface members to your own project and map them onto controls that exist within the environment.

Size the TreeView control to fill the user control pane (jot down the height and width settings of the DimensionView user control and set the TreeView control's height and width properties to the same values). Also set the Style property for the TreeView control to 7 – tvwTreelinesPlusMinusPictureText and set the ImageList property for the TreeView control to point to the imlIcons image list (using the property pages for the tvwDimensions control). This ensures that the control will display a small plus/minus icon, allowing the user to expand or contract the tree, as well as showing a small graphic denoting the type of item being displayed. The control should look similar to the screen shown in Figure 7.6.

FIGURE 7.6:

Design-time view of Dimension View control

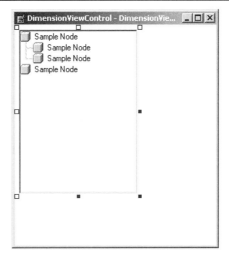

We're now ready to add code to the project!

TIP To actually recreate the control as we built it, you'll need to add the bitmaps for all of the cube icons to the ImageList. You'll probably find it easier to copy the ImageList from the sample project than to go through the effort of recreating it on your own. In fact, you can reference the entire project from the sample code in the DimensionView.vbg project group.

Control Initialization

The code for the Dimension View control fills most of the rest of this chapter, interspersed with comments where appropriate. You can also find it on the companion CD in the DimensionViewControl.vbp project file. We start with code to initialize the control and set the enumerations and constants for the project. Listing 7.2 shows this code.

Listing 7.2:   DimensionView.ctl

```
'/////////////////////////////////////////////////////////////////////
'OLAP Dimension View ActiveX Control 1.0
'Copyright (c) 1999-2001 Tim Sneath / Sybex Inc.
'
'This control provides access to the dimensions and levels of a
'specified cube using ADOMD. The control contains a TreeView control,
```

```
'together with associated code to populate it with the relevant levels
'and produce an output of the relevant unique name for the dimension
'selected.
'
'Properties available:
'    DataSource   - OLE DB connection string for the OLAP db
'    Cube         - the name of the (virtual) cube within the database
'    SelectedItem - the fully-qualified name of the level selected
'    ViewStyle    - show either dimensions, measures, or both...
'/////////////////////////////////////////////////////////////////////
Option Explicit
Option Base 0

'Event Declarations:
Event Click()'MappingInfo=tvwDimensions,tvwDimensions,-1,Click
Event DblClick()'MappingInfo=tvwDimensions,tvwDimensions,-1,DblClick
Event KeyDown(KeyCode As Integer, Shift As Integer)
➥'MappingInfo=tvwDimensions,tvwDimensions,-1,KeyDown
Event KeyPress(KeyAscii As Integer)
➥'MappingInfo=tvwDimensions,tvwDimensions,-1,KeyPress
Event KeyUp(KeyCode As Integer, Shift As Integer)
➥ 'MappingInfo=tvwDimensions,tvwDimensions,-1,KeyUp
Event MouseDown(Button As Integer, Shift As Integer, x As Single, y As Single)
➥'MappingInfo=tvwDimensions,tvwDimensions,-1,MouseDown
Event MouseMove(Button As Integer, Shift As Integer, As Single, y As Single)
➥'MappingInfo=tvwDimensions,tvwDimensions,-1,MouseMove
Event MouseUp(Button As Integer, Shift As Integer,x As Single, y As Single)
➥'MappingInfo=tvwDimensions,tvwDimensions,-1,MouseUp

'Error Declarations:
Const dvErrSource = "OLAP Dimension View Control"
Const dvGeneralFailure = 1024
Const dvConnectionFail = 1025
Const dvNoSuchCube = 1026
Const dvObjectNotFound = 1027

'ImageViewTypes public enum
Public Enum ImageViewTypes
    ivCube = 1
    ivDimension = 2
    ivHierarchy = 3
    ivLevelAll = 4
    ivLevel1 = 5
    ivLevel2 = 6
    ivLevel3 = 7
    ivLevel4 = 8
    ivLevel5 = 9
    ivLevel6 = 10
    ivLevel7 = 11
    ivLevel8 = 12
    ivLevel9 = 13
```

```
            ivLevel10 = 14
            ivLevel11 = 15
            ivLevel12 = 16
            ivLevel13 = 17
            ivLevel14 = 18
            ivLevel15 = 19
            ivLevel16 = 20
            ivMember = 21
            ivCalcMeasure = 22
            ivClosedFolder = 23
            ivOpenFolder = 24
            ivFunction = 25
    End Enum

    'ViewStyles public enum
    Public Enum ViewStyles
            vsShowAll = 0
            vsShowDimensionsOnly = 1
            vsShowMeasuresOnly = 2
    End Enum

    'Default Property Values:
    Const m_def_DataSource = ""
    Const m_def_Cube = ""
    Const m_def_ViewStyle = vsShowAll

    'Property Variables:
    Dim m_DataSource As String
    Dim m_Cube As String
    Dim m_ViewStyle As ViewStyles

    Private adoCat As New ADOMD.Catalog
    Private adoOpenCub As ADOMD.CubeDef
```

The eight events listed above will be mapped directly to the equivalent events within the TreeView control. The MappingInfo comments allow the ActiveX Control Interface Wizard to store its own state, allowing you to run the Wizard again. However, they are not required for the successful execution of the control.

We then set up the enumerations. The values contained within the ImageViewTypes enumeration are used to select the appropriate image from the imlIcons ImageList control and insert the image into the relevant node of the TreeView control. The ViewStyles enumeration is used as the type for the ViewStyle property and presents the user with one of three choices for displaying dimensions, measures, or both within the control.

Last, we declare some internal variables used to hold the property values during the control's execution, and two variables (adoCat and adoOpenCub) used to hold the current ADO/MD session. These variables will be used whenever we need a pointer into the Analysis Services database.

The next step is to add code to handle the properties of the control, as shown in Listing 7.3.

Listing 7.3:   DimensionView.ctl continued

```
'/////////////////////////////////////////////////////////////////////
'User Control Event Handlers
'/////////////////////////////////////////////////////////////////////
Private Sub UserControl_Initialize()
    Dim nodX As MSComctlLib.Node
    tvwDimensions.Nodes.Clear
    Set nodX = tvwDimensions.Nodes.Add(, , "r", UserControl.Name)
End Sub

Private Sub UserControl_InitProperties()
    m_DataSource = m_def_DataSource
    m_Cube = m_def_Cube
    m_ViewStyle = m_def_ViewStyle
End Sub

'Load property values from storage
Private Sub UserControl_ReadProperties(PropBag As PropertyBag)
    'Properties that map onto TreeView control
    tvwDimensions.Enabled = PropBag.ReadProperty("Enabled", True)
    Set tvwDimensions.Font = PropBag.ReadProperty("Font", Ambient.Font)

    'User-defined properties
    m_DataSource = PropBag.ReadProperty("DataSource", m_def_DataSource)
    m_Cube = PropBag.ReadProperty("Cube", m_def_Cube)
    m_ViewStyle = PropBag.ReadProperty("ViewStyle", m_def_ViewStyle)
End Sub

'Write property values to storage
Private Sub UserControl_WriteProperties(PropBag As PropertyBag)
    'Properties that map onto TreeView control
    Call PropBag.WriteProperty("Enabled", tvwDimensions.Enabled, True)
    Call PropBag.WriteProperty("Font", tvwDimensions.Font, Ambient.Font)

    'User-defined properties
    Call PropBag.WriteProperty("DataSource", m_DataSource, m_def_DataSource)
    Call PropBag.WriteProperty("Cube", m_Cube, m_def_Cube)
    Call PropBag.WriteProperty("ViewStyle", m_ViewStyle, m_def_ViewStyle)
End Sub

'Ensure that TreeView control is always the same size as its parent control
Private Sub UserControl_Resize()
    With tvwDimensions
        .Top = 0
        .Left = 0
        .Height = UserControl.Height
        .Width = UserControl.Width
    End With
End Sub
```

Listing 7.3 shows the code that handles the key intrinsic events of the user control. The `Initialize()` function clears the tvwDimensions TreeView control and gives it a default node. This will be replaced when the DataSource and Cube properties are set. The `InitProperties()` function sets each of the internal functions used to store property values to default values, as set in the Const statements previously.

The `ReadProperties()` and `WriteProperties()` functions are used to persist the state of the control as it moves between design time and runtime execution. The contents of the properties are streamed into the FRM file into which the control is placed. Keep in mind that an ActiveX control effectively executes both at runtime *and at design time*. As a user of a control sets properties on that control from within their environment, so the events above will be triggered.

The Resize() event is triggered whenever the user control is resized. This may occur either at design time, as a developer modifies the layout of their form, or at runtime, as a user resizes a window containing the custom control. Either way, the ActiveX control must handle this to ensure that any changes affect not just the container control but its contents; that is, the tvwDimensions TreeView control. The ImageList control used within the form need not be resized as it is not visible outside of the control design-time view.

Handling Control Events and Properties

Listing 7.4 contains the code used to handle each of the events our control supports.

Listing 7.4:   DimensionView.ctl continued

```
'/////////////////////////////////////////////////////////////////////////////
'Event Handlers
'/////////////////////////////////////////////////////////////////////////////
Private Sub tvwDimensions_Click()
    RaiseEvent Click
End Sub

Private Sub tvwDimensions_DblClick()
    RaiseEvent DblClick
End Sub

Private Sub tvwDimensions_KeyDown(KeyCode As Integer, Shift As Integer)
    RaiseEvent KeyDown(KeyCode, Shift)
End Sub

Private Sub tvwDimensions_KeyPress(KeyAscii As Integer)
    RaiseEvent KeyPress(KeyAscii)
End Sub

Private Sub tvwDimensions_KeyUp(KeyCode As Integer, Shift As Integer)
```

```
        RaiseEvent KeyUp(KeyCode, Shift)
End Sub

Private Sub tvwDimensions_MouseDown(Button As Integer,
➥Shift As Integer, x As Single, y As Single)
        RaiseEvent MouseDown(Button, Shift, x, y)
End Sub

Private Sub tvwDimensions_MouseMove(Button As Integer,
➥Shift As Integer, x As Single, y As Single)
        RaiseEvent MouseMove(Button, Shift, x, y)
End Sub

Private Sub tvwDimensions_MouseUp(Button As Integer,
➥Shift As Integer, x As Single, y As Single)
        RaiseEvent MouseUp(Button, Shift, x, y)
End Sub

Private Sub tvwDimensions_Expand(ByVal Node As MSComctlLib.Node)
        ExpandNode Node
End Sub
```

The above section of code simply maps several events that can be trapped by the tvwDimensions control onto the equivalent events raised by the DimensionView control. This "bubbling up" of events allows applications using our control to themselves choose whether to handle such events. Since our control itself does not need to do anything with these events, they can simply be passed up directly using the RaiseEvent method. The only exception is the Expand event, which calls an associated function ExpandNode, listed below.

Listing 7.5 contains the code that handles each of the properties exposed by the ActiveX control.

Listing 7.5:   DimensionView.ctl continued

```
'//////////////////////////////////////////////////////////////////////////
'Property Handlers
'//////////////////////////////////////////////////////////////////////////

'WARNING! DO NOT REMOVE OR MODIFY THE FOLLOWING COMMENTED LINES!
'MappingInfo=tvwDimensions,tvwDimensions,-1,Enabled
Public Property Get Enabled() As Boolean
        'NB To work the same way other controls' Enabled properties do, Enabled
        'must have the correct Procedure ID. This must be done manually, using
        'the Property Attributes dialog, accessed from the Tools menu,
        'to set Procedure ID to Enabled for the Enabled property. See the
        'ActiveX Control Interface Wizard's log for further information.
        Enabled = tvwDimensions.Enabled
End Property
```

```
Public Property Let Enabled(ByVal New_Enabled As Boolean)
    tvwDimensions.Enabled() = New_Enabled
    PropertyChanged "Enabled"
End Property

'WARNING! DO NOT REMOVE OR MODIFY THE FOLLOWING COMMENTED LINES!
'MappingInfo=tvwDimensions,tvwDimensions,-1,Font
Public Property Get Font() As Font
    Set Font = tvwDimensions.Font
End Property

Public Property Set Font(ByVal New_Font As Font)
    Set tvwDimensions.Font = New_Font
    PropertyChanged "Font"
End Property

'WARNING! DO NOT REMOVE OR MODIFY THE FOLLOWING COMMENTED LINES!
'MappingInfo=tvwDimensions,tvwDimensions,-1,Refresh
Public Sub Refresh()
    tvwDimensions.Refresh
End Sub

'WARNING! DO NOT REMOVE OR MODIFY THE FOLLOWING COMMENTED LINES!
'MemberInfo=13,0,0,0
Public Property Get DataSource() As String
    DataSource = m_DataSource
End Property

Public Property Let DataSource(ByVal New_DataSource As String)
    'Switch on error handling
    On Error GoTo ErrorTrap

    Dim nodX As MSComctlLib.Node

    m_DataSource = New_DataSource
    PropertyChanged "DataSource"

    'When the control is added for the first time, m_DataSource will not yet
    'be set. We therefore don't want to hook our Catalog object up yet.
    'Whenever the DataSource property is changed, we reset the m_Cube field
    'to nothing to avoid a mismatch between the two properties.
    tvwDimensions.Nodes.Clear
    If m_DataSource <> m_def_DataSource Then 'this is being set to something
        adoCat.ActiveConnection = m_DataSource
        m_Cube = m_def_Cube
        Set nodX = tvwDimensions.Nodes.Add(, , "r", "No cube selected")
    End If
    Exit Property
```

```vb
ErrorTrap:
    Select Case Err.Number
        'This section could be extended, and is shown for demonstration
        'purposes only
        Case -2147467259
Err.Raise vbObjectError + dvConnectionFail, dvErrSource, Err.Description
        Case Else
            Err.Raise Err.Number, , Err.Description
    End Select
End Property

'WARNING! DO NOT REMOVE OR MODIFY THE FOLLOWING COMMENTED LINES!
'MemberInfo=13,0,0,0
Public Property Get Cube() As String
    Cube = m_Cube
End Property

Public Property Let Cube(ByVal New_Cube As String)
    m_Cube = New_Cube
    PropertyChanged "Cube"

    'So long as the DataSource property is a meaningful value then we can
    'go ahead and populate the TreeView control.
    If m_DataSource <> m_def_DataSource Then
        Call ResetCube
    Else
        Dim nodX As MSComctlLib.Node
        tvwDimensions.Nodes.Clear
        Set nodX = tvwDimensions.Nodes.Add(, , "r", "No data source selected")
    End If
End Property

'WARNING! DO NOT REMOVE OR MODIFY THE FOLLOWING COMMENTED LINES!
'MemberInfo=9,1,2,0
Public Property Get SelectedItem() As Object
    'This function is also useful internally, so we've shifted
    'it into a separate associated function, which this property
    'function calls...

    Set SelectedItem = GetSelectedItemAsObject()
End Property

Public Property Set SelectedItem(ByVal New_SelectedItem As Object)
    'Property is read-only so raise an error depending on current mode
    'See Visual Basic error code reference for further details...
    If Ambient.UserMode Then 'run-time
        'Raise error "'Item' property cannot be set at run time"
        Err.Raise 382
    Else 'design-time
        'Raise error "'Item' property is read-only"
        Err.Raise 383
    End If
End Property
```

```
Public Property Get ViewStyle() As ViewStyles
    ViewStyle = m_ViewStyle
    If tvwDimensions.Nodes.Count > 1 Then
        'The dimensions are already being displayed; therefore the
        'TreeView control will need to be cleared and repopulated.
        ResetCube
    End If
End Property

Public Property Let ViewStyle(ByVal New_ViewStyle As ViewStyles)
    m_ViewStyle = New_ViewStyle
    PropertyChanged ("ViewStyle")
End Property
```

We can support several of the properties in the same way as we did earlier for the events; in other words, by mapping them directly to the TreeView control contained within our own control. Many custom controls draw themselves, or act as containers for other intrinsic controls. If our control fell into such a category, we would need to do more work to support basic properties such as Font. We would have to either redraw our control, taking the new setting into account, or pass the setting over to the underlying controls and possibly rescale them accordingly.

Since our control contains just one visible control itself, we can simply pass standard properties directly to the TreeView control, which will handle the changes using its own precompiled code. This approach is used for the Enabled, Font, and Refresh properties, so for both assignment and retrieval of the properties, we simply need to read or write the appropriate setting from tvwDimensions.

WARNING   In fact, things are slightly more complex for the Enabled property. For this property to be handled in the same way as other controls, we need to set the appropriate Procedure ID using the Tools ➤ Procedure Attributes menu option. See the Visual Basic documentation for further information on the use of the Enabled property within custom controls.

The DataSource and Cube properties are used to set the OLE DB connection string and select the cube we wish to use within the control. Although we could combine the two properties into one, it is slightly more elegant (as well as consistent with other similar components) to keep the connection string separate. However, this presents a problem. How do we know that both properties have been set? We obviously don't want to try to populate the control until both have been set to matching values, because otherwise we will receive an error.

To solve this problem, we add two safeguards. First, we presume (and insist) that the Data-Source property is set prior to the Cube property. This means that we need only attempt to populate the tree control when both have been set, thus preventing a mismatch from occurring. Second, we check in the Cube Let property that the DataSource property is not still set to the default. This provides elegant degradation should a program set the wrong property first. If the DataSource is set to its default, the cube property sets an appropriate status message within the tree control to inform the developer/user of what actions have been taken.

The SelectedItem property is used to return the currently selected object. The client application can then use this in any way it chooses, perhaps by setting it to another object and testing for its type, in the following manner:

```
Dim objX As Object
'We won't know what type this object is until it is set,
'so we bind it as late as possible.

Set objX = dv.SelectedItem
If TypeOf objX Is ADOMD.CubeDef Then
    Debug.Print "The user selected a cube called " & _
        objX.Name
ElseIf TypeOf objX Is ADOMD.Dimension Then
    'and so on...
End If
```

The control code calls a function, `GetSelectedItemAsObject`, which rather unsurprisingly returns the selected item as an object. It simply sets that object to the return property. The function itself is slightly involved, so we'll cover it separately in Listing 7.9 below.

One last thing to say about the SelectedItem property is that it is read-only at both design time and runtime. Since the underlying object model is read-only, setting this property has no semantic meaning. If an attempt is made to set this property, the control raises an error (*which* error depends on whether the control is active at design time or runtime).

Last, the ViewStyle property allows us to choose whether we show dimensions or members. As we mentioned when discussing the Dimensions collection, members are treated as if they were a special kind of dimension as far as the ADO/MD syntax goes. While this reduces complexity within the object model, many client applications will not want to expose both to an end user at the same time. The ViewStyle property is used later in the code, when we handle the Expand event for the tvwDimensions control.

Drilling Down the Object Model

The next section of the code, shown in Listing 7.6, contains several functions that are heavily dependent on ADO/MD and provide the functionality for drilling down through the object model. Table 7.15 shows the functions.

TABLE 7.15: Dimension View Function Details

Name	Explanation
ResetCube	This function clears the TreeView control, before repopulating it with a root node corresponding to the currently selected cube. It is called when the Cube property is changed.
ExpandNode	This function takes as a parameter a pointer to a node within the TreeView control. It expands that node and populates it with any underlying members, as necessary. It is called from tvwDimensions_Expand( ).
PopulateLevels	This function is called by ExpandNode( ) and is used for expanding dimension or hierarchy nodes with underlying levels.
PopulateMembers	This recursive function populates a level node with its underlying members. It is called by ExpandNode( ).
ShowAboutBox	This function displays an About dialog for our ActiveX control in design-time view.

Listing 7.6:   **DimensionView.ctl continued**

```
'/////////////////////////////////////////////////////////////////
'General Functions
'/////////////////////////////////////////////////////////////////
Private Sub ResetCube()
    'This function is called when the cube or data source changes. It
    'resets the TreeView control to the initial starting point for the
    'relevant cube.

    'Switch on error handling
    On Error GoTo ErrorTrap

    Set adoOpenCub = adoCat.CubeDefs(m_Cube)

    Dim adoDim As ADOMD.Dimension
    Dim nodX As MSComctlLib.Node, nodY As MSComctlLib.Node

    'Clear anything remaining in the treeview
    tvwDimensions.Nodes.Clear

    'Create a root node
    Set nodX = tvwDimensions.Nodes.Add(, , "r", m_Cube, ivCube)
    Set nodX = tvwDimensions.Nodes.Add(nodX, tvwChild)

    Exit Sub

ErrorTrap:
    Select Case Err.Number
        Case 3265
```

```
        Err.Raise vbObjectError + dvNoSuchCube,
    ➥dvErrSource, "The data source does not contain a cube
    ➥with the specified name."
            Case Else
                Err.Raise Err.Number, , Err.Description
        End Select
End Sub
```

The ResetCube function, shown in Listing 7.6, is called whenever the control is pointed to a new cube. It resets the adoOpenCub form-level variable to the newly connected cube; it also resets the TreeView control contained within our own component.

When using the TreeView control to store large (or unknown) quantities of data, it is important to think carefully about how and when that information will be populated to avoid degrading the performance of your application. Users may never choose to see many of the items within the hierarchy, so it makes a lot of sense to only populate a node when it is expanded for the first time, rather than populating all nodes up front. This will minimize the processing time necessary to fill the control with data, and avoid over-usage of memory and graphical resources.

But if a node hasn't been populated with data in advance, how will the control know that there is more information to display? This is an issue because, unless a particular node contains a child node, the TreeView control will not display an expand (+) symbol, thus making it impossible to view the underlying information.

One way to get around this issue is by creating a dummy node, as follows:

```
Dim nod As MSComctlLib.Node
Set nod = tvwDimensions.Nodes.Add(Key:="root", Text:="Root Node", _
    Image:=ivRoot)
Set nod = tvwDimensions.Nodes.Add(Relative:=nod, _
    Relationship:=tvwChild)
```

In this code, we create two nodes, the "real" node and a dummy node, which will represent the underlying nodes. The dummy node will force the TreeView control into displaying the expand symbol. We can remove the dummy node when the real node is expanded, as shown in the following code snippet:

```
Private Sub TreeView1_Expand(ByVal Node As MSComctlLib.Node)
    If Node.Child.Text = "" Then
        'Remove dummy node
        TreeView1.Nodes.Remove Node.Child.Index
        Call PopulateNode(Node)
    Else
        'Don't need to do anything: node has already been
        'expanded once!
    End If
End Sub
```

This approach is the one used within our own code, as shown in Listing 7.7.

Listing 7.7:   DimensionView.ctl continued

```
Private Sub ExpandNode(ByVal Node As MSComctlLib.Node)
    Dim nodX As MSComctlLib.Node, nodY As MSComctlLib.Node
    Dim adoDim As ADOMD.Dimension
    Dim adoHier As ADOMD.Hierarchy
    Dim iLoop As Integer

    If Node.Child.Text = "" Then
        tvwDimensions.Nodes.Remove Node.Child.Index
        Select Case Node.Image
        Case ivCube
'Iterate through Dimensions collection,adding each entry to tree view
            For Each adoDim In adoOpenCub.Dimensions
                If (m_ViewStyle = vsShowMeasuresOnly
                ➥And adoDim.Name = "Measures") _
                    Or (m_ViewStyle =
                    ➥vsShowDimensionsOnly And adoDim.Name <> "Measures") _
                    Or (m_ViewStyle = vsShowAll) Then

                    Set nodX = tvwDimensions.Nodes.Add
                    ➥("r", tvwChild, , adoDim.Name, ivDimension)
                    nodX.Tag = adoDim.UniqueName

                    'Create a dummy "child" node without a
                    'name, so that the +(expand) symbol is
                    'present. When the node is expanded, we check to
                    'see whether a nameless child exists: if so,
                    'we delete and repopulate.
                    'This saves us having to populate
                    'every level of every node
                    'from the beginning.
                    Set nodY = tvwDimensions.Nodes.Add(nodX, tvwChild)
                End If
            Next adoDim

        Case ivDimension
            'Hierarchies are used to allow the display of different
            'breakdowns of a particular dimension in SQL Server 2000.
            If adoOpenCub.Dimensions(Node.Text).Hierarchies.Count = 1 Then
                PopulateLevels
                ➥adoOpenCub.Dimensions(Node.Text).Hierarchies(0).Levels, Node
            Else
                For Each adoHier In adoOpenCub.Dimensions(Node.Text).Hierarchies
                    Set nodX = tvwDimensions.Nodes.Add(Node, tvwChild, ,
                    ➥adoHier.Name, ivHierarchy)
                    nodX.Tag = adoHier.UniqueName
                    Set nodY = tvwDimensions.Nodes.Add(nodX, tvwChild)
                Next adoHier
            End If
```

```
            Case ivHierarchy
                PopulateLevels adoOpenCub.Dimensions(Node.Parent.Text)
                  .Hierarchies(Node.Text).Levels, Node

            Case ivLevelAll To ivLevel16
                Dim sDimension As String, sHierarchy As Variant

                sHierarchy = 0
                Set nodX = Node
                Do
                    If nodX.Image = ivHierarchy Then sHierarchy = nodX.Text
                    Set nodX = nodX.Parent
                Loop While nodX.Image <> ivDimension
                sDimension = nodX.Text

                PopulateMembers adoOpenCub.Dimensions(sDimension).Hierarchies
                  ➥(sHierarchy).Levels(Node.Image - 4).Members, Node
            End Select
        End If
End Sub

Private Sub PopulateLevels(ByVal Levels As
➥ADOMD.Levels, ByVal Node As MSComctlLib.Node)
    Dim adoLev As ADOMD.Level
    Dim nodX As MSComctlLib.Node, nodY As MSComctlLib.Node

    For Each adoLev In Levels
        Set nodX = tvwDimensions.Nodes.Add(Node,
        ➥tvwChild, , adoLev.Name, ivLevelAll + adoLev.Depth)
        nodX.Tag = adoLev.UniqueName
        Set nodY = tvwDimensions.Nodes.Add(nodX, tvwChild)
    Next adoLev
End Sub

Private Sub PopulateMembers(ByVal Members As Members,
➥ByVal Node As MSComctlLib.Node)
    Dim adoMem As ADOMD.Member
    Dim nodX As MSComctlLib.Node, nodY As MSComctlLib.Node

    For Each adoMem In Members
        Set nodX = tvwDimensions.Nodes.Add(Node,
        ➥tvwChild, , adoMem.Name, ivMember)
        nodX.Tag = adoMem.UniqueName
        If adoMem.Children.Count > 0 Then PopulateMembers adoMem.Children, nodX
    Next adoMem
End Sub
```

When a user clicks the plus (+) symbol next to a node to expand it, the tvwDimensions _Expand() function will be called, with a single parameter identifying the node that has been expanded. As mentioned earlier, the first time the node has been expanded it will contain a single dummy entry to improve performance at startup. The problem we face is that to identify the children of a node, we must first hold a pointer to the node itself within the ADO/MD object model. But all we have been passed is the TreeView node. How do we find the appropriate ADO/MD object?

One simple way would be to store the ADO/MD object representing the node in some structure allied to the TreeView control (perhaps using the .Tag property). Unfortunately, the performance and memory hit necessary to store what could be tens of thousands of objects is prohibitive.

Fortunately we can store sufficient information in a populated Node object to allow ourselves to navigate dynamically to the equivalent ADO/MD object. In particular, the Node.Text value contains the name of the node, the Node.Tag value contains the fully qualified unique name of the node, and the Node.Image value contains an image representing the type of object shown by the node. Using this information, we know how many levels deep we are within the control, and we can use the Node.Parent property to find information on the node's parents.

The code to perform these tasks, shown in Listing 7.7, is not nearly as daunting as it might first appear. Ultimately the function is just one Select statement. Unfortunately for us, the collection containing the children of an object has a different name for each object (a Dimension contains a Hierarchies collection, a Hierarchy object contains a Levels object, and so on). This adds complexity to the code, because we can't simply use syntax such as objX.Children.

In this version of the code, we populate all the members at one time. A database can contain a hierarchy of up to 64 members, each representing a different level. As a result, the PopulateMembers function is recursive, calling itself to add members to the selected node's children until no more members are left.

The last method of the control is a ShowAboutBox method, shown in Listing 7.8.

Listing 7.8:   DimensionView.ctl continued

```
Public Sub ShowAboutBox()
    'Set using Tools / Procedure Attributes
    dlgAbout.Show vbModal
    Unload dlgAbout
    Set dlgAbout = Nothing
End Sub
```

Finally, the ShowAboutBox() function in Listing 7.8 is called to display our customized "About box" whenever the (About) button is clicked within the control's Properties window. The About box is shown in Figure 7.7.

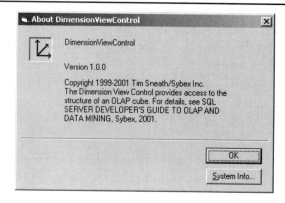

The ShowAboutBox() function must be connected manually to the (About) button. This can be done from within Tools ➤ Procedure Attributes by setting the ProcedureID field to AboutBox for the function.

Now we'll return to the GetSelectedItemAsObject function that we skipped over when discussing the control's SelectedItem property. Listing 7.9 shows the code for this function.

Listing 7.9:   DimensionView.ctl continued

```
Private Function GetSelectedItemAsObject() As Object
    Dim obj As Object
    Dim bHier As Boolean

    With tvwDimensions.SelectedItem
        Select Case .Image
            'The top three are easy: we can determine the
            'position based on the current node
            Case ivCube
                Set obj = adoOpenCub
            Case ivDimension
                Set obj = adoOpenCub.Dimensions(.Text)
            Case ivHierarchy
                Set obj = adoOpenCub.Dimensions(.Parent.Text).Hierarchies(.Text)

            Case ivLevelAll To ivLevel16
                'When we built the treeview control up, we hid the
                'hierarchies if none existed. So to present the object,
                'we have to find out whether we are using hierarchies or
                'not, and modify the Set statement accordingly.
                bHier = IIf((.Parent.Image = ivHierarchy), True, False)
                If bHier Then
                    Set obj = adoOpenCub.Dimensions(
                    ➥.Parent.Parent.Text).Hierarchies(.Parent.Text)
                    ➥.Levels(.Text)
```

```
    Else
        Set obj = adoOpenCub.Dimensions(.Parent.Text)
        ➡.Hierarchies(0).Levels(.Text)
    End If

Case ivMember
    'This is the fun one! Members can be children of members...
    'We need to firstly create a stack, iterating up the Treeview
    'until there are no more member parents left. Then we can create
    'the object, building back down the tree using the code from
    'above for finding the level, and then iterating through the
    'array to bring us back to the original member.
    Dim nodX As MSComctlLib.Node
    Dim sMembers() As String
    Dim iLoop As Integer

    ReDim sMembers(0)
    Set nodX = tvwDimensions.SelectedItem

    Do Until nodX.Image <> ivMember
        ReDim Preserve sMembers(UBound(sMembers) + 1)
        'NB Very Important! Must store UniqueName here...
        sMembers(UBound(sMembers) - 1) = nodX.Tag
        Set nodX = nodX.Parent
    Loop

    'At this stage, nodX.Image should be a level identifier, and
    'we should have a populated array sMembers. So we can now
    'work back down the tree to build the SelectedItem object. The
    'following six lines of code should be familiar from above.
    bHier = IIf((nodX.Parent.Image = ivHierarchy), True, False)
    If bHier Then
        Set obj = adoOpenCub.Dimensions(nodX.Parent.Parent.Text)
        ➡.Hierarchies(nodX.Parent.Text).Levels(nodX.Text)
    Else
        Set obj = adoOpenCub.Dimensions(nodX.Parent.Text)
        ➡.Hierarchies(0).Levels(nodX.Text)
    End If

    'Work back down the tree
    For iLoop = UBound(sMembers) - 1 To 0 Step -1
        If TypeOf obj Is ADOMD.Level Then
            Set obj = obj.Members.Item(sMembers(iLoop))
        Else 'type must be ADOMD.Member
            Set obj = obj.Children.Item(sMembers(iLoop))
        End If
    Next iLoop

    'And at last, we should have the right member!

Case Else
```

```
                    'Error
                    Set obj = Nothing
                    Err.Raise vbObjectError + dvObjectNotFound,
                    ➥ dvErrSource,
                    ➥"The selected item could not be retrieved as an object."
            End Select
            Set GetSelectedItemAsObject = obj
        End With
    End Function
```

Listing 7.9 shows the `GetSelectedItemAsObject()` function. This function is used to retrieve the object representing the currently selected node via the .SelectedItem property. The code is thoroughly commented, but a few additional comments are in order.

The primary operation of the function is to traverse up through the nodes within the Tree-View control until it reaches the root node. Where the currently selected item is a CubeDef, Dimension, or Hierarchy, this task is relatively simple: we know exactly how many levels deep within the TreeView control we are, and we can find the root node as a known ancestor of the currently selected node.

This task becomes slightly more complex for a Level object; depending on the dimension, a Hierarchy object may (or may not) be displayed for that object. This means that we must examine the type of the parent node to establish how many levels deep we are within the TreeView. Once this is understood, we can generate the selected object as before.

When a Member object is selected, the challenge is further magnified. A Member object may have an indeterminate number of other Member objects as its immediate ancestors. To regenerate this object from the node, we must first navigate back up the structure to find the first non-member object, pushing each node's unique names to a stack as we go. Once we get to the Level object, we can retrieve it using the techniques as described above; we can then work back down the tree to the selected member, using the stack to retrieve the names of the appropriate child node.

We eventually return whichever ADO/MD object is finally selected to the parent function and ultimately to the client application. Since the calling application doesn't know exactly what type of object it will receive, we use the generic type identifier Object and bind it late. The client application can use the TypeOf keyword to identify the object and call the appropriate properties or methods.

There are undoubtedly more elegant ways of writing the function above that present a generic solution to navigate through the hierarchy for any given member of that hierarchy, but from a performance standpoint, this method is probably slightly faster.

So that's it! We've developed a fully functional ActiveX control that provides access to the full ADO/MD schema and allows a user to navigate through the structure. Phew!

Using the Dimension View Object

Now that we've finally got all the code for the Dimension View control, let's put together a small test harness that shows the control working in practice. The program we present uses the Dimension View control to display the properties, as exposed through the ADODB.Properties collection, for any object selected within the control. This program is based on that shown in Listing 7.1, which showed the properties of a CubeDef object. By using our custom component, we can very easily extend this to show properties for any entity in the OLAP database. Figure 7.8 shows the test program in operation.

FIGURE 7.8:

OLAP Information Center test program

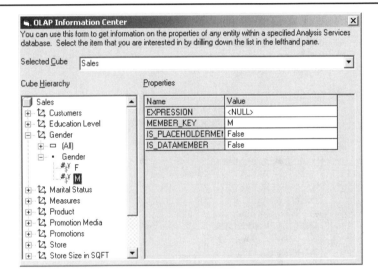

To recreate the form, add the labels as shown above, along with a drop-down listbox *cboCubes* (for displaying a list of available cubes), a Dimension View control *dvCube* (to show the cube schema), and a Hierarchical FlexGrid control *grdProperties* (to show the actual properties exposed). Set the form's BorderStyle to vbFixedDialog, to ensure it is displayed as a dialog box.

Listing 7.10 shows the code for the test harness.

Listing 7.10:   frmOLAPInformationCenter.frm

```
'//////////////////////////////////////////////////////////////////
'OLAP Dimension View Sample Application
'Copyright (c) 1999-2001 Tim Sneath / Sybex Inc.
'
'This application briefly demonstrates the capabilities of the Sybex
'Dimension View Control (see DimensionView.vbg) for accessing
'members of a cube hierarchy. It shows how the Properties collection,
```

```
'contained within each significant ADO MD object, can be used to
'display extended information about that object.
'//////////////////////////////////////////////////////////////////
Option Explicit
Option Base 0

Private sConn As String                      'OLE DB connection string

Private Sub Form_Load()
    Dim adoCat As New ADOMD.Catalog
    Dim adoCub As ADOMD.CubeDef

    sConn = InputBox("Please enter a valid OLE DB connection " & _
      "string representing the OLAP database to which you wish " & _
      "to connect.", _
      "OLAP Database Info", _
      "Provider=MSOLAP;Data Source=localhost;Initial Catalog=Foodmart")
    adoCat.ActiveConnection = sConn

    'Populate cboCubes drop-down list box with appropriate values
    For Each adoCub In adoCat.CubeDefs
        cboCubes.AddItem adoCub.Name
    Next adoCub

    With grdProperties
        .TextMatrix(0, 0) = "Name": .ColWidth(0) = 1800
        .TextMatrix(0, 1) = "Value": .ColWidth(1) = 2560
    End With

    'Setting ListIndex to 0 will initialize cboCubes and should
    'also call cboCubes_Click() automatically to set up dvCube.
    cboCubes.ListIndex = 0
End Sub

Private Sub cboCubes_Click()
    dvCube.DataSource = sConn
    dvCube.Cube = cboCubes.List(cboCubes.ListIndex)
End Sub

Private Sub dvCube_Click()
    Dim adoProp As ADODB.Property

    With grdProperties
        .Redraw = False
        .Rows = 1: .FixedRows = 0
        For Each adoProp In dvCube.SelectedItem.Properties
            .Rows = .Rows + 1
            .TextMatrix(.Rows - 1, 0) = adoProp.Name
            .TextMatrix(.Rows - 1, 1) =
            ➥ IIf(IsNull(adoProp.Value), "<NULL>", adoProp.Value)
        Next adoProp
```

```
            .FixedRows = 1
            .Redraw = True
        End With
    End Sub
```

We can now use this program to view properties for any database on our system. To try out the program, select the default OLE DB connection string (i.e., the local FoodMart 2000 OLAP database). Choose the Sales cube, and browse to the Customers dimension. Figure 7.9 shows the output.

FIGURE 7.9:

Customers dimension properties

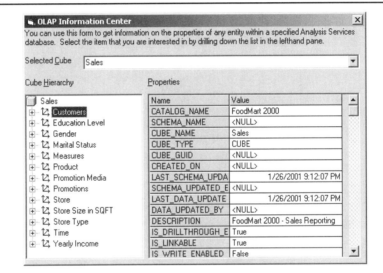

Here you can see the properties exposed by the OLAP Services OLE DB provider for a dimension. (Check Table 7.7 for a description of each property listed.) Now change the current cube to Warehouse, and navigate down the tree to view Store 13, as shown in Figure 7.10.

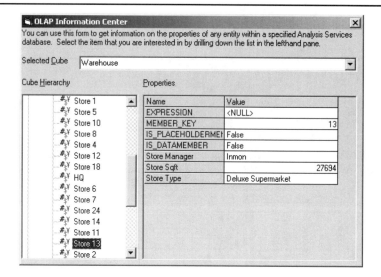

Here you can see the individual custom properties that have been set for the store, including store size, type, and manager's name. Last, navigate to the Profit measure back in the Sales cube, as shown in Figure 7.11.

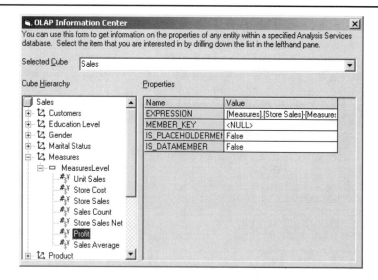

The EXPRESSION property here describes the calculation necessary to arrive at this calculated member (Profit = Sales Price – Cost).

One problem will become immediately apparent if you drill down any large dimension into its measures (e.g., the Customers dimension). The performance offered by the recursive `PopulateMembers()` function of the Dimension View control (see Listing 7.7) is still too slow. We need to populate each level of members dynamically at runtime to avoid this performance hit. Listing 7.11 presents a revised version of the necessary functions. This revised code is what's actually in the sample project on the companion CD.

Listing 7.11:   Revised PopulateMembers function

```
Private Sub PopulateMembers(ByVal Members As Members,
➥ByVal Node As MSComctlLib.Node)
    Dim adoMem As ADOMD.Member
    Dim nodX As MSComctlLib.Node, nodY As MSComctlLib.Node

    For Each adoMem In Members
        Set nodX = tvwDimensions.Nodes.Add(Node,
        ➥tvwChild, , adoMem.Name, ivMember)
        nodX.Tag = adoMem.UniqueName
        If adoMem.Children.Count > 0 Then PopulateMembers adoMem.Children, nodX
    Next adoMem
End Sub
```

Summary

In this chapter, we've seen how you can use the ADO/MD object model to query the Analysis Services engine for information about the dimensions, levels, and members contained within a cube. By using the appropriate ADO/MD objects, you can retrieve complete information about the structure of any cube stored by Analysis Services.

In the next chapter, we'll cover the remaining ADO/MD objects and, in particular, look at how you can send MDX queries and retrieve their results with ADO. We'll also add to the Dimension View control created in this chapter by building an MDX Query Analyzer application using the control.

CHAPTER **8**

Building OLAP Services Applications with ADO/MD Part II: Query Retrieval Objects

- ADO/MD Query Retrieval Objects

- OLAP Workbench

The previous chapter described the use of the ADO/MD object model to drill down and examine the object schema within an OLAP database. This chapter takes ADO/MD a stage further by looking at its use for querying an Analysis Services database. We'll also look at how you can use the object model to interpret the resulting dataset using the Cellset object.

ADO/MD Query Retrieval Objects

This section describes the remaining objects in the ADO/MD object model. As well as allowing a program to examine the metadata (the structure of the Analysis Services cube), ADO/MD also provides features to support querying of an Analysis Services cube using the MDX syntax discussed in Chapter 6, "Querying Analysis Services with MDX." Results from querying a cube are returned in a structure called a Cellset, which you can think of as a multidimensional analog to the familiar ADO recordset. In this section, we'll go through the objects pertaining to multidimensional Cellset manipulation.

Finally, at the end of this chapter, we'll provide a fully fledged application that allows users to auto-generate MDX queries and display them, pulling together the various examples we've used up to this point.

Figure 8.1 shows the entire ADO/MD object model. In this chapter, we'll be concerned with the objects on the right-hand side of the diagram: Cellset, Cell, Axis, Position, and Member.

FIGURE 8.1:

ADO/MD object model

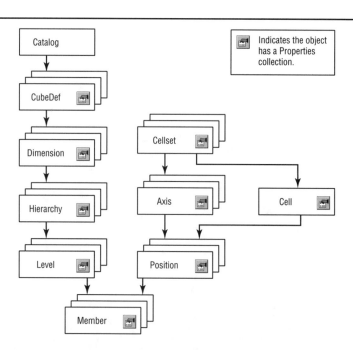

The Cellset Object

In the same way as the ADO object model contains a Recordset object that can be used to store the results of a (relational) SQL query, ADO/MD contains an equivalent *Cellset* object, which can be used to store the results of a multidimensional MDX query.

A Cellset object can be broken down into its component axes, a position within an axis, and ultimately an individual cell. Table 8.1 shows the member properties and methods contained within the Cellset object.

TABLE 8.1: Cellset Object Details

Name	Type	Explanation
ActiveConnection	P	A valid OLE DB connection string or ADO Connection object, against which MDX queries should be executed
Axes	C	A collection containing an Axis object for each of the axes within the result set
Close	M	Closes the currently open connection
FilterAxis	P	An Axis object containing information about the slicer dimensions used to return this Cellset
Item	*P*	*An individual cell, specified by index or array*
Open	M	Opens the connection and returns a Cellset based on the results of an MDX query against the active connection
Properties	C	A collection containing an object for each property relating to the Cellset that has been exposed by the data provider (read-only)
Source	P	Sets the MDX query used to generate the resultant Cellset
State	P	Indicates whether the Cellset is open or closed

Cellset objects are created based on a MDX query to an active connection. To activate a Cellset, you must complete the following steps:

- Create a new Cellset object.

- Set the *ActiveConnection* property to a valid OLE DB connection string or existing ADO Connection object.

- Set the *Source* property to a valid MDX query string.

- Call the *Open* method on the Cellset object to perform the query and populate the object.

The following code snippet demonstrates this:

```
Set cst = New ADOMD.Cellset
cst.ActiveConnection = _
 "Provider=MSOLAP.2;Data Source=localhost;Initial Catalog=FoodMart 2000"
cst.Source = "SELECT" & vbCrLf & _
 "{[Product]} ON COLUMNS," & vbCrLf & _
 "{[Store Type]} ON ROWS" & vbCrLf & _
 "FROM Sales"
cst.Open
```

TIP   You'll find this and the other code snippets from this chapter in the Chapter8.vbp sample project on the companion CD.

Note that the ActiveConnection and Source properties can be given as optional parameters to the Open method, allowing the above sample to be reduced to two lines of code:

```
Set cst = New ADOMD.Cellset
cst.Open "SELECT" & vbCrLf & _
 "{[Product]} ON COLUMNS," & vbCrLf & _
 "{[Store Type]} ON ROWS" & vbCrLf & _
 "FROM Sales", _
 "Provider=MSOLAP.2;Data Source=localhost;Initial Catalog=FoodMart 2000"
```

Use whichever form you prefer; there is no performance or resource difference. If you're opening many Cellsets in the same code, you should consider creating an explicit ADO Connection object and assigning it to the ActiveConnection property of each Cellset object; otherwise, your code will create a hidden Connection object anew with every Cellset.

Once you have finished using a Cellset object, you should close it in order to release the resources it was holding. This is as simple as the following statement:

```
cst.Close
```

The State property of a Cellset object can be used to indicate whether a particular Cellset is open or closed. It returns 0 (adStateClosed) or 1 (adStateOpen) accordingly.

Once a Cellset is open, you have two choices: you can either read individual cells in a random access fashion, selecting the desired cell by an index representing its location, or use the inherent structure of the Cellset to break the cells down by axis, position, and ultimately, member. The former option can be achieved by using the Item property, the latter through the Axes collection of Axis objects, which is described under the next heading.

The Item property is comparatively simple to use. You simply specify the cell you want, either as an ordinal number index starting from 0 and working along columns and then rows, or as an array index. Figure 8.2 shows a sample Cellset.

FIGURE 8.2:

Two-dimensional Cellset

Unit Sales	Desktop PCs	Laptop PCs	Printers	Other
Business	5394	2673	3125	5071
Personal	6214	1708	7406	3311
Educational	2401	2	430	6610
Governmental	1021	45	612	4565

Using this figure, the same cell could be specified in any of the following ways:

```
Set cll = cst(11)
Set cll = cst.Item(3,2)
Set cll = cst("Educational", "Other")
```

Where an MDX query is phrased in terms of ROWS and COLUMNS, you can access a cell by providing a tuple in the form (columns, rows). Of course, the same applies where an *n*-dimensional Cellset is returned; you can continue to specify the Cellset in the same way.

TIP   The Item collection, like other ADO/MD collections, is numbered starting at zero.

The FilterAxis property contains a single Axis object that provides information on the slice (i.e., filter) used to select the Cellset. For example, take the following MDX query against the FoodMart Sales cube:

```
WITH MEMBER [Measures].[Store Profit Rate] AS
'([Measures].[Store Sales]-[Measures].[Store Cost])/[Measures].[Store Cost]',
format = '#.00%'
SELECT {[Measures].[Store Cost],[Measures].[Store Sales],
[Measures].[Store Profit Rate]} ON COLUMNS,
Order([Product].[Product Department].Members,
[Measures].[Store Profit Rate], BDESC) ON ROWS
FROM Sales
WHERE ([Time].[1997])
```

For this query, the FilterAxis property contains one position containing several members, as follows:

```
All Stores
1997
All Media
All Promotions
All Customers
All Education Level
All Gender
```

```
All Marital Status
All Store Size in SQFT
All Store Type
All Yearly Income
```

Here you can see that all the dimensions that are not returned in the Cellset (that is, all except for the products dimension) are shown at a particular level. The original query has a WHERE clause restricting the returned Cellset to entries relating to 1997; therefore, the member relating to Time within FilterAxis shows the restriction.

NOTE   The Axis object exposed by the FilterAxis property is not a standard, cell data–containing axis. As a result, this special axis is not available through the Axes collection for the Cellset.

The FilterAxis property can be particularly useful when you are displaying the result set in graphical or tabular form and want to easily show what result set is displayed. You can use properties exposed by the members to find out information about a particular query. For example, the following function lists only the filtered dimensions in a particular Cellset:

```
Private Sub ShowFilter(cst As ADOMD.Cellset)
    Dim mem As ADOMD.Member
    For Each mem In cst.FilterAxis.Positions(0).Members
        If Instr(mem.LevelName, "[(All)]") = 0 Then
            Debug.Print mem.LevelName & "=" & _
                mem.Caption & vbCrLf
        End If
    Next mem
End Sub
```

This works by looking for the special name "[(All)]" that Analysis Services assigns to any All dimension, no matter how the caption for the dimension is set. For the Cellset returned by the above MDX query, this function will print the following:

```
[Time].[Year]=1997
```

You might be wondering at this point why we couldn't just get the same information by parsing the MDX query itself. The main benefit of the object model approach is that the results are returned in a consistent format that doesn't rely on the MDX query itself being structured in a particular way. If you are writing an application that supports user input or modification of a query, you can't guarantee how the query will be formed. There's little point in writing a complex MDX query parser to extract this information when ADO/MD gives you the facility out of the box.

The Properties collection stored for a Cellset gives you extended information on that Cellset. However, the versions of the MSOLAP provider included in SQL Server 7.0 and SQL Server 2000 expose no custom properties through the collection; in the future, other providers supplied with OLE DB for OLAP-compliant databases may include properties here.

The Cell Object

The Cell object represents a single unit of the data contained within the Cellset (and is therefore analogous to the Field object within ADO). Ultimately any code that works with a Cellset will operate on a cell to display the values of the Cellset, usually by iterating through the Cellset and retrieving cells individually.

A cell can be retrieved from the parent Cellset using the Cellset.Item property, as described above. Table 8.2 shows the properties and collections that can be accessed on the Cell object.

TABLE 8.2: Cell Object Details

Name	Type	Explanation
FormattedValue	P	Returns a string containing the value in the appropriate format for that value (e.g., "3,344.82") as defined by the FORMAT_STRING property associated with a cell.
Ordinal	P	A number representing the index of the cell within its parent Cellset (starting with 0).
Positions	C	A collection containing the individual positions that together represent the location of the cell on an axis.
Properties	C	A collection of extended properties relating to the cell; this is populated by the appropriate OLE DB provider.
Value	P	*The value of a cell in raw, unformatted form (e.g., 3344.8166).*

It shouldn't surprise you to discover that the Cell object contains two kinds of information: the location of the cell (as provided by the Ordinal and Positions properties), and the data contained within the cell (as provided by the FormattedValue and Value properties).

The Ordinal property matches the ordinal numbering that can be used to retrieve the cell from its parent Cellset. For example, this code snippet will print the value 5 to the Immediate window:

```
Dim cst As ADOMD.Cellset
Dim cll As ADOMD.Cell

Set cst = New ADOMD.Cellset
cst.ActiveConnection = _
  "Provider=MSOLAP.2;Data Source=localhost;Initial Catalog=FoodMart 2000"
cst.Source = "SELECT" & vbCrLf & _
  "{[Product].Children} ON COLUMNS," & vbCrLf & _
  "{[Store Type].Children} ON ROWS" & vbCrLf & _
  "FROM Sales"
cst.Open

Set cll = cst.Item(5)
Debug.Print cll.Ordinal
```

TIP

If you are displaying the contents of a Cellset in a grid, the ordinal property is an ideal target for storage in the Tag for each cell in the grid. Once you have this stored, you can quickly and easily reference the cell at a later date, perhaps to get additional information on the cell.

The choice of using FormattedValue or Value will likely depend on whether you are planning to use the output for display or for further manipulation.

WARNING

The ADO/MD documentation suggests that the FormattedValue property takes care of currency symbols. In our experimentation, this does not seem to be true. It does properly handle percentages.

The MSOLAP provider also exposes the properties above in the Cell object's Properties collection, as Table 8.3 shows for completeness. These properties are defined by the OLE DB provider, so they could change if you use a different provider. Providers can also add other properties such as BACK_COLOR and FORE_COLOR to this list.

TABLE 8.3: Cell Properties Collection

Name	Description
VALUE	The value of the cell
FORMATTED_VALUE	The value of the cell formatted for display
CELL_ORDINAL	The ordinal number of the cell in the parent Cellset

The Axis Object

An Axis object corresponds to an individual axis from an MDX query. The axes are specified within an MDX statement as ON <axis>, as shown in the following example:

```
SELECT
{[Product].Children} ON COLUMNS,
{[Store Type].Children} ON ROWS,
{[Customers].Children} ON PAGES
FROM Sales
```

The above example has three axes: columns, rows, and pages; if we executed the statement above, the resultant Cellset would contain an Axes collection of three Axis objects: Cellset.Axis(0), Cellset.Axis(1), and Cellset.Axis(2), denoting columns, rows, and pages, respectively.

Table 8.4 shows the member properties, methods, and collections contained within the Axis object.

TABLE 8.4: Axis Object Details

Name	Type	Explanation
DimensionCount	P	Returns the number of dimensions contained within the axis
Name	P	Returns the name of the axis, if stored
Positions	*C*	*A collection containing a Position object for each slice or point within the axis*
Properties	C	A collection containing extended properties for the object as exposed by the provider

ADO/MD itself does not supply any properties for the Properties collection of an Axis object. The underlying OLE DB provider for a Cellset is free to define its own properties in this collection. The MSOLAP provider does not define any properties for an Axis object.

The Position Object

We've seen already that an axis contains one or more dimensions and that the corresponding Axis object contains a collection of positions. An individual position is simply a point along the axis. Each position may contain one or more members, depending on the level of the position.

Table 8.5 shows the member properties and methods contained within the Position object.

TABLE 8.5: Position Object Details

Name	Type	Explanation
Members	*C*	*A collection containing a Member object for each member contained within the position*
Ordinal	P	A number representing the index of the position within the axis (read-only)

The Position object has no major function of its own but is, rather, a classification as part of the hierarchy.

Unlike most of the other ADO/MD objects, the Position object has no Properties collection. Because each position has at least one corresponding Member object, the properties are contained within the member itself.

The Member Object (Reprise)

The Member object was described in Chapter 7, "Building Analysis Services Applications with ADO/MD Part I: Cube Schema Objects," when we reviewed techniques for accessing an OLAP schema through ADO/MD. In fact, the Member object is available from both schema and Cellset parts of the ADO/MD object model, through the Level and Position objects, respectively.

Accessed through the Level object, the Members collection contains an entry for each entity within that level. For example, a Month level would contain members January, February, March, and so on. Accessed through the Position object, the Members collection contains information on the same members, but based on their location within the axis of a returned Cellset.

Some properties exposed by the Member object are only available through one of the two routes. Table 8.6 shows which properties can be used from a Member object that has been retrieved from a Level or Position.

TABLE 8.6: Availability of Member Properties through Level and Position Objects

Name	Level	Position
Caption	Available	Available
ChildCount	Available	Available
Children	Available	Available, but never contains information
Description	Available	Available
DrilledDown	Not Available	Available
LevelDepth	Available	Available
LevelName	Available	Available
Name	Available	Available
Parent	Available	Not Available
ParentSameAsPrev	Not Available	Available
Properties	Available	Available
Type	Available	Not Available
UniqueName	Available	Available

OLAP Workbench

In the course of this and the previous chapter, we've seen that ADO/MD allows Visual Basic programmers full access to the structure of an OLAP cube, as well as the ability to send MDX queries to the server and handle the resultant Cellsets returned.

To take these features a stage further, we present below a more comprehensive application that uses the functionality of ADO/MD in an OLAP setting. The application, OLAP Workbench, provides a primitive equivalent to the SQL Query Analyzer program included in SQL Server but supports MDX queries rather than Transact-SQL.

OLAP Workbench provides a user interface that allows the user to enter an MDX query and see the results presented in a tabular or graphical fashion. It also includes a Wizard that automatically builds an MDX query based on choices selected from a graphical interface.

WARNING   As it exists on the companion CD, OLAP Workbench is not a professional-quality application. The code is meant to demonstrate the basic operations in generating and executing an MDX query, rather than to be bombproof. Check the Sybex web site for updates and bug fixes to this application in the future.

Figure 8.3 shows the application running. The code for the application can be found on the companion CD in the OLAPWorkbench.vbp project and is also presented here.

FIGURE 8.3:

OLAP Workbench

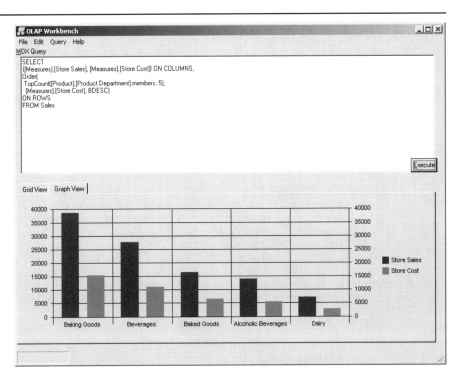

The application uses several Microsoft Common Control libraries, as well as the Dimension View control described in Chapter 7. Make sure you have the following controls installed on your machine before attempting to run OLAP Workbench (all of these controls except the DimensionView control are installed as part of Visual Basic):

- Microsoft Chart Control 6.0
- Microsoft Common Dialog Control 6.0
- Microsoft Hierarchical FlexGrid Control 6.0
- Microsoft Tabbed Dialog Control 6.0
- Microsoft Windows Common Controls 6.0
- Microsoft Windows Common Controls-2 6.0
- Microsoft Windows Common Controls-3 6.0
- DimensionViewControl (you'll need to compile the DimensionView project from Chapter 7 to install this control, or use the compiled version from the companion CD)

The main window for the application is a single, resizable form that allows users to enter an MDX query and view the end results. The code for the window, frmMain, is shown in Listing 8.1.

Listing 8.1:   frmMain.frm

```
'/////////////////////////////////////////////////////////////////////
'OLAP Workbench 1.0
'Copyright (c) 1999-2001 Tim Sneath / Mike Gunderloy / Sybex Inc.
'
'This application provides a suitable testbed for running MDX queries
'against an OLAP server. It supports query entry and execution, with
'results returned in either tabular or graphical form.
'
'Known limitations:
'   - Although any valid MDX query can be entered within the appropriate
'     textbox, the application only supports the display of a two-
'     dimensional cellset. The usage of PAGES, SECTIONS and CHAPTERS
'     clauses is unsupported.
'   - No active parsing of invalid MDX queries is conducted.
'
'Queries or comments to tim.sneath@russley.com
'/////////////////////////////////////////////////////////////////////

Option Explicit
Option Base 0

'Connection string details
Public sProvider As String
Public sDataSource As String
Public sInitialCatalog As String
```

```
'Currently open catalog / cube
Public adoCat As New ADOMD.Catalog

'Currently open file
Public sFilename As String

'////////////////////////////////////////////////////////////////////
'Form Management
'////////////////////////////////////////////////////////////////////
Private Sub Form_Load()
    sFilename = ""
    cdlgFileMgmt.Filter = "MDX Query Files (*.mdx)|*.mdx|Text Files
    ➡(*.txt)|*.txt|All Files (*.*)|*.*"

    'We need a default database, so we call up the appropriate dialog
    mnuFileConnect_Click
End Sub

Private Sub Form_Resize()
    With frmMain
        'Set minimum height / width
        If .Height < 3000 Then .Height = 3000
        If .Width < 4000 Then .Width = 4000

        'Reset widths
        txtMDX.Width = .Width - 495
        cmdExecute.Left = .Width - 990
        tabView.Width = .Width - 345
        grdView.Width = .Width - 550
        chtView.Width = .Width - 550

        'Reset heights
        txtMDX.Height = (.Height - 1290) / 2.5
        cmdExecute.Top = txtMDX.Top + txtMDX.Height - cmdExecute.Height
        tabView.Height = .Height - 1700 - txtMDX.Height
        tabView.Top = txtMDX.Height + 465
        grdView.Height = tabView.Height - 505
        chtView.Height = tabView.Height - 505
    End With
End Sub

Private Sub cmdExecute_Click()
    'This function executes a specific MDX query against OLAP Services.
    'We open a Cellset object adoCst, which is passed to other
    'functions as appropriate.
    Dim adoCst As New ADOMD.Cellset

    If Not (adoCat.ActiveConnection Is Nothing) Then
        'It's quite possible that we'll get an error here if the MDX query
        'has a syntax error, so we handle it discretely with the
        'appropriate warning...
        On Error GoTo Err_Handler
```

```
        adoCst.Open txtMDX.Text, adoCat.ActiveConnection

        Screen.MousePointer = vbHourglass
        DrawGridView adoCst
        DrawChartView adoCst
        adoCst.Close
        Screen.MousePointer = vbDefault
    Else
        MsgBox "No connection open. Please reconnect to a valid data source and
        ➥try again.", vbExclamation
    End If
    Exit Sub

Err_Handler:
    MsgBox "Error in MDX query:" & vbCrLf & Err.Description, vbOKOnly +
    ➥vbExclamation, "OLAP Workbench"
End Sub

Private Sub DrawGridView(adoCst As ADOMD.Cellset)
    Dim col As Integer, row As Integer

    With grdView
        'Switching off redraw greatly improves performance when populating a
        ➥grid
        .Redraw = False

        'Prepare the grid
        .Cols = adoCst.Axes(0).Positions.Count + 1
        .Rows = adoCst.Axes(1).Positions.Count + 1

        'Set col headings
        For col = 0 To adoCst.Axes(0).Positions.Count - 1
            .TextMatrix(0, col + 1) = _
            adoCst.Axes(0).Positions(col).Members(0).Caption
        Next col

        'Set row headings
        For row = 0 To adoCst.Axes(1).Positions.Count - 1
            .TextMatrix(row + 1, 0) =
            ➥adoCst.Axes(1).Positions(row).Members(0).Caption
        Next row

        'Iterate through the grid, adding data
        For col = 0 To adoCst.Axes(0).Positions.Count - 1
            For row = 0 To adoCst.Axes(1).Positions.Count - 1
                .TextMatrix(row + 1, col + 1) = adoCst(col, row).FormattedValue
            Next row
        Next col
```

```
                .Redraw = True
        End With
End Sub

Private Sub DrawChartView(adoCst As ADOMD.Cellset)
      Dim col As Integer, row As Integer

      With chtView
            'Switching off redraw greatly improves performance when populating a
            ➡grid
            .Repaint = False

            'Prepare the grid
            .chartType = VtChChartType2dBar
            .ColumnCount = adoCst.Axes(0).Positions.Count
            .RowCount = adoCst.Axes(1).Positions.Count
            .ShowLegend = True

            'Set col headings
            For col = 0 To adoCst.Axes(0).Positions.Count - 1
                  .Column = col + 1
                  .ColumnLabel = adoCst.Axes(0).Positions(col).Members(0).Caption
            Next col

            'Set row headings
            For row = 0 To adoCst.Axes(1).Positions.Count - 1
                  .row = row + 1
                  .RowLabel = adoCst.Axes(1).Positions(row).Members(0).Caption
            Next row

            'Iterate through the grid, adding data
            For col = 0 To adoCst.Axes(0).Positions.Count - 1
                  For row = 0 To adoCst.Axes(1).Positions.Count - 1
                        .Column = col + 1
                        .row = row + 1
                        .Data = adoCst(col, row).Value
                  Next row
            Next col

            .Repaint = True
      End With
End Sub

Private Sub Initialize()
      'Now make connection and navigate to appropriate cube
      If sProvider <> "" And sDataSource <> "" And sInitialCatalog <> "" Then
            adoCat.ActiveConnection = "Provider=" & sProvider & "; Data Source=" &
            ➡sDataSource & "; Initial Catalog=" & sInitialCatalog
            sbrMain.SimpleText = "Connected to " & sInitialCatalog & " on " &
            ➡sDataSource & " using " & sProvider & " OLE DB Provider."
      Else
```

```
            Set adoCat.ActiveConnection = Nothing
            sbrMain.SimpleText = "Disconnected."
        End If
    End Sub


    '///////////////////////////////////////////////////////////////////
    'Menu Commands
    '///////////////////////////////////////////////////////////////////
    Private Sub mnuFileConnect_Click()
        'Allow user to select database connection and provider
        dlgOpenDb.Show vbModal, Me

        'Open cube and fill out screen controls with appropriate values
        Initialize
    End Sub

    Private Sub mnuFileDisconnect_Click()
        Set adoCat.ActiveConnection = Nothing
        sbrMain.SimpleText = "Disconnected."
    End Sub

    Private Sub mnuFileInfo_Click()
        frmDbInfo.Show vbModal, Me
    End Sub

    Private Sub mnuFileOpen_Click()
        Dim fso As New Scripting.FileSystemObject
        Dim stream As Scripting.TextStream

        On Error GoTo Err_Handler

        'Show common dialog box
        cdlgFileMgmt.ShowOpen
        sFilename = cdlgFileMgmt.FileName

        'Load selected file into txtMDX textbox
        Set stream = fso.OpenTextFile(FileName:=sFilename, IOMode:=ForReading)
        txtMDX.Text = stream.ReadAll
        stream.Close

        Exit Sub
    Err_Handler:
        'User cancelled File/Open operation.
        Exit Sub
    End Sub

    Private Sub mnuFileSave_Click()
        Dim fso As New Scripting.FileSystemObject
        Dim stream As Scripting.TextStream

        On Error GoTo Err_Handler
```

```
        'If filename is empty, then no file is currently open: therefore
        'show Save dialog box
        If sFilename = "" Then
            cdlgFileMgmt.ShowSave
            sFilename = cdlgFileMgmt.FileName
        End If

        Set stream = fso.CreateTextFile(FileName:=sFilename, Overwrite:=True)
        stream.Write txtMDX.Text
        stream.Close

        Exit Sub
Err_Handler:
        'User cancelled File/Save operation.
        Exit Sub
End Sub

Private Sub mnuFileSaveAs_Click()
    Dim fso As New Scripting.FileSystemObject
    Dim stream As Scripting.TextStream

    On Error GoTo Err_Handler

    cdlgFileMgmt.ShowSave
    sFilename = cdlgFileMgmt.FileName

    Set stream = fso.CreateTextFile(FileName:=sFilename, Overwrite:=True)
    stream.Write txtMDX.Text
    stream.Close

    Exit Sub
Err_Handler:
        'User cancelled File/Save operation.
        Exit Sub
End Sub

Private Sub mnuFileExit_Click()
    Unload Me
End Sub

Private Sub mnuEditCut_Click()
    Clipboard.Clear
    Clipboard.SetText txtMDX.SelText
    txtMDX.SelText = ""
End Sub

Private Sub mnuEditCopy_Click()
    Clipboard.Clear
    Clipboard.SetText txtMDX.SelText
End Sub
```

```
Private Sub mnuEditPaste_Click()
    txtMDX.SelText = Clipboard.GetText
End Sub

Private Sub mnuEditSelectAll_Click()
    txtMDX.SelStart = 0
    txtMDX.SelLength = Len(txtMDX.Text)
End Sub

Private Sub mnuQueryExecute_Click()
    cmdExecute_Click
End Sub

Private Sub mnuQueryWizard_Click()
    dlgMDXWizard.Show vbModal, Me
End Sub

Private Sub mnuHelpAbout_Click()
    frmAbout.Show vbModal, Me
End Sub
```

Much of the code provided above does not require further explanation. When the application is started, the Form_Load() subroutine displays a dialog box dlgOpenDB to allow the user to select an active OLAP database. It then calls the Initialize() routine, which sets up a publicly accessible Catalog object, adoCat, to point to the active connection, which is used throughout to obtain references to the current cube.

When a user attempts to enter an MDX query, the application creates a Cellset based on the Catalog object. If successful, two subroutines are called to display the results: DrawGridView and DrawChartView. Each of these functions iterates through the Cellset in a nested loop, populating the appropriate display control with the data from the Cellset. If the query generates an error, this is handled by the application and the user is prompted to amend the MDX query.

The application allows users to save MDX queries to disk; this is handled through the file operations provided as part of the new FileSystemObject library. It supports the use of common dialog boxes to prompt for a file location.

Figure 8.4 and Listing 8.2 show dlgOpenDB, which is called at the start of the application and whenever the user chooses the File ➤ Connect menu option.

FIGURE 8.4:

Database connection
dialog box

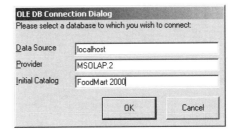

Listing 8.2:   dlgOpenDB.frm

```
Option Explicit

Private Sub CancelButton_Click()
    Unload Me
End Sub

Private Sub OKButton_Click()
    With frmMain
        .sDataSource = txtDataSource
        .sProvider = txtProvider
        .sInitialCatalog = txtInitialCatalog
    End With
    Unload Me
End Sub
```

One useful feature provided by the application is the ability to auto-generate MDX based on a Wizard-driven user interface. The code for this Wizard is contained in a separate part of the program, for which the upcoming listing is shown. The Query Wizard dialog box includes several tabs:

- Introduction/cube selection
- Dimension selection
- Measure selection
- Calculated measure builder
- MDX preview option

Figure 8.5 shows the Query Wizard in operation.

FIGURE 8.5:

FIGURE 8.5:

Query Wizard dialog box

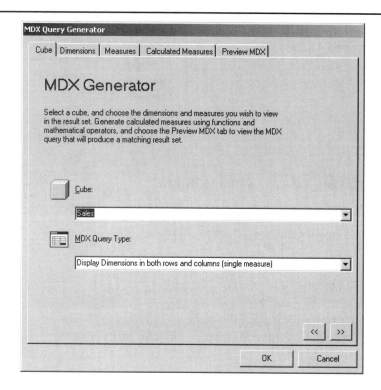

The code for the MDX query generator is shown in Listing 8.3.

Listing 8.3: **dlgMDXWizard.frm**

```
'////////////////////////////////////////////////////////////////////
'MDX Query Generator Wizard 1.0
'Copyright (c) 1999-2001 Tim Sneath / Mike Gunderloy / Sybex Inc.
'
'This series of property pages allows an end-user to automatically
'generate MDX code for a chosen set of dimensions and levels,
'specifying measures from within the cube and generating calculated
'measures directly from within the wizard. It produces a "preview" MDX
'view which can then be executed directly against the OLAP server.
'
'Known limitations:
'   - Not overly sophisticated in the queries it generates; demonstrates
'     the structure of an MDX query rather than the full extent of
'     potential usage.
'   - Does not check for deliberate attempts to break the wizard.
'
'For the latest updates to this application, visit the website for this
'book at http://www.sybex.com.
'////////////////////////////////////////////////////////////////////
```

```
Option Explicit
Option Base 0

'/////////////////////////////////////////////////////////////////
'Global Scope Logic
'/////////////////////////////////////////////////////////////////
Private Sub Form_Load()
    Dim adoCub As ADOMD.CubeDef        'for looping purposes only

    'First test whether we are connected to a valid data source
    If Not (frmMain.adoCat.ActiveConnection Is Nothing) Then
        'Iterate through CubeDefs collection
        For Each adoCub In frmMain.adoCat.CubeDefs
            cboCubes.AddItem adoCub.Name
        Next adoCub
        cboCubes.ListIndex = 0
        cboQueryType.ListIndex = 0

        InitMDXFunctionStruct    'in modMDXFunctions.bas
        InitMDXFunctionListbox   'in dlgMDXWizard.frm
        cboOrderBy.ListIndex = 0

        tabMDXWizard.Tab = 0     'set default tab
    Else
        MsgBox "No connection open. Please reconnect to a valid data source and
        ➡try again.", vbExclamation
        Unload Me
    End If
End Sub

Private Sub tabMDXWizard_Click(PreviousTab As Integer)
    'Only update MDX string when we click on that tab
    Select Case tabMDXWizard.Tab
        Case 4: txtMDX.Text = CreateMDX
    End Select
End Sub

Private Sub cmdPrevTab_Click()
    'Navigate through the tabs, enabling or disabling the command
    'buttons as appropriate.
    tabMDXWizard.Tab = tabMDXWizard.Tab - 1
    If tabMDXWizard.Tab = 0 Then
        cmdPrevTab.Enabled = False
    End If
    cmdNextTab.Enabled = True
End Sub

Private Sub cmdNextTab_Click()
    'Navigate through the tabs, enabling or disabling the command
    'buttons as appropriate.
    tabMDXWizard.Tab = tabMDXWizard.Tab + 1
    If tabMDXWizard.Tab = tabMDXWizard.Tabs - 1 Then
        cmdNextTab.Enabled = False
```

```
        End If
        cmdPrevTab.Enabled = True
    End Sub

    Private Sub cmdOK_Click()
        'Fill out MDX query textbox with generated query and return
        frmMain.txtMDX.Text = CreateMDX()
        Unload Me
    End Sub

    Private Sub cmdCancel_Click()
        Unload Me
    End Sub

    '///////////////////////////////////////////////////////////////////
    'Tab 1: Cubes
    '///////////////////////////////////////////////////////////////////
    Private Sub cboCubes_Click()
        lstColDim.Clear: lstRowDim.Clear
        dvDimensions.DataSource = frmMain.adoCat.ActiveConnection
        dvDimensions.Cube = cboCubes.List(cboCubes.ListIndex)
        BuildMeasureView lstMeasures
        BuildMeasureView lstMeasures2
        BuildMeasureView cboOrderBy
    End Sub

    Private Sub cboQueryType_Click()
        'We offer two choices of query type:
        '  - those with dimensions along both rows and columns, with one
        '    measure used to display the cell data
        '  - those with dimensions along rows only, with different
        '    measures along the columns
        '
        'Depending on which of the options are selected, we selectively
        'enable or disable user controls as appropriate.
        lstColDim.Enabled = IIf((cboQueryType.ListIndex = 0), True, False)
        cmdToCol.Enabled = lstColDim.Enabled
        cmdFromCol.Enabled = lstColDim.Enabled
    End Sub

    '///////////////////////////////////////////////////////////////////
    'Tab 2: Dimensions
    '///////////////////////////////////////////////////////////////////
    Private Sub cmdToCol_Click()
        If TypeOf dvDimensions.SelectedItem Is ADOMD.CubeDef Then
            lstColDim.AddItem dvDimensions.SelectedItem.Name
        Else
            lstColDim.AddItem dvDimensions.SelectedItem.UniqueName
        End If
    End Sub

    Private Sub cmdFromCol_Click()
        If lstColDim.ListIndex <> -1 Then
```

```
            lstColDim.RemoveItem lstColDim.ListIndex
        End If
End Sub

Private Sub cmdToRow_Click()
    If TypeOf dvDimensions.SelectedItem Is ADOMD.CubeDef Then
        lstRowDim.AddItem dvDimensions.SelectedItem.Name
    Else
        lstRowDim.AddItem dvDimensions.SelectedItem.UniqueName
    End If
End Sub

Private Sub cmdFromRow_Click()
    If lstRowDim.ListIndex <> -1 Then
        lstRowDim.RemoveItem lstRowDim.ListIndex
    End If
End Sub

'///////////////////////////////////////////////////////////////
'Tab 3: Measures
'///////////////////////////////////////////////////////////////
'No code required here.

'///////////////////////////////////////////////////////////////
'Tab 4: Calculated Measures
'///////////////////////////////////////////////////////////////
Private Sub cmdPlus_Click()
    txtFunction = txtFunction & "+"
End Sub

Private Sub cmdMinus_Click()
    txtFunction = txtFunction & "-"
End Sub

Private Sub cmdMultiply_Click()
    txtFunction = txtFunction & "*"
End Sub

Private Sub cmdDivide_Click()
    txtFunction = txtFunction & "/"
End Sub

Private Sub lstMeasures2_DblClick()
    txtFunction.SelText = "[Measures].[" &
    ➥lstMeasures2.List(lstMeasures2.ListIndex) & "]"
End Sub

Private Sub lstFunctions_DblClick()
    txtFunction.SelText = lstFunctions.List(lstFunctions.ListIndex)
End Sub

Private Sub cmdAddCalcMeasure_Click()
    lstMeasures.AddItem txtCalcName
End Sub
```

```
'///////////////////////////////////////////////////////////////
'General Functions and Procedures
'///////////////////////////////////////////////////////////////
Private Sub BuildMeasureView(objX As Object)
    Dim adoMbr As ADOMD.Member

    'objX must support .AddItem and .Clear
    Debug.Assert ((TypeOf objX Is ListBox) Or _
                (TypeOf objX Is ComboBox))

    objX.Clear

    'Measures are accessible through ADOMD as a special kind of
    '"dimension". The dimension characteristics are fixed for all
    'cubes, however, so we can hard-code the location of the measures.
    'We treat them as a special case, since there is of course a
    'significant difference in the way the two can be used.
    For Each adoMbr In
frmMain.adoCat.CubeDefs(cboCubes.List(cboCubes.ListIndex)).
➡Dimensions("Measures").Hierarchies(0).Levels("MeasuresLevel").Members
        objX.AddItem adoMbr.Name
    Next adoMbr
End Sub

Private Function CreateMDX() As String
    Dim sFormulaClause As String
    Dim sAxisClause() As String
    Dim sCubeClause As String
    Dim sSlicerClause As String
    Dim sError As String
    Dim iAC As Integer, iLoop As Integer
    sError = ""

    'MDX SELECT statement syntax:
    '
    '    [WITH [<formula_specification>]]
    '    SELECT [<axis_specification>[, <axis_specification>...]]
    '    FROM [<cube_specification>]
    '    [WHERE [<slicer_specification>]]
    '
    '    We generate an MDX statement by building up each clause
    '    individually.

    '*** [WITH [<formula_specification>]] ***
    sFormulaClause = "MEMBER [Measures].[" & txtCalcName.Text & "] AS '" &
➡txtFunction.Text & "' "

    '*** SELECT [<axis_specification>[, <axis_specification>...]] ***
    '    An axis can be any of COLUMNS, ROWS, PAGES, CHAPTERS, SECTIONS
    '    or even an arbitrary axis specified as AXIS(<index>)
    '
    '    Within this sample application, we will just use COLUMNS and
    '    ROWS, but this could easily be extended...
    iAC = 0
    ReDim sAxisClause(2)
```

```
'Generate MDX if dimensions selected for columns
If cboQueryType.ListIndex = 0 Then
    sAxisClause(iAC) = sAxisClause(iAC) & "{"
    If lstColDim.ListCount > 0 Then
        For iLoop = 0 To lstColDim.ListCount - 1
            sAxisClause(iAC) = sAxisClause(iAC) & _
                lstColDim.List(iLoop) & ".members, "
        Next iLoop
        'Strip off trailing ", "
        sAxisClause(iAC) = Mid(sAxisClause(iAC), 1,
        ➥Len(sAxisClause(iAC)) - 2) & "} ON COLUMNS"
    Else
        sError = sError & "  - No dimensions selected for the column axis."
        ➥& vbCrLf
    End If

'Generate MDX if measures selected for columns
Else
    sAxisClause(iAC) = sAxisClause(iAC) & "{"
    For iLoop = 0 To lstMeasures.ListCount - 1
        If lstMeasures.Selected(iLoop) Then
            sAxisClause(iAC) = sAxisClause(iAC) & "[Measures].
            ➥[" & lstMeasures.List(iLoop) & "], "
        End If
    Next iLoop
    'Strip off trailing concatenation, so long as we added
    'a measure in the first place...
    If lstMeasures.SelCount > 0 Then
        sAxisClause(iAC) = Mid(sAxisClause(iAC), 1,
        ➥Len(sAxisClause(iAC)) - 2) & "} ON COLUMNS"
    Else
        sError = sError & "  - No measures selected." & vbCrLf
    End If
End If

iAC = iAC + 1
'Generate MDX if dimensions selected for rows
If lstRowDim.ListCount > 0 Then
    sAxisClause(iAC) = sAxisClause(iAC) & "{"
    If lstRowDim.ListCount > 0 Then
        For iLoop = 0 To lstRowDim.ListCount - 1
            sAxisClause(iAC) = sAxisClause(iAC) & lstRowDim.List(iLoop) &
            ➥".members, "
        Next iLoop
        sAxisClause(iAC) = Mid(sAxisClause(iAC), 1,
        ➥Len(sAxisClause(iAC)) - 2) & "} ON ROWS"
    Else
        sError = sError & "  - No dimensions selected for the row axis." &
        ➥vbCrLf
    End If
End If
```

```
'*** FROM [<cube_specification>] ***
sCubeClause = cboCubes.List(cboCubes.ListIndex)

'*** [WHERE [<slicer_specification>]] ***
'We use this section to select a measure when we are using the wizard in 2D
➥mode...
If cboQueryType.ListIndex = 0 Then
    If lstMeasures.SelCount = 1 Then
        For iLoop = 0 To lstMeasures.ListCount - 1
            sSlicerClause = "[Measures].[" & lstMeasures.List(iLoop) & "]"
        Next iLoop
    Else
        sError = sError & "  - Only one measure can be selected if
        ➥dimensions are displayed on both rows and columns." & vbCrLf
    End If
End If


'Lastly, build the MDX select statement from its constituent parts
CreateMDX = ""
If sError = "" Then
    If sFormulaClause <> "" Then
        CreateMDX = CreateMDX & "WITH " & sFormulaClause & vbCrLf
    End If
    CreateMDX = CreateMDX & "SELECT " & vbCrLf
    For iLoop = 0 To UBound(sAxisClause) - 1
        CreateMDX = CreateMDX & sAxisClause(iLoop) & _
        IIf((UBound(sAxisClause) - iLoop > 1), ", ", "") & vbCrLf
    Next iLoop
    CreateMDX = CreateMDX & " FROM " & sCubeClause & vbCrLf
    If sSlicerClause <> "" Then
        CreateMDX = CreateMDX & " WHERE " & sSlicerClause
    End If
Else
    CreateMDX = "Automatic MDX query generation failed for the following
    ➥reasons: " & vbCrLf & sError
End If
End Function

Private Sub InitMDXFunctionListbox()
    Dim iLoop As Integer

    For iLoop = 1 To collMDX.Count
        lstFunctions.AddItem collMDX.Item(iLoop)
    Next iLoop
End Sub
```

Many of the functions required in this Wizard support the basic "plumbing" of the user interface, and the manipulation of the various controls based on choices made by the user.

The most important function of this Wizard is CreateMDX(), which builds an MDX query based on the various controls elsewhere in the tabbed dialog box.

CreateMDX() builds up a string variable using the following syntax:

```
[WITH [<formula_specification>]]
SELECT [<axis_specification>[, <axis_specification>...]]
FROM [<cube_specification>]
[WHERE [<slicer_specification>]]
```

The application allows for two different kinds of MDX queries to be created:

- Queries with one or more dimensions drilled down along the row axis, with one or more measures spread across the columns

- Queries with dimensions along both row and column axes, showing one measure in the Cellset

Supporting both types of query adds to the complexity of the function that generates MDX, since they are handled differently in the resultant MDX. As a result, the code to define measures is present both in the ON COLUMNS clause and in the WHERE clause. The other issue that needs careful attention is the use of a comma symbol to delimit various parts of the MDX statement—be careful not to add a comma at the end of a clause, because it would cause a syntax error.

To build up a valid MDX expression, at least one dimension and a measure must be selected. The function uses a string variable sError to store any errors as they occur (such as the absence of any required elements). At the end of the function, this variable is tested: if it is not empty, then the function returns the error statement.

You can try out the MDX Wizard by following these steps:

1. Connect to the FoodMart 2000 database on the local machine.

2. Choose Query ➢ Wizard to start the Wizard itself.

3. Choose the Sales cube and select the second query type option (Display Dimensions In Rows, And Multiple Measures In Columns).

4. Select the Dimensions tab and add Product Department to the rows listbox.

5. Select the Preview MDX tab, and note the error message.

6. Select the Calculated Measures tab, and enter a name for the calculated measure of Total Store Sales.

7. Either type or use the built-in facilities to enter the following function: Sum(Ytd(), [Measures].[Store Sales]).

8. Choose Add Calculated Measure To Cube to create this measure.

9. Go back to the Measures tab, and select this new calculated measure as well as the Store Sales measure.

10. Click OK to return to the main OLAP Workbench form.

The resultant MDX query should read as follows:

```
WITH MEMBER [Measures].[Total Store Sales] AS
    'Sum(Ytd(),[Measures].[Store Sales])'
SELECT
{[Measures].[Store Sales], [Measures].[Total Store Sales]} ON COLUMNS,
{[Product].[Product Department].members} ON ROWS
 FROM Sales
```

Go ahead and execute it, and see the results in the grid. Your screen should match that shown in Figure 8.6.

FIGURE 8.6:

Auto-generated MDX query

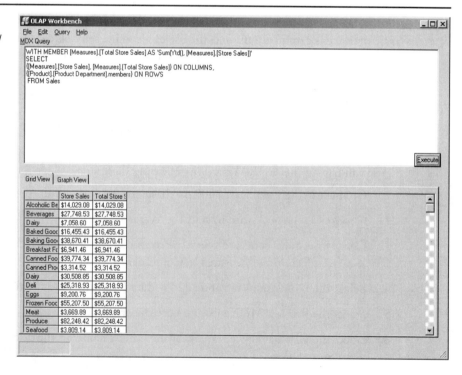

The OLAP Workbench application is certainly not an exhaustive demonstration of the capabilities of ADO/MD coupled with MDX, but it offers a useful starting point and demonstrates many of the techniques necessary to build your own applications.

Conclusion

In this chapter we have seen how ADO/MD can be used to write applications that use the capabilities of OLAP Services to support multidimensional analysis. ADO/MD is pivotal to the development of OLAP applications; together with MDX, it provides Visual Basic with a powerful library for writing data-aware applications that support detailed analysis.

In the next chapter, we'll proceed to look at some of the ways you can use the PivotTable Service in conjunction with ADO/MD to build and manage local cubes without using an Analysis Services server.

CHAPTER 9

Advanced Usage of the PivotTable Service

- Architecture of the PivotTable Service

- Creating and Using Local Cubes

- Handling Writeback from Clients

- Redistributing the PivotTable Service

The PivotTable Service is an essential client-side component of the Microsoft OLAP architecture. In this chapter, we'll explore how the PivotTable Service fits into the big picture of Analysis Services and then explore how you can use it in your own applications—whether or not Analysis Services is actually available to the client computers.

> **NOTE**   The PivotTable Service also plays an integral role in client applications that use the new data mining features in the SQL Server 2000 implementation of Analysis Services. We'll cover those PivotTable features in Chapter 11, "Building Data Mining Solutions with Analysis Services."

Architecture of the PivotTable Service

Figure 9.1 presents a reminder of the overall architecture of Analysis Services, as we discussed in Chapter 2, "Analysis Services Architecture." In this chapter, we'll be dealing exclusively with the PivotTable Services component of this architecture. Note that all client communication with Analysis Services flows through PivotTable Services.

FIGURE 9.1:

Analysis Services architecture

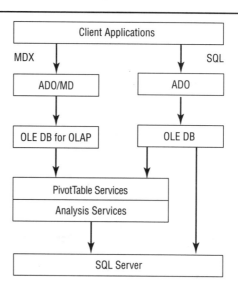

As you'll see in this chapter, the PivotTable Service plays a dual role in Microsoft's OLAP architecture. On the one hand, it is a layer of software that every request from a client to an Analysis Services server must pass through. On the other, it is an independent multidimensional engine that contains code to perform many of the tasks that the full version of Analysis Services can perform, although generally with less data and at a slower rate.

In its first role as a pipeline from a client application to Analysis Services, the PivotTable Service maintains its own client-side cache of user queries, returned data, and metadata. Caching the metadata means that the PivotTable Service is aware of the structure of the returned data and can use it to answer new queries without necessarily retrieving more data from the Analysis Services server. For example, suppose a user requests inventory data for California, Nevada, Oregon, and Washington, and that those states jointly make up the company's Western Region. If the user then asks for data aggregated over the entire Western Region, the PivotTable Service can answer that request directly from its cache. Being able to return the answer from RAM, instead of from a server somewhere across the network, greatly speeds the process of returning data to the user. If the user then wants to look at comparisons between the Western Region and the Eastern Region, only the Eastern Region data needs to be retrieved over the network.

In its second role as an OLAP calculation engine, the PivotTable Service delivers the ability to create, populate, and query *local cubes*. A local cube is the equivalent of an Analysis Services database kept in a disk file. By using the PivotTable Service, client applications such as Excel can perform multidimensional analyses on the contents of a local cube file.

Connections to Analysis Services

Figure 9.2 shows the connection architecture when using the PivotTable Service with an Analysis Services server. In this case, the PivotTable Service is used to mediate requests and data between the client application and Analysis Services. All communication with the actual data, whether it is stored in ROLAP or MOLAP format, is done by Analysis Services itself (possibly, as in the case of ROLAP data, by using SQL Server to retrieve the actual data).

FIGURE 9.2:

Connecting to an Analysis Services server

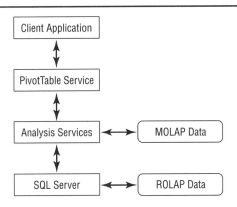

The nature of the connection between the PivotTable Service and Analysis Services depends on whether the two components are running on a single computer. If both the PivotTable Service and Analysis Services are on the same computer (for example, when you're working directly at the computer running Analysis Services), then communication between the two is via a block of shared memory. More often, the PivotTable Service will be installed on a client computer and Analysis Services will be running on a server computer elsewhere on the network. In this case, communication between the two is via a network protocol, most often TCP/IP.

Connecting via HTTP

The SQL Server 2000 version of Analysis Services also adds the ability for the PivotTable Service to connect to an Analysis Server via HTTP. Figure 9.3 shows the architecture of such an HTTP connection.

FIGURE 9.3:

Connecting to an Analysis Services server via HTTP

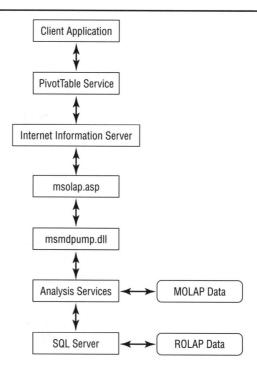

If you compare Figure 9.3 with Figure 9.2, you'll see that connecting via HTTP simply adds several layers of "plumbing" to the path that would otherwise be used by the PivotTable Service:

- Internet Information Server handles the incoming HTTP requests and returns data to the PivotTable Service as a formatted HTML stream.

- msolap.asp is an Active Server Page that's created when you install Analysis Services. By default, it's installed to the bin folder of the Analysis Services tree. This ASP page brokers requests between IIS and the server.

- msmdpump.dll is the Analysis Services server IIS pump. This is a COM component that's instantiated by the msolap.asp page to make the connection to Analysis Services.

Listing 9.1 shows the contents of msolap.asp. Note that, for the most part, you should not modify the contents of this page. However, if you're having problems with Analysis Services timing out on large requests, you may want to increase the pump.Timeout property from its default of 60 (seconds) to a larger value.

Listing 9.1:   msolap.asp

```
<%@ LANGUAGE="VBSCRIPT"%>
<%' ************** Do not change this file ***************
   '  changing of this file can bring unexpected results
   '  NEVER add any HTML tags. Places that are allowed to
   '  change will be specified explicitly in the comments.
   ' *********************************************************
%>
<%Response.Expires = 0%>
<%Response.Buffer=FALSE%>
<%Server.ScriptTimeout=3600%>
<HTML><%
    On Error Resume Next
    Call ReadData
    ' This is error handling code and should not be modified
    ' This code will take care of the potentional errors in
    ' this asp page.
    if ( Err.Number <> 0 ) Then
        errstr = "<Error>" + CStr(-8) + "</Error>"
        errstr = errstr + "<SysError>" + CStr(err.Number) + "</SysError>"
        errstr = errstr + "<Note>" + err.Description + "</Note>"
        Response.AddHeader "Pump-Error", errstr
        Response.Flush
        Response.End
    End if

    Function ReadData
        ' ****** You can modify code of this function,
        ➥but we don't recommend doing it. **************
```

```
        if (isEmpty(Session("StoredPump"))) Then
            Set pump = Server.CreateObject("PUPump.PUPump.1")
            Set Session("StoredPump") = pump
        else
            Set pump = Session("StoredPump")
        End if
        ' This value can be changed.
        pump.Timeout=60
        pump.ReadData
        Response.Flush
        Response.End
    End Function
    %>
```

To connect to an Analysis Services database via HTTP, follow these steps:

1. Add the folder containing msolap.asp to your IIS server as a new virtual directory. Give this virtual directory a name such as msolap and turn on Read and Run Scripts permissions on the virtual directory.

2. To connect to the Analysis Services server via HTTP, use the URL of the virtual directory containing the msolap.asp page as the Datasource property. For example, a valid HTTP connection string might look like this:

```
"Provider=MSOLAP.2;Datasource=
➥http://www.schmoop.com/msolap/;Initial Catalog = FoodMart 2000;"
```

Once you've connected to Analysis Services via HTTP, the connection is transparent to the client application. That is, you do not need to do any special programming in the client as a result of using HTTP as the transport protocol. The PivotTable Service takes care of all the details of sending requests and returning data.

Connections to an OLE DB Provider

When the PivotTable Service is used with a local ROLAP cube (as opposed to a ROLAP cube from an Analysis Services server), it employs the hybrid architecture shown in Figure 9.4.

FIGURE 9.4:

Connecting to a local
ROLAP cube

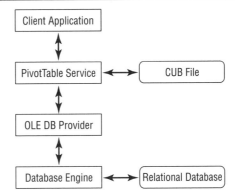

FIGURE 9.4:

Connecting to a local
ROLAP cube

In the case of a local ROLAP cube, the CUB file stores the metadata describing the cube, but not any actual data or aggregations. The data remains in a relational database accessible via OLE DB, and the PivotTable Service makes a connection to the appropriate provider whenever it is asked to return data from the cube.

Compared to local MOLAP cubes, local ROLAP cubes are smaller (because they do not store precalculated aggregations) but slower (because they must connect to the relational database to retrieve data).

Connecting to a Local Cube

Finally, Figure 9.5 shows the architecture used when the PivotTable Service retrieves data from a local MOLAP cube.

FIGURE 9.5:

Connecting to a local
MOLAP cube

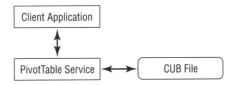

A local MOLAP cube contains the data, metadata, and aggregations necessary to answer MDX queries from the cube. After it's been created and processed, a local MOLAP cube does not require any connection to the database containing the data. The PivotTable Service can answer queries directly from the CUB file.

Note that local MOLAP cube files are completely portable. After you've created a local MOLAP cube file, you can move it to another computer and it can still be used by the PivotTable Service, even if the original relational data is unavailable.

PivotTable Service Properties

The PivotTable Service exposes a large number of properties that can be used to fine-tune your applications' connections to Analysis Services (or local CUB files). These properties can be specified as part of the OLE DB connection string for the MSOLAP provider. Table 9.1 lists the available properties.

WARNING   Some of the properties contain spaces in their names and some do not. You must match the format exactly when setting properties, despite this annoying inconsistency.

TABLE 9.1: PivotTable Service Properties

Property Name	Default Value	Description
ArtificialData	None	Reserved for future use.
Authenticated User	None	Reserved for future use.
Auto Synch Period	10000	Frequency (in milliseconds) of synchronization between client and server.
Cache Policy	None	Reserved for future use.
Cache Ratio	None	Reserved for future use.
Client Cache Size	25	Limits space used by the client cache. When set to 1–99, uses that percentage of available memory. If set to over 100, the client can use up to that much memory in KB.
CompareCaseNotSensitiveStringFlags	0	Overrides the current value in the registry and changes the way case-insensitive string comparisons work for Katagana, Hiragana, and Hindi for the current client connection.
CompareCaseSensitiveStringFlags	0	Overrides the current value in the registry and changes the way case-sensitive string comparisons work for Katagana, Hiragana, and Hindi.
Connect Timeout	60	Number of seconds to wait before a connection attempt times out.
CreateCube	None	Used with InsertInto and Source_DSN and contains the CREATE CUBE statement to build a local cube.
Data Source	None	Source for cube data: server name, HTTP connect string, or local cube filename.
Datasource Connection Type	None	Read this property to determine the type of the currently active connection: 1 for an Analysis Services server, 2 for a local cube, 4 for a connection via HTTP.
Default GUID Dialect	DBGUID_SQL	GUID that indicates which query parser to use with this connection: SQL, MDX, or data mining.

Continued on next page

TABLE 9.1 CONTINUED: PivotTable Service Properties

Property Name	Default Value	Description
Default Isolation Mode	None	If set to Y, T, or a nonzero number, forces all transactions for rowsets on this connection to be serializable.
Default MDX Visual Mode	None	Specifies whether totals should include all cells or only visual cells.
Distinct Measures By Key	None	Reserved for future use.
Do Not Apply Commands	None	Reserved for future use.
Execution Location	0	Determines whether queries are resolved on the client or the server.
Initial Catalog	None	Analysis Services database to use.
InsertInto	None	Used with CreateCube and Source_DSN and contains the INSERT INTO statement to build and populate a local cube.
Large Level Threshold	1000	Most members that will be sent to the client cache in one burst.
Locale Identifier	Null	LCID for the connection (defaults to LCID for the computer).
Log File	None	File to store MDX queries performed over this connection.
MDX Calculated Members Mode	None	Reserved for future use.
MDX Compatability	0	If 0 or 1, placeholder members in ragged hierarchies are not exposed. If 2, placeholder members are exposed.
MDX Object Qualification	None	Set by provider to indicate how fully qualified object names are constructed.
MDX Unique Name Style	0	Set by provider to indicate how unique object names are constructed.
Mining Execution Location	0	Determines the location of data mining query execution.
Mining Location	None	Directory for local data mining models.
Mining Persistence Format	0	If 0 or 2, mining models are stored in proprietary binary format. If 1, mining models are stored in XML.
OLE DB for OLAP Version	None	Set by provider to indicate the supported version of the OLE DB for OLAP specification.
Password	None	Password used to connect to the data when using HTTP.
Provider	MSOLAP	OLE DB Provider to use for connections.
Read Only Session	None	Reserved for future use.
Roles	None	Comma-delimited string of role names to use in connecting to the server.

Continued on next page

TABLE 9.1 CONTINUED: PivotTable Service Properties

Property Name	Default Value	Description
Safety Options	Allow safe	Controls whether functions that are not safe for scripting or initialization can be used.
Secured Cell Value	#N/A	Controls the data returned when you attempt to access a cell that you cannot read due to cell-level security.
Show Hidden Cubes	None	Reserved for future use.
Source_DSN	None	Contains a connection string or DSN and is used with CreateCube and InsertInto to build a local cube.
Source_DSN_Suffix	None	Allows specification of a portion of the Source_DSN property that is not stored in the local cube.
SQL Compatibility	None	Reserved for future use.
SSPI	None	Specifies the security package to use when authenticating users.
UseExistingFile	False	Determines whether to overwrite an existing file when creating a local cube.
User ID	None	User ID used to connect to the data when using HTTP.
Writeback Timeout	0	Number of seconds to wait for a writeback to succeed.

As you can see, many of these properties are fairly obscure or reserved for future use. Here are some additional comments on the ones that you're most likely to want to change in the current release of Analysis Services.

The Auto Synch Period controls the synchronization of the client cache with the data on the Analysis Services server (assuming you're dealing with a remote cube). By default, this is set to 10,000 milliseconds, or 10 seconds. This does not mean, however, that the cache is synchronized every 10 seconds. Rather, when a query is sent to the PivotTable Service that can be resolved from the local cache, it checks whether the local cache is more than 10 seconds old. If it is, then the cache is synchronized with the server before the query is answered. If you want to make sure that recent updates are used, you can reduce the value of this property. The minimum valid value is 250 (1/4 second); if you set the property to a value from 1 to 249, then the PivotTable Service will set it to 250. A value of zero disables the automatic synchronization and lets the PivotTable Service answer any queries from the cache that it can, without ever checking for more recent data on the server.

The Client Cache Size property controls the amount of memory that the PivotTable Service will use for caching. However, the values for this property are somewhat obscure:

- 0 allows the client cache to use unlimited memory.
- 1 to 99 allow the client cache to use that percentage of total virtual memory.
- 100 or more allow the client cache to use that many kilobytes of memory.

The CreateCube, InsertInto, and Source_DSN properties fall into a class by themselves. Rather than setting parameters for the connection, they are values that are passed to the PivotTable Service when you wish to create a local cube, and they contain all of the information necessary to create the cube. You'll see these properties in action in the next section, "Creating and Using Local Cubes."

The Data Source property contains the name of the Analysis Services server or local cube file where the data that you wish to analyze is located. There is also one special value for this property. If you set the Data Source property to null when creating a cube, then the cube is created as a temporary local cube and is deleted when you end the PivotTable Service session.

The Default GUID Dialect property controls the way in which the PivotTable Service attempts to parse SQL statements that it receives. The PivotTable Service implements three different parsers, one each for SQL, MDX, and data mining. You can set this property to these special values:

- DBGUID_SQL gives precedence to the SQL parser.
- MDGUID_MDX gives precedence to the MDX parser.
- MDGUID_DM gives precedence to the data mining parser.

The Execution Location property gives you some control over whether queries are resolved by the PivotTable Service or passed back to the server. If it's set to 0 or 1, the PivotTable Service will select the execution location that it thinks will return the answer most quickly. A value of 2 forces client-side execution, and a value of 3 forces server-side execution.

If you're curious as to just what the PivotTable Service is doing, or if you're trying to troubleshoot a problem, you can use the Log File property. This property allows you to keep a disk file with all of the queries that are executed on a particular connection. To use the property, you just include it in the connection string, as in this example:

```
Dim cst As ADOMD.Cellset

Set cst = New ADOMD.Cellset
cst.ActiveConnection = _
 "Provider=MSOLAP.2;Data Source=localhost;" & _
 "Initial Catalog=FoodMart 2000;Log File=c:\PTS.log"
```

```
cst.Source = "SELECT" & vbCrLf & _
 "{[Product]} ON COLUMNS," & vbCrLf & _
 "{[Store Type]} ON ROWS" & vbCrLf & _
 "FROM Sales"
cst.Open

MsgBox "LogFile created"

cst.Close
Set cst = Nothing
```

If you execute this code (it's in the sample project for this chapter), you'll find that it creates a file named c:\PTS.log. The file contents will consist of entries that look something like this:

```
VB6:2500    2/16/2001    4:38:32 PM    MDX    SELECT
{[Product]} ON COLUMNS,
{[Store Type]} ON ROWS
FROM Sales
```

The file includes the process name, process ID, date and time of the query, type of the query (MDX, SQL, or DM), and the actual query text (here spread over multiple lines because of the vbCrLf characters in the source).

Creating and Using Local Cubes

In this section, we'll look at the use of the PivotTable Service to create a local cube file. Local cube files are useful in situations when you don't have a full Analysis Services server available. For example, any copy of Microsoft Excel 2000 can create a local cube file, even if no Analysis Services server is on your network. We'll cover three ways in which you can do this:

- By invoking the OLAP Cube Wizard from Microsoft Excel
- By invoking the OLAP Cube Wizard from your own code
- By sending a connection string directly to the PivotTable Service

Using the OLAP Cube Wizard

The easiest way to get started with local cubes is to use the OLAP Cube Wizard. This is a component of Microsoft Excel that first shipped as part of Excel 2000. Assuming that you have Office 2000 installed on your computer, you can create a local cube file by following these steps:

1. Launch Excel 2000.

2. Choose Data ➢ Get External Data ➢ New Database Query.

3. Make sure the box for Use The Query Wizard To Create/Edit Queries is checked, choose <New Data Source> on the Databases tab of the Choose Data Source dialog, and click OK.

4. In the Create New Data Source dialog box, name the new data source Northwind, select the Microsoft Access Driver, and click Connect.

5. In the ODBC Microsoft Access Setup dialog box, click the Select button.

6. Navigate to the `c:\Program Files\Microsoft Office\Office\Samples` folder, and choose Northwind.mdb. Click OK.

7. Click OK to dismiss the ODBC Microsoft Access Setup dialog box.

8. In the Create New Data Source dialog box, click OK (do not select a default table).

9. In the Choose Data Source dialog box, make sure the new Northwind data source is selected and click OK.

10. On the Choose Columns panel of the Query Wizard, select the entire Customers table, the EmployeeID and LastName fields from the Employees table, and the entire Orders table. Click Next.

11. Do not choose any fields to filter by. Click Next.

12. Do not choose any fields to sort by. Click Next.

13. On the Finish panel of the Query Wizard, select Create An OLAP Cube From This Query and click Finish. This will launch the OLAP Cube Wizard.

14. As with other Wizards, the OLAP Cube Wizard opens with a welcome panel. Read this and click Next.

15. On Step 1 of the OLAP Cube Wizard, select Count Of OrderID and Sum Of Freight as the fields to summarize. Click Next. Although the OLAP Cube Wizard doesn't use the term, these are the measures for your cube. Figure 9.6 shows this panel of the OLAP Cube Wizard.

16. On Step 2 of the OLAP Cube Wizard, drag the Region field to the Drop Fields Here To Create A Dimension node. Then drag and drop City on Region, Address on City, and CompanyName on Address. What you're doing here is building up a dimension, one level at a time. You can right-click the topmost node of a dimension and click Rename to assign a name such as Geography. Drag the OrderDate field to the Drop Fields Here node to create a date hierarchy. Click Next. Figure 9.7 shows this panel of the Cube Wizard.

FIGURE 9.6:

Defining measures in the OLAP Cube Wizard

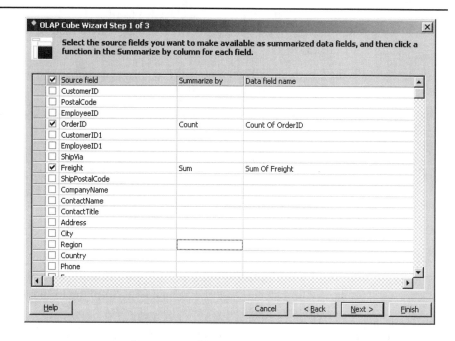

FIGURE 9.7:

Defining dimensions in the OLAP Cube Wizard

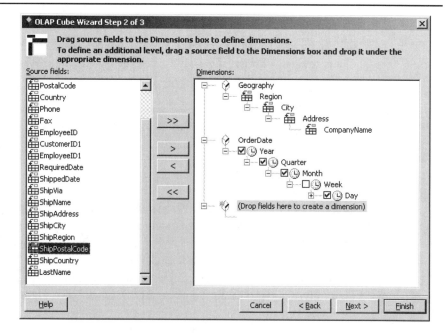

17. On the final panel of the OLAP Cube Wizard, select a storage option. The first two options create ROLAP cubes; the third creates a MOLAP cube. Assign a name to the cube file and click Finish. You'll also be prompted to save an OQY file, which is Excel's pointer to a cube file.

18. You'll be returned to Excel, at Step 3 of the PivotTable and PivotChart Wizard. Click Finish to create a Pivot Table based on the cube in the Excel worksheet.

Although the interface used by the OLAP Cube Wizard is unique, by now the concepts should be familiar to you. The Office 2000 designers chose to hide much of the complexity and terminology of Analysis Services from their users.

A local cube can be used just like a remote cube, once you've connected to it. The cubes created by the OLAP Cube Wizard use OCWCube as the name of both the catalog and the cube itself. Thus, you can use code like this to open a cube created with the OLAP Cube Wizard:

```
Dim cst As ADOMD.Cellset

On Error GoTo HandleErr

Set cst = New ADOMD.Cellset
cst.ActiveConnection = _
  "Provider=MSOLAP.2;Data Source=" & App.Path & _
  "\Northwind.cub;Initial Catalog=OCWCube"
cst.Source = "SELECT" & vbCrLf & _
  "{[OrderDate]} ON COLUMNS," & vbCrLf & _
  "{[Geography]} ON ROWS" & vbCrLf & _
  "FROM OCWCube"
cst.Open

MsgBox cst.Axes.Count

cst.Close
Set cst = Nothing
```

You'll find this code, together with a local MOLAP cube to use in testing, as part of this chapter's sample code on the accompanying CD-ROM.

Automating the OLAP Cube Wizard

The OLAP Cube Wizard would just be a minor sidelight to using OLAP, except for one key undocumented feature: you can use it in your own applications. That's because the Cube Wizard is implemented as a COM server with public interfaces that you can call from your own code.

WARNING   Note that you do not have the right to redistribute the OLAP Cube Wizard. To use the technique demonstrated in this section, you'll need to have Office 2000 installed on the computer where the code is run.

To use the OLAP Cube Wizard from a Visual Basic application, select Project ➤ References. Browse to the `Program Files\Microsoft Office\Office` folder and add a reference to MSOWCW.DLL to your project. This will show up as Microsoft Office Web Component Wizards in the References dialog box.

If you open the Object Browser and select the mce library, you'll find that it contains several classes. The OLAP Cube Wizard is contained in a class named MiniCubeEditor, which was the beta name of the Wizard. The only member visible for the MiniCubeEditor by default is ShowHelp. However, if you right-click in the Members pane of the Object Browser and choose Show Hidden Members, you'll discover the rest of the interface.

Table 9.2 lists the important methods and properties of the MiniCubeEditor object.

TABLE 9.2: MiniCubeEditor Interface

Name	Type	Explanation
Caption	P	Caption to use for the OLAP Cube Wizard window.
CreateCube	M	Launch the OLAP Cube Wizard to create a cube.
CubeFileName	P	Filename chosen for the local cube file.
CubeFilePath	P	Path to the local cube file.
CubeName	P	Name of the cube being constructed.
DCubeConnectionString	P	Connection string created by the Wizard.
DeferData	P	Setting for the defer data option.
DeferDimensions	P	Setting for the defer dimensions option.
EditCube	M	Launch the Wizard to edit an existing cube.
EnableFinishButton	P	True to display a finish button on the final panel.
FinishMessage	P	Text to show as a message on finish.
LastErrorText	P	Text of any error that halts the Wizard.
LocaleID	P	LCID to use when creating the cube.
NoHoverSelect	P	Set to True to turn off hover select in the treeview.
RDBCommandString	P	Relational query that retrieves columns for the Wizard.
RDBConnectionString	P	Connection string for the source of the cube's data.
ShowHelp	E	Callback event to show cube help.
ShowOverview	P	Set to True to show the Welcome pane.
ShowStepNumbers	P	Set to True to show step numbers in the Wizard caption.

The minimum steps necessary to use the OLAP Cube Wizard from your own code are to instantiate a MiniCubeEditor object, set its RDBCommandString and RDBConnection-String properties, and call its CreateCube method. This will show the Wizard, using the query and connection that you specified to initialize the user interface.

TIP   All fields in the RDBCommandString property must be qualified with the name of the table that contains the field. For example, if you're referring to a field named CustomerName in the Customers table, you must always refer to it as Customers.CustomerName.

There are three possibilities for the exit from the Wizard:

- If the user clicks Cancel, the CreateCube method returns the mceCancel constant.
- If an error occurs, the CreateCube method returns the mceError constant, and the LastErrorText property will contain the description of the error.
- If the user finishes the Wizard successfully, the CreateCube method returns the mce-Success constant, and the DCubeConnectionString property will contain a connection string that you can use with the PivotTable Service to create the specified cube.

The Chapter 9 sample project (Chapter9.vbp) contains the example code shown in Listing 9.2 to demonstrate the use of the OLAP Cube Wizard from Visual Basic. This code depends on being run on the same computer as a SQL Server that contains the BookSamples database from the companion CD-ROM.

Listing 9.2:   Calling the OLAP Cube Wizard from your own code

```
Private Sub cmdOLAPCubeWizard_Click()
    Dim objWizard As mce.MiniCubeEditor
    Dim intStatus As Integer

    On Error GoTo HandleErr

    Set objWizard = New mce.MiniCubeEditor

    With objWizard
        .Caption = "Chapter 9 Wizard"
        .EnableFinishButton = True
        .FinishMessage = "Press Finish to return a Cube connection string"
        .NoHoverSelect = False
        .ShowOverview = True
        .ShowStepNumbers = True

        .DeferData = True
        .DeferDimensions = True
```

```
            .RDBConnectionString = "Provider=SQLOLEDB;Data Source=(local);" & _
             "Initial Catalog=BookSamples;Integrated Security=SSPI"
            .RDBCommandString = "SELECT tblCalls.CallID, tblCalls.CallTypeID, " & _
             "tblCalls.LeadSourceID, " & _
             "tblCalls.ProductID, tblCalls.RegionID, tblCalls.CallDate, " & _
             "tblCallType.CallTypeID, tblCallType.CallType, " & _
             "tblCallType.CallSubType, " & _
             "tblLeadSource.LeadSourceID, tblLeadSource.LeadSource, " & _
             "tblProduct.ProductID, tblProduct.ProductGroup, " & _
             "tblProduct.Product, " & _
             "tblProduct.ItemName, " & _
             "tblRegion.RegionID, tblRegion.Continent, tblRegion.Country, " & _
             "tblRegion.City " & _
             "FROM (((tblCalls INNER JOIN tblCallType " & _
             "ON tblCalls.CallTypeID = tblCallType.CallTypeID) " & _
             "INNER JOIN tblLeadSource " & _
             "ON tblCalls.LeadSourceID = tblLeadSource.LeadSourceID) " & _
             "INNER JOIN tblProduct " & _
             "ON tblCalls.ProductID = tblProduct.ProductID) " & _
             "INNER JOIN tblRegion " & _
             "ON tblCalls.RegionID = tblRegion.RegionID "

            intStatus = .CreateCube()
            Select Case intStatus
                Case mceCancel
                    MsgBox "You cancelled the Wizard"
                Case mceError
                    MsgBox "An error occurred: " & .LastErrorText
                Case mceSuccess
                    Debug.Print .DCubeConnectionString
            End Select
        End With

ExitHere:
    Exit Sub

HandleErr:
    MsgBox "Error " & Err.Number & ": " & _
     Err.Description, "cmdOLAPCubeWizard"
    Resume ExitHere
    Resume

    End Sub
```

Using a Connection String

The OLAP Cube Wizard does not itself create a cube file. Rather, it returns a connection string that uses the MSOLAP OLE DB provider. Using this connection string with the provider is what actually creates the cube, either as a temporary cube for the duration of the session, or as a permanent cube file.

For example, if you run the code shown in Listing 9.2, and make some reasonable choices on the OLAP Cube Wizard interface, you'll get back a DCubeConnectionString property something like this (reformatted for clarity):

```
Provider=MSOLAP;
Initial Catalog=[Cube1];
Data Source=Cube1.cub;
CreateCube=CREATE CUBE [Cube1] (
    DIMENSION [CallType],
        LEVEL [All] TYPE ALL,
        LEVEL [CallType],
        LEVEL [CallSubType],
    DIMENSION [LeadSource],
        LEVEL [All] TYPE ALL,
        LEVEL [LeadSource],
    DIMENSION [ProductGroup],
        LEVEL [All] TYPE ALL,
        LEVEL [ProductGroup],
        LEVEL [Product],
        LEVEL [ItemName],
    DIMENSION [Continent],
        LEVEL [All] TYPE ALL,
        LEVEL [Continent],
        LEVEL [Country],
        LEVEL [City],
    MEASURE [Count Of CallID]
        FUNCTION COUNT
);
InsertInto=INSERT INTO Cube1([Count Of CallID],
SKIPONECOLUMN, SKIPONECOLUMN, SKIPONECOLUMN,
SKIPONECOLUMN, SKIPONECOLUMN, SKIPONECOLUMN,
[CallType].[CallType], [CallSubType], SKIPONECOLUMN,
[LeadSource].[LeadSource], SKIPONECOLUMN,
[ProductGroup].[ProductGroup], [Product], [ItemName],
SKIPONECOLUMN, [Continent].[Continent], [Country], [City])
OPTIONS ATTEMPT_ANALYSIS
SELECT tblCalls.CallID, tblCalls.CallTypeID,
tblCalls.LeadSourceID, tblCalls.ProductID, tblCalls.RegionID,
tblCalls.CallDate, tblCallType.CallTypeID, tblCallType.CallType,
tblCallType.CallSubType, tblLeadSource.LeadSourceID,
tblLeadSource.LeadSource, tblProduct.ProductID,
tblProduct.ProductGroup, tblProduct.Product, tblProduct.ItemName,
tblRegion.RegionID, tblRegion.Continent, tblRegion.Country,
tblRegion.City FROM (((tblCalls INNER JOIN tblCallType ON
tblCalls.CallTypeID = tblCallType.CallTypeID) INNER JOIN
tblLeadSource ON tblCalls.LeadSourceID =
tblLeadSource.LeadSourceID) INNER JOIN tblProduct ON
```

```
tblCalls.ProductID = tblProduct.ProductID)
INNER JOIN tblRegion ON tblCalls.RegionID = tblRegion.RegionID ;
Source_DSN="Provider=SQLOLEDB;Data Source=(local);
Initial Catalog=BookSamples;Integrated Security=SSPI";
```

As you can see, a complex syntax is used in MSOLAP connection strings to create local cubes. This connection string is made up of these properties:

- The Provider property, which specifies the MSOLAP provider.

- The Initial Catalog property, which specifies the database name for the cube.

- The Data Source property, which specifies the disk filename for the cube.

- The CreateCube property, which specifies a SQL-like string that describes the structure of the cube.

- The InsertInto property, which specifies a SQL-like string that maps the columns of a SELECT query to the parts of the structure described in the CreateCube property.

- The Source_DSN property, which specifies an OLE DB connection string for the relational database that is the source of the cube's data.

- The Source_DSN_Suffix property (not used in this example), which contains an extra part of the Source_DSN that is not stored in the local cube. This is intended to hold username and password parameters that the PivotTable Service needs to access the original data but which should not be stored to disk.

The CreateCube Property

The CreateCube property contains a CREATE CUBE statement. CREATE CUBE is an extension to the SQL language developed by Microsoft's OLAP team to define the structure of a cube, by analogy with the standard CREATE TABLE statement.

The formal definition of CREATE CUBE contains many optional clauses, but the basics are easy to understand by looking at an example. The statement always starts with the CREATE CUBE keywords and the name of the cube:

```
CREATE CUBE [Cube1] (
```

Note that all identifiers within a CREATE CUBE statement must be quoted with square brackets if they contain spaces or if they conflict with SQL keywords. Brackets are always allowed, and the Cube Wizard takes the conservative approach of using brackets around all identifiers.

The next part of the CREATE CUBE statement is a series of one or more DIMENSION clauses. Each of these clauses defines a dimension in the cube, by listing the levels within the dimension:

```
DIMENSION [Continent],
        LEVEL [All] TYPE ALL,
        LEVEL [Continent],
        LEVEL [Country],
        LEVEL [City]
```

Note that both the Dimension and the second level within the dimension are named Continent. The PivotTable Service (and Analysis Services in general) allows multiple objects to share the same name as long as they are at distinct places within the cube's hierarchical structure.

The [All] level is defined with the TYPE ALL keyword, which tells the PivotTable Service that this is a level that rolls up all levels from within this dimension. Other keywords can also be used to indicate the levels of time dimensions:

```
DIMENSION [CallDate] TYPE TIME,
    LEVEL [All] TYPE ALL,
    LEVEL [Year] TYPE YEAR,
    LEVEL [Quarter] TYPE QUARTER,
    LEVEL [Month] TYPE MONTH,
    LEVEL [Day] TYPE DAY
```

These special level types allow client applications to properly aggregate the data in the dimension into natural time units.

After all of the dimension definitions, the CREATE CUBE statement contains one or more measure definitions:

```
MEASURE [Count Of CallID]
    FUNCTION COUNT,
MEASURE [Sum Of CallDuration]
    FUNCTION SUM
```

Each measure is defined by assigning it a measure and a function. The allowable functions are SUM, MIN, MAX, and COUNT.

Although the CREATE CUBE statement defines the structure of the cube, it doesn't actually connect that structure to fields in the source database. That's the job of the INSERT INTO statement.

The InsertInto Property

The InsertInto property contains an INSERT INTO statement. As with CREATE CUBE, this is a Microsoft-defined SQL extension particularly for OLAP.

For the most part, an INSERT INTO statement is a listing of objects in a cube matched to fields in a relational database query. The keyword SKIPONECOLUMN can be used in the cube object listing to indicate that a relational field has no place in the cube. For example, here's a part of an INSERT INTO statement:

```
INSERT INTO Cube1([Count Of CallID],
SKIPONECOLUMN, SKIPONECOLUMN …
OPTIONS ATTEMPT_ANALYSIS …
SELECT tblCalls.CallID, tblCalls.CallTypeID,
tblCalls.LeadSourceID …
```

This statement indicates that the [Count of CallID] measure in the cube should be populated from the tblCalls.CallID field of the database, and that the tblCalls.CallTypeID and tblCalls.LeadSourceID fields are not used in the cube.

The INSERT INTO statement also has an OPTIONS clause that can contain one or more options that dictate the way in which the PivotTable Service should process the statement:

- DEFER_DATA tells the PivotTable Service to execute the query only when a user requests data from the cube. This option creates a ROLAP cube.

- ATTEMPT_DEFER tells the PivotTable Service to attempt to create a ROLAP cube but, if anything goes wrong with this process, to execute the query as if you had specified the PASSTHROUGH option.

- PASSTHROUGH tells the PivotTable Service to use exactly the query supplied in the INSERT INTO statement when retrieving data for this cube. If you omit PASSTHROUGH, the PivotTable Service may reformulate the query or break it into multiple queries for more efficient processing.

- ATTEMPT_ANALYSIS tells the PivotTable Service to attempt to break the query into more efficient pieces but to revert to PASSTHROUGH if this is impossible.

NOTE   For more details on the CREATE CUBE and INSERT INTO statements, including full BNF definitions, refer to SQL Server Books Online under Analysis Services Programming/PivotTable Service/PivotTable Service Programmer's Reference/Data Definition Language and Analysis Services Programming/PivotTable Service/PivotTable Service Programmer's Reference/Data Manipulation Language.

Handling Writeback from Clients

In Chapter 5, "Advanced Analysis Services," we discussed the use of writeback to allow client applications to change the data stored as part of a cube. Writeback operations are managed by the PivotTable Service. In this section, we'll explore the programming syntax involved in using writeback and look at some of the issues involved.

Leaf Writeback

To change a value in a leaf cell of the cube (that is, a cell that is at the lowest level in all dimensions of the cube), you can make changes directly to the Value property of an ADOMD Cell object. Listing 9.3 shows the code from the Chapter9 sample project that demonstrates this technique.

Listing 9.3:   cmdLeafWriteback_Click

```
Private Sub cmdLeafWriteback_Click()
    Dim cst As ADOMD.Cellset
    Dim cll As ADOMD.Cell
    Dim cllTotal As ADOMD.Cell

    On Error GoTo HandleErr

    lstResults.Clear

    Set cst = New ADOMD.Cellset
    cst.ActiveConnection = "Provider=MSOLAP.2;Data Source=localhost;" & _
     "Initial Catalog=FoodMart 2000"
    cst.Source = "SELECT " & _
     "{[Account].[Net Income].[Total Expense],[Account].
    ➡[Level 04].Members} " & _
     "ON COLUMNS, " & _
     "{[Store].[Store Name].Members} ON ROWS " & _
     "From [Budget] " & _
     "Where " & _
     "([Time].[1997].[Q4].[12], " & _
     "[Category].[All Category].[Current Year's Actuals]) "
    cst.Open

    Set cll = cst.Item(4, 14)
    Set cllTotal = cst.Item(0, 14)
    lstResults.AddItem "Before writeback:"
    lstResults.AddItem "  Store 24 Information Systems = " & cll.FormattedValue
    lstResults.AddItem "  Store 24 Total Expense = " & cllTotal.FormattedValue
    cll.Value = 20
    lstResults.AddItem "After writeback:"
    lstResults.AddItem "  Store 24 Information Systems = " & cll.FormattedValue
    lstResults.AddItem "  Store 24 Total Expense = " & cllTotal.FormattedValue

    lstResults.AddItem "Attempting writeback to total..."
    cllTotal.Value = 1000

    Set cll = Nothing
```

```
        Set cllTotal = Nothing
        cst.Close
        Set cst = Nothing

    ExitHere:
        Exit Sub

    HandleErr:
        MsgBox "Error " & err.Number & ": " & _
          err.Description, , "cmdLeafWriteback"
        Resume ExitHere
        Resume

    End Sub
```

Figure 9.8 shows the cube that this procedure works with, open in the MDX Sample Application, with the two cells that the procedure uses highlighted. Figure 9.9 shows the results of running the procedure.

FIGURE 9.8:

Data used by the Leaf Writeback example

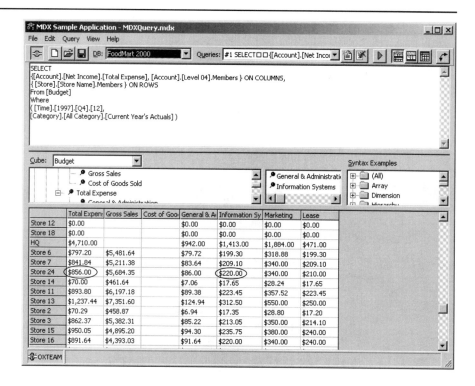

FIGURE 9.9:

Results of writing back to
leaf and non-leaf cells

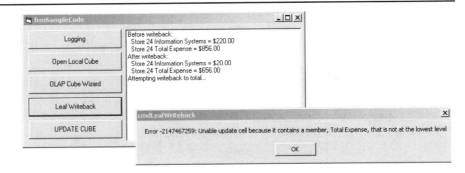

When you use writeback to alter the contents of a cell, you must refer to the cell by specifying all of its indexes in the Cellset.Item collection, rather than its ordinal number. In this example, the cell is referred to by its column and row indexes:

```
Set cll = cst.Item(4, 14)
cll.Value = 20
```

The equivalent code using the ordinal position of the cell won't work properly:

```
Set cll = cst.Item(102)
cll.Value = 20
```

Even though this refers to the exact same cell in the cellset as the previous code snippet, it won't work properly. Even worse, the second code snippet will not give you a runtime error. Rather, it will allow you to set the cell value, but then if you immediately retrieve the cell value, you'll get the old value rather than the new value, which is apparently discarded!

Note that the MDX statement that retrieves the cellset includes an explicit reference to every dimension in the cube:

```
SELECT
{[Account].[Net Income].[Total Expense],
[Account].[Level 04].Members } ON COLUMNS,
{ [Store].[Store Name].Members } ON ROWS
From [Budget]
Where
( [Time].[1997].[Q4].[12],
[Category].[All Category].[Current Year's Actuals] )
```

Every dimension in the cube appears as either an axis (Account, Store) or a slicer dimension (Time, Category). This is necessary to return cells that are at the lowest level of aggregation in all dimensions. If you omit any dimensions from the MDX statement, you won't get any updateable cells.

Finally, note from Figure 9.9 that attempting to update an aggregated cell raises a runtime error. In fact, the PivotTable Service does allow you to write back to non-leaf cells, but you must use an entirely different method, which we'll demonstrate in the next section.

UPDATE CUBE

The reason the PivotTable Service does not allow simply changing the value of a non-leaf cell in a cube is that this would lead to inconsistent data in the cube. When a non-leaf cell is changed, the leaf cells that contribute to the total in the non-leaf cells must be changed as well. The PivotTable Service provides the UPDATE CUBE statement to handle these changes consistently.

Listing 9.4 demonstrates the use of the UPDATE CUBE statement in the Chapter9.vbp sample project. Figure 9.10 shows the results of running this procedure.

Listing 9.4:   cmdUpdateCube_Click

```
Private Sub cmdUpdateCube_Click()

    Dim cnn As ADODB.Connection
    Dim cst As ADOMD.Cellset
    Dim cll As ADOMD.Cell
    Dim cllTotal As ADOMD.Cell
    Dim strUpdate As String

    On Error GoTo HandleErr

    lstResults.Clear

    Set cnn = New ADODB.Connection
    cnn.ConnectionString = "Provider=MSOLAP.2;Data Source=localhost;" & _
     "Initial Catalog=FoodMart 2000"
    cnn.Open
    Set cst = New ADOMD.Cellset
    Set cst.ActiveConnection = cnn
    cst.Source = "SELECT " & _
     "{[Account].[Net Income].[Total Expense],[Account].
    ➥[Level 04].Members} " & _
     "ON COLUMNS, " & _
     "{[Store].[Store Name].Members} ON ROWS " & _
     "From [Budget] " & _
     "Where " & _
```

```
        "([Time].[1997].[Q4].[12], " & _
        "[Category].[All Category].[Current Year's Actuals]) "

    cst.Open

    Set cll = cst.Item(4, 14)
    Set cllTotal = cst.Item(0, 14)
    lstResults.AddItem "Before UPDATE CUBE:"
    lstResults.AddItem "  Store 24 Information Systems = " & cll.FormattedValue
    lstResults.AddItem "  Store 24 Total Expense = " & cllTotal.FormattedValue

    cst.Close

    strUpdate = "UPDATE CUBE [Budget] " & _
      "SET " & _
      "([Total Expense],[Store 24]," & _
      "[Time].[1997].[Q4].[12],[Current Year's Actuals]) " & _
      " = 1000 USE_EQUAL_INCREMENT"

    cnn.Execute strUpdate

    cst.Open

    Set cll = cst.Item(4, 14)
    Set cllTotal = cst.Item(0, 14)
    lstResults.AddItem "After UPDATE CUBE:"
    lstResults.AddItem "  Store 24 Information Systems = " & cll.FormattedValue
    lstResults.AddItem "  Store 24 Total Expense = " & cllTotal.FormattedValue

    Set cll = Nothing
    Set cllTotal = Nothing
    cst.Close
    Set cst = Nothing

ExitHere:
    Exit Sub

HandleErr:
    MsgBox "Error " & err.Number & ": " & _
     err.Description, , "cmdUpdateCube"
    Resume ExitHere
    Resume

End Sub
```

FIGURE 9.10:

Results of updating non-leaf data with an UPDATE CUBE statement

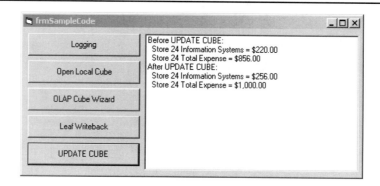

The key to this procedure, of course, is the UPDATE CUBE statement. Here's the statement that's used in this example:

```
UPDATE CUBE [Budget]
 SET
 ([Total Expense],[Store 24],
 [Time].[1997].[Q4].[12],[Current Year's Actuals])
  = 1000
 USE_EQUAL_INCREMENT
```

The UPDATE CUBE statement is designed to parallel the SQL UPDATE statement. It consists of these parts:

- The UPDATE CUBE keyword and the name of the cube to update.

- The SET keyword.

- An identifier for the cell to update. This should consist of a member of each dimension in the cube. If any dimension is omitted, then the PivotTable Service uses the default member for that dimension (usually the ALL member).

- The new value for the cell to update.

- A clause specifying how the updates should be distributed to the leaf cells that make up the cell being updated (here, USE_EQUAL_INCREMENT).

Table 9.3 lists the possible update distribution clauses for the UPDATE CUBE statement.

TABLE 9.3: Methods for Distributing Updates to Leaf Cells

Clause	Effect
USE_EQUAL_ALLOCATION	Every leaf cell in the aggregate being updated is set to the same value, the total divided by the number of leaf cells.
USE_EQUAL_INCREMENT	Every leaf cell in the aggregate is changed by the same percentage so that their total makes up the new value.
USE_WEIGHTED_ALLOCATION BY <expression>	Every leaf cell in the aggregate is multiplied by the result of the given expression.
USE_WEIGHTED_INCREMENT BY <expression>	Every leaf cell in the aggregate is changed by its proportion of the current total multiplied by the result of the given expression.

WARNING   If you choose USE_WEIGHTED_ALLOCATION or USE_WEIGHTED_INCREMENT as an update distribution clause, you are responsible to make sure that the changes made by the distribution expression add up to the new total you specify. Otherwise, you can end up with inconsistent data in the cube. You also need to beware of rounding errors when making a weighted change to a total made up of integer values.

Transaction Issues

Whenever you connect to a cube using the PivotTable Service, the PivotTable Service starts a new OLE DB transaction by implicitly calling the Connection.BeginTrans method. Changes made within this transaction are held privately for use by the current session until and unless the ADO Connection.CommitTrans method is used. If the CommitTrans method isn't explicitly called before the end of the session, then all changes made to the cube are automatically rolled back—the PivotTable Service never performs an implicit commit.

This strategy allows the PivotTable Service to support local "what-if" analyses via temporary writeback even in circumstances where actual writeback can never happen:

- When a cube is not write-enabled

- When a cube is local (local cubes cannot be write-enabled)

- When a cube is read-only

To see PivotTable Service transactions in action, you can run the leaf writeback example that we discussed earlier in the chapter twice in succession. You'll find that the changes from the first run vanish, because the transaction is never committed. In fact, this transaction can't be committed, because the Budget cube is not enabled for writeback.

Redistributing the PivotTable Service

Your SQL Server license includes the right to redistribute the files making up the PivotTable Service. This allows you to develop applications that use this service for creating and analyzing data cubes and to make them available, with full functionality, to your customers.

NOTE   This does not allow you to redistribute Analysis Services itself. Applications you redistribute with the PivotTable Service will work exclusively with local cubes unless the user has their own licensed copy of Analysis Services.

Your SQL Server CD-ROM contains two files designed for redistributing the PivotTable Service. These files are in the MSOLAP\INSTALL\PTS folder:

- Ptslite.exe installs the core PivotTable Service files.
- Ptsfull.exe installs the core PivotTable Service files, plus the Microsoft Data Access Components (MDAC) files.

TIP   You should use Ptslite.exe plus the latest MDAC setup from www.microsoft.com/data, because the MDAC files have been updated since the SQL Server CD-ROMs were manufactured.

Either Ptslite.exe or Ptsfull.exe may be executed from the Windows user interface or from a command line. If you execute one of these files from a command line, you can supply any of these optional parameters:

-r   To generate a response file containing a record of the choices made during an installation.

-f1<response file>   To use a previously generated response file.

-s   To perform an unattended installation. (This is generally only useful if you already have a response file. In this case, you can either use the -f1 parameter to specify a response file, or place the response file in the same directory as setup.exe.)

-f2<logfile>   To generate a log of the installation in a directory that you specify instead of the default systemroot directory.

-z   To work around a bug that otherwise causes setup to fail on a computer with more than 256MB of memory.

Conclusion

In this chapter we've covered some of the details of programming the PivotTable Service. The PivotTable Service functions as both an interface to Analysis Services and as an OLAP data provider in its own right. You learned how to create and use local cubes without needing Analysis Services, and how to programmatically use writeback in local or remote cubes.

In the next chapter, we'll introduce Decision Support Objects (DSO). DSO provides a way to manage all the objects that appear in the Analysis Manager interface, allowing you to programmatically perform tasks that are difficult or impossible with the libraries that we've already covered.

Managing an Analysis Services Environment Using DSO

- The DSO Architecture

- Interfaces and Collections in DSO

- Building a Cube Using DSO

- Aggregations and Processing

- The Call Center Cube

In Chapters 7, "Building Analysis Services Applications with ADO/MD Part I: Cube Schema Objects," and 8, "Building OLAP Services Applications with ADO/MD Part II: Query Retrieval Objects," we discussed how OLAP cubes could be queried and manipulated using ADO/MD. ADO/MD is not the only object model delivered with Analysis Services, however. You can also use the Decision Support Objects (DSO) library to perform any action that you could perform through the Analysis Manager interface.

You're probably already familiar with SQL-DMO (Distributed Management Objects), a COM-based object library for the core SQL Server engine that provides the ability to manage any aspect of the SQL Server environment and database structure. In fact, the SQL Server Enterprise Manager administrative console itself uses SQL-DMO to interact with the database engine. In the same way, DSO provides the management capabilities of Analysis Services for OLAP database and data mining models (and, in fact, Analysis Manager uses DSO to do its work). Here are some of the things you can do programmatically through DSO:

- Query the state of an Analysis Services server, obtaining information as to its name, version and edition.

- Start and stop the MSSQLServerOLAPService service within Windows NT or 2000.

- Create, modify, and delete databases, cubes, aggregations, and data mining models.

- Design and populate shared, private, and virtual dimensions, levels, measures, and commands.

- Design and process aggregations and storage options for the database.

- Manage security at a cell-level basis using role-based permission settings.

- Process full and incremental data updates.

But why use DSO? Why not simply create cubes, dimensions, and so on through the Analysis Manager user interface? Here are a few reasons for taking this approach:

- By using DSO, you can quickly write a small application that offers a limited subset of the functionality in Analysis Manager. This can be useful when you wish to offer analysis capabilities along with a shrink-wrapped or dedicated application you have written, or when you want to reduce the complexity of the management tool for a less technical user.

- DSO can be viewed as a scripting language for Analysis Manager, allowing you to codify a series of tasks for repeated execution at a later stage. For instance, you may wish to use DSO for an automated process to create and build cubes, which can then be scheduled via the Windows 2000 Scheduled Tasks facility.

- A DSO program can provide good documentation on the structure of an OLAP database; it can be used as a means of ensuring that the entire design is understood and no properties are hidden that could impact on the operations of the resultant cube.

This chapter explains how to use DSO from Visual Basic, using some sample applications that provide for remote administration of a database without requiring the Analysis Manager. You can also find information on using DSO for data mining purposes in Chapter 11, "Building Data Mining Solutions with Analysis Services."

The DSO Architecture

Let's start by taking a quick look at the DSO architecture. One easy way to figure out the main objects and methods within a library is to use the Visual Basic Object Browser. Here's how to view the objects and methods in the DSO library from within a Visual Basic project:

1. Choose the Project ➤ References menu item to bring up the References dialog box.

2. Scroll down the list of available references until you find Microsoft Decision Support Objects, and check the box next to this reference. This library will only be present if you have installed Analysis Services on your development machine.

3. Click OK to close the dialog box and set the reference in your project.

4. To access the Object Browser from Visual Basic, choose View ➤ Object Browser, or press the F2 shortcut key.

The Object Browser will show you all of the objects in the DSO library. Figure 10.1 shows the most important objects within DSO and the relationships between them.

NOTE   For the complete DSO object model, refer to Appendix C, "DSO Object Model."

In many ways, the DSO object model doesn't look too different from the ADO/MD object model we've seen in previous chapters. There are several key differences, however:

- ADO/MD is primarily designed for passing MDX queries through to a server and retrieving a response or for exploring the structure of a cube, whereas DSO interacts directly with the server.

- ADO/MD and MDX together are written to support the OLE DB for OLAP specification; therefore, strictly speaking, they are non-proprietary, as they can be used with other back-end database servers that support OLE DB for OLAP. In contrast, DSO is a proprietary object model that is designed to work exclusively with Analysis Services.

- The DSO object model matches the internal workings of the Analysis Server very closely: the hierarchy of DSO should look very familiar to anyone who has spent any time within the Analysis Manager console. In contrast, ADO/MD is more generic and matches a more general concept of OLAP structures.

FIGURE 10.1:

Basic DSO object model

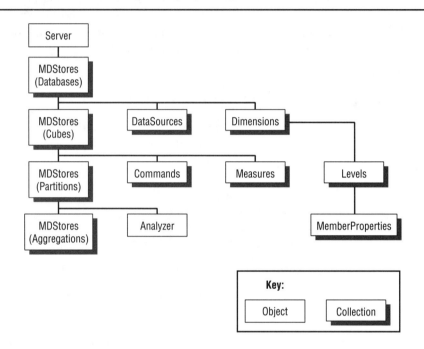

There's a certain amount of functionality overlap between the two object models, yet they don't compete. In the same way that ADO and SQL-DMO coexist, so also are ADO/MD and DSO both likely to continue into future incarnations of Analysis Services.

In choosing the right object model, consider whether your application requires primarily administrative or user-focused access. If your code needs to query a database, use ADO/MD in conjunction with MDX. If it needs to process cubes, automate the creation of new cubes, or manage the service as a whole, use DSO. Occasionally, you may need to consider using both object models together.

WARNING   Unlike the client components described earlier in this book (such as the PivotTable Service), DSO cannot be installed on Windows 95, 98, or Millennium Edition, even if the OLAP database runs on a remote computer. You therefore need to be running either Windows NT or 2000 to successfully execute the demonstration programs in this chapter.

Interfaces and Collections in DSO

If you spend any amount of time with the documentation for DSO, you'll find many references to interfaces. DSO implements six interfaces in Analysis Services:

- Command
- Dimension
- Level
- MDStore
- Measure
- Role

Interfaces provide a way for different objects to expose similar functionality. For example, consider the Dimension interface. Some dimensions belong to a database as a whole (shared dimensions), while other dimensions belong to an individual cube (private dimensions). The DSO designers could have chosen to create two entirely separate objects for these two types of dimensions, but then the two objects would have had nearly identical properties. Instead, they've created two different objects that share a single interface, the Dimension interface.

If you're working in Visual Basic code, you can for the most part safely ignore the difference between an object and an interface. An object variable within Visual Basic can be declared as type DSO.Dimension and used to represent any Analysis Services object that exposes the Dimension interface. If you need to know precisely which object you're dealing with through a particular Dimension object, you can check the Dimension's ClassType property, which returns a read-only constant indicating the underlying object.

In this section, we'll discuss the most important of the DSO interfaces, the MDStore interface. We'll also look at the somewhat idiosyncratic way in which DSO implements collections. Equipped with this information, we'll be ready to start demonstrating some DSO code.

The MDStore Interface

Many of the most important objects within DSO implement a single interface called MDStore. MDStore is short for Multidimensional Store and represents any object that contains multidimensional data. This includes databases, cubes, partitions, and aggregations. The ClassType property of an MDStore object will return a constant indicating which of these underlying objects is being queried via this particular instance:

- clsDatabase
- clsCube
- clsPartition
- clsAggregation

As a result, you usually find that these objects are passed around and accessed using the interface MDStore, rather than the class name itself.

Although you'll find objects such as Database, Cube, Partition, and Aggregation in the DSO library, you should not use these objects in your code. If you do, you'll find that the functionality present on the MDStore interface is not available. That is, you should declare these objects using the MDStore interface rather than using the specific object types.

Using Collections in DSO

DSO uses the concept of a Collection as a means of storing groups of objects, but in contrast to ADO/MD, DSO does not use standard Visual Basic collections, instead implementing a custom set of properties and methods into an object called an *OlapCollection*. Fortunately, an OlapCollection object is fairly similar to a Visual Basic Collection. Tables 10.1 and 10.2 list the methods and properties exposed by an OlapCollection object.

TABLE 10.1: OlapCollection Methods

Name	Description
Public Sub Add (Item As Object, Optional sKey As String, Optional Before As Variant)	Adds an instantiated object to the collection. The sKey parameter defaults to the Item's Name property, and if you supply a value, it must equal the value of the Item's Name property. If the Before parameter is specified, adds the item to the collection at the position specified, moving all following items along by one position.
Public Function AddNew (Name As String, Optional SubClassType As SubClassTypes = sbclsRegular) As Object	Creates a new object and adds it to the collection. The Name parameter specifies the name of the item; the optional SubClassType parameter can be used to specify a particular subclass for the object. For instance, you can specify that a cube is a linked cube by specifying the subclass to be sbclsLinked from the SubClassTypes enum. By default, the subclass is set to sbclsRegular. The function returns the created object.
Public Function Find (vKey As Variant) As Boolean	Attempts to find an object with name (or index) matching vKey in the current collection. You can think of the vKey parameter as either the key in the OLAPCollection or the Name of the object to find, because DSO requires the key to match the name. The function returns a Boolean value indicating the success or otherwise of the operation. Note that it does not return the item found.
Public Function Item (vntIndexKey As Variant) As Variant	Identifies and returns an object from within the current collection matching the name (or index) specified in vntIndexKey. The function returns the identified object.
Public Sub Remove (vntIndexKey As Variant)	Identifies and deletes an item, if it exists, matching the name or index specified in vntIndexKey.

TIP In addition to the visible methods in Table 10.1, the OLAPCollection object also exposes the hidden NewEnum method, so you can iterate through the objects in an OLAPCollection with the For Each syntax.

TABLE 10.2: OlapCollection Properties

Name	Description
Public Property ClassType As Integer	Returns an integer value from the ClassTypes enum. This is the class type of the collection itself, not of the contained objects.
Public Property ContainedClassType As ClassTypes	Returns a value from the ClassTypes enumeration indicating the type of objects held within the collection.
Public Property Count As Long	Counts the number of items within the collection. Note that all collections in DSO are 1-based, so items are numbered from 1 to Count.

NOTE Some of the method parameter names and types are a bit confusing here: why should some Variants be prefixed with *v* and others with *vnt*, whilst other parameters have no prefix at all? However, this makes little difference to the usage of this object.

Probably the most striking difference between an OlapCollection object and a standard Visual Basic collection is that the former is more strongly typed. A standard collection can contain any kind of object, whereas an OlapCollection can only contain objects of a single type. Furthermore, the AddNew method automatically creates an object of the relevant type based on the type of collection that will contain it.

Obtaining Database Information Using DSO

Armed with this basic knowledge of DSO, we're ready to start using it to interact with Analysis Services. Listing 10.1 shows a brief demonstration of DSO, providing some basic information about the local server and the databases and cubes that it is storing. You'll find this code, and the rest of the sample code for this chapter, in the Chapter10.vbp project on the companion CD-ROM.

Listing 10.1:   cmdBasicInformation_Click

```
Private Sub cmdBasicInformation_Click()
    Dim dsoServer As New DSO.Server
    Dim dsoDb As DSO.MDStore
    Dim dsoCube As DSO.MDStore
```

```
    On Error GoTo HandleErr

    dsoServer.Connect "localhost"

    lstInfo.AddItem "Server " & dsoServer.Name
    lstInfo.AddItem vbTab & "Version " & dsoServer.Version
    If dsoServer.Edition = olapEditionUnlimited Then
        lstInfo.AddItem vbTab & "Enterprise Edition"
    ElseIf dsoServer.Edition = olapEditionNoPartitions Then
        lstInfo.AddItem vbTab & "Standard Edition"
    Else
        lstInfo.AddItem vbTab & "(Unknown Edition)"
    End If

    ' Iterate through the MDStores collection of the Server
    ' object, which contains Databases
    For Each dsoDb In dsoServer.MDStores
        lstInfo.AddItem "Database: " & dsoDb.Name & " (" & _
         dsoDb.Description & ")"
        ' Iterate through the MDStores collection of the Database
        ' object, which contains Cubes
        For Each dsoCube In dsoDb.MDStores
            lstInfo.AddItem vbTab & "Cube: " & dsoCube.Name & " (" & _
             dsoCube.Description & ")"
        Next dsoCube
    Next dsoDb

    dsoServer.CloseServer
    Set dsoServer = Nothing

ExitHere:
    Exit Sub

HandleErr:
    MsgBox "Error " & Err.Number & ": " & _
     Err.Description, , "cmdBasicInformation"
    Resume ExitHere
    Resume

End Sub
```

The nested For Each...Next loops in Listing 10.1 demonstrate the use of OlapCollection objects. Note that both Databases and Cubes are stored in collections referenced from the MDStores property of their parent objects. Figure 10.2 shows the results of running this procedure.

FIGURE 10.2:

Retrieving information
with DSO

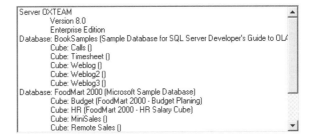

```
Server OXTEAM                                                                    ▲
        Version 8.0
        Enterprise Edition
Database: BookSamples (Sample Database for SQL Server Developer's Guide to OLA
        Cube: Calls ()
        Cube: Timesheet ()
        Cube: Weblog ()
        Cube: Weblog2 ()
        Cube: Weblog3 ()
Database: FoodMart 2000 (Microsoft Sample Database)
        Cube: Budget (FoodMart 2000 - Budget Planing)
        Cube: HR (FoodMart 2000 - HR Salary Cube)
        Cube: MiniSales ()
        Cube: Remote Sales ()                                                    ▼
```

It should be noted that a similar routine for viewing the structure of an OLAP database could be written in ADO/MD, although some information, such as the server version, is not available through ADO/MD. The big difference here is that as a result of using DSO, it is possible to make changes to the structure: unlike the ADO/MD CubeDef object, the DSO MDStore object is read/write.

Building a Cube Using DSO

In this section, we'll walk through the steps necessary to create a cube within a database using the DSO object model. The examples presented here can be adapted easily for your own cubes and databases or used with increased parameterization as a more generic toolset. There are six basic steps to creating a cube with DSO:

1. Create a database.

2. Add a cube to a database.

3. Set new data sources.

4. Build dimensions and levels.

5. Add measures to the cube.

6. Finalize the cube properties.

Of course, you won't always need all of these steps. For example, you can skip the first step if you're creating a new cube in an existing Analysis Services database.

NOTE   We'll go through the entire process in this section with short code snippets. Later in the chapter, and in the sample project, you'll find an example that builds a cube from start to finish.

Creating a Database

To do anything within DSO, it is first necessary to create and initialize the DSO.Server object and use this to connect to an existing Analysis Services instance. Note that, unlike ADO/MD, DSO cannot be used to connect to a local (offline) cube. Remember that DSO is purely a server-based API: it is not installed with the client PivotTable Service and does not execute under Windows 95, 98, or Me. When connecting to a server, it is necessary to specify the server's hostname directly: neither a URL nor an IP address is suitable. You can, however, use the special name localhost if the server is running on the same computer as the DSO code.

You can make a DSO connection to an Analysis Services server by instantiating the DSO.Server object and calling its Connect method. The collections within the Server object can then be accessed. To build a new cube, we'll work almost exclusively with the MDStores collection at various levels within the DSO object model.

Earlier we mentioned that databases, cubes, partitions, and aggregations all implement the MDStore interface. Taking that one step further, several objects (server, database, cube, and partition) contain an MDStores collection that holds a number of MDStore-implementing objects. Figure 10.3 shows how these various elements fit together within the DSO object model.

FIGURE 10.3:

Usage of MDStore within DSO object model

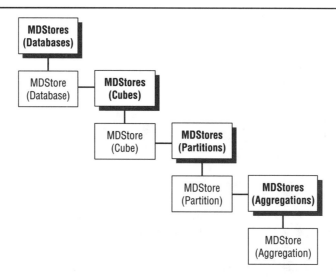

To create a new database, you must call the AddNew method on the MDStores collection of the Server object. The syntax looks like this (where dsoServer is a reference to the connected DSO.Server object):

```
dsoServer.MDStores.AddNew "Expenses"
```

This statement creates a new database called Expenses within the OLAP environment. You can then go ahead and make other changes to the properties of the database (for example, setting the default storage mode or a description for the database) in the following way:

```
dsoServer.MDStores("Expenses").Description = "Corporate Expenses Database"
dsoServer.MDStores("Expenses").OlapMode = olapmodeMolapIndex
dsoServer.MDStores("Expenses").Update
```

WARNING Note that the Update method shown above *must* be used in order to persist changes made to the properties of a database (or any other object that implements the MDStore interface) into the metadata repository.

Perhaps a more efficient way to write the above statements takes advantage of the fact that the AddNew method returns the newly created object. Thus the following is also valid:

```
Dim dsoDb As DSO.MDStore
Set dsoDb = dsoServer.MDStores.AddNew("Expenses")
dsoDb.Description = "Corporate Expenses Database"
dsoDb.OlapMode = olapmodeMolapIndex
dsoDb.Update
```

The above is more efficient since it reduces the need for Analysis Services to repeatedly search through the metadata repository for an object with the specified key.

As an example of all the above put together, Listing 10.2 shows the code to create an Analysis Services database based on the options specified by the user.

Listing 10.2:   cmdCreateDatabase_Click

```
Private Sub cmdCreateDatabase_Click()
    Dim dsoServer As DSO.Server
    Dim dsoDb As DSO.MDStore

    On Error GoTo HandleErr

    'Connect to server
    Set dsoServer = New DSO.Server
    dsoServer.Connect txtServer.Text

    'Now add the new database with the specified options
    Set dsoDb = dsoServer.MDStores.AddNew(txtDbName.Text)
    dsoDb.Description = txtDbDescription.Text
```

```
    If optDbStorage(0).Value = True Then
        dsoDb.OlapMode = olapmodeMolapIndex
    ElseIf optDbStorage(1).Value = True Then
        dsoDb.OlapMode = olapmodeHybridIndex
    Else
        dsoDb.OlapMode = olapmodeRolap
    End If
    dsoDb.Update

    MsgBox "Database " & txtDbName & " successfully created."

ExitHere:
    Exit Sub

HandleErr:
    Select Case Err.Number
        Case -2147221424
            MsgBox "A connection to the Analysis server could " & _
                "not be established. Please try again later. " & _
                "The database " & txtDbName & " could not be created.", _
                , , "cmdCreateDatabase"
        Case Else
            MsgBox "Error " & Err.Number & ": " & _
                Err.Description, , "cmdCreateDatabase"
    End Select
    Resume ExitHere
    Resume
End Sub
```

Service Management

You can use DSO as a way to start or stop the Analysis Services engine. The Server object contains a ServiceState property that you can use to start, stop, or pause the MSSQLServerOLAPService service. Unusually for the DSO service, the values you can use are not provided as an enumeration. If you want to use this property, you should create your own enumeration to hold the possible values:

```
Public Enum ServiceStates
    serviceStopped = 1
    serviceStartPending = 2
    serviceStopPending = 3
    serviceRunning = 4
    serviceContinuePending = 5
    servicePausePending = 6
    servicePaused = 7
End Enum
```

Continued on next page

To start, stop, or pause the service, set the ServiceState property to `serviceRunning`, `serviceStopped`, or `servicePaused`, respectively, as in the following:

```
dsoServer.ServiceState = serviceRunning    'start the service
```

You can also read the value of this property, which will give you the current status of the service. If it is starting, pausing, or stopping, you may be returned one of the additional constants `serviceStartPending`, `serviceStopPending`, `serviceContinuePending`, or `servicePausePending`. Setting the state to one of these values will cause an error.

Adding a Cube to a Database

Having created a database, creating a cube is extremely easy. Just as a database is created using the AddNew method on a Server.MDStores collection, a cube is created using the AddNew method on a Database.MDStores collection. Here's an example (assuming that dsoDb is a valid MDStore object pointing to a database):

```
Dim dsoCube As DSO.MDStore
Set dsoCube = dsoDb.MDStores.AddNew("EmployeeExpenses")
```

The above statement creates a new cube called "EmployeeExpenses" within the existing database.

One question that may be crossing your mind is, "How does DSO know what type of object to create when an AddNew method is called?" After all, we've created a database and a cube using exactly the same syntax in the above two sections.

The answer to this lies in the use of the ClassType and ContainedClassType properties. Every object in DSO has a ClassType property, which returns a value from the ClassTypes enumeration that identifies the object. As far as the MDStores collection is concerned, a strict parent-child hierarchy exists between the various objects that implement the MDStore interface, and this hierarchy is maintained by the AddNew method. The hierarchy is shown in Table 10.3.

TABLE 10.3: MDStores Parent-Child Hierarchy

obj.ClassType	obj.MDStores.ContainedClassType
clsServer	clsDatabase
clsDatabase	clsCube
clsCube	clsPartition
clsPartition	clsAggregation

So whenever you call AddNew on a DSO MDStores collection, the appropriate object type is created based on the ContainedClassType for the collection. Note that a DSO collection is special in this regard: you *cannot* store objects with different ClassTypes in the same collection. To do so might invite impossible combinations within the structure of the database (e.g., a database object containing aggregations rather than cubes). Arguably, it might have made more sense if the DSO object model had done away with the MDStores interface altogether and accepted some duplication for the sake of simplicity, but we have to deal with things the way they are.

Setting a Data Source for a Database

The next stage in the creation of a cube is to identify one or more data sources that contain the data for the cube. As you may remember from working with Analysis Manager, data sources are created at the database level; when you create a new cube, you specify one (and only one) data source that you will use for that cube.

You can create new data sources using another collection within the Database object with the name DataSources (intuitively enough). Like all collections in DSO, it is not a standard Visual Basic collection but is instead of type OlapCollection (see earlier in this chapter for further details). To add a new data source, you simply call the AddNew method of the DataSources collection, adding the relevant properties, including the connection string, as in the following code snippet:

```
Dim dsoServer AsDSO.Server
Dim dsoDb As DSO.MDStore
Dim dsoDataSrc As DSO.DataSource

Set dsoServer = New DSO.Server
dsoServer.Connect "localhost"
Set dsoDb = dsoServer.MDStores.Item("Expenses")

Set dsoDataSrc = dsoDb.DataSources.AddNew("EmployeeData")
dsoDataSrc.ConnectionString = "Provider=SQLOLEDB.1;" & _
    "Data Source=(local);Initial Catalog=Employees;" & _
    "Integrated Security=SSPI"
dsoDataSrc.Update
```

If you use the Visual Basic Object Browser against the DSO library to explore the DataSource class, you may notice that the class contains an IsValid property. Don't be fooled into thinking that this property checks that the data source connection string given is valid; instead, this property simply tests that the Name, ConnectionString, and Parent properties contain some (any) value, without checking to see that those strings actually point to a reachable server.

To test that a data source connection string is valid, you can use the IsConnected method. This method returns a Boolean indicating whether the data source can be reached and takes as a parameter an optional string that will return an error message if the data source is unreachable.

```
Dim sErr As String
If dsoDataSrc.IsConnected(sErr) Then
    'Connection successful
    MsgBox "Test connection for data source " & dsoDataSrc.Name & " succeeded."
Else
    'Connection failed for some reason
    MsgBox "Test connection for data source " & dsoDataSrc.Name & " failed. " &
    ➥vbCrLf & "Error: " & sErr
End If
```

One interesting point to note is that while you might expect DSO to alleviate some of the idiosyncrasies of the Analysis Manager user interface, this is often not the case. While this is reasonable because Analysis Manager itself uses DSO, it can be perplexing. For instance, once a data source has been created within Analysis Manager, you can't rename it; this restriction also applies within DSO. An attempt to make a change such as the following,

```
dsoDataSrc.Name = "NewName"
dsoDataSrc.Update
```

fails with error –2147221498, "Cannot rename object." The lesson here is to ensure that you enable error handling within your code and test in a range of situations.

Having created one or more data sources within your database (and tested the connections if necessary), the next stage is to associate a particular data source with the cube you are creating. Once again, this is almost identical to the process of creating the data source in the first place. All that needs to be done is for the cube's DataSources collection to be populated, as in the following example:

```
dsoCube.DataSources.AddNew dsoDb.DataSources("EmployeeData").Name
```

or, more simply,

```
dsoCube.DataSources.AddNew "EmployeeData"
```

Note that this is not the place to create new data sources: if you attempt to add a data source with a name that does not exist in the current database, Analysis Services will throw an error, as in the following:

```
dsoCube.DataSources.AddNew "NewEmployeeData"    'does not work
```

Unlike the original data source definition, we don't need to store the return value for this AddNew method call: we already have the data source definition available to us in the database itself.

Specifying the Fact Table

This is a good time to set some other properties on the cube, including the location of the fact table within the data source. The *Source Table* property of the MDStore interface allows us to set this, as in the following:

```
dsoCube.SourceTable = """sales_fact"""
```

NOTE   Don't forget that in a Visual Basic string, you can include the quote character by placing two together. Thus the above property is set to a string 12 characters long, beginning and terminating with a double-quote character (").

Quoting Issues with Query Processors

Whenever you specify a table or field, you should take care to ensure that the value is quoted. This avoids any issues with special characters (such as spaces) or reserved words confusing the query processor of the source database.

Different databases use different characters to delimit identifiers. For example, SQL Server supports the use of double quotation marks or square brackets; other databases use single quotation marks.

If you want to be absolutely safe, you can determine the correct way of quoting for a given data source using the *OpenQuoteChar* and *CloseQuoteChar* properties exposed by the Data-Source object. Here's an example of using this to write a database-agnostic property:

```
Dim sOQ As String, sCQ As String

sOQ = dsoDataSrc("EmployeeData").OpenQuoteChar
sCQ = dsoDataSrc("EmployeeData").CloseQuoteChar

dsoCube.SourceTable = sOQ & "sales_fact" & sCQ
```

Although this is slightly longer-winded the first time you access a data source, the code will work across any source database platform. As Analysis Services gradually expands the number of supported databases, this will become more of an issue.

To make this chapter easier to read, we've cheated and made the reasonable presumption that the double-quote character is valid. If it gives you errors against a particular database platform when you implement examples based on the given code, simply use the above properties to establish the correct quote characters and use these instead.

To maximize the quality of the designed aggregations generated by the Partition Analyzer (see the section "Aggregations and Processing" later in this chapter), we should also specify a value for the *EstimatedRows* property of the cube, which tells Analysis Services how many rows we expect in the fact table.

If the table is already fully populated with a sample set of data, we can use a SQL statement such as the following to retrieve this information:

```
SELECT COUNT(*) FROM sales_fact
```

We could do this dynamically using ADO to establish a runtime value for this figure if it were likely to change. Having established this, we can simply set the EstimatedRows property in the following way:

```
dsoCube.EstimatedRows = 215500
```

Last, we should ensure that any changes to the cube's properties are updated back to the metadata store with the following statement:

```
dsoCube.Update
```

Creating Dimensions

Now comes the fun bit! Having created a database together with an associated cube and data sources, we can now proceed to build up the structure of the cube itself. This is slightly more complicated than previous steps, since we have to map the level-based structure to the original source database, but the DSO object model is fairly simple here.

Starting with the dimensions, it will come as no surprise to discover that a collection called Dimensions exists within the Database object. You can therefore create a new dimension using the following commands:

```
Dim dsoDim As DSO.Dimension
Set dsoDim = dsoDB.Dimensions.AddNew("Customer")
```

The above command creates a new Dimension object and sets it to the result of the AddNew method, producing a regular dimension with the name Customer. From here, we can set the other properties of the dimension (for example, allowing dimension writeback).

In the Dimension Wizard within Analysis Manager, five different types of dimension are offered: star, snowflake, parent-child, virtual, and mining model. For the moment, we'll describe the creation of a dimension (and the levels) using star and snowflake schema types. Afterward, we'll talk about creating other types of dimensions.

TIP   Keep the dialogs in Analysis Manager's Dimension Wizard in mind when you think about the properties that need to be completed within DSO: they match up well.

For a star schema, we need to specify just one property, called FromClause. This is used to specify the table in which the level information resides (i.e., the dimension table), as in the following example:

```
dsoDim.FromClause = "customer"
```

Things are slightly more complex in a snowflake schema. Here we will need to specify more than one table in the FromClause and also specify an additional property, JoinClause, which describes how the two tables are related. The following example demonstrates this:

```
dsoDim.FromClause = """customer", "customer_sector"""
dsoDim.JoinClause = _
  "(""customer"".""custsect_id""=""customer_sector"".""custsect_id"")"
```

Don't forget that wherever you put a single quotation mark in the statement, you must put two to ensure that Visual Basic doesn't terminate the string prematurely, just as in the above example.

Properties Exposed by the Dimension Interface

Table 10.4 shows the major properties that you might consider setting for a dimension at the database level. These are all properties implemented by the Dimension interface.

TABLE 10.4: Dimension Object Properties

Name	Description
AllowSiblingsWithSameName	Boolean value, indicating whether more than one member can have both the same name and the same parent member (useful where the member name is a person's name). This setting applies across the dimension.
AreMemberKeysUnique	Specifies if member keys are unique across the dimension. If true, specifying this will result in improved efficiency in the generation of unique names.
AreMemberNamesUnique	Specifies if member names are unique across the entire dimension.
DefaultMember	MDX expression evaluating to a single member within the dimension. If not specified, defaults to the first member at the top level (usually the All member unless otherwise specified).
DependsOnDimension	Specifies the name of another dimension on which a dependency exists (i.e., where two dimensions are based ultimately on the same source table). For virtual dimensions, contains the name of the source dimension.
Description	Provides a short description of the dimension.
DimensionType	Specifies (from the DimensionTypes enumeration) what kind of information is held within the dimension (e.g., geographic, organizational, employees).
FromClause	Specifies the table or tables from which the source data is drawn (a comma-separated list).
JoinClause	For a dimension stored in a snowflake schema, specifies how the tables are linked, by equating the primary and foreign keys.

Continued on next page

TABLE 10.4 CONTINUED: Dimension Object Properties

Name	Description
SourceTableFilter	Provides a WHERE clause for the dimension table, so that you can select only certain rows from the source table to create the dimension. For example, you might use this for indicating test values on the source table by adding a field to the structure and querying on this.
StorageMode	Specifies how dimension contents are to be stored. If set to storeasMOLAP, the dimension is stored in a MOLAP structure; if set to storeasROLAP, the dimension is stored in a ROLAP structure. The latter option is useful for creating a database that keeps all but the largest dimensions in a multidimensional structure, which promotes maximum scalability.

Adding Levels to Dimensions

The next step after creating the dimension is to add the levels for the dimension. This is again simply a matter of working with the Levels collection object within the current dimension object. So you can simply write the following (presuming the dimension object dsoDim already exists):

```
Dim dsoLev As DSO.Level
Set dsoLev = dsoDim.Levels.AddNew("Class")
dsoLev.Description = "Overall category for a product"
dsoLev.MemberKeyColumn = """Products"".""ProductClass"""
dsoDim.Update
```

When creating a level, it is essential that the property MemberKeyColumn be specified. This property should contain a SQL expression that dictates the specific column from which the level's data (i.e., the key) is retrieved. Once again, don't forget to quote the table and field names.

In addition to specifying the member key column, it is often necessary to specify the member *name* column. The reason behind this is that on many occasions, the machine key will not be a "friendly" name that the user can easily recognize. For example, an employee may be referenced by a unique employee ID, yet this gives few clues to a human browser as to the actual identity of that individual.

The member name can easily be specified, therefore, by using the MemberNameColumn property. In the same way as for MemberKeyColumn, this property can contain the name of a column within a table, or alternatively a SQL expression that returns a string value. Thus the following code might be used to create the lowest level for an employee dimension:

```
Dim dsoLev As DSO.Level
Set dsoLev = dsoDim.Levels.AddNew("Employee Name")
```

```
dsoLev.Description = "Individual employee name"
dsoLev.MemberKeyColumn = """"employees"".""emp_id"""
dsoLev.MemberNameColumn = """"employees"".""emp_lname"" + ', '
➡ + ""employees"".""emp_fname"""
dsoDim.Update
```

Another property that is worth including is the *EstimatedSize* property. This property should contain a rough approximation of the number of members that will exist at the chosen level, as in the following snippet:

```
dsoLev.EstimatedSize = 50000
```

It's not essential to specify this, but it will enhance the performance of the final cube if you do. When you tell Analysis Services to design the storage and perform the aggregation analysis, the partition analyzer uses the estimated sizes for each level to determine the potential performance benefit of precalculating a particular aggregation. Without this information, Analysis Services is forced to treat different aggregations based on a default algorithm, which may or may not match the way you will actually load the database.

NOTE One minor idiosyncrasy to note in the examples given here is that changes to a level don't take effect until the *parent dimension* is updated with the Update method. There is no corresponding Update method for level objects, so both dimensions and levels are really treated as one whole by DSO.

For a basic star or snowflake schema dimension in a MOLAP or HOLAP store, that's all you need to do to define the dimensions and levels. If the aggregations are going to be stored in a relational database (in other words, if the dimension or cube is a ROLAP store), you also need to specify two other properties, *ColumnType* and *ColumnSize*. These are used by Analysis Services to create a table structure that can hold the aggregations on the remote database. The ColumnType property is used to provide the data type (integer, Boolean, date, etc.) and should be a value from the ADODB.DataTypesEnum enumeration. The ColumnSize property should be the storage requirements in bytes for that field. If these properties are not specified, Analysis Services will attempt to identify the appropriate data types and field lengths for you based on the existing data, but it will not take account of future database changes (for example, the existing database columns may increase in size). So if you want to be safe, you should always set these properties.

Properties Exposed by the Level Interface

Table 10.5 summarizes the main properties you might consider setting for the Level object. For further details on other properties available, check the documentation in SQL Server Books Online.

TABLE 10.5: Level Object Properties

Name	Description
AreMemberKeysUnique	Specifies if member keys are unique across the level. If true, specifying this will result in improved efficiency in the generation of unique names.
ColumnSize	Indicates the size of the column in bytes. Used in a ROLAP dimension to create an aggregation table that is used for storing member values.
ColumnType	Indicates the type of the column; used in a ROLAP dimension to indicate the data type used for storing the column within the aggregations. This property should contain an enumerated value derived from ADODB.DataTypeEnum.
CustomRollupColumn	Contains the name of a column in the source database that contains instructions for processing custom rollups.
CustomRollupExpression	Contains an MDX expression that is used to roll up members within a level.
Description	Contains a string that describes the level.
EstimatedSize	Provides a rough approximation of the number of members within the current level.
Grouping	Set to a value from the GroupingValues enumeration to describe how members within very large levels (i.e., a level with >64,000 members) should be grouped. If set to groupingAutomatic, such levels will be split into hidden subgroups, each containing no more than 64,000 members. If set to groupingNone, no such changes will be made and the level will be limited to a maximum of 64,000 members.
HideMemberIf	Specifies the circumstances under which a level will be hidden. This property is used to provide support for ragged hierarchies, where one or more levels may be missing for certain members. The classic example of this is for geographic dimensions, where some countries may not have zip/postal code information or the concept of states/provinces. This property is set to a value from the HideIfValues enumeration.
IsVisible	Used to hide a level from user access. The level will be present within the database but will not be exposed to applications that are OLE DB for OLAP clients (including those that use ADO/MD). At least one level in a dimension must be visible.
LevelType	Set to a value from the LevelTypes enumeration to provide semantic information on the contents of this level (for example, levCustomerGroup, levGeoCountry, etc.). Should be used in combination with the DimensionType property of the parent dimension. The values set in these properties can be used by a client application to add extra facilities based on the type of information (for example, members of type levGeo-PostalCode could be used to link into an external mapping application).
MemberKeyColumn	Contains the column from which the member's key value is taken within the source database.
MemberNameColumn	Contains the column from which the member's name value is taken within the source database.
Ordering	Specifies how the members should be ordered within the level (set to a value from the OrderTypes enumeration). If set to orderKey, members are ordered by their key column; if set to orderName, members are ordered by their display name column; if set to orderMemberProperty, members are ordered by the member property specified in Level.OrderingMemberProperty.
OrderingMemberProperty	Contains the name of a member property whose values are used to order the members within a level.
UnaryOperatorColumn	Refers to a column that contains a mathematical operator that can be used to aggregate the members of this level (by default, members are added together). Values can be +, -, *, /, or ~ (ignored). Useful for financial accounting cubes, among other things.

Ordering of Levels within a Dimension

Levels are placed in the dimension in the order they are created. The *OrdinalPosition* property for each level contains the position within the hierarchy of that level. If there is an (All) level, it has an OrdinalPosition value of 1, with other levels numbered sequentially beyond that point.

The OrdinalPosition property is read-only; this means that once a level has been inserted into a dimension with the AddNew method, its position in the hierarchy cannot be changed without creating a new dimension. For this reason, it is important to ensure that the levels are correct from the start (that is, created from the most general to the least general), rather than taking a "design and modify" approach.

Special Case Dimensions

Before leaving the subject of the creation of dimensions and levels, let's briefly look at a couple of special cases that you may come across when building cubes.

Time-Based Dimensions

A time dimension is constructed in exactly the same way as any other star schema dimension, with levels corresponding to the different ways of breaking up time (by years, months, quarters, and so on).

Usually when you build a time dimension, the field containing the relevant information is held in a column in the fact table that has a data type of *datetime*. This is the only significant difference between time-based dimensions and other dimensions: time dimensions typically store information for all the levels within the one field, whereas other dimensions usually contain a separate table with columns for each of the levels in the created dimension.

The process of building the levels within a time dimension is therefore one of extracting the relevant level-based information from this field. For instance, the Year level needs a key column that relates to the year alone. The simplest way to extract such information is to use the *DatePart* function, which returns an integer representing the selected portion of the date. The syntax for this function is as follows:

```
DatePart(part, date)
```

The *date* parameter contains the date from which you wish to extract an element, naturally. The *part* parameter specifies which part of the date you wish to return. Table 10.6 shows the possible options for this parameter.

TABLE 10.6: DatePart Parameters

Expression	Returns
yyyy, yy	Year
q, qq	Quarter
m, mm	Month
wk, ww	Week
y, dy	Day of year
dw	Day of week
d, dd	Day
h, hh	Hour
mi, n	Minute
s, ss	Second
ms	Millisecond

WARNING Remember, the SQL statements you use for the MemberNameColumn and MemberKeyColumn properties are executed by the OLE DB Provider for the relational database. So the technique shown here will only work if the provider involved supports the datepart() function!

With this knowledge in mind, you can easily construct a given time-based level from a datetime field using code similar to the following:

```
Dim dsoLev As DSO.Level
Set dsoLev = dsoDim.Levels.AddNew("Quarter")
dsoLev.Description = "Time broken down by quarter"
dsoLev.MemberKeyColumn = "DatePart('q',""sales_fact"".""date_sold"")"
dsoLev.MemberNameColumn = "'Quarter ' + " & _
    "Format$(DatePart('q',""sales_fact"".""date_sold""))"
dsoDim.Update
```

That's not quite all as far as time-based dimensions are concerned. We mentioned above the use of the *DimensionType* and *LevelType* properties to specify the content of a particular dimension or level. This is especially important for a time dimension, as Analysis Services can use this information to make a special case for certain time-based processing.

Another thing to note is that, by default, members of levels are ordered alphabetically by member name; this makes no sense for months unless you want to see them ordered as {April, August, December, February ...}. Instead, we need to manually set the *Ordering* property to *orderKey*. Since the keys should be set to numbers from 1 to 12, this will order months appropriately. So the following line should be included:

```
dsoLev.Ordering = orderKey
```

Last, keep in mind that most time-based dimensions do not contain unique members, because the same names and keys will be used for each period. For example, in a database containing three years of data, three members will have the name January. Thus it would be ambiguous to specify a member as [Time].[January]; instead, it would have to be specified as (for instance) [Time].[1999].[January]. The following two properties should therefore be set for repeating levels to warn Analysis Services of the duplication and force the use of fully qualified names:

```
dsoLev.AreMemberKeysUnique = False
dsoLev.AreMemberNamesUnique = False
```

Parent-Child Dimensions

Parent-child dimensions are identified using the *subclass* of the dimension class. This means that to create a dimension where the data is structured with a parent-child relationship, you simply specify an additional parameter to the AddNew method, as in the following example:

```
Dim dsoDim As DSO.Dimension
Set dsoDim = dsoDB.Dimensions.AddNew("Employee", sbclsParentChild)
```

This ensures that the dimension is created properly and set to contain a hierarchy that will vary in the number of levels, depending on the relationship between members set in the source data.

A parent-child dimension can contain no more than two levels. First, it may optionally include an (All) level, which contains all the members within the dimension; second, it must include a level that holds each of the members and the relationships between members within that level. This is then used by Analysis Services to create the hierarchical structure a user sees when querying a cube.

In the same way as for other dimensions, a parent-child dimension must contain a *from* clause that specifies the names of the tables from which dimensional data is drawn, and optionally a *join* clause that specifies how those tables are linked. Typically parent-child dimensions rely on only one table for their data, although member properties can often be stored in a separate table.

The main level within a parent-child dimension should have values for the *MemberKeyColumn* and *MemberNameColumn* properties set, as for any other level; it should, however, also include a value for the *ParentKeyColumn*, which specifies the column where the parent key for a given member may be found. Table 10.7 shows some additional properties beyond those given in Table 10.5 that pertain especially to levels in parent-child dimensions.

TABLE 10.7: Level Object Properties for Parent-Child Dimensions

Name	Description
LevelNamingTemplate	Specifies names for the hierarchy of levels created using a parent-child dimension. For example, an employee dimension might have levels such as Non-Executive Board, Executive Board, Senior Management, Middle Management, etc.
RootMemberIf	This property determines how the top of a parent-child dimension's hierarchy is determined. The value comes from the RootIfValues enumeration and can be set to any of the values rootifParentIsBlank (the parent key column will contain a null or empty value), rootifParentIsMissing (the parent key column will point to a non-existent key), rootifParentIsSelf (the parent key column will point to the member's own key) or rootifParentIsBlankOrSelfOrMissing (any of the above).
SkippedLevelsColumn	Provides support for a ragged hierarchy within parent-child dimensions, by specifying the name of a column in the source database table that contains the number of empty levels between the current member and its parent. If this is set to a number greater than 0, its parent key column is considered to point to an ancestor *n* levels above the current member. For example, a CEO's personal assistant is extremely unlikely to be on the board, yet all other direct descendants will list the CEO's key as their ParentKeyColumn. Specifying a higher value in this column of the source data enables the separation to be kept, while retaining the correct relationship between parent and child members.

The *LevelNamingTemplate* property can be used either to provide specific names for each level in the created hierarchy or to provide a template for the creation of names. In the former case, each level name is specified with a semicolon acting as a separator, as in the following:

```
dsoLev.levelNamingTemplate = "Director;Senior Manager;Manager;Supervisor;
➥Team Leader;Worker"
```

In the latter case, the asterisk (*) sign is used to indicate a name that can be used for multiple levels, as in the following:

```
dsoLev.levelNamingTemplate = "Level *"
```

In this example, levels within the parent-child hierarchy will be named Level 1, Level 2, Level 3, and so on.

The following example demonstrates the creation of a parent-child dimension from start to finish, using the properties described above.

```
'Presumes the prior instantiation of an object dsoDb that
'contains a data source "Timesheet"

'Create the Employees dimension
Set dsoDim = dsoDb.Dimensions.AddNew("Employees", sbclsParentChild)
With dsoDim
    .Description = "Registered employees of the company"
    .DimensionType = dimOrganization
```

```
        .FromClause = """employees"""
        .JoinClause = ""
End With

'Now create the (All) level
Set dsoLev = dsoDim.Levels.AddNew("All")
With dsoLev
        .Description = "Contains all employees."
        .LevelType = levAll

        'For levels of type levAll, MemberKeyColumn can be a static value
        .MemberKeyColumn = "All Employees"
End With

'Lastly, create the parent-child level containing the employees
Set dsoLev = dsoDim.Levels.AddNew("Employees", sbclsParentChild)
With dsoLev
        .MemberKeyColumn = """employees"".""emp_id"""
        .MemberNameColumn = """employees"".""emp_lname""" & _
            " + ', ' + ""employees"".""emp_fname"""
        .ParentKeyColumn = """employees"".""parent_emp_id"""
        .Ordering = orderName
        .RootMemberIf = rootifParentIsSelf
        .LevelNamingTemplate = "Grade *"
        .SkippedLevelsColumn = """employees"".""parent_distance"""
End With
dsoDim.Update
```

Virtual Dimensions

A *virtual dimension* is a dimension that is based on the member properties of another dimension or on one or more columns from that dimension source table.

Virtual dimensions have changed considerably since the original release of OLAP Services with SQL Server 7.0. They no longer need to be based on a member property, they can contain multiple levels, and they can be edited in the Dimension Editor within Analysis Manager. They are now materialized and act far more like regular dimensions. As a result, the DSO object model has changed in terms of virtual dimensions. The new version is backwardly compatible as far as code is concerned, but the virtual dimensions created with 7.0 code are treated differently within the internals of the Analysis Services engine and retain the same restrictions as before.

TIP   If you have virtual dimensions left in 7.0 format, you should take the time to "upgrade" them to 2000 format by deleting and recreating them.

To create a new-style virtual dimension, set the IsVirtual property of the Dimension object to True and indicate that it is a dependent dimension using the DependsOnDimension property. You can then create the dimension in the same way as for other dimensions, with a couple of notable differences. First, there is no need to specify the properties FromClause, JoinClause, SourceTableFilter, and SourceTableAlias, since they are all taken from the parent dimension. The IsChanging property is always set to True for virtual dimensions, and the StorageMode property is always set to storeasMOLAP. Last, you don't need to specify an EstimatedSize property for the levels within a virtual dimension.

The following code can therefore be used to create a virtual dimension (presuming that an active connection to database dsoDb exists):

```
'Create the virtual dimension
Set dsoDim = dsoDb.Dimensions.AddNew("Employee Grade")
Set dsoDim.DataSource = dsoDb.DataSources(1)
With dsoDim
    dsoDim.Description = "Employee Grade"
    dsoDim.DimensionType = dimRegular
    dsoDim.IsVirtual = True
    dsoDim.DependsOnDimension = "Employees"
End With

'Create the (All) top level
Set dsoLevel = dsoDim.Levels.AddNew("All")
dsoLevel.LevelType = levAll
dsoLevel.MemberKeyColumn = "All Grades"

'Now create the grade level to match the member prop.
Set dsoLevel = dsoDim.Levels.AddNew("Employee Grade")
With dsoLevel
    .MemberKeyColumn = """"employee""""."""grade"""""
    .ColumnType = adVarChar
    .ColumnSize = 15
End With
dsoDim.Update
```

Private (Non-Shared) Dimensions

Any dimension can be marked as private to a cube, if so chosen. Once this is done, the dimension cannot be used within any cube apart from the one in which it has been created. If another cube wishes to use the same dimension, it must be duplicated.

There is no special property within a dimension that can be used to mark it as "private." To create such a dimension, simply prefix the actual name of the dimension with the cube's name, followed by a caret (^). Thus the following code can be used to create a dimension:

```
Dim dsoDim As DSO.Dimension
Set dsoDim = dsoDB.Dimensions.AddNew("Sales^Customer")
```

Although private dimensions are specified as such through their name, a given dimension can be queried to ascertain whether it is private or shared by using the dimension's IsShared property, in the following way:

```
If dsoDim.IsShared Then
    MsgBox "The dimension is shared."
Else
    MsgBox "The dimension is private."
End If
```

However, the IsShared property is read-only at all times and cannot be set using code.

In every other way, private dimensions are handled the same as shared dimensions; thus, you can create a private, parent-child dimension with the following code:

```
Dim dsoDim As DSO.Dimension
Set dsoDim = dsoDB.Dimensions.AddNew("Timesheet^Employee", sbclsParentChild)
```

Member Properties

As you learned in Chapter 5, "Advanced Analysis Services," member properties are a great way to add additional information about a single member within a level. For instance, an Employee dimension could contain extra information about individual employees' job titles, salary levels, years of service, and so on, if this information is not already stored as a level within the dimension. Or you could use it to embed some additional information in HTML or XML format, which a client application could display at some point.

Member properties can be added using the by now familiar process of using an AddNew method, as in the following example (where dsoLev is an object of type DSO.Level):

```
Dim dsoMemProp As DSO.MemberProperty
Set dsoMemProp = dsoLev.MemberProperties.AddNew("Email")
With dsoMemProp
    .Description = "Employee's company email address"
    .SourceColumn = """"employees"".""email"""
    .PropertyType = propWebMailAlias
    .ColumnType = adVarChar
    .ColumnSize = 50
End With
```

This code creates a new member property based on an existing level for an individual's e-mail address. The address itself is taken from the "email" field from the Employees table and can be up to 50 characters long. The property type is also set to a suitable value from the PropertyTypeValue enumeration in the DSO type library; this will assist client applications in the identification of this property's purpose. In this case, an aware application could present the e-mail address as a hyperlink that, when clicked, executes a mail program to send an e-mail to that individual.

Member properties can be stored for any level within the dimension, although they are most commonly used on the lowest level in the hierarchy. Once set, a member property can be used to provide the sort order for the members. To do this, use the Ordering and OrderingMemberProperty properties in the parent level, as in the following example:

```
dsoLev.Ordering = orderMemberProperty
dsoLev.OrderingMemberProperty = "Salary"
```

The above example orders the current level by the member property Salary.

Member Properties in Multiple Languages

In SQL Server 2000, member properties can be used to help with the internationalization of a cube. You can create multiple properties that have the same content but are expressed in different languages.

To do this, follow these steps:

- Create two separate member properties, each containing a column with the appropriate language information and a descriptive name in the native language.

- Add a Caption property for each of the member properties, set to an identical string value for each (often this will be the name in English or the primary language).

- Add a Language property for each of the member properties from the LanguageValues enumeration, set to the appropriate language for the member property content.

When displaying the member property's name and contents, Analysis Services will automatically detect the client's locale ID as presented to it and attempt to match this to the appropriate language, if one exists.

Adding and Removing Dimensions in a Cube

The process of adding dimensions to a cube is identical to that of adding data sources to a cube. Once you have created the dimensions, it's simply a matter of establishing that we want them to be used within the cube itself. So the following code adds three dimensions to a cube dsoCube:

```
With dsoCube
    .Dimensions.AddNew "Customer"
    .Dimensions.AddNew "Project"
    .Dimensions.AddNew "Timesheet^Employee"
End With
```

Simple stuff!

For the sake of completeness, we should note that the Remove method on a collection provides a mechanism to take dimensions out of that collection; hence the following code,

```
dsoCube.Dimensions.Remove "Project"
```

removes the Project dimension from the dsoCube cube. It will, however, remain a shared dimension for use within other cubes (assuming it was not created as a private dimension in the first place).

Creating Measures for a Cube

We've nearly covered everything necessary to build a cube. What remains is to create some measures so that users will have data to browse. Unsurprisingly enough, there's an object in the DSO library called *Measure* that you can populate and add to your cube to define the measures for that cube.

As part of the process of creating a cube, you must update the SourceTable property to point to the fact table for the cube; you should also specify the estimated number of rows within the fact table. When it comes to specifying the measures, you can take advantage of these properties to ensure that the measures are correct.

To add in a measure, you must do two things: first you need to specify the location, type, and size of the measure within the source database; second, you need to specify how the measure will be aggregated. Also, you can optionally specify other information that will determine how the measure is displayed.

Here's an example of measure creation, using a cube that has already been defined as dsoCube:

```
Dim dsoMeasure As DSO.Measure
Set dsoMeasure = dsoCube.Measures.AddNew("Time Worked")
dsoMeasure.Description = "Number of hours worked (including non-chargeable
➥time)."
dsoMeasure.SourceColumn = dsoCube.SourceTable & "."""worked_hours"""
dsoMeasure.SourceColumnType = adBigInt
dsoMeasure.AggregateFunction = aggSum
```

This code snippet begins by adding a new measure using the *AddNew* method with the cube's Measures collection. Once the measure exists, you can set any properties you choose, such as the *Description* property.

The *SourceColumn* property describes the specific field that contains the measure information you want to show. You need to also specify the table, but since that information is already contained in the cube's SourceTable property, you can specify this value by concatenating the existing table name with a column name to give something like "timesheet_fact_1999"."worked_hours".

You should also specify the data type of the column, so that Analysis Services can allocate the appropriate storage for the aggregations. This is specified in the *SourceColumnType* property; the constant values come from the DataTypeEnum enumeration found within the main ADO type library. One way to determine the appropriate value is to use ADO directly to query the source table, in the following way:

```
Dim adoRs As New ADODB.Recordset
adoRs.Open dsoCube.SourceTable, _
    dsoDataSrc.ConnectionString, , , adCmdTable
dsoMeasure.SourceColumnType = adoRs.Fields(dsoMeasure.SourceColumn).Type
```

The last step in the example above is to set the function used to aggregate the measure across a series of members by using the *AggregateFunction* property. This value can be set to any of the values in the AggregatesTypes enumeration, as shown in Table 10.8.

TABLE 10.8: AggregateTypes Enumeration

Name	Description
aggSum	(Default.) To aggregate, sum the measure for all rows in the current subset of the fact table.
aggCount	To aggregate, count the number of instances of this measure for all rows in the current subset of the fact table.
aggMin	To aggregate, identify the minimum value of this measure for all rows in the current subset of the fact table.
aggMax	To aggregate, identify the maximum value of this measure for all rows in the current subset of the fact table.
aggDistinctCount	To aggregate, count the number of distinct instances of this measure for all rows in the current subset of the fact table.

TIP   The cube can only support writeback if all measures use the aggSum aggregation type.

We can optionally set the formatting options for the measure at this point, using the *FormatString* property. This operates in the same way as the Visual Basic Format() function and accepts the same parameters for specified or custom properties. Thus the following are all valid:

```
dsoMeasure.FormatString = "Currency"
dsoMeasure.FormatString = "Standard"
dsoMeasure.FormatString = "$#,##0;($#,##0);\Z\e\r\o"
```

Finally, having created all the measures you plan to include in the cube, don't forget to update the cube to ensure that the changes are propagated into the metadata repository.

Finalizing the Cube Structure

You're nearly there! There's just one task that's left before you've covered all the stages necessary to build a fully populated cube, and that's to specify the cube's source tables and join statement. The two relevant properties are *FromClause* and *JoinClause*, respectively, and both are used as part of the cube processing to ensure that all the relevant tables are mapped together.

The FromClause property simply contains a comma-separated list of all the tables that are used to create any of the dimensions. Make sure when using this property that you don't forget any related tables when adding a dimension based on a snowflake schema. Also don't forget to add the fact table.

The JoinClause property is used to connect the various tables to each other. This should follow a simple JOIN syntax, as in the following example:

```
("timesheet_fact"."emp_id"="employees"."emp_id")
AND
("timesheet_fact"."client_id"="clients"."client_id")
AND
("timesheet_fact"."worktype_id"="worktypes"."worktype_id")
AND
("timesheet_fact"."project_id"="project"."project_id")
AND
("project"."projclass_id"="project_class"."projclass_id")
```

Ensure that each table in the FromClause property is linked to another table in some way in the JoinClause property.

TIP   The JoinClause property uses the older syntax for joins in a WHERE clause, not the newer INNER JOIN syntax.

And that's it! Over the last few pages, we've shown you all the pieces needed to build an entire cube structure up through the use of DSO.

Aggregations and Processing

Of course, building the structure of a cube is only part of the work necessary to make the data in the cube available to end users. You must also design the storage for the cube and process the cube so that it actually picks up the source data and creates any aggregations that are necessary for efficient data processing. In this section, we'll show you how you can use DSO for these purposes.

Using the PartitionAnalyzer Aggregation Designer

The Storage Design Wizard in Analysis Manager provides a wonderful graphical design tool to allow you to design aggregations for your cube. Not only is the underlying functionality for this available within DSO, but the facility also exists to design your own custom aggregations, going way beyond what the user interface itself supports. Using DSO is the only way to specify exactly which aggregations are to be created.

Aggregations are constructed at the partition level, rather than at the cube level. This gives you the flexibility to choose the appropriate aggregations on a partition-by-partition basis. For example, you might know that the end users of your cube are more likely to query the data for the most recent financial year than for preceding years; by splitting the data into partitions and optimizing the aggregations accordingly, you can maximize the performance of your cube with minimum overhead during the processing stages.

The easiest way to design the aggregations for a cube is to use the PartitionAnalyzer object to select and add aggregations until a threshold you have set is reached. Once complete, you can add the chosen aggregations into your partition, at which stage the partition (and therefore your cube) is ready for processing.

Multiple Partitions in SQL Server Enterprise Edition

The Enterprise Edition of SQL Server adds several additional features to Analysis Services. One of these is the ability to create and manage multiple permanent partitions for a single cube. This is particularly suitable for cubes that contain a large quantity of data or that are time-consuming to process. If a cube has multiple partitions, you can specify separate data sources for each partition, as well as individually defining the OLAP storage model (MOLAP, ROLAP, or HOLAP).

Since the Partition object implements the MDStore interface, the methods and operations for partitions are similar to those for cubes. Thus, to create a new partition, the following command can be issued:

```
Dim dsoNewPartition As DSO.MDStore
Set dsoNewPartition = dsoCube.MDStores.AddNew("Partition2")
```

Continued on next page

Once a new partition has been created, its contents can be cloned from an existing partition using the Clone method, as follows:

```
dsoOldPartition.Clone dsoNewPartition, cloneMinorChildren
```

This partition can now be modified to point to a different data source and/or have different source columns and joins.

The following steps are required to utilize the PartitionAnalyzer object in this way:

1. Create a new PartitionAnalyzer object from an existing partition.

2. Call the InitializeDesign method to check the partition's structure and prepare for aggregation design.

3. Repeatedly call the NextAnalysisStep to add another aggregation to the design, until the required threshold has been reached in terms of number of aggregations, percentage improvement, or estimated partition size.

4. Add each of the designed aggregations into the partition itself.

5. Free up the partition analysis object's resources by calling its CloseAggregationsAnalysis method.

Listing 10.3 wraps these steps up into a single function that you can use with any cube. You'll see an example of using this function later in this chapter, when we use DSO to create an entire cube.

Listing 10.3: DoAggregation

```
Option Explicit

Public Enum Targets
    targetPercentageImprovement = 1
    targetAccumulatedSize = 2
    targetAggregationsCount = 3
End Enum

Public Sub DoAggregation(dsoCube As DSO.Cube, Target, TargetType As Targets)
    Dim dsoPartition As DSO.MDStore
    Dim dsoPartitionAnalyzer As DSO.PartitionAnalyzer
    Dim dsoAggregation As DSO.MDStore
    Dim dPercent As Double, dSize As Double, lAggs As Long

    On Error GoTo HandleErr
```

```
        'Aggregate the default partition (the only partition in Standard Edition)
        Set dsoPartition = dsoCube.MDStores(1)
        Set dsoPartitionAnalyzer = dsoPartition.Analyzer
        dsoPartitionAnalyzer.InitializeDesign

        'Repeatedly add aggregations until we hit a target point
        Do While dsoPartitionAnalyzer.NextAnalysisStep(dPercent, dSize, lAggs)
            If ((TargetType = targetPercentageImprovement) And _
            (dPercent >= Target)) _
            Or ((TargetType = targetAccumulatedSize) And (dSize >= Target)) _
            Or ((TargetType = targetAggregationsCount) And (lAggs >= Target)) _
            Then
                Exit Do
            End If
        Loop

        'Now add the designed aggregations to the partition
        For Each dsoAggregation In dsoPartitionAnalyzer.DesignedAggregations
            dsoPartition.MDStores.Add dsoAggregation
        Next dsoAggregation

        'Inform the analyzer that its job is done; update the partition
        dsoPartitionAnalyzer.CloseAggregationsAnalysis
        dsoPartition.Update

ExitHere:
    Exit Sub

HandleErr:
    MsgBox "Error " & Err.Number & ": " & _
     Err.Description, , "DoAggregation"
    Resume ExitHere
    Resume

End Sub
```

A couple of points are worth noting in this code. To start with, the NextAnalysisStep method returns four separate outputs. The first of these is the return parameter, which is a Boolean value indicating whether it was possible to design an aggregation. If no more aggregations can be added (which generally happens in small cubes when every possible aggregation has already been created), this value will return False (hence the need to wrap this function in a Do...Loop). The remaining three are by-reference variables dPercent, dSize, and lAggs, which on exit of the method return the current percentage improvement, the partition size, and the number of aggregations designed, respectively. In the above function, we test all three and allow the calling application to choose one as a threshold; you can use these values however you want. The Analysis Manager uses these values to generate the dynamic graph you see when designing aggregations.

The second thing to note is that the partition analyzer object doesn't add the aggregations to the partition by itself; you must remember to do this by hand at the end. If you have some existing custom or predefined aggregations that you want to build into the partition, you can do so at this stage. Last, we must of course update the partition object with the `dsoPartition.Update` statement to commit the transaction to the database. Note that the current function contains no error handling beyond a simple error trap, but it could be extended easily to add this facility.

To call this function from within your own code, select the threshold type you wish to use (percentage improvement, accumulated size, or aggregation count) and provide the relevant value as a parameter to the function, along with the value you wish to use as the limit; for example,

```
DoAggregation dsoBudget, 50#, targetPercentageImprovement
```

The above call will create aggregations for the default partition of cube dsoBudget until it reaches a 50 percent performance improvement over direct fact table querying or all possible aggregations have been created, whichever comes first.

Processing the Cube

The last step is the easiest: to process a cube, simply call the Process method of the Cube object:

```
dsoCube.Process
```

This method initiates the processing of your cube, including the calculation of any members or designed aggregations. You can choose how the cube is processed by specifying an optional parameter to the Process method. By default, the cube's data is refreshed unless it has never been processed in the first place, in which case a full process is performed. It is possible to manually specify the type of process operation performed using a value from the ProcessTypes enumeration (part of the DSO type library), as in the following example:

```
dsoCube.Process processFull
```

This performs a full cube process, discarding and repopulating the data within the cube from the original data source specified at design time. Table 10.9 shows the possible values for the processing type parameter from the ProcessTypes enum.

TABLE 10.9: Cube Processing Constants

Constant	Meaning
processBuildStructure	Build the cube's structure, but do not populate it with data.
processDefault	Leaves the processing decision to Analysis Services. Normally this means to refresh the data if the cube already exists, or to process it completely if it does not exist.

Continued on next page

TABLE 10.9 CONTINUED: Cube Processing Constants

Constant	Meaning
processFull	Rebuild the cube from scratch.
processReaggregate	Rebuild all MOLAP partitions.
processRefreshData	Refresh data only.
processRefreshDataAndIndex	Refresh data, and rebuild partition indexes.
processSuspend	Stop responding to user queries for five minutes or until a processResume command is received.
processResume	Resume responding to user queries.

Troubleshooting Processing Failures

If you have missed any of the steps listed in this chapter for the creation of a cube, expect to get an error message from DSO. Here are a few steps that people often fail to remember:

- Setting the EstimatedSize for the members within a dimension
- Setting the DataSource property for the dimensions and/or the cube
- Adding the shared dimensions created into the cube
- Making sure all tables in the cube are included in the JoinClause property so that there are no orphaned tables

If you have missed a crucial step, such as one of those above, it will not usually become apparent until you process the cube. You will often then get an error, either on the first call to PartitionAnalyzer.NextAnalysisStep or on the call to the Process method of your cube. In the former instance, the error message will usually give you some useful information on the cause of the message (for example, informing you of a conflict between the AreMemberKeysUnique property in the dimension and the levels). In the latter case, you will often be given a generic error message indicating that the cube could not be processed or, worse, that an unspecified OLE DB error occurred.

One useful troubleshooting tip at this stage is to view your created cube within Analysis Manager. Try processing the shared dimensions individually, to establish which of them is causing an error. When you identify the failing dimension, review the code and compare it with other, successful dimensions to identify the problem. But don't forget to delete your existing cube before running the program to build it from scratch again!

The Call Center Cube: From Start to Finish

Having gone through each of the steps necessary to create and process a cube, it makes sense to summarize what we have described by presenting a code listing that takes the process from beginning to end. Listing 10.4 creates a cube containing information on calls received by a call center, similar to that used in many of the examples in Chapter 6, "Querying Analysis Services with MDX." This cube contains four dimensions, as follows:

- Products
- Call Type
- Geography
- Time

It contains a single measure, Call Count, which shows the number of calls made for a particular slice of the cube. The code sample puts together all of the pieces we've just discussed. Feel free to use this as a template for your own cube scripts.

Listing 10.4:   Creating a cube with DSO

```
Private Sub cmdCeateCube_Click()
    Dim dsoServer As DSO.Server
    Dim dsoDb As DSO.MDStore
    Dim dsoDataSrc As DSO.DataSource
    Dim dsoCube As DSO.MDStore
    Dim dsoMeasure As DSO.Measure

    On Error GoTo HandleErr

    lstInfo.Clear
    Screen.MousePointer = vbHourglass

    'Connect to a server and set a log for processing errors
    Set dsoServer = New DSO.Server
    dsoServer.Connect "localhost"
    dsoServer.ProcessingLogFileName = "c:\dso_process_errors.txt"
    dsoServer.Update

    'If we've got this database already, delete it
    If dsoServer.MDStores.Find("Robin Hood Computers") Then
        dsoServer.MDStores.Remove ("Robin Hood Computers")
    End If

    'Create a new database
    Set dsoDb = dsoServer.MDStores.AddNew("Robin Hood Computers")
    dsoDb.Description = "Computers so good, the Sheriff wants them banned."
    dsoDb.OlapMode = olapmodeMolapIndex
```

```
'Now add a data source
Set dsoDataSrc = dsoDb.DataSources.AddNew("Call Center")
dsoDataSrc.ConnectionString = "Provider=SQLOLEDB.1;" & _
  "Data Source=(local);Initial Catalog=BookSamples;" & _
  "Integrated Security=SSPI;"
dsoDataSrc.Update
oQ = dsoDataSrc.OpenQuoteChar
cQ = dsoDataSrc.CloseQuoteChar

lstInfo.AddItem "Data source initialized"

' Create the dimensions
CreateProductDimension dsoDb
lstInfo.AddItem "tblProduct dimension created"
CreateTimeDimension dsoDb
lstInfo.AddItem "Time dimension created"
CreateCallTypeDimension dsoDb
lstInfo.AddItem "Call type dimension created"
CreateGeographyDimension dsoDb
lstInfo.AddItem "Geography dimension created"

'Create the cube itself
Set dsoCube = dsoDb.MDStores.AddNew("Call Center")
With dsoCube
    .DataSources.AddNew dsoDb.DataSources(1).Name
    .Description = "Incoming calls received by the corporate call center"
    .SourceTable = oQ & "tblCalls" & cQ
    .EstimatedRows = 95000
    .Dimensions.AddNew "Region"
    .Dimensions.AddNew "CallType"
    .Dimensions.AddNew "Product"
    .Dimensions.AddNew "Time"
    .FromClause = oQ & "tblCalls" & cQ & ", " & _
                  oQ & "tblCallType" & cQ & ", " & _
                  oQ & "tblRegion" & cQ & ", " & _
                  oQ & "tblLeadSource" & cQ & ", " & _
                  oQ & "tblProduct" & cQ
    .JoinClause = _
    "(" & oQ & "tblCalls" & cQ & "." & oQ & "RegionID" & cQ & _
    "=" & oQ & "tblRegion" & cQ & "." & oQ & "RegionID" & cQ & ")" & _
    " AND " & _
    "(" & oQ & "tblCalls" & cQ & "." & oQ & "LeadSourceID" & cQ & _
    "=" & oQ & "tblLeadSource" & cQ & "." & oQ & _
    "LeadSourceID" & cQ & ")" & _
    " AND " & _
    "(" & oQ & "tblCalls" & cQ & "." & oQ & "ProductID" & cQ & _
    "=" & oQ & "tblProduct" & cQ & "." & oQ & "ProductID" & cQ & ")" & _
    " AND " & _
    "(" & oQ & "tblCalls" & cQ & "." & oQ & "CallTypeID" & cQ & _
    "=" & oQ & "tblCallType" & cQ & "." & oQ & "CallTypeID" & cQ & ")"
End With
```

```
        lstInfo.AddItem "Cube created"

        'Add the Call Count measure
        Set dsoMeasure = dsoCube.Measures.AddNew("Call Count")
        With dsoMeasure
            .Description = "Number of calls received by the center."
            .SourceColumn = dsoCube.SourceTable & "." & oQ & "CallID" & cQ
            .SourceColumnType = adInteger
            .AggregateFunction = aggSum
        End With
        lstInfo.AddItem "Measure created"

        'Aggregate for 50% performance improvement
        DoAggregation dsoCube, 50#, targetPercentageImprovement
        lstInfo.AddItem "Aggregations determined"

        'Process the aggregations for the cube
        dsoCube.Process
        lstInfo.AddItem "Cube processed and ready to query!"

        'Finally, release the connection to the target server
        dsoServer.CloseServer

ExitHere:
        Screen.MousePointer = vbNormal
        Exit Sub

HandleErr:
        MsgBox "Error " & Err.Number & ": " & _
         Err.Description, , "cmdCreateCube"
        Resume ExitHere
        Resume

End Sub

Private Sub CreateProductDimension(dsoDb As DSO.MDStore)
        Dim dsoDim As DSO.Dimension
        Dim dsoLev As DSO.Level
        Dim dsoMemProp As DSO.MemberProperty

        On Error GoTo HandleErr

        'Create the tblProduct dimension
        Set dsoDim = dsoDb.Dimensions.AddNew("Product")
        Set dsoDim.DataSource = dsoDb.DataSources(1)
        With dsoDim
            .Description = "Different products for which calls have been received."
            .FromClause = oQ & "tblProduct" & cQ
            .JoinClause = ""
            .DimensionType = dimRegular
        End With
```

```
    'Create the tblProduct (All) level
    Set dsoLev = dsoDim.Levels.AddNew("All")
    With dsoLev
        .LevelType = levAll
        .MemberKeyColumn = "All Products"
    End With

    'Create the tblProduct group level
    Set dsoLev = dsoDim.Levels.AddNew("Product Line")
    With dsoLev
        .Description = "Overall Product Group"
        .MemberKeyColumn = oQ & "tblProduct" & cQ & "." & oQ & _
         "ProductGroup" & cQ
        .ColumnType = adChar
        .ColumnSize = 50
        .EstimatedSize = 2
    End With

    'Create the tblProduct Product level
    Set dsoLev = dsoDim.Levels.AddNew("Product")
    With dsoLev
        .Description = "Product line"
        .MemberKeyColumn = oQ & "tblProduct" & cQ & "." & oQ & "Product" & cQ
        .ColumnType = adChar
        .ColumnSize = 50
        .EstimatedSize = 6
    End With

    'Create the individual tblProduct level
    Set dsoLev = dsoDim.Levels.AddNew("Item Name")
    With dsoLev
        .Description = "Physical item (i.e. SKU level)"
        .MemberKeyColumn = oQ & "tblProduct" & cQ & "." & oQ & "ItemName" & cQ
        .ColumnType = adChar
        .ColumnSize = 50
        .EstimatedSize = 23
        .LevelType = levProduct
    End With

    'Update the dimension
    dsoDim.Update

ExitHere:
    Exit Sub

HandleErr:
    MsgBox "Error " & Err.Number & ": " & _
     Err.Description, , "CreateProductDimension"
    Resume ExitHere
    Resume
```

```
    End Sub

    Private Sub CreateTimeDimension(dsoDb As DSO.MDStore)
        Dim dsoDim As DSO.Dimension
        Dim dsoLev As DSO.Level

        On Error GoTo HandleErr

        'Create the time dimension
        Set dsoDim = dsoDb.Dimensions.AddNew("Time")
        Set dsoDim.DataSource = dsoDb.DataSources(1)
        With dsoDim
            .Description = "Date on which the call took place"
            .FromClause = oQ & "tblCalls" & cQ
            .JoinClause = ""
            .DimensionType = dimTime
        End With

        'Create the time (All) level
        Set dsoLev = dsoDim.Levels.AddNew("All")
        With dsoLev
            .LevelType = levAll
            .MemberKeyColumn = "All Time"
        End With

        'Create the time year level
        Set dsoLev = dsoDim.Levels.AddNew("Year")
        With dsoLev
            .LevelType = levTimeYears
            .EstimatedSize = 4
            .MemberKeyColumn = "DatePart(yyyy," & oQ & "tblCalls" & cQ & "." & _
                oQ & "CallDate" & cQ & ")"
        End With

        'Create the time month level
        Set dsoLev = dsoDim.Levels.AddNew("Month")
        With dsoLev
            .LevelType = levTimeMonths
            .EstimatedSize = 48
            .MemberKeyColumn = "DatePart(mm," & oQ & "tblCalls" & cQ & "." & _
                oQ & "CallDate" & cQ & ")"
        End With

        dsoDim.Update

    ExitHere:
        Exit Sub
```

```
HandleErr:
    MsgBox "Error " & Err.Number & ": " & _
     Err.Description, , "CreateTimeDimension"
    Resume ExitHere
    Resume

End Sub

Private Sub CreateCallTypeDimension(dsoDb As DSO.MDStore)
    Dim dsoDim As DSO.Dimension
    Dim dsoLev As DSO.Level

    'Create the call type dimension
    Set dsoDim = dsoDb.Dimensions.AddNew("CallType")
    Set dsoDim.DataSource = dsoDb.DataSources(1)
    With dsoDim
        .Description = "Information on the reason for the incoming call"
        .FromClause = oQ & "tblCallType" & cQ
        .JoinClause = ""
        .DimensionType = dimRegular
    End With

    'Create the (All) level
    Set dsoLev = dsoDim.Levels.AddNew("All")
    With dsoLev
        .LevelType = levAll
        .MemberKeyColumn = "All Call Types"
    End With

    'Create the call type level
    Set dsoLev = dsoDim.Levels.AddNew("Call Type")
    With dsoLev
        .Description = "Type of call received (e.g. sales, support request)"
        .LevelType = levRegular
        .MemberKeyColumn = oQ & "tblCallType" & cQ & "." & oQ & _
         "CallType" & cQ
        .MemberNameColumn = oQ & "tblCallType" & cQ & "." & oQ & _
         "CallType" & cQ
        .ColumnType = adChar
        .ColumnSize = 30
        .EstimatedSize = 2
    End With

    'Create the call subtype level
    Set dsoLev = dsoDim.Levels.AddNew("Issue Type")
    With dsoLev
        .Description = "Specific issue category"
        .LevelType = levRegular
        .MemberKeyColumn = oQ & "tblCallType" & cQ & "." & oQ & _
         "CallSubType" & cQ
        .MemberNameColumn = oQ & "tblCallType" & cQ & "." & oQ & _
```

```
            "CallSubType" & cQ
            .ColumnType = adChar
            .ColumnSize = 50
            .EstimatedSize = 9
        End With

        dsoDim.Update

ExitHere:
    Exit Sub

HandleErr:
    MsgBox "Error " & Err.Number & ": " & _
     Err.Description, , "CreateCallTypeDimension"
    Resume ExitHere
    Resume

End Sub

Private Sub CreateGeographyDimension(dsoDb As DSO.MDStore)
    Dim dsoDim As DSO.Dimension
    Dim dsoLev As DSO.Level

    On Error GoTo HandleErr

    'Create the tblRegion dimension
    Set dsoDim = dsoDb.Dimensions.AddNew("Region")
    Set dsoDim.DataSource = dsoDb.DataSources(1)
    With dsoDim
        .Description = "Location of the customer placing the inbound call."
        .FromClause = oQ & "tblRegion" & cQ
        .JoinClause = ""
        .DimensionType = dimGeography
    End With

    'Create the (All) level
    Set dsoLev = dsoDim.Levels.AddNew("All")
    With dsoLev
        .LevelType = levAll
        .MemberKeyColumn = "All Geography"
    End With

    'Create the continent level
    Set dsoLev = dsoDim.Levels.AddNew("Country")
    With dsoLev
        .Description = "Continent in which the call originated"
        .LevelType = levGeoCountry
        .MemberKeyColumn = oQ & "tblRegion" & cQ & "." & oQ & "Continent" & cQ
        .ColumnType = adChar
        .ColumnSize = 50
        .EstimatedSize = 3
    End With
```

```
    'Create the country level
    Set dsoLev = dsoDim.Levels.AddNew("State")
    With dsoLev
        .Description = "Country in which the call originated (where applicable)"
        .LevelType = levGeoStateOrProvince
        .MemberKeyColumn = oQ & "tblRegion" & cQ & "." & oQ & "Country" & cQ
        .ColumnType = adChar
        .ColumnSize = 50
        .EstimatedSize = 12
    End With

    'Create the city level
    Set dsoLev = dsoDim.Levels.AddNew("City")
    With dsoLev
        .Description = "City in which the call originated"
        .LevelType = levGeoCity
        .MemberKeyColumn = oQ & "tblRegion" & cQ & "." & oQ & "City" & cQ
        .ColumnType = adChar
        .ColumnSize = 50
        .EstimatedSize = 16
    End With

    dsoDim.Update

ExitHere:
    Exit Sub

HandleErr:
    MsgBox "Error " & Err.Number & ": " & _
     Err.Description, , "CreateGeographyDimension"
    Resume ExitHere
    Resume

End Sub
```

Conclusion

Over the course of this chapter, you've seen that DSO provides an extensible mechanism that can be used to control every aspect of the Analysis Services engine. Using DSO, you can programmatically create and administer cubes, design aggregations, and process partitions, as well as everything in between.

DSO also provides a way to specify design options that cannot be set directly through the user interface. For example, you can build custom aggregations and add them to a partition.

DSO is a large object model with many other options that fall beyond the scope of our coverage here. Armed with the knowledge in this chapter, you'll find that the documentation in Books Online provides a useful resource for advanced DSO topics such as partition and aggregation management.

Nearly everything we've covered in this book so far applies to both SQL Server 7.0 OLAP Services and SQL Server 2000 Analysis Services. Now, though, it's time to move on to one of the new features of Analysis Services that was introduced only with the SQL Server 2000 version: data mining.

Building Data Mining Solutions with Analysis Services

- Understanding Data Mining Models

- The PivotTable Service and Data Mining

- DSO and Data Mining

- Making Predictions with a Data Mining Model

As you've seen in the last 10 chapters, Analysis Services is a wonderfully powerful way to look at aggregated data. If you'd like to know how many toothbrushes were sold in March at your Seattle and Redmond stores, for example, it's the perfect tool. By slicing and dicing your data, you can quickly find the numbers that you're looking for.

But what if you don't know what you're looking for? What if you'd like to figure out why people bought those toothbrushes? Was it the advertising campaign for dental health? The seasonal colors of the handles? The fact that those stores are patronized by more children than the others in your chain?

Even with the ability to aggregate data easily, human beings aren't always good at spotting the trends and correlations within large amounts of data. That's where *data mining* enters the picture. Data mining allows you to find the important factors and hidden trends in a large mass of data. With the SQL Server 2000 version of Analysis Services, Microsoft has extended its reach to data mining. In this chapter, we'll see how data mining works in Analysis Services, first from the user interface and then from the various available programming interfaces.

TIP   It can be difficult to find working examples of data mining to learn from, because the technology is so new. One place to look is the OLE DB for Data Mining Resource Kit, available from `www.microsoft.com/data/oledb/DMResKit.htm`. It includes some interesting ActiveX controls such as a decision tree viewer and cluster viewer.

Understanding Data Mining Models

The core concept of data mining in Analysis Services is the *data mining model*. A data mining model is a structure created by Analysis Services that represents the groupings of data found within a cube or within a relational data source. In this section, we'll explore the concepts and terminology used in data mining models in Analysis Services, look at the algorithms that Microsoft implemented to create data mining models, and see how you can use the Analysis Manager user interface to create and explore data mining models.

What Is a Data Mining Model?

In Analysis Services, data mining is based on a data mining model. Conceptually, a data mining model is similar to a cube: it is a persistent data structure that Analysis Services constructs based on low-level data. Like a cube, a data mining model can be browsed to see the data and relationships that it contains.

Data mining models are constructed of *cases* and *attributes*. The entity that the data mining model is designed to analyze is called a case. For example, if you are mining customer information from a database of sales, each customer together with all of the sales for that customer would make up a case. Note that the concept of "entity" here is looser than it is in the traditional relational database world. The data for a single case might be spread across multiple tables within a relational database. A customer case, for example, might draw on information from Customers, Orders, Order Details, and Products tables.

Attributes are information about cases. A Customer case, for example, might have attributes such as age, education level, and total number of orders placed. One of the main tasks of data mining is to determine the relationships between attributes of cases. For example, in this hypothetical database of sales, older customers might prove to make more purchases. Data mining could help you discover and even quantify this relationship.

The collection of cases in a particular data mining model is called the *case set* for that data mining model. You can construct multiple data mining models, each with its own case set, from the same basic data. Given a database of Customers and Orders, you might choose any of these as a case set, to name just a few examples:

- All Customers
- All Orders
- Customers in Maine
- 1998 Orders

After choosing the cases and attributes for a data mining model, you must *train* the model. Training a mining model is analogous to processing a cube. During the training process, Analysis Services looks at the cases and attributes in many ways, hunting for relationships with predictive power and for clusters in the data. These are the same processes that a human analyst might follow. The advantage to using data mining is that Analysis Services can take a systematic look at a large number of alternative possible relationships before settling on the ones that best explain the patterns in the data.

In Analysis Services, data mining models can be based either on existing cubes or directly on data in a relational database.

The algorithm used to construct a data mining model is not fixed. Rather, Microsoft has defined a new standard, the OLE DB for Data Mining specification. Any vendor is free to supply an OLE DB provider that meets this specification, and any such provider can be used by Analysis Services to create a data mining model. Microsoft ships two such providers with Analysis Services:

- Microsoft Decision Trees
- Microsoft Clustering

As you'll see, these two providers do occupy a privileged position in the Analysis Services user interface, and they can each be used to construct models from the same data.

> **TIP** The data mining algorithms used by Analysis Services were developed by a team at Microsoft Research. You can read some of the technical details of their work at research.microsoft.com/dmx/DataMining/default.asp.

Microsoft Decision Trees

A *decision tree* is a set of questions arranged in a branching series designed to allow the prediction of some independent variable. For example, given information on a family's location, total income, and number of children, you might develop the decision tree shown in Figure 11.1.

FIGURE 11.1:

Predicting truck ownership
with a decision tree

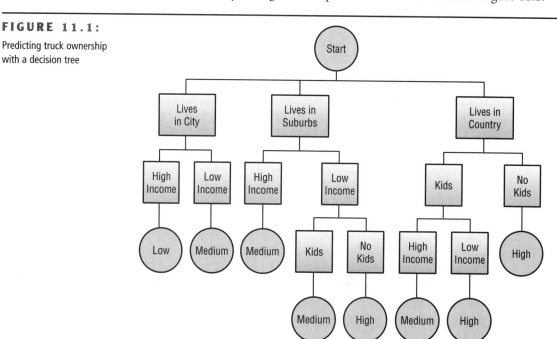

To use this decision tree, start at the top and follow the path for the case that you're interested in. Given a family that lives in the country and has kids but low income, you'd predict a high probability of truck ownership.

> **NOTE** This decision tree is based on fictitious data. One of the co-authors lives in the country and owns a truck, so you shouldn't jump to any conclusions about how we feel about trucks.

The Microsoft Decision Trees algorithm is designed to build decision trees from a large amount of data. It structures the tree so that the most important factors are located toward the root of the tree and the least important factors are toward the leaves of the tree. By convention, Analysis Services orients these trees to read from left to right. Figure 11.2 shows how a decision tree for truck ownership might look in the Data Mining Model Browser. Here the nodes in the tree are color-coded, with the darker nodes having a higher probability of truck ownership.

FIGURE 11.2:

Decision tree in Data Mining Model Browser

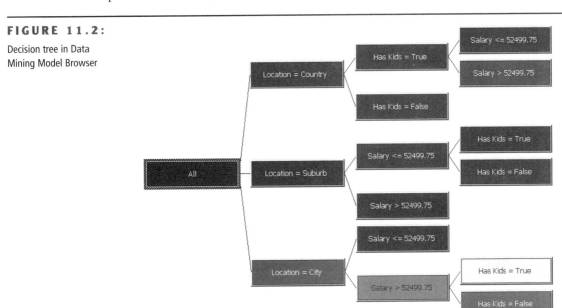

Note that the importance of factors in a decision tree may change depending on other factors. In our truck ownership example, income is a more important predictor of truck ownership than children for owners in the suburbs, while children are a more important predictor of truck ownership than income for owners in the country.

The Microsoft Decision Tree algorithm is designed to make you less likely to ask additional questions the deeper you go into the tree. This helps keep the algorithm from *overfitting* the data, the process of finding spurious correlations based on too few cases to actually draw a conclusion. The algorithm has also been tuned to be efficient even when working with large datasets including millions of cases.

Microsoft Clustering

The other data mining algorithm that's available in Analysis Services is Microsoft Clustering. As the name suggests, this algorithm looks for clusters of cases in the data. Roughly speaking, this means that it finds sets of cases that are more similar to one another than they are to cases in other sets.

Figure 11.3 should give you a taste of the Microsoft Clustering algorithm. This graph shows two variables: household income plotted against type of vehicle owned. As the ovals on the figure show, it's easy to see how owners of a particular type of vehicle tend to have similar incomes in this example.

FIGURE 11.3:

Locating clusters in the data

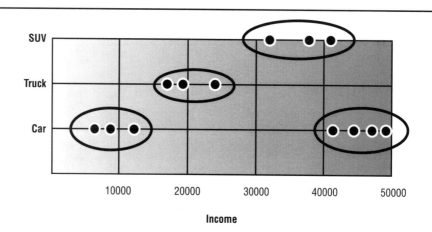

In this case, the clusters are easy to see because the data fit neatly into two dimensions, and the clusters are easily separated just by inspection. However, if you've got a dozen or more variables in your data, it can be impossible to find the clusters by looking at a graph. That's where the Microsoft Clustering algorithm comes in. It can find clustered data in multi-dimensional datasets that defy human ability to visualize a graph.

Clustering is typically used to make predictions about new cases based on existing cases. For example, a bank might inspect the information it has about customers who have bought certificates of deposit. If they find that a cluster of people in a single zip code tends to buy one particular type of CD, they might decide to do a promotional mailing to potential customers in that same zip code.

Like Microsoft Decision Trees, the Microsoft Clustering algorithm has been designed to perform efficiently even on large datasets.

NOTE   Despite the similarity in names, the Microsoft Clustering algorithm has nothing to do with Microsoft Cluster Services.

Creating and Browsing Data Mining Models

To demonstrate data mining, we'll use the United States Department of Agriculture Nutrient Database. This is a collection of information on the nutrients in foods, and the USDA makes it freely available on the web. The following sidebar explains how you can download a copy of this database and modify it to follow along with our examples here if you'd like.

Obtaining the Standard Nutrient Database

The USDA Nutrient Database for Standard Reference, Release 13, can be downloaded from the Internet. After you've downloaded it, you'll need to add some queries to make the database useful for the examples in this chapter. Follow these steps to download and modify the database. You'll need to have Microsoft Access 2000 installed.

1. Open www.nal.usda.gov//fnic/foodcomp/Data/SR13/dnload/sr13dnld.html with your web browser.

2. Use the link for the Access version of the full database to download a copy. Save the resulting sr13acc.zip file to your hard drive.

3. Unzip the file. This will give you the sr13.mdb database and some documentation. The full database is about 25 MB, so make sure you have plenty of disk space available.

4. Open sr13.mdb with Microsoft Access 2000.

5. Switch to the Queries pane of the Database Container.

6. Right-click in the Database Container and choose Import.

7. Browse to the Chapter 11 samples on the companion CD. Choose the NutrientObjects.mdb file to import from. Click Import.

8. Select all queries in the Import Objects dialog box and click OK.

9. Select the MakeAllNutrientsTable query and click Open. Confirm that you want to run the query to build a new table. Click Yes on the dialog informing you that you're about to paste rows into a table. Note that this query may take several minutes to run.

10. Select the MakeSelectedNutrientsTable query and click Open. Confirm that you want to run the query to build a new table. Click Yes on the dialog informing you that you're about to paste rows into a table. Note that this query may take several minutes to run.

That's it. You're now ready to use the modified sr13.mdb database as a source of data for data mining.

We'll demonstrate three separate data mining models in the remainder of this section:

- A decision tree based on an OLAP cube
- A clustering model based on an OLAP cube
- A decision tree based directly on the relational database

To begin, we'll create an OLAP cube from part of the relational database. Follow these steps to create the cube:

1. In Analysis Manager, create a new data source using the Microsoft Jet 4.0 OLE DB provider to pull data from the sr13.mdb database. You can create this new data source in an existing Analysis Services database, or create a new database just for this sample.

2. Launch the Cube Wizard to create a new cube. Skip the introductory panel if it's displayed.

3. Choose the SelectedNutrientValues table from the sr13.mdb data source as the fact table and click Next.

4. Choose Energy as the numeric column to define a measure and click Next.

5. Click New Dimension to launch the Dimension Wizard. Skip the introductory panel if it's displayed.

6. Choose Star Schema and click Next.

7. Choose the SelectedNutrientValues table and click Next.

8. Select FDGP_DESC and then DESC as the levels for this dimension. Click Next.

9. Click Next to accept the suggested member key columns.

10. Leave the advanced options unchecked and click Next.

11. Name the dimension Foods and click Finish.

12. Back in the Cube Wizard, click Next. Tell the Wizard Yes, count the fact table.

13. Name the cube SelectedNutrients and click Finish.

14. In the Cube Editor, save the cube. Close the Cube Editor. Do not set storage options at this time.

15. In Analysis Manager, right-click the Foods dimension and click Edit.

16. Right-click the Desc level and choose New Member Property.

17. In the Insert Member Property dialog box, choose Ash and click OK.

18. Create three more member properties, one each from the Carbohydrate, Protein, and Total Lipid columns.

19. Save the Dimension and close the Dimension Editor.

20. Right-click the SelectedNutrients cube and select Process. Click OK to process the cube. Click Close when Analysis Services has finished processing the cube.

Figure 11.4 shows this cube in the Cube Browser. Note that the totals really don't mean anything: they're the sum of calories in the foods in each category. For data mining purposes, we don't care about this, because we'll only be dealing with the lowest-level data rather than with aggregated data.

FIGURE 11.4:

Browsing the SelectedNutrients cube

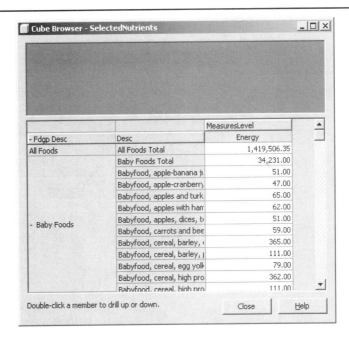

Now that the cube exists, we're ready to build a data mining model based on the data that the cube contains. To do so, follow these steps:

1. In Analysis Manager, right-click the Mining Models node and choose New Mining Model. This will launch the Mining Model Wizard. Read the introductory panel and click Next.

2. On the Source Type panel, select OLAP Data and click Next.

3. On the Select Source Cube panel, select the SelectedNutrients cube and click Next.

4. Select Microsoft Decision Trees as the technique and click Next.

5. On the Select Case pane, choose the Desc level of the Foods dimension. This will make each row of the source cube on that level (each food in the original database) a case for data mining analysis. Click Next.

6. As a predicted entity for the cube, select the Energy measure. This tells Analysis Services to build the decision tree so as to best predict the Energy measure, based on other factors that you'll specify on the next pane. Click Next.

7. On the Select Training Data pane, uncheck the Fdgp Desc box, but leave all of the measures checked. Figure 11.5 shows this pane. By checking all of the measures, you're giving Analysis Services the freedom to use any or all of them in building the decision tree. Click Next.

FIGURE 11.5:

Selecting training data for
the mining model

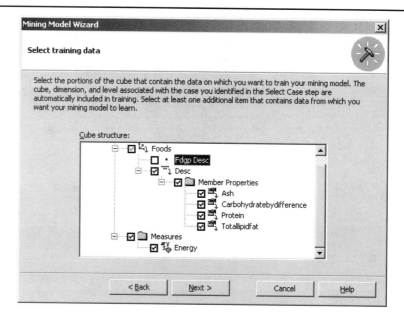

8. Leave the boxes checked to create a new dimension and a virtual cube. Name the dimension NutrientMining and the virtual cube ExtendedNutrients. Click Next.

9. Name the model NutrientModel. Select the option to save and process the model. Click Finish.

10. The Process dialog box will open and show you the progress of creating the mining model and the virtual cube. When Analysis Manager is finished processing the cube, click Close. This will open the mining model in the Mining Model Editor. Figure 11.6 shows this model in the Mining Model Editor.

FIGURE 11.6:

The Mining Model Editor

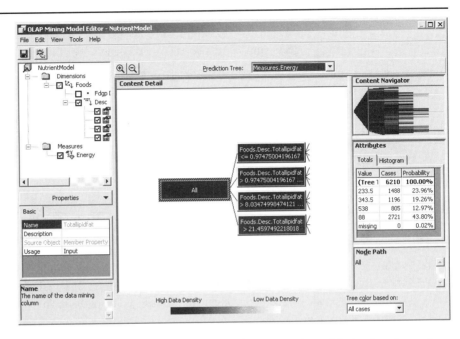

The Mining Model Editor offers you many choices for interacting with the data in a mining model. The editor consists of these pieces:

- The Model Structure window in the upper-left corner shows the structure of the model, including the Dimensions and Measures that are included in the model's analysis. You can use the check boxes in this treeview to adjust the attributes that are included in the analysis. If you change the attributes, you'll have to reprocess the model before you can continue exploring it.

- The Properties window shows you the properties of the object currently selected in the Model Structure window.

- The Prediction Tree combo box allows you to choose which attribute to predict if the model has more than one predictable attribute.

- The Content Detail window shows you a portion of the decision tree. Each node in the decision tree is colored according to the number of cases it represents, with the darker colors corresponding to more cases. Each node also shows the decision that it corresponds to. In Figure 11.6, the second level of decisions splits the cases according to the Totallipidfat attribute. This means that, for the purpose of predicting energy content, total fats is the most important factor.

- The Content Navigator window shows a bird's-eye view of the entire model. In Figure 11.6, you can see that up to six levels are in the decision tree, with the data growing progressively less dense as you proceed farther into the tree.

- The Attributes window shows the attributes of the currently selected node in the Content Detail window. In particular, it gives you the number of cases for each measure in the current node.

- The Node Path window shows the decisions that led to the currently selected node in the Content Detail window.

- The Tree Color Based On combo box allows you to select whether the coloring should be based on all values in the measure or only on particular values.

In the case of this initial model, Microsoft Decision Trees has split up all of the potential Energy values into four "buckets" labeled 88, 233.5, 343.5, and 538. You can think of these as low, medium, and high energy content. Let's focus on low calorie foods for a moment. Choose 88 in the Tree Color Based On combo box. The tree nodes will change color in both the Content Detail and Content Navigator windows. If you look at the densest color, you'll see that these foods are concentrated along a few paths in the decision tree. As you click farther down into the tree, the Node Path window will show you which decisions you've made.

Now choose 538 (the high calorie bucket) for the tree coloring. You'll see that these cases are concentrated in a different portion of the tree from the low calorie cases. This shows that the decision tree is doing an effective job of separating the high calorie foods from the low calorie foods.

When you're done exploring the decision tree, choose File ➤ Exit to close the Mining Model Editor.

Now let's look at the same data a different way, by using the Microsoft Clusters algorithm. To create a model that uses Microsoft Clusters, follow these steps:

1. In Analysis Manager, right-click the SelectedNutrients cube and choose New Mining Model. This will launch the Mining Model Wizard, with the SelectedNutrients cube already chosen as the source.

2. Choose Microsoft Clustering as the data mining technique and click Next.

3. Choose the Desc level of the Foods dimension to identify the case, and click Next.

4. Select the Energy measure and all of the Member Properties as the training data for the mining model. Click Next.

5. Name the model NutrientCluster. Select the option to save and process and click Finish.

6. When Analysis Services is done processing the model, click Close to dismiss the Process dialog box. This will load the mining model into the Mining Model Editor, as shown in Figure 11.7.

FIGURE 11.7:

Microsoft Clusters algorithm data mining model

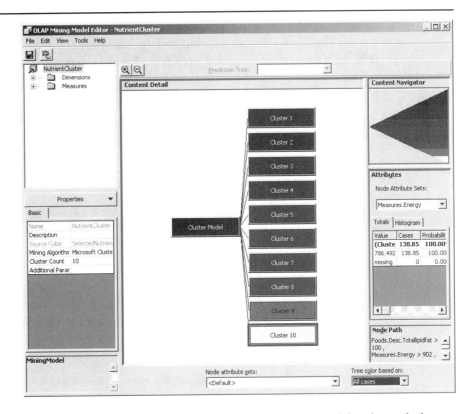

Note that the cluster model has only one level of decomposition. Each box beneath the root of the cluster tree represents one cluster of cases. In this particular model, you can see from the color coding that Cluster 9 and Cluster 10 contain substantially fewer cases than the other clusters. This indicates that the default cluster count of 10 was too high for this particular data. To fix this, change the Cluster Count property in the property pages for this mining model from 10 to 8, then save and reprocess the model.

Clicking an individual cluster will show you the details of that cluster. For example, after reprocessing with eight clusters, clicking Cluster 2 will show an average value for energy around 38, meaning that this is a cluster of low calorie foods. Inspecting the Node Path window will show you that these particular foods are low in fat, protein, and other nutrients as well.

When you're done exploring the clustering model, close the Mining Model Editor window to return to Analysis Manager.

Each of these first two data mining models was based on an OLAP cube. Sometimes, though, you'll want to go back to the relational database containing raw data to create a mining model. This makes sense for two reasons. First, as you saw above, mining models deal with individual pieces of data, and so don't require the aggregations found in cubes. Second, the relational database will frequently contain additional information that's ignored when building a cube.

To see how this works, we'll build a decision tree based on the sr13.mdb relational database. To build this mining model, follow these steps:

1. Right-click the Mining Models node in Analysis Manager and choose New Mining Model. If it displays the welcome panel, click Next.

2. Select Relational Data as the source type and click Next.

3. Choose the option to have all the data pulled from a single table. Choose the AllNutrientsTable table and click Next.

4. Select Microsoft Decision Trees as the technique and click Next.

5. Select DESC as the case key column and click Next.

6. Select as many columns as you like to be predictable columns in the data mining model. The more columns you choose, the more relationships Analysis Manager may find in your data. But choosing more columns will increase the processing time as well. Click Next when you finish selecting columns.

7. Name the model AllNutrients. Select the option to save and process and click Finish.

8. When Analysis Services is done processing the model, click Close to dismiss the Process dialog box. This will load the mining model into the Relational Mining Model Editor.

9. Click the Content tab at the bottom of the Relational Mining Model Editor to see the actual decision tree.

Note that you can use the Prediction Tree combo box to select any of the columns you chose as the basis for the decision tree. This data mining model contains many decision trees in a single package. Use the Prediction Tree combo box and the Content Navigator to explore the data mining model. When you're finished, close the Relational Mining Model Editor.

When you have a model with many interrelated factors, another tool is available for exploring the relationships. That's the dependency network for the model. Right-click the AllNutrients model in the Analysis Manager window and choose Browse Dependency Network. This will open the window shown in Figure 11.8.

FIGURE 11.8:

Dependency Network for the AllNutrients model

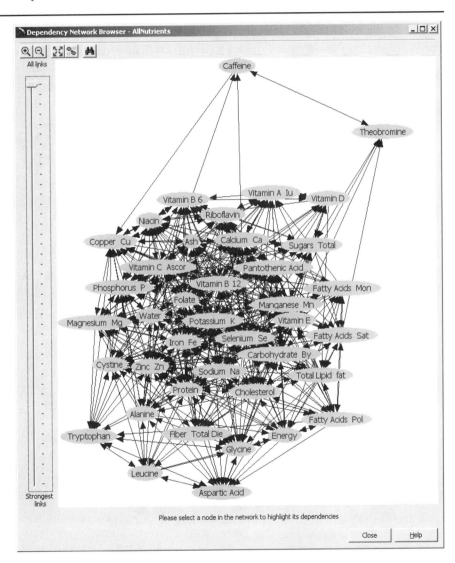

The dependency network shows you exactly what factors are useful in predicting other factors within the data mining model. As you can see, if you have many attributes, this can be a mess. You can do two things to focus on the portion of the dependency network that interests you. First, you can click an individual node to see only the links for that node. Second, you can use the slider on the left side of the Dependency Network Browser to control how many links are shown in the network. As you move the slider down, weaker correlations are eliminated from the network display.

Figure 11.9 shows the same dependency network after selecting the Vitamin E node and reducing the number of links. From this view, you can see that the amount of Vitamin E in the food is a good predictor of the amount of copper in the food, and that Vitamin E itself is well-predicted by several factors including the amount of Vitamin B-12 and the amount of tryptophan.

FIGURE 11.9:

Dependencies of a single node

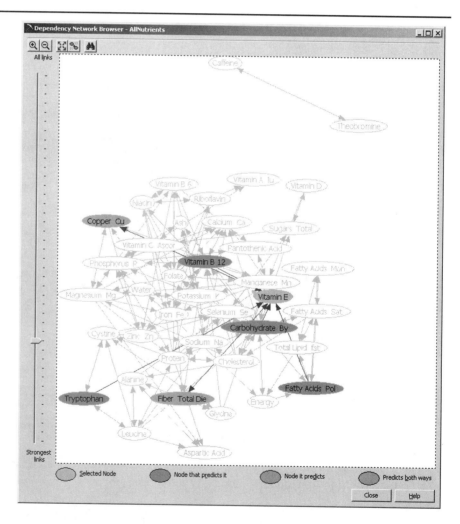

The PivotTable Service and Data Mining

Of course, Analysis Services includes programmatic as well as graphical access to data mining models. In fact, most of the interfaces supported by Analysis Services have been extended with data mining concepts. We'll start with the PivotTable Service. You'll recall from Chapter 9, "Advanced Usage of the PivotTable Service," that the PivotTable Service can be used to create, populate, and retrieve data from local cubes. With SQL Server 2000, the PivotTable Service can also be used to create, train, and retrieve data from a data mining model. In this section we'll show you how these activities work.

NOTE   By putting these capabilities into the PivotTable Service, Microsoft has made it possible to create and use local data mining models that do not depend on a connection to an Analysis Services server.

Creating and Training a Data Mining Model

To create a local data mining model from an OLAP Cube, you use the CREATE OLAP MINING MODEL statement. This is a SQL extension that's supported only by the PivotTable Service, so you must have a connection to the PivotTable OLE DB provider to use this statement.

WARNING   The PivotTable Service can only create local data mining models. To create a new data mining model on an Analysis Services server, you must use DSO, as we'll demonstrate later in this chapter.

Here's the general format for the CREATE OLAP MINING MODEL statement:

```
CREATE OLAP MINING MODEL ModelName
  FROM CubeName
  (
   CASE
   DimensionList,
   MeasureList
  )
  USING Algorithm
```

The CREATE OLAP MINING MODEL statement takes these parameters:

- *ModelName* is the name to use for the new model.

- *CubeName* is the name of an existing OLAP cube on the server to which the PivotTable service is connected.

- *DimensionList* is a list of dimensions, levels, and properties that should be used in the model.

- *MeasureList* is a list of measures that should be used in the model.

- *Algorithm* is either `Microsoft_Decision_Trees` or `Microsoft_Clustering`.

For example, to build a local mining model that has the same structure as the Nutrient-Model model we created earlier in the chapter, you could use this statement:

```
CREATE OLAP MINING MODEL [NutrientModelLocal]
  FROM [SelectedNutrients]
  (
   CASE
   DIMENSION [Foods]
   Level [DESC]
   PROPERTY [Ash],
   PROPERTY [Carbohydratebydifference],
   PROPERTY [Protein],
   PROPERTY [Totallipidfat],
   MEASURE [Energy] PREDICT
  )
USING Microsoft_Decision_Trees
```

Once you've created a data mining model, you must train it. You do this with the INSERT INTO statement:

```
INSERT INTO ModelName
```

You don't need to include any structural detail with the INSERT INTO statement, because the CREATE OLAP MINING MODEL already tells the PivotTable Service exactly what data to use for the new data mining model.

NOTE   You may recall from Chapter 9 that to create a cube with the PivotTable Service you construct a special connection string that includes the CreateCube and InsertInto parameters. This is not the procedure used to create a mining model. To create a mining model, you simply execute the CREATE OLAP MINING MODEL and INSERT INTO statements on an ADO connection to the Analysis Server containing the source cube.

Retrieving Information from a Data Mining Model

Once you've created a local data mining model, you'll probably want to extract the information it contains. One way to do this is to extract a schema rowset using the MINING_MODEL_CONTENT constant to choose the schema rowset for the model.

Schema rowsets were designed as a way for ADO to return metadata from an OLE DB provider. Each different schema rowset is designated by a constant (which is actually a GUID). For example, every OLE DB provider supports returning a schema rowset of the type DBSCHEMA_TABLES that lists all the tables available over the current connection.

The OLE DB for Data Mining standard defines some additional schema rowsets. One of these, MINING_MODEL_CONTENT, contains the actual mining model nodes.

To open a schema rowset, you use the ADO OpenSchema method:

```
Connection.OpenSchema(QueryType, Criteria, SchemaID)
```

The OpenSchema method takes three parameters:

- QueryType can be a schema constant that's built into ADO, or adProviderSpecific for constants that ADO doesn't know about. For data mining, this is always adProviderSpecific.

- Criteria is an array of constraints that's used to limit the schema information returned. For example, you could use this to limit a schema rowset of columns to return only columns for a particular table. In the case of a data mining model, we'll use this to return only the information for a particular model.

- SchemaID is the constant specifying a particular schema. This is only used when QueryType is adProviderSpecific.

Table 11.1 shows the information returned in the MINING_MODEL_CONTENT schema rowset. This rowset contains one row for each node in the data mining model.

TABLE 11.1: The MINING_MODEL_CONTENT Schema Rowset

Column Name	Description
MODEL_CATALOG	Name of the catalog (database) containing the model
MODEL_SCHEMA	Name of the schema containing the model
MODEL_NAME	Name of the model
ATTRIBUTE_NAME	Name of the attribute for this node
NODE_NAME	Name of the node
NODE_UNIQUE_NAME	Fully qualified name of the node
NODE_TYPE	Constant indicating the type of the node
NODE_GUID	GUID associated with this node, if any
NODE_CAPTION	Display label for the node
CHILDREN_CARDINALITY	Estimated number of children of the node
PARENT_UNIQUE_NAME	Fully qualified name for the parent node of this node
NODE_DESCRIPTION	Human-readable description of the node
NODE_RULE	XML description of the rule for this node
MARGINAL_RULE	XML description of the rule for moving from the parent to this node
NODE_PROBABILITY	Percent of overall cases in this node
MARGINAL_PROBABILITY	Percent of cases from the parent in this node
NODE_DISTRIBUTION	Returns a recordset with information on the histogram for this node
NODE_SUPPORT	Number of cases that this node was built from

TIP The XML description of the node's rule is returned in a format known as Predictive Model Markup Language (PMML). You can find more information about PMML and the other details of the schema rowsets available from OLE DB for Data Mining in the OLE DB for Data Mining Specification, which is available for download from www.microsoft.com/data.

The Chapter11.vbp sample project contains a procedure to create a local data mining model and display the information from its nodes in a TreeView control. You can right-click any node in the TreeView control to see the rule for that node. Figure 11.10 shows the tree-view plus one of the rules. Listing 11.1 shows the code that was used to create this treeview.

FIGURE 11.10:

Displaying a local data mining model

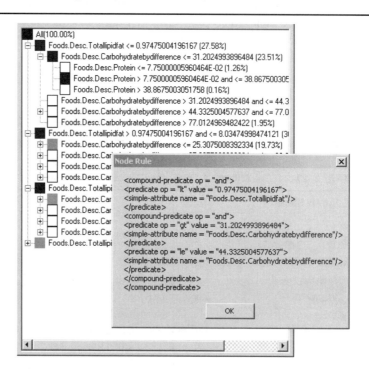

Listing 11.1:   Creating a local data mining model

```
Option Explicit

Const MINING_MODEL_CONTENT As String = _
  "{3ADD8A76-D8B9-11D2-8D2A-00E029154FDE}"

Private Sub cmdCreateOLAPMiningModel_Click()
```

```
Dim cnn As ADODB.Connection
Dim cmd As ADODB.Command
Dim strCreate As String
Dim strTrain As String
Dim rstModel As ADODB.Recordset
Dim strModel As String
Dim nod As Node
Dim nodparent As Node
Dim nodRoot As Node
Dim intImage As Integer
Dim varRestrict As Variant

On Error GoTo HandleErr

Screen.MousePointer = vbHourglass

Set cnn = New ADODB.Connection
' Change the Initial Catalog name if you used a different
' database for the Nutrient data
cnn.ConnectionString = "PROVIDER=MSOLAP.2;Data Source=localhost;" & _
  "Initial Catalog=BookSamples"
cnn.Open

Set cmd = New ADODB.Command
Set cmd.ActiveConnection = cnn

' Create the model
strCreate = "CREATE OLAP MINING MODEL [NutrientModelLocal] " & _
  "FROM [SelectedNutrients] " & _
  "( " & _
  "CASE " & _
  "DIMENSION [Foods] " & _
  "Level [DESC] " & _
  "PROPERTY [Ash], " & _
  "PROPERTY [Carbohydratebydifference], " & _
  "PROPERTY [Protein], " & _
  "PROPERTY [Totallipidfat], " & _
  "MEASURE [Energy] PREDICT " & _
  ") " & _
  "USING Microsoft_Decision_Trees"

cmd.CommandText = strCreate
cmd.Execute

' Train the model
strTrain = "INSERT INTO [NutrientModelLocal]"
cmd.CommandText = strTrain
cmd.Execute

Set rstModel = New ADODB.Recordset
```

```vb
        ' Open a schema recordset for the model
        varRestrict = Array(Empty, Empty, "NutrientModelLocal")
        Set rstModel = cnn.OpenSchema(adSchemaProviderSpecific, varRestrict, _
            MINING_MODEL_CONTENT)

        ' Populate the TreeView from the schema recordset
        Do While Not rstModel.EOF
            If rstModel.Fields("NODE_UNIQUE_NAME") <> "0" Then
                If rstModel.Fields("PARENT_UNIQUE_NAME").Value = 0 Then
                    Set nod = tvwModel.Nodes.Add(, , _
                     "K" & rstModel.Fields("NODE_UNIQUE_NAME").Value, _
                     rstModel.Fields("NODE_CAPTION").Value & "(" & _
                     Format(rstModel.Fields("NODE_PROBABILITY").Value, _
                     "Percent") & ")", 5)
                    nod.Tag = rstModel.Fields("NODE_RULE").Value
                    Set nodRoot = nod
                Else
                    Select Case rstModel.Fields("NODE_PROBABILITY").Value
                        Case Is < 0.1
                            intImage = 1
                        Case Is < 0.2
                            intImage = 2
                        Case Is < 0.3
                            intImage = 3
                        Case Else
                            intImage = 4
                    End Select
                    Set nodparent = tvwModel.Nodes( _
                     "K" & rstModel.Fields("PARENT_UNIQUE_NAME").Value)
                    Set nod = tvwModel.Nodes.Add(nodparent, tvwChild, _
                     "K" & rstModel.Fields("NODE_UNIQUE_NAME").Value, _
                     rstModel.Fields("NODE_CAPTION").Value & "(" & _
                     Format(rstModel.Fields("NODE_PROBABILITY").Value, _
                     "Percent") & ")", intImage)
                    nod.Tag = rstModel.Fields("NODE_RULE").Value
                End If
            End If
            rstModel.MoveNext
        Loop

        nodRoot.Expanded = True

        Screen.MousePointer = vbDefault

    ExitHere:
        Exit Sub

    HandleErr:
        MsgBox "Error " & Err.Number & ": " & _
         Err.Description, , "cmdCreateOLAPMiningModel"
        Resume ExitHere
        Resume
```

```
End Sub

Private Sub mnuShortcutRule_Click()
    MsgBox tvwModel.SelectedItem.Tag, , "Node Rule"
End Sub

Private Sub tvwModel_MouseDown(Button As Integer, _
 Shift As Integer, x As Single, y As Single)
    ' Select the clicked-on node and display the rule stored in its Tag
    Dim nod As Node
    Set nod = tvwModel.HitTest(x, y)
    If Not nod Is Nothing Then
        nod.Selected = True
        If Button = vbRightButton Then
            PopupMenu mnuShortcut
        End If
    End If
End Sub
```

TIP You can also create a local data mining model from a relational database, using the CREATE MINING MODEL statement. For information on the syntax of CREATE MINING MODEL, refer to SQL Server Books Online.

DSO and Data Mining

In Chapter 10, "Managing an Analysis Services Environment Using DSO," you saw how the Decision Support Objects (DSO) library could be used to retrieve metadata about existing objects from Analysis Services, and how it could be used to create new objects. In SQL Server 2000 Analysis Services, DSO has also been extended to work with data mining models. You can retrieve information about existing models, or create entirely new models, using DSO. In this section, we'll show how DSO works with data mining.

Retrieving Data Mining Metadata with DSO

The DSO object model contains several objects that are useful for retrieving information about data mining models. These are the MiningModel and Column objects. Each database contains a collection of MiningModels, and each MiningModel contains a collection of Columns. Figure 11.11 shows the portion of the DSO object model that's used for investigating mining models.

FIGURE 11.11:

Data mining model objects
in DSO

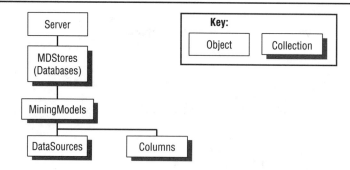

The MiningModel object represents, as you would guess, a single data mining model. Table 11.2 shows the methods and properties available from the MiningModel object.

TABLE 11.2: Details of the MiningModel Object

Member	Type	Description
AreKeysUnique	P	True if key column values are unique across all cases in the model (relational model only)
CaseDimension	P	Dimension that contains the cases for the model (OLAP model only)
CaseLevel	P	Level that contains the cases for the model (OLAP model only)
ClassType	P	Indicates that this object represents a mining model
Clone	M	Duplicate an existing mining model
Description	P	Human-readable description of the model
Filter	P	SQL expression to filter the rows used for training the model (relational model only)
FromClause	P	SQL FROM clause to return the rows used for training the model (relational model only)
IsVisible	P	True if the mining model is visible to client applications
JoinClause	P	SQL JOIN clause the SQL query uses to return the rows used for training the model (relational model only)
LastProcessed	P	Date and time that the model was last processed.
LastUpdated	P	Not used by Analysis Services
LockObject	M	Prevent multiple users from updating the mining model
MiningAlgorithm	P	The mining algorithm used in the model (clustering or decision trees)
Name	P	The name of the model
Parameters	P	Parameters used by the mining algorithm
Parent	P	Pointer to the MDStore object holding this model

Continued on next page

TABLE 11.2 CONTINUED: Details of the MiningModel Object

Member	Type	Description
SourceCube	P	Returns to the name of the cube that contains the data for this model (OLAP model only)
State	P	Status of the model
SubClassType	P	Constant indicating whether the model is based on relational or OLAP data
TrainingQuery	P	Query used to return data for training the model
UnlockObject	M	Allow users to access the mining model
Update	M	Save and update the model's metadata
ValidateStructure	M	Validates all properties of the model and its columns
XML	P	PMML representation of the model

Each MiningModel contains a collection of Column objects. Each Column object represents a single piece of data that the model can use for input or prediction or both. Because columns in a data mining model can be complex tables in their own right when cases span multiple tables, a Column too has a Columns collection. The MiningModel object also has collections of CustomProperties, Roles, and DataSources. These collections are not unique to mining models, and behave just as they do for the other DSO objects that we discussed in Chapter 10. Table 11.3 shows the methods and properties of the Column object.

TABLE 11.3: Details of the Column Object

Member	Type	Description
AreKeysUnique	P	True if key column values are unique across all cases in the column (relational model only)
ClassType	P	Type of the object
ContentType	P	Flags indicating the type of content in the column (relational model only)
DataType	P	Type of data the column contains (relational model only)
Description	P	Description of the column
Distribution	P	Statistical distribution of data in the column
Filter	P	Filter for rows in a nested table (relational model only)
FromClause	P	SQL FROM clause for rows in a nested table (relational model only)
IsDisabled	P	True if the column should be ignored when training the model
IsInput	P	True if the column accepts input for training the model

Continued on next page

TABLE 11.3 CONTINUED: Details of the Column Object

Member	Type	Description
IsKey	P	True if the column is the key of a nested table (relational model only)
IsParentKey	P	True if the column is a foreign key back to the parent table (relational model only)
IsPredictable	P	True if the column is to be predicted by the model
JoinClause	P	SQL JOIN clause for rows in a nested table (relational model only)
ModelingFlags	P	Options for a column
Name	P	Name of the column
Num	P	Ordinal position of the column in the collection
Parent	P	Parent mining model or column for this column
RelatedColumn	P	Column to which this column is related (relational model only)
SourceColumn	P	Name of the relational database column that holds the data for this column (relational model only)
SourceOlapObject	P	Name of the DSO object that contains the data for this column (OLAP model only)
SpecialFlag	P	Used by DSO to specify statistical properties for the column
SubClassType	P	Indicates the type of a nested column

To use the MiningModel and Column objects in your code, you need to include a reference to the Microsoft Decision Support Objects library. Once you've done this, it's easy to iterate the collections, as shown in this snippet from the sample project for this chapter:

```
Dim dsoServer As DSO.Server
Dim dsoDb As DSO.MDStore
Dim dsoMiningModel As DSO.MiningModel
Dim dsoColumn As DSO.Column
...

' Iterate through the MDStores collection of the Server
' object, which contains Databases
For Each dsoDb In dsoServer.MDStores
    lstInfo.AddItem "Database: " & dsoDb.Name & " (" & _
    dsoDb.Description & ")"
    ' Iterate through the MiningModels collection
    For Each dsoMiningModel In dsoDb.MiningModels
        lstInfo.AddItem vbTab & "Model: " & dsoMiningModel.Name & " (" & _
        dsoMiningModel.Description & ")"
        ' Iterate through the columns of the model
        For Each dsoColumn In dsoMiningModel.Columns
```

```
            lstInfo.AddItem vbTab & vbTab & "Column: " & dsoColumn.Name
            ➡& "( " & _
             dsoColumn.Description & ")"
         Next dsoColumn
      Next dsoMiningModel
   Next dsoDb
```

Figure 11.12 shows the result of running the procedure that contains this code.

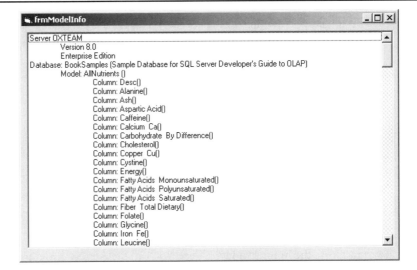

Creating a New Data Mining Model with DSO

You can also use DSO to create entirely new mining models from scratch. While this can involve a good deal of code, you'll find that most of the code is a repetitive definition of Column objects. Here's an outline of the process you'll need to use to create a mining model with DSO:

1. Connect to an Analysis Services server and get an object pointer to the database where you wish to create the new mining model.

2. Create the new MiningModel object.

3. Set properties for the MiningModel object.

4. Create a Column object for the first column in the mining model.

5. Set the properties for the Column object.

6. Repeat steps 4 and 5 for the remaining columns in the mining model.

7. Use the MiningModel.Update method to save the mining model.

8. Use the MiningModel.LockObject method to lock the mining model so users don't try to update it while it is being trained.

9. Use the MiningModel.Process method to train the mining model.

10. Use the MiningModel.UnlockObject method to make the new model available to users.

In the rest of this section, we'll present the Visual Basic code to build a copy of the NutrientModel data mining model using these steps.

First, getting a pointer to the correct database is code you've seen before. If you have the Nutrient data in a separate database, replace the BookSamples catalog with that name:

```
Dim dsoServer As DSO.Server
Dim dsoDb As DSO.MDStore
Dim dsoMiningModel As DSO.MiningModel
Dim dsoColumn As DSO.Column
Dim dsoCube As DSO.MDStore

    …

' Connect to the local server and retrieve the
' sample database
Set dsoServer = New DSO.Server
dsoServer.Connect "localhost"

Set dsoDb = dsoServer.MDStores("BookSamples")
```

To create the mining model object, you call the AddNew method on the Database's Mining-Models collection. This method takes a required parameter to specify whether the mining model will be based on OLAP or relational data (here, we're going to use OLAP data):

```
' Create a new MiningModel object
' For sample purposes, delete the object if it already exists
If Not dsoDb.MiningModels("NutrientModel2") Is Nothing Then
    dsoDb.MiningModels.Remove "NutrientModel2"
End If
Set dsoMiningModel = dsoDb.MiningModels.AddNew("NutrientModel2", _
    sbclsOlap)
```

Once the mining model exists, you need to set some properties. Which properties you need to set depends on whether the model is based on OLAP or relational data. Refer back to Table 11.2 to see which properties apply to each type of mining model.

```
' Set some mining model properties
With dsoMiningModel
    .SourceCube = "SelectedNutrients"
    Set dsoCube = dsoDb.MDStores("SelectedNutrients")
    .DataSources.Add (dsoCube.DataSources(1))
    .MiningAlgorithm = "Microsoft_Decision_Trees"
    .CaseDimension = "Foods"
    .Description = "Model created with DSO"
```

```
    .Update
End With
```

There are a few things to note about this block of code. First, you need to specify both the source cube and the data source for the mining model if it's based on an OLAP cube. To make sure no inconsistency exists between these two properties, this code retrieves the data source from the cube and uses it for the mining model.

Second, note the call to the mining model's Update method. When you call Update after adding a source cube, DSO automatically adds all of the levels and measures from the source cube to the mining model's Columns collection and sets their IsDisabled property to False. This may seem like wasted effort, but it makes the next task, that of adding a column and setting its properties, much easier:

```
' Create a column in the model
Set dsoColumn = dsoMiningModel.Columns("DESC")
' And set its properties
With dsoColumn
    .IsDisabled = False
End With
```

Because the Update method added the column to the mining model, you can retrieve the column by name from the Columns collection. To make it active in the mining model, you just have to set its IsDisabled property to False. Because this particular column is the lowest enabled level in the mining model's case dimension, it will define the cases for the mining model.

Adding additional columns to the model is just a matter of enabling them and setting appropriate properties:

```
' Repeat for other columns
Set dsoColumn = dsoMiningModel.Columns("Ash")
With dsoColumn
    .IsDisabled = False
    .IsInput = True
End With

Set dsoColumn = dsoMiningModel.Columns("Carbohydratebydifference")
With dsoColumn
    .IsDisabled = False
    .IsInput = True
End With

Set dsoColumn = dsoMiningModel.Columns("Protein")
With dsoColumn
    .IsDisabled = False
    .IsInput = True
End With
```

```
Set dsoColumn = dsoMiningModel.Columns("Totallipidfat")
With dsoColumn
    .IsDisabled = False
    .IsInput = True
End With

Set dsoColumn = dsoMiningModel.Columns("Energy")
With dsoColumn
    .IsDisabled = False
    .IsPredictable = True
End With
```

Note that you need to set the IsPredictable property to True for at least one of the columns. Otherwise the model would have nothing to predict.

The remaining steps (saving, locking, processing, and unlocking the model) take one line of code each:

```
' Save the model
dsoMiningModel.Update

' Lock the model
dsoMiningModel.LockObject olapLockProcess, "Processing model"

' Process the model
dsoMiningModel.Process processFull

' Unlock the model
dsoMiningModel.UnlockObject
```

You'll find the complete procedure attached to frmCodeSamples in the Chapter11.vbp sample project. If you run this procedure and then open Analysis Manager, you should find the new data mining model in the treeview.

TIP   If Analysis Manager is already running when you execute this code, you'll need to select the Analysis Services database and click the Refresh button on the Analysis Manager toolbar to see the new mining model.

Making Predictions with a Data Mining Model

One of the uses of a data mining model is to make predictions. Suppose you have a data mining model with six input columns and a predicted column. If you were supplied with values for the input columns, you could use the data mining model to determine the most likely value for the predicted column. Analysis Services has added a SQL extension, PREDICTION JOIN, to do just that. A PREDICTION JOIN takes a data mining model and specifies how it relates to new data, and then uses the model to make predictions for the new data.

It's easy to think of uses for data mining predictions. For example, suppose you had a database of customer information that included the average time customers took to pay their bills. You could build a data mining model that used other information about customers, such as the length of time you'd been doing business with them or their average monthly purchase, and use this model to predict the time to pay bills. Then, when a new customer applied for credit, you'd be able to predict whether they were a good credit risk based on past experience with similar customers as captured in the data mining model.

In this section, you'll see how to make data mining predictions in two different ways. First, we'll explore the user interface that is present in SQL Server Data Transformation Services to perform this task. Second, we'll show you how to do the same thing in code, by sending an appropriate SQL statement to Analysis Services and retrieving the results.

To demonstrate the use of a data mining model for predictions, we'll use the simple relational data shown in Figure 11.13. This table shows the subject, level, and length for various textbooks. We'll create a data mining model that uses the subject and level to predict the length, and then use it to predict lengths for some new books.

FIGURE 11.13:

Relational table for the BookLengths mining model

BookID	BookSubject	BookLevel	BookLength
1	Health	Junior High	83
2	Astronomy	College	120
3	Astronomy	College	172
4	Astronomy	College	187
5	Math	High School	128
6	Astronomy	College	143
7	Chemistry	College	142
8	Chemistry	College	124
9	Philosophy	College	126
10	Philosophy	College	153
11	Philosophy	Junior High	24
12	History	College	149
13	Math	High School	76
14	Philosophy	College	96
15	History	High School	80
16	Literature	Junior High	57
17	Chemistry	High School	114
18	Literature	Junior High	20
19	Physics	College	196
20	Social Studies	Junior High	89

Record: 1 of 1000

To build the BookLengths mining model, follow these steps:

1. Right-click the Data Sources folder in the BookSamples database in Analysis Manager and choose New Data Source. Select the Microsoft Jet 4.0 OLE DB Provider and click Next. Browse to the Books.mdb sample database from the companion CD and click OK to create the data source.

2. Right-click the Mining Models folder and choose New Mining Model. Skip the introductory panel if it appears.

3. Choose Relational Data and click Next.

4. Choose the tblBooks table in the data source that you just created as the single table containing the data for the model and click Next.

5. Choose Microsoft Decision Trees and click Next.

6. Choose BookID as the Case key column and click Next.

7. Choose BookLength as the predictable column, and BookSubject and BookLevel as the input columns. Click Next.

8. Name the model BookLength, choose to save and process, and click Finish.

9. Click Close to close the Process dialog box.

10. When you're done browsing the model, close the Relational Mining Model Editor to return to Analysis Manager.

WARNING   You may wonder, as we did, what the connection is between local data mining models created through the PivotTable Service and prediction with a data mining model. Being able to create a local mining model and then immediately use it for prediction would be useful in cases where you're not connected to an Analysis Services server. Unfortunately, you'll need to wait for the next version of SQL Server to get this capability. Predictions from local data mining models are not supported in SQL Server 2000; the syntax simply isn't implemented.

Using Data Transformation Services for Predictions

One way to use a data mining model for predictions is to create a specialized Data Transformation Services (DTS) task. We mentioned DTS in Chapter 2, "Analysis Services Architecture," as part of the overall architecture of creating a data warehouse. But in SQL Server 2000, DTS can do much more than just move data between different data sources. A wide variety of specialized tasks are available to help you clean up or otherwise modify data now incorporated in DTS.

Figure 11.14 shows another table in the Books.mdb database. This table contains information on book subjects and levels, but not on their lengths. We'll use our BookLength data mining model to predict the length for these books.

To make a data mining prediction for this data using DTS, follow these steps:

1. Open SQL Server Enterprise Manager.

2. Expand the Enterprise Manager treeview to view the Data Transformation Services folder.

3. Right-click the Data Transformation Services folder and select New Package. This will open the DTS Package Editor.

4. Select Task ➤ Data Mining Prediction Task. This will insert an icon for the Data Mining Prediction Task and open the Properties dialog box for this task.

5. Type a name and a description for the task.

6. On the Mining Model tab, type in **localhost** as the server name and select the BookSamples database. Select the BookLength data mining model. Figure 11.15 shows the DTS Package Editor at this point.

7. On the Query tab, use the browse button to select the Books.mdb file as the data source. Use the Jet 4.0 OLE DB provider.

8. Click the New Query button to launch the Prediction Query Builder.

9. Choose tblNewBooks as the case table. This is the table that contains the data we wish to use in the prediction.

10. Choose the source columns that correspond to the model columns.

11. Choose Book Length as the predicted column. Click Finish to return to the Properties dialog box for the prediction task.

12. On the Output tab, leave the output data source set to the same table as the input data source. Name the output table PredictionResultsDTS. Click OK.

FIGURE 11.15:

Choosing a mining model for the DTS package

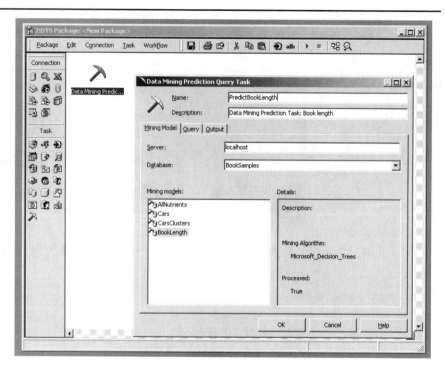

At this point, you've created the DTS task to perform a prediction of values in the tblNew-Books table. The prediction is based on the BookLength data mining model, which is itself based on the tblBooks table. You could go on to save the DTS package if you like. Or, you can just choose Package ➤ Execute in the DTS Package Editor to run the package.

After running the package, open the Books.mdb file in Microsoft Access. You'll find that the DTS task has created a new table named PredictionResultsDTS. This table has the exact same structure as the tblNewBooks table, with the addition of length estimates.

Making Predictions in Code

The secret to making a prediction from a data mining model is the PREDICTION JOIN extension to SQL. This is yet another of the extensions added by the PivotTable Service (so you need to connect via the PivotTable Service to perform a prediction). If you return to the properties of the Data Mining Prediction Task in the DTS Editor, you'll find the SQL statement that the Prediction Query Builder constructed for you. Here's the SQL statement for this particular case (somewhat reformatted):

```
SELECT FLATTENED
  [T1].[Book Id], [T1].[Book Level], [T1].[Book Subject],
```

```
  [T1].[Book Length], [BookLength].[Book Length]
FROM
  [BookLength]
PREDICTION JOIN
  OPENROWSET(
    'Microsoft.Jet.OLEDB.4.0',
    'Provider=Microsoft.Jet.OLEDB.4.0;Data Source=C:\Books.mdb; \
    ➡Persist Security Info=False',
    'SELECT `BookID` AS `Book Id`, `BookLevel` AS `Book Level`,
    `BookSubject` AS `Book Subject`, `BookLength` AS `Book Length`
     FROM `tblNewBooks` ORDER BY `BookID`'
    ) AS [T1]
ON
  [BookLength].[Book Id] = [T1].[Book Id] AND
  [BookLength].[Book Level] = [T1].[Book Level] AND
  [BookLength].[Book Subject] = [T1].[Book Subject] AND
  [BookLength].[Book Length] = [T1].[Book Length]
```

Though this statement looks a bit imposing, it's really not much worse than any other SELECT statement with a JOIN. Let's go through the syntax piece by piece. First comes the SELECT keyword itself, together with another PivotTable Service extension:

```
SELECT FLATTENED
```

The FLATTENED keyword tells the PivotTable Service to return a two-dimensional recordset rather than an *n*-dimensional cellset. You'll see later in this section that this allows you to use ADO rather than ADO/MD to execute the statement.

Next comes a list of fields to return:

```
[T1].[Book Id], [T1].[Book Level], [T1].[Book Subject],
  [T1].[Book Length], [BookLength].[Book Length]
```

This list includes all of the fields from the new table that we're going to use as the prediction input (here aliased from tblNewBooks to T1, for reasons that you'll see in a moment) and the Book Length column of the BookLength data mining model.

The first part of the FROM clause specifies the name of the data mining model to use:

```
FROM
  [BookLength]
```

Then comes the keyword that tells the PivotTable Service that it should use this model to make a prediction:

```
PREDICTION JOIN
```

But what can the model be joined to? It can't be just the name of a table, because the Pivot-Table Service uses the Analysis Service database as its data source. Instead, the PivotTable Service supports the OPENROWSET statement from Transact-SQL. OPENROWSET is a Microsoft extension to SQL that allows you to create a rowset (virtual table) from any OLE DB data source. Here's the syntax in this case:

```
OPENROWSET(
  'Microsoft.Jet.OLEDB.4.0',
  'Provider=Microsoft.Jet.OLEDB.4.0;Data Source=C:\Books.mdb;
➥Persist Security Info=False',
  'SELECT `BookID` AS `Book Id`, `BookLevel` AS `Book Level`,
  `BookSubject` AS `Book Subject`, `BookLength` AS `Book Length`
  FROM `tblNewBooks` ORDER BY `BookID`'
  ) AS [T1]
```

The OPENROWSET statement takes three parameters. The first is the name of the OLE DB provider that will supply the data. The second is the connection string to use with the provider to locate the exact database (the connection string that you saw in the DTS Package Editor might be slightly different, depending on which folder holds your copy of Books.mdb). The third parameter is the SELECT statement to use to retrieve records from the database referred to by the connection string. Note the use of back quotes (`) within this third parameter to represent any forward quotes in the SELECT statement.

TIP   For more information on the OPENROWSET statement, refer to Mike Gunderloy and Joseph L. Jorden's book, *Mastering SQL Server 2000* (Sybex, 2000).

Finally, there's an ON clause that specifies how columns from the data mining model should be matched with the columns returned by the OPENROWSET statement:

```
ON
  [BookLength].[Book Id] = [T1].[Book Id] AND
  [BookLength].[Book Level] = [T1].[Book Level] AND
  [BookLength].[Book Subject] = [T1].[Book Subject] AND
  [BookLength].[Book Length] = [T1].[Book Length]
```

TIP   Although this example is based on a relational data mining model, you can also use an OLAP data mining model as the basis for a data mining model prediction. To do so, you'll need to use the Microsoft Shape Provider in the OPENROWSET statement to create a shaped rowset with the same structure as the source data for the data mining model. You can find an example of this in the OLE DB for Data Mining Specification.

The Chapter11.vbp sample project shows how you can use this SQL statement in your Visual Basic code. The key idea is to open an ADO Recordset object whose source is this SQL statement. Listing 11.2 demonstrates the details. The sample prints the contents of the predicted recordset to the Immediate Window.

Listing 11.2:   **cmdMakePrediction_Click**

```
Private Sub cmdMakePrediction_Click()
    Dim cnn As ADODB.Connection
    Dim strPredict As String
    Dim rstPredict As ADODB.Recordset
    Dim fld As ADODB.Field

    On Error GoTo HandleErr

    Set cnn = New ADODB.Connection
    cnn.ConnectionString = "PROVIDER=MSOLAP.2;Data Source=localhost;" & _
     "Initial Catalog=BookSamples"
    cnn.Open

    Set rstPredict = New ADODB.Recordset
    strPredict = "SELECT FLATTENED " & _
     "[T1].[Book Id] , [T1].[Book Level], [T1].[Book Subject], " & _
     "[T1].[Book Length], [BookLength].[Book Length] " & _
     "FROM " & _
     "[BookLength] PREDICTION JOIN " & _
     "OPENROWSET( " & _
     "'Microsoft.Jet.OLEDB.4.0'," & _
     "'Provider=Microsoft.Jet.OLEDB.4.0;Data Source=" & App.Path & _
     "\Books.mdb;Persist Security Info=False'," & _
     "'SELECT `BookID` AS `Book Id`, `BookLevel` AS `Book Level`, " & _
     "`BookSubject` AS `Book Subject`, `BookLength` AS `Book Length` " & _
     "FROM `tblNewBooks` ORDER BY `BookID`')" & _
     "AS [T1] " & _
     "ON " & _
     "[BookLength].[Book Id] = [T1].[Book Id] AND " & _
     "[BookLength].[Book Level] = [T1].[Book Level] AND " & _
     "[BookLength].[Book Subject] = [T1].[Book Subject] AND " & _
     "[BookLength].[Book Length] = [T1].[Book Length]"

    rstPredict.Open strPredict, cnn
    For Each fld In rstPredict.Fields
        Debug.Print fld.Name & vbTab;
    Next fld
    Debug.Print
    Do Until rstPredict.EOF
        For Each fld In rstPredict.Fields
            Debug.Print fld.Value & vbTab;
        Next fld
        Debug.Print
        rstPredict.MoveNext
    Loop

ExitHere:
    Exit Sub
```

```
HandleErr:
    MsgBox "Error " & Err.Number & ": " & _
     Err.Description, , "cmdCreateOLAPMiningModel"
    Resume ExitHere
    Resume

End Sub
```

Conclusion

Data mining is the most complex subject in SQL Server 2000 Analysis Services. Because it's a new addition to the product, it can also be difficult to find working data mining examples to learn from. In this chapter we began by demonstrating the user interface that Analysis Manager provides for data mining. Then we showed how you can use the PivotTable Service to create a local data mining model, or the Decision Support Objects library to create a persistent data mining model on the server. Finally, we introduced the concept of using a data mining model for predicting future data.

In the final chapter, we'll look at one of the other products that is included with SQL Server 2000: Microsoft English Query. You may have played with English Query in a previous version of SQL Server, but you'll discover that it has been vastly improved and changed for SQL Server 2000. In particular, you can now use English Query to retrieve data from an OLAP cube using natural language querying.

CHAPTER 12

Supporting Natural Language Queries with English Query

- What Is English Query?

- English Query Components

- Creating an English Query Application

- Deploying an English Query Application

One of the problems that end users have with Analysis Services is the difficulty of learning the MDX language. Developers have invested many hours coming up with interfaces that hide the details of this process from users. SQL Server 2000 includes a tool named Microsoft English Query that's designed to make interacting with databases and OLAP cubes simpler. The SQL Server 2000 version of English Query is completely overhauled from the tool of the same name that shipped with SQL Server 7.0. In particular, English Query can now use OLAP cubes directly to answer questions. By creating an English Query application, you can make it possible for your end users to extract information from a database by using plain English instead of MDX or SQL queries.

In this chapter, we'll explain the basic concepts of English Query and show how you can use it to enable natural language querying for an Analysis Services application.

What Is English Query?

English Query is a tool that builds specialized applications based on a relational database (the database may be stored on either SQL Server or Oracle) or an OLAP cube (the cube must be stored on an Analysis Server). These applications allow the user to pose questions in plain English instead of in MDX or SQL. For example, instead of submitting the MDX query

```
SELECT
  {[Measures].[Unit Sales]} ON COLUMNS,
  {[Store].[All Stores].[USA].[OR]} ON ROWS
FROM [Sales]
```

an English Query user could just type the question

```
What were the total sales for Oregon in 1997?
```

Of course, English Query isn't magic. English Query applications are constructed in the Model Editor, a tool that's hosted in the familiar Visual Studio shell. This may indicate that future versions of Visual Studio will ship with English Query, although Microsoft has made no announcement to that effect yet. The Model Editor includes Wizards that do most of the work of building an application based on reasonable assumptions. It's your job as developer to fine-tune the results. For example, if your source data uses OR to indicate Oregon, you'd want to add "Oregon" as a synonym for "OR" to make the model more useful.

Once your English Query model is complete, you use the Model Editor to create a compiled version of the model. This compiled version can be used together with the English Query runtime files and (of course) the original data source to answer the user's questions. The compiled model can be accessed in a variety of ways, including from a dedicated application written in a language such as Visual Basic or from a set of web pages. Later in this chapter, you'll see how to deploy an English Query application to an IIS-based web site.

English Query Components

English Query consists of a number of interrelated components. These include the following:

- The English Query model, which captures the semantic information from your database in a form that English Query can understand

- The Question Builder, a control that lets you integrate English Query into other applications

- The English Query runtime, a set of files that you can redistribute when you need to use English Query

In this section, we'll briefly describe each of these components.

English Query Models

A great deal of knowledge about the English language is already built into English Query. For example, it knows that customers buy items and that employees work for companies. However, what it doesn't know is how these concepts connect with your data: whether there are customers, items, employees, and companies in your database and, if so, where they are stored. The job of an English Query model is to capture the structure of your data in a form that makes it useful to English Query.

An English Query model consists of both database objects and semantic objects. Database objects are the familiar schema objects from your Analysis Services cube and the underlying SQL Server (or Oracle) database: dimensions, measures, levels, tables, fields, joins, data types, keys, and so on. Semantic objects hold information that connects these database objects with English Query's knowledge of the language. Three main types of semantic object exist:

Entity   An entity is a noun represented by a database object. This might be a person such as a customer, a place such as a city, a thing such as an inventory item, or an idea such as a schedule. Entities typically map directly to members of a level or to measures.

Relationship   A relationship is a phrase expressing the connection between two entities. For example, "customers purchase tickets" would express the relationship between customer entities and ticket entities.

Phrasing   A phrasing is a way of expressing a relationship in English. A single relationship might give rise to multiple phrasings. For example, "customers purchase tickets" and "tickets are sold to customers" are two phrasings for the same relationship. The more phrasings you include in your English Query model, the better that model will be at answering questions phrased in English.

Question Builder

The Question Builder is an ActiveX control that can be used to integrate an English Query application with any ActiveX host language: Visual Basic, Visual C++, ASP pages, and so on. The Question Builder is new in the version of English Query that's shipped with SQL Server 2000 and is designed to help users determine the types of questions they can ask an English Query application.

Figure 12.1 shows the Question Builder in action (here connected to an application based on the Sales cube in the FoodMart 2000 Analysis Services database). The leftmost pane of the Question Builder lists all the entities and relationships in the current English Query model. The center pane is a drag-and-drop target. The user can drag entities and drop them here to see the relationships between those entities. The rightmost pane suggests typical questions that can be answered using the entity or relationship that is selected in the center pane.

FIGURE 12.1:

The Question Builder
ActiveX control

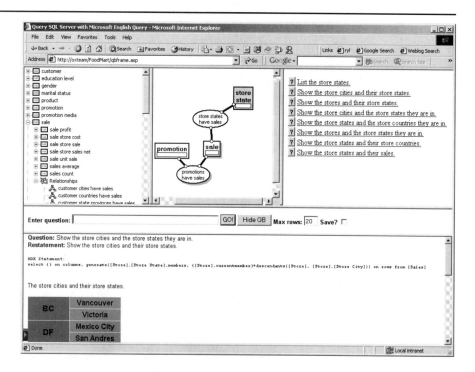

> **TIP**   Figure 12.1 shows the Question Builder hosted by an ASP page that also contains other controls. The Question Builder control displays the three panes that are spread across the top of this web page.

The Question Builder can help you avoid one of the typical problems with natural language applications. It's sometimes difficult for users of such applications to determine just what "natural" language the application understands. This results in frustration and, ultimately, a user's refusal to use the application. By suggesting appropriate terms and questions, the Question Builder can help make users more comfortable with your English Query application.

The box at the bottom of each entity allows the user to enter a specific value for an entity in the model. If the user enters a value, the proposed questions change to include that value. Figure 12.2 shows this process in action.

FIGURE 12.2:

Asking questions about a particular state

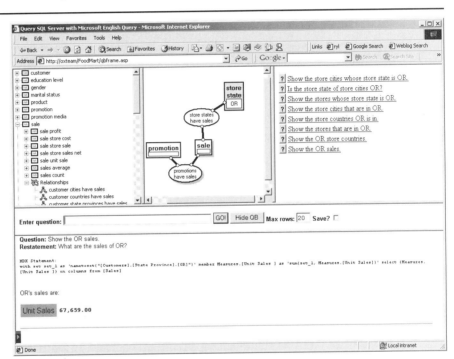

> **TIP**
>
> If you'd like to see English Query in action without the trouble of building an English Query application, check the Program Files\Microsoft English Query\Samples\Models directory for several sample applications.

The English Query Runtime

Depending on how you deploy your English Query application, you may need to redistribute the English Query runtime files. If you're shipping a stand-alone English Query application written in C++, Visual Basic, or another programming language, you need to make sure that all the users of the application have these libraries installed:

- `Mseqole.dll`
- `Mseqbase.dll`
- `Mseqsql.dll`
- `Mseqmsg.dll`
- `Mseqconn.dll`
- `Mseqcore.eqd`

English Query installs these files by default in the `Program Files\Common Files\ Microsoft Shared\EQ80` folder on your development computer. You can copy them to client computers from that folder. Be sure to use regsvr32 to register `Mseqole.dll`:

```
Regsvr32 Mseqole.dll
```

If you're using a web server for deploying your application, those libraries need to be installed only on the web server.

If your application uses the Question Builder, you also need to make sure your users have the appropriate ActiveX control installed. For stand-alone applications, you can install and register `Mseqgrqb.ocx` to deliver this control. For web applications, you should include `Mseqgrqb.cab` in the web application. This file contains the ActiveX control and the help file and will automatically be downloaded by the user's browser when they load a page that uses the control.

WARNING   It's also your responsibility to make sure that every user of an English Query application has a SQL Server client access license. This is required even if the English Query application only uses Analysis Services data and never retrieves data directly from a SQL Server database.

Creating an English Query Application

In this section, we'll walk through the process of creating a typical English Query application, using the Northwind sample database from SQL Server 2000 as the underlying database. We'll cover four steps in this process:

1. Creating an English Query project
2. Adding synonyms to the English Query model
3. Adding relationships to the English Query model
4. Testing the application

Each of these steps is covered in more detail in the remainder of this section.

Creating a Project

The first step in working with English Query is to create a new English Query project. Start by launching English Query itself by choosing Start ➤ Programs ➤ Microsoft SQL Server ➤ English Query ➤ Microsoft English Query. This will open the Visual Studio interface with English Query loaded and launch the New Project dialog box shown in Figure 12.3. If the dialog box doesn't open, you can open it manually by choosing File ➤ New Project.

TIP If you can't find English Query on the Start menu, check to make sure that it was installed on your computer. Installing English Query requires running a separate setup program after the main SQL Server installation is complete.

FIGURE 12.3:

The New Project dialog box

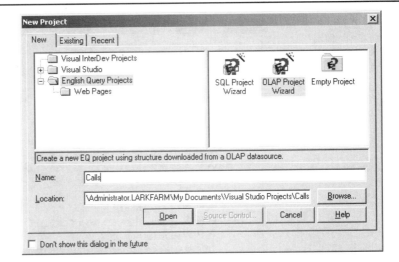

For your first project, you should choose the OLAP Project Wizard. Enter a name for the project and either accept the location that the dialog box proposes or type in your own location. Then click Open to launch the Wizard.

The Wizard will open a dialog box to allow you to select the Analysis Server and database that you want to use as the data source for this English Query project. You can use "localhost" as the database name if English Query is running on the same computer as Analysis Services; otherwise you'll need to supply a computer name here. When you enter the computer name, the database combo box will be populated with the names of the Analysis Services databases on that computer. For this chapter, we'll use the BookSamples database with the Calls cube that you first saw in Chapter 6, "Querying Analysis Services with MDX." After selecting the database, click OK to launch the Wizard itself.

The OLAP Project Wizard uses only two panes (and it doesn't use the familiar Next/Back/Finish Wizard interface). In the first pane, you select the cubes that you would like to use in your English Query project.

TIP   You can base an English Query project on multiple OLAP cubes. This is most useful if the cubes are drawing data from a single relational database. For example, both the Sales and Warehouse cubes from the FoodMart 2000 sample database use the same Access database for their underlying data and would work well together in a single English Query project.

When you click OK after selecting cubes, English Query will retrieve schema information from your database for each of the selected cubes. The OLAP Project Wizard will then display the proposed entities and relationships that it will create, as shown in Figure 12.4.

FIGURE 12.4:

Entities and relationships in the OLAP Project Wizard

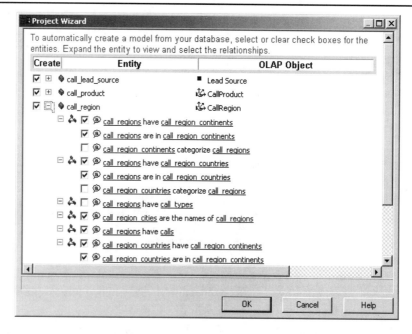

Generally, the OLAP Project Wizard will propose an entity for each measure, level, and dimension in the cubes that you've chosen to include. You can control which of these entities the Project Wizard will actually create by selecting or deselecting the check box to the left of the entity name. You can also click the plus signs (+) to expand the entity and see a list of relationships (the call_region entity is expanded in Figure 12.4). The OLAP Project Wizard will propose several alternative ways to express various relationships.

You can click the icons indicating entities or relationships, or the hyperlinked terms within a relationship, to view additional details. Once you've chosen which entities and relationships to use in your model, click OK to proceed. The OLAP Project Wizard will generate your English Query project and open it in the main English Query interface, as shown in Figure 12.5.

FIGURE 12.5:

New project in English Query

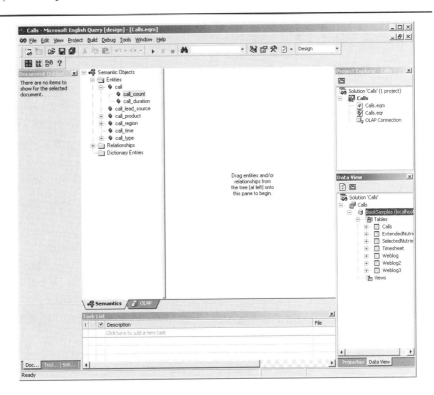

English Query inherits all the windows and controls of the Visual Studio shell in this release of SQL Server. However, you'll find that English Query is not an exceptionally good fit in this shell, and you can simply ignore most of the windows (in the future, you may well include an English Query project in a larger Visual Studio solution, of course, which makes the rest of this interface more useful). Here's what you'll see when you open an English Query project:

- The Document Outline window is not used with English Query projects. We suggest closing this window.

- The Task List window lets you keep a to-do list that's saved as part of your English Query project. If you have some other means of keeping track of tasks, you should close this window as well.

- The Project Explorer shows you all the files that are part of your English Query project. Usually you won't need this information. This window comes in handy if you deploy your English Query project to a web server, because it provides a handy launching point for the web pages. You'll also need this window if you happen to close the main English Query window; to reopen the main window you can double-click the EQM file in the Project Explorer.

- The Data View window shows the database connection that your English Query project is using to retrieve data. This is normally also extraneous information. However, if you're using data from multiple sources in a single English Query project, the Data View window will help you keep the various data sources straight.

- The Semantics tab in the main document window shows the English Query entities and relationships that are part of your project, and provides you with a way to create new relationships. This is where you'll do most of your work.

- The OLAP tab in the main document window shows the Analysis Services objects that are used in your English Query model.

If you close all the extraneous windows to get more working space, your English Query environment will resemble that shown in Figure 12.6. If you later decide you want to show some or all of the other windows, you can reopen them from the View menu.

FIGURE 12.6:

English Query with extra windows closed

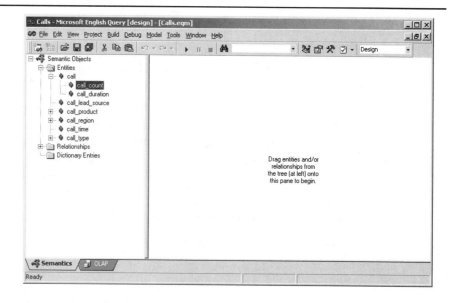

Adding Synonyms

After you've created the English Query model, you can use the English Query design environment to refine the model. One refinement you'll often need to make is to add synonyms for entities. For example, in the Calls model, the Project Wizard will automatically create an entity named call_duration from the CallDuration measure in the Calls cube. English Query will automatically recognize the phrase "call duration" as referring to this entity. However, your users may well use "call length" when asking about the duration of calls. So, it's useful to add call length as a synonym for this entity. To do so, follow these steps:

1. Expand the Call object in the Entities folder in the Semantic Objects tree by clicking the plus sign to its left.

2. Double-click the call_duration entity to open the properties of this object. You'll see the dialog box shown in Figure 12.7.

3. Click the text box labeled Words (that currently contains the phrase call duration). This will open a data-entry area beneath the text box. Type in **call length** and hit Enter. The text box should display call duration, call length.

4. Click OK to save your changes.

FIGURE 12.7:

Setting properties for the call_duration entity

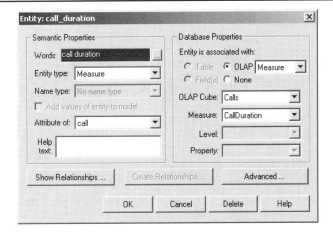

Adding Entities

Although the OLAP Project Wizard does a good job of identifying the entities for an English Query project, there are times when you'll need to add more entities manually. For example, you might have modified the OLAP cube itself, and now want to mirror your modifications into the English Query model. While it would be nice if everything automatically stayed synchronized, in practice you need to take care of these details yourself.

Let's look at a concrete example by adding a member property to the Calls cube and then modifying the English Query model to contain an entity for the property. The property we'll choose is the Product ID, which can be represented in the Calls cube as a member property for the Item Name level of the CallProduct dimension.

To add the Product ID member property to the Calls cube, follow these steps:

1. Launch Analysis Manager and expand the treeview to show the individual shared dimensions in the sample database.

2. Right-click the CallProduct dimension and choose Edit.

3. In the Dimension Editor, expand the Item Name node in the treeview to show its Member Properties folder.

4. Right-click the Member Properties folder and choose New Member Property.

5. In the Insert Member Property dialog box, select the ProductID field and click OK.

6. Choose File ➢ Save to save the dimension.

7. Choose Tools ➢ Process Dimension. You'll need to choose whether to perform an incremental update or a full rebuild of the dimension structure; for this example it doesn't matter which of these options you choose.

8. When Analysis Services is done processing the dimension, close the Dimension Editor.

9. Right-click the Calls cube and select Process. Do a full process of the cube.

At this point, you've created the new member property, but English Query doesn't know anything about it yet. To add a Product ID member property to English Query, follow these steps:

1. Switch to the OLAP tab of the English Query model.

2. Right-click the Calls cube and choose Refresh Cube. This step is necessary to force English Query to reread the cube's metadata.

3. Switch to the Semantics tab of the English Query model.

4. Right-click the Entities folder and choose Add Entity.

5. Set the Words property of the new entity to Product ID.

6. Set the entity type to None.

7. Set the name type to Unique ID.

8. Set the new entity to be an attribute of the call_product entity.

9. Associate the entity with an OLAP property.

10. Select CallProduct as the Dimension, Item Name as the level, and Product Id as the property. Figure 12.8 shows the completed New Entity dialog box.

11. Click OK to create the new entity and add it to the model.

FIGURE 12.8:

Adding a new entity to the model

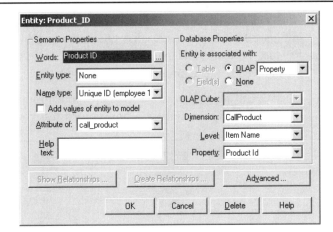

WARNING When you're refreshing the metadata in the English Query model, be sure to do the refresh on the OLAP tab of the English Query model. If you choose to refresh in the Visual Studio data view, the data view will show the new property but the property will still be unavailable to English Query.

Adding Relationships

You can also use the English Query design environment to add relationships to a model. For example, the newly created Product_ID entity should have a relationship to the Call_Product entity. To create this relationship, follow these steps:

1. Drag the call_product entity and drop it on the right-hand panel of the design surface.

2. Drag the Product_ID entity and drop it on top of the call_product entity. This will open the New Relationship dialog box.

3.   Click the Add button to the right of the Phrasings box. Note that two Add buttons are on this dialog box.

4.   On the Select Phrasing dialog box, choose the appropriate type of phrasing. In this particular case, you want to create a Name/ID Phrasing. Click OK when you've selected a type of phrasing.

5.   On the Name/ID Phrasing dialog box, choose the appropriate subject and object. In this case, the final phrase is "Product_IDs are the names of call_products," which will appear at the bottom of the Trait Phrasing dialog box.

6.   Click OK to add the phrasing to the New Relationship dialog box. The result is shown in Figure 12.9. Note that English Query is smart enough to notice the ID part of the Product_ID name, and that this causes it to change the phrasing to "Product_IDs are the unique ids of call_products."

7.   Click OK to add the relationship to the model. English Query will display the relationship as an oval between the two boxes on its design surface.

FIGURE 12.9:

Creating a new relationship

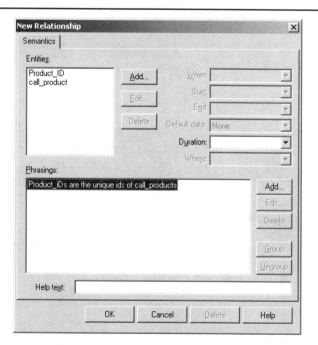

Adding SQL Support

Using English Query to ask questions based on an OLAP cube is fine if the data is actually in the cube. But your users may want to drill down to a level of detail that's not contained in the aggregate information in the cube. For example, with the Calls cube, they might want details of individual calls. These details exist only in the underlying relational database, not in the cube.

Fortunately, English Query lets you have multiple data connections in a single project. In particular, you can add a SQL connection to an English Query project based on OLAP data. By directing the SQL connection to the relational database that underlies the cube, you give English Query the flexibility to use either the aggregated data or the raw data to answer questions.

NOTE   English Query will attempt to use an MDX query to the OLAP database first, using a SQL query to the relational database only when the requested data is not in the OLAP database.

To add a SQL connection to the Calls English Query project, follow these steps:

1. Select Project ➤ ProjectName Properties from the English Query menus.

2. On the Data Connection tab of the Project Properties dialog box, check the Enable SQL check box.

3. Click the Change button in the SQL Connection section to open the Data Link Properties dialog box.

4. Select the OLE DB Provider for SQL Server and click Next.

5. Select the server that holds the BookSamples database, enter your login information, and select the BookSamples database. Click OK to return to the Project Properties dialog box.

6. Click OK to dismiss the Project Properties dialog box. English Query will warn you that it needs to connect as an administrator. Click Yes.

7. English Query will connect to the Analysis Server to determine which relational tables hold the source data for each Cube object, and then return control to the English Query interface.

TIP   English Query uses DSO to retrieve data from the underlying relational database. You must be a member of the OLAP Administrators group to enable this functionality.

Testing the Model

Once you've finished fine-tuning your English Query model, you should test it to make sure that you get the expected answers to questions, and that it can answer all the questions you think are reasonable. To test the model, follow these steps:

1. Select Debug ➤ Start or press F5 to compile and run the model. This will open the Model Test dialog box.

2. Type a question into the Query box and hit Enter, or click the Submit Query button on the Model Test toolbar.

3. Model Test will analyze the question and supply a phrasing that it understands as equivalent, a caption for the results, and the MDX or SQL statement that it will use to answer the question.

4. Click the View Results button or press Ctrl+R to see the results of the query.

Figure 12.10 shows the Model Test dialog box in action.

FIGURE 12.10:

Testing a model

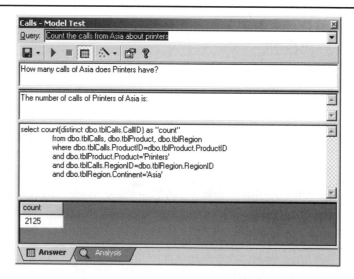

You can see which pieces of the model English Query used to answer your question by clicking the Analysis tab in the Model Test dialog box.

Note that the rephrasing that English Query comes up with may not make much sense to you. But that doesn't matter, as long as it gets the correct result. While you're testing the model, you may wish to keep a copy of the Analysis Services cube browser open so you can check the results.

If English Query is unable to answer a question, you can supply more information by clicking the Suggestion Wizard toolbar button or pressing Ctrl+W. This will open the Suggestion Wizard dialog box, as shown in Figure 12.11. You can supply additional information here so that English Query can figure out what you're asking. When you click OK, the information you supply will be added to the English Query model.

FIGURE 12.11:

Clarifying a question for English Query

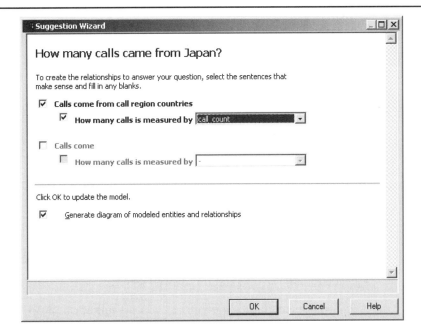

Once you have dismissed the Suggestion Wizard dialog box, you can use the Submit Query button to see the results of asking your question with the new information. English Query will automatically recompile the model before answering the question.

When you're done testing the model, simply close the Model Test dialog box to return to the main English Query interface.

Deploying an English Query Application

When you're done developing an English Query application, the final task you need to perform is to deploy the application so that end users can benefit from it. This requires performing two tasks: building the application and deploying the application. In this section, we'll show you how to perform those two tasks.

We'll deploy our sample application as a web site using Internet Information Server. You can also use a COM-aware programming tool (such as Visual C++ or Visual Basic) to create a stand-alone English Query application.

Building the Application

Building an English Query application takes the model and converts it into a compiled form that can be used along with the English Query runtime to answer questions on a computer that does not have the full English Query development interface installed. To build your application, follow these steps:

1. Choose Project ➢ ProjectName Properties from the English Query menus.

2. On the Data Connection tab, check the Sample Data check box.

3. Click OK to dismiss the Project Properties dialog box.

4. Select Build ➢ Build to compile the model.

Deploying to the Web

English Query has a built-in Wizard to deploy your application to a web site. To use this Wizard, though, you need to meet certain requirements:

- You must have installed Microsoft Visual Interdev on the computer where you're working with Microsoft English Query.

- You must have the FrontPage extensions installed on your web server.

- You must have permission to write to the root on the web server.

- You must be an operator on the web server.

Once you've met these requirements, you can follow this procedure to deploy your application to the web server:

1. Select Project ➢ Deploy to Web.

2. On the first step of the Web Project Wizard, choose the server that you wish to use to deploy your English Query application. Select Master Mode for the deployment and click Next.

3. On the second step of the Web Project Wizard, choose whether to deploy to a new or existing web application and specify the name for the application. This name will be part of the URL for accessing your English Query application via the web, so be sure you make note of it. You can also choose to create a web page to enable full text searching on your database if you'd like. Click Next.

4. On the third step of the Web Project Wizard, choose any navigation controls that you want to use with your application and click Next.

5. On the fourth step of the Web Project Wizard, choose a theme for your application and click Finish.

The Web Project Wizard will create several ASP and HTM pages for your application and then prompt you for connection information. You can supply separate information for design-time and runtime authentication. If you're concerned about security, be sure to prompt for connection information at runtime.

If you'd like to allow anonymous access to your Web Project, the simplest solution is to add your IIS anonymous user to an Analysis Services role that has access to the cube where the data is located. The anonymous user will have a name of the form IUSR_*computername*, using the name of the computer where IIS is installed. You can add this user to Analysis Services by right-clicking the Database Roles folder in Analysis Manager and selecting Manage Roles.

TIP   See Chapter 5, "Advanced Analysis Services," for a discussion of roles.

To see the pages that the Web Project Wizard builds, open the Project Explorer window in English Query. You'll find a set of nodes in the treeview for the web portion of the application.

To use your deployed application, use your web browser to navigate to `servername/applicationname`. For example, if you named the application Calls and deployed it to a server named OXTEAM, you'd use `OXTEAM/Calls` to show the application.

The interface to your application will resemble that shown in Figure 12.12. The user can type a question into the left frame and click Go or just hit Enter, or the user can use the Show QB button to invoke the Question Builder. Results are displayed in the right frame.

FIGURE 12.12:

Using English Query in a web browser

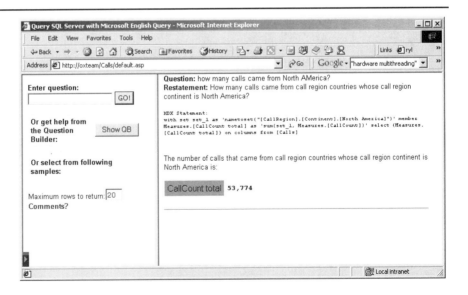

Using an English Query Domain from Visual Basic

When you build an English Query project, the output is an EQD (English Query Domain) file. English Query also supplies redistributable libraries that let you use this file to answer questions from any COM host. In this section, we'll show you how to use your English Query Domain file from within a Visual Basic program. The code for this section is contained within the Chapter12.vbp sample project on the companion CD.

> **TIP**   For details of the English Query object model, refer to Appendix D.

The main functionality of English Query is contained in the Microsoft English Query Type Library 2.0. To use English Query from Visual Basic, you need to set a reference to this library from Project ➤ References. To include the Question Builder, you can select Project ➤ Components and include the graphical_qb 1.0 Type Library. If this library doesn't appear in the list of available controls, use the Browse button on the Components dialog box to locate the file MSEQGRQB.OCX.

> **TIP**   English Query installs several other type libraries that are used by the English Query design interface. You won't need a reference to those libraries to use English Query functionality from your application.

The first step in using English Query from Visual Basic is to instantiate an Mseq.Session object and call its InitDomain method with the name of an EQB file. The sample application allows you to enter the name of an EQB file, and then uses this code to set up the English Query session:

```
Dim objsession As Mseq.Session
…
Set objsession = New Mseq.Session
objsession.InitDomain (txtModel.Text)
```

Once you've initialized the Session object to use an English Query domain, processing a query is easy. Just use the ParseRequest method of the Session object to return a Response object, and check the Type property of the returned Response object to find out whether English Query handled the question:

```
Set objResponse = objsession.ParseRequest(txtQuestion.Text)

Select Case objResponse.Type
    Case nlResponseCommand
        txtQuery.Text = objResponse.Commands(0).QueryText
    Case nlResponseUserclarify
        txtQuery.Text = _
          "English Query cannot answer the question as stated"
    Case nlResponseError
        txtQuery.Text = "An internal error occurred"
End Select
```

From a Visual Basic developer's point of view, the Response object is peculiar. Its properties and subsidiary objects change depending on the Type property. What's actually going on here is that English Query is creating a variety of different objects that inherit from a single Response object. There are three broad categories of response:

CommandResponse   Provides SQL or MDX commands that can be executed to answer the question that was submitted via the ParseRequest method. A CommandResponse contains a collection of Command objects, each of which has a QueryText property. (There are actually multiple varieties of Command objects as well, but we won't go into those details.) In the sample application, we return (in the case of a successfully parsed query) the QueryText from the first Command object. Note that English Query collections are numbered starting at zero. Figure 12.13 shows the sample application displaying the equivalent MDX statement for a question, with the MDX taken from the QueryText of a Command object.

FIGURE 12.13:

Sample English Query application in Visual Basic

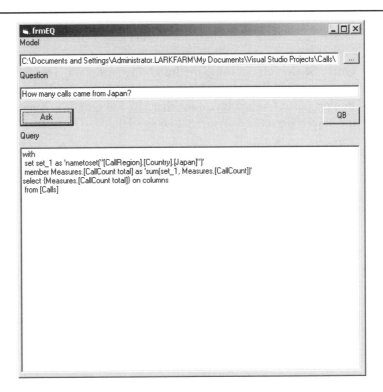

UserClarifyResponse   Indicates that English Query needs more information. In the sample application, we just display an error message when this happens, but you can actually do a great deal more. That's because the UserClarifyResponse contains subsidiary objects that allow the user to supply more information.

ErrorResponse   Indicates an internal error somewhere. There's not much to do about this other than to display an error message.

NOTE   The QueryText property of a Command object returns an MDX or SQL query. It does not return actual database results. To get the corresponding database results, you'll need to use ADO/MD or ADO to submit the QueryText to the database.

The other technique demonstrated in this application is the use of the QuestionBuilder control. Using the QuestionBuilder only takes a few lines of code:

```
Dim objsession As Mseq.Session
Set objsession = New Mseq.Session
objsession.InitDomain (txtModel.Text)

Load frmQB
frmQB.GraphicalQB1.QBEngine = objsession.DomainInfo.QuestionBuilder
frmQB.Show vbModal
```

Here, frmQB is a Visual Basic form containing a QuestionBuilder control named Graphical-QB1. To initialize the QuestionBuilder control, you first create and initialize an English Query Session object, using the InitDomain method. Then you set the control's QBEngine property to use the QuestionBuilder property that's available from the Session's Domain-Info property. Once you've done that, the full Question Builder interface is available, with the objects from the domain that you specified.

The QuestionBuilder control supports several events. The important one is the Select-Example event. This event is triggered when the user chooses a question from the Question Builder. It returns a string with the text of the question:

```
Private Sub GraphicalQB1_SelectExample(ByVal szExample As String)
    frmEQ.txtQuestion.Text = szExample
    Unload Me
End Sub
```

Of course, this sample contains only the bare bones of English Query functionality. In a real application, you need to be prepared to handle all the possible variants of Response and Command objects. But there's no point to writing this code yourself, because Microsoft supplies it with every copy of English Query. The directory Program Files\Microsoft English Query\SAMPLES\Applications contains sample code in ASP, Visual Basic, and Visual C++ that you're free to reuse in your own applications. The Visual Basic code includes a module named VBUILib.bas that contains several useful general-purpose procedures. The most important of these procedures are listed in Table 12.1.

TABLE 12.1: Procedures in VBUILib.bas

Procedure	Description
Startup	Initializes the Visual Basic code from an English Query project, rebuilding the English Query Domain file and prompting for database login information if necessary.
Shutdown	Cleanly closes open objects and resources.
SubmitQuery	Submits a query to the English Query engine and returns any answers.
Clarify	Uses the information in a UserClarifyResponse object to prompt the user for further input.
ExecuteQuery	Takes a command and displays the actual results on the user interface.

Conclusion

In this chapter, you've learned how to use English Query, Microsoft's natural language querying tool, with data stored by Analysis Services. You saw how you could use English Query to enable your users to ask questions in plain English instead of Transact-SQL, and how to create and deploy an English Query application to a web server. We also showed you how to use an English Query domain from a COM application of your choice.

That takes us to the end of our exploration of Analysis Services in SQL Server 2000. We hope that over the course of the book we've convinced you of the power of the Analysis Services engine and the flexibility of the various programmatic interfaces for retrieving OLAP data that it supports.

MDX Reference

This appendix documents the MDX statements and functions included within Analysis Services, along with a brief description of their results. We provided information on the operation of MDX in Chapter 6, "Querying Analysis Services with MDX." In that chapter we covered only some of the details of MDX. For a complete reference, refer to the MDX book under Analysis Services in the SQL Server Books Online.

Statement Reference

This appendix gives you the format of the statements that MDX understands. To read these syntax diagrams, you need to be aware of the conventions shown in Table A.1.

TABLE A.1: Syntax Diagram Conventions

Symbol	Meaning
< >	User-supplied parameter. Do not type the angle brackets.
[ ]	Optional item. Do not type the brackets.
|	Alternatives. Choose one of the items separated by vertical bars.
…	Repeat any number of times. Do not type the ellipsis. Separate items by commas.
::=	Composed of. For example, `<slicer_specification> ::= <tuple>` indicates that a slicer specification is composed of a tuple, and you can look in the diagram to see the components of a tuple in more detail.

SELECT

The SELECT statement is the primary means in MDX for retrieving data from a cube. Specify the dimensions and measures to be retrieved on each axis, using calculated members as necessary, and using additional clauses to describe the presentation of the result set, the source cube, and any filters or ways in which the data will be "sliced."

```
<select_statement> ::= [WITH <single_formula_specification>
[<single_formula_specification>...]]
SELECT [<axis_specification> [, <axis_specification>...]]
FROM <cube_specification>
[WHERE <slicer_specification>]
[<cell_props>]
<single_formula_specification> ::= <member_specification>
| <set_specification>
| <cache_specification>
<member_specification> ::= MEMBER <parent_of_member>.<member_name> AS
➡ '<value_expression>'
```

```
[, <solve_order_specification>]
[, <member_property_definition>...]
<solve_order_specification> ::= SOLVE_ORDER = <unsigned_integer>
<member_property_definition> ::= <member_property_name> = <value_expression>
<set_specification> ::= SET <set_name> AS '<set>'
<cache_specification> ::= CACHE AS '(<set> [,<set>])'
<axis_specification> ::= [NON EMPTY] <set> [<dim_props>] ON <axis_name>
<set> ::= member:member
| <set_value_expression>
| {<set> | <tuple> [,<set> | <tuple>...]}
| (<set>)
<tuple> ::= <member> | (<member>[,<member>...]) | <tuple_value_expression>
<axis_name> ::= COLUMNS | ROWS | PAGES | SECTIONS | CHAPTERS | AXIS(<index>)
<dim_props> ::= [DIMENSION] PROPERTIES <property> [, <property>...]
<property> ::= <dimension_property> | <level_property> | <member_property>
<dimension_property> ::= <dimension_name>.ID | <dimension_name>.KEY |
➥<dimension_name>.NAME
<level_property> ::= [<dimension_name>.]<level_name>.ID
| [<dimension_name>.]<level_name>.KEY
| [<dimension_name>.]<level_name>.NAME
<member_property> ::= <level_name>.<member_property_name>
<cube_specification> ::= <cube_name>
<slicer_specification> ::= <tuple>
<cell_props> ::= [CELL] PROPERTIES <cell_property> [, <cell_property>...]
<cell_property> ::= <mandatory_cell_property>
| <optional_cell_property>
| <provider_specific_cell_property>
<mandatory_cell_property> ::= CELL_ORDINAL | VALUE | FORMATTED_VALUE
<optional_cell_property> ::= FORMAT_STRING | FORE_COLOR | BACK_COLOR | FONT_NAME
➥| FONT_SIZE | FONT_FLAGS
<provider_specific_cell_property> ::= <identifier>
```

DRILLTHROUGH

The DRILLTHROUGH statement can be appended to SELECT statements to drill down
to the original source data used in aggregation to reach the subtotals originally displayed.

```
<drillthrough>      ::= DRILLTHROUGH [<Max_Rows>] [<First_Rowset>] <MDX
                    ➥select>
    <Max_Rows>      ::= MAXROWS <positive number>
    <First_Rowset>  ::= FIRSTROWSET <positive number>
```

ALTER CUBE

The ALTER CUBE statement can be used on a cube to specify the default member for a dimension, and it can be used on parent-child dimensions to create, modify, move, or delete the members within that dimension.

```
<Alter Cube> ::= ALTER CUBE <cube> [<update dim list>]
    | [<Alter List>]
<update dim list> ::= <update dimension>[,<update dimensions list>]
<update dimension> ::= UPDATE DIMENSION <dimension name> [Default Member] =
➥'<MDX rule>'
<dimension name> ::= <dim name>
    | <dim name. Hierarchy name>
<alter_list>     ::= [<alter_statement> [, <alter_list>]]
<alter_statement> ::= <create_statement>
    | <remove_statement>
    | <move_statement>
    | <update_statement>
<create_statement> ::= CREATE DIMENSION MEMBER
    <parent_unique_name>.<member_name> [AS '<MDX expr.>'],
    KEY='<key_value>' [, <property_name> =
<value>' [, <property_name> = '<value>' ... ]]
<remove_statement> ::= DROP DIMENSION MEMBER <member_unique_name>
➥[WITH DESCENDANTS]
<move_statement> ::= MOVE DIMENSION MEMBER <member_unique_name>
    [, SKIPPED_LEVELS = '<value>']
    [WITH DESCENDANTS] UNDER <member_unique_name>
<update_statement> ::= UPDATE DIMENSION MEMBER <member_unique_name>
    {AS '<MDX expr.>'
        | ,<property_name> = '<value>'}
    [, <property_name> = '<value>' ...]
<member_unique_name> ::= <dimension_name>.&[[]<key>[]]
```

CREATE CUBE

The CREATE CUBE statement is used to create local cubes. It must be used in conjunction with the INSERT INTO statement as part of a PivotTable connection string. For details, see Chapter 9, "Advanced Usage of the PivotTable Service."

TIP   This statement can only be used to create local cubes. For information on creating server cubes, see Chapter 10, "Managing an Analysis Services Environment Using DSO."

```
<create-cube-statement > ::= CREATE CUBE <cube name> <open paren> <dimensions
➥def> <measures def> [<command expression>] <close paren>
```

```
<dimensions def> :: = DIMENSION <dimension name> [<time def>]
➡[DIMENSION_STRUCTURE <sub_type>][<hidden def>] <options def> <comma>
➡<hierarchy def  list>
<time def> ::= TIME | ...
<dimension name> ::= <legal name>
<sub_type>::= PARENT_CHILD
<hidden_def> ::= HIDDEN
<options def> ::= OPTIONS <open paren> <dim options list> <close paren>
<dim options list> ::= <dim option> [ < comma> <dim options list>]
<dim option> ::= UNIQUE_NAME | UNIQUE_KEY | NOTRELATEDTOFACTTABLE |
➡ALLOWSIBLINGSWITHSAMENAME
<hierarchy def list> ::= <hierarchy def> [ <comma> <hierarchy def  list>
<hierarchy def> ::= [HIERARCHY <hierarchy name> [<hidden_def>] <comma>]
➡<level def>
<hierarchy name> ::= <legal name>
<level def > ::= <parent-child level def> | <normal level def list >
<parent-child level def> ::= [<all level def> <comma>] LEVEL <Template>
➡// if dimension is parent-child
<normal level def list> ::= <normal level def> [ <comma> <normal level def list> ]
<all level> ::= LEVEL <level name> TYPE ALL
<level name> ::= <legal name>
<normal level def> ::= [<all level> <comma>] LEVEL <level name> [TYPE <level
➡type>] [<level format def>] [<level options def>] [<hidden def>] [<hole def>]
➡[<root member def>] [<custom_rollup_expr def>] [<comma> <level prop def list>]
<level type> ::= YEAR | QUARTER | MONTH | WEEK | DAY
| DAYOFWEEK | DATE | HOUR | MINUTE | SECOND
<level format def> ::= FORMAT_NAME <expression> [FORMAT_KEY <expression>]
<level options def> ::= OPTIONS ( [<sort option> <comma>] <level option list> |
➡[<level option list> <comma>] <sort option>)
<level option list> :: = <option> [<comma> <level option list>]
<sort option> ::= SORTBYNAME
| SORTBYKEY
| SORTBYPROPERTY <property name>
<option> ::= UNIQUE
| UNIQUE_NAME
| UNIQUE_KEY
| NOTRELATEDTOFACTTABLE
<hole def> ::= HIDE_MEMBER_IF <hide values>
<hide values> ::= ONLY_CHILD_AND_BLANK_NAME
| ONLY_CHILD_AND_PARENT_NAME
| BLANK_NAME
| PARENT_NAME
<root member def> ::= ROOT_MEMBER_IF <root values>
<root values> ::= ROOT_IF_PARENT_IS_BLANK
  | ROOT_IF_PARENT_IS_MISSING
  | ROOT_IF_PARENT_IS_SELF
  | ROOT_IF_PARENT_IS_BLANK_OR_SELF_OR_MISSING
```

```
<custom_rollup_exp> ::= CUSTOM_ROLLUP_EXPRESSION <MDX expression>
<level prop def list> ::= <level prop def> [<comma> <level prop def list>]
<level prop def> ::= PROPERTY <legal name> [<prop type def>] [<hidden def>]
➡[<prop caption def>]
<prop type def> ::= TYPE <prop type value>
<property_type value>::= REGULAR | ID | RELATION_TO_PARENT
   | ORG_TITLE | CAPTION | CAPTION_SHORT
   | CAPTION_DESCRIPTION | CAPTION_ABBREVIATION
   | WEB_URL | WEB_HTML | WEB_XML_OR_XSL | WEB_MAIL_ALIAS
   | ADDRESS | ADDRESS_STREET | ADDRESS_HOUSE
   | ADDRESS_CITY | ADDRESS_STATE_OR_PROVINCE
   | ADDRESS_ZIP | ADDRESS_QUARTER | ADDRESS_COUNTRY
   | ADDRESS_BUILDING | ADDRESS_ROOM | ADDRESS_FLOOR
   | ADDRESS_FAX | ADDRESS_PHONE
   | GEO_CENTROID_X | GEO_CENTROID_Y | GEO_CENTROID_Z
   | GEO_BOUNDARY_TOP | GEO_BOUNDARY_LEFT
   | GEO_BOUNDARY_BOTTOM | GEO_BOUNDARY_RIGHT
   | GEO_BOUNDARY_FRONT | GEO_BOUNDARY_REAR
   | GEO_BOUNDARY_POLYGON
   | PHYSICAL_SIZE | PHYSICAL_COLOR | PHYSICAL_WEIGHT
   | PHYSICAL_HEIGHT | PHYSICAL_WIDTH | PHYSICAL_DEPTH
   | PHYSICAL_VOLUME | PHYSICAL_DENSITY
   | PERSON_FULL_NAME | PERSON_FIRST_NAME
   | PERSON_LAST_NAME | PERSON_MIDDLE_NAME
   | PERSON_DEMOGRAPHIC | PERSON_CONTACT
   | QTY_RANGE_LOW | QTY_RANGE_HIGH
   | FORMATTING_COLOR | FORMATTING_ORDER
   | FORMATTING_FONT | FORMATTING_FONT_EFFECTS
   | FORMATTING_FONT_SIZE | FORMATTING_SUB_TOTAL
   | DATE | DATE_START | DATE_ENDED | DATE_CANCELED
   | DATE_MODIFIED | DATE_DURATION
   | VERSION
<prop caption def> ::= CAPTION <any string>
<measures def> :: = MEASURE <measure name> <measure function def> [<measure
➡format def>] [<measure type def>] [<hidden def>] [<comma> <measures def>]
<measure function def> ::= FUNCTION <function name>
<function name> ::= SUM | MIN | MAX | COUNT
<measure format def> ::= FORMAT <expression>
<measure type def> ::= TYPE <supported OLE DB numeric types>
<supported OLEDB numeric types> :: = DBTYPE_NUMERIC
    | DBTYPE_I1 | DBTYPE_I2 | DBTYPE_I4 | DBTYPE_I8
 | DBTYPE_UI1 | DBTYPE_UI2 | DBTYPE_UI4 | DBTYPE_UI8
 | DBTYPE_R4 | DBTYPE_R8
 | DBTYPE_CY | DBTYPE_DECIMAL | DBTYPE_DATE
<command expression> ::= COMMAND <expression> [ <comma> <command expression>]
```

DROP CUBE

The DROP CUBE statement deletes a cube from the current OLAP database. Use with care!

```
<drop-cube-statement> ::= DROP CUBE <cube-name>
```

INSERT INTO

The INSERT INTO statement copies data into a local cube from a MOLAP or ROLAP data source. For more information, see Chapter 9.

```
<insert-into-statement> ::= INSERT INTO <target-clause> [<options-clause>]
➥[<bind-clause>] <source-clause>
    |INSERT INTO <model> (<mapped model columns>) <source data query>
    |INSERT INTO <model> (<mapped model columns>) VALUES <constant list>
    |INSERT INTO <model>.COLUMN_VALUES(<mapped model columns>) <source data
    ➥query>
<mapped model columns> ::= <column identifier> | <table identifier>(<column
➥identifier> | SKIP), ...
<target-clause> ::= <cube-name> <open-paren> <target-element-list> <close-paren>
<target-element-list> ::= <target-element>[, <target-element-list>]
<target-element> ::= [<dim-name>.[<hierarchy-name>.]]<level-name>
    | <time-dim-name> | <parent-child-dim-name>
    | [Measures.]<measure-name>
    | SKIPONECOLUMN
<level-name> ::= <simple-level-name>
    | <simple-level-name>.NAME
    | <simple-level-name>.KEY
    | <simple-level-name>.Custom_Rollup
    | .parent
    | <simple-level-name>.SkipLevelColumn
<time-dim-name> ::= <dim-name-type-time>
    | <dim-name-type-time>.NAME
    | <dim-name-type-time>.KEY
<options-clause> ::= OPTIONS <options-list>
<options-list> ::= <option>[, <options-list>]
<option> ::= <defer-options>
    | < analysis-options>
<defer-options> ::= DEFER_DATA
    | ATTEMPT_DEFER
<analysis-options> ::= PASSTHROUGH
    | ATTEMPT_ANALYSIS
<bind-clause> ::= BIND (<bind-list>)
<bind-list> ::= <simple-column-name>[,<simple-column-name>]
<simple-column-name> ::= <identifier>
<source-clause> ::= SELECT <columns-list>
    FROM <tables-list>
    [ WHERE <where-clause> ]
```

```
    | DIRECTLYFROMCACHEDROWSET <hex-number> | DIRECTLYFROMMARSHALLEDROWSET
    ↪<hex number>
<columns-list> ::= <column-expression> [, < columns-list> ]
<column-expression> ::= <column-expression-name>
<column-expression-name> ::= <column-name> [AS <alias-name>]
    | <alias name> <column-name>
<column-name> ::= <table-name>.<column-name>
    | <column-function>
    | <ODBC scalar function>
    | <braced-expression>
<column function> ::= <identifier>(. . .)
<ODBC scalar function> ::= {FN<column-function>}
<braced-expression> ::= (. . .)
<tables -ist> ::= <table-expression> [, <tables-list>]
<table-expression> ::= <table-name> [ [AS] <table-alias>]
<table-alias> ::= <identifier>
<table-name> ::= <identifier>
<where-clause> ::= <where-condition> [AND <where-clause>]
<where-condition> ::= <join-constraint>
    | <application constraint>
<join-constraint> ::= <column-name> = <column-name>
    | <open-paren><column-name> = <column-name><close-paren>
<application-constraint> ::= (. . .)
    | NOT (. . .)
    | (. . .) OR (. . .)
<identifier> ::= <letter>{<letter>
    |<digit>
    |<underline>
    |<dollar>
    |<sharp>}. . .
```

USE LIBRARY

The USE LIBRARY statement specifies and initializes external libraries (i.e., COM components in DLLs) to be used in the construction of calculated members and other custom facilities.

```
<use_library> ::= USE LIBRARY <lib_list> | ALL
    <lib_list> ::= <lib_def> [, <lib_list>]
    <lib_def> ::= <prog_id> | <lib_name>
```

DROP LIBRARY

The DROP LIBRARY statement acts as a destructor for the specified libraries that have been initialized by the USE LIBRARY statement within the current user session.

```
<drop_library> ::= DROP LIBRARY <lib_list> | ALL
    <lib_list> ::= <lib_def> [, <lib_list>]
    <lib_def> ::= <prog_id> | <lib_name>
```

The statement DROP LIBRARY ALL unloads all user-defined function libraries.

Function Reference

Table A.2 describes the functions available within MDX. These functions can be used to create calculated members, actions, and custom rollups within MDX statements.

TABLE A.2: MDX Functions

Function	Description
AddCalculatedMembers(«Set»)	Returns a set containing the specified members and any sibling calculated members. Thus, `AddCalculatedMembers([Measures].Members)` returns the set of all measures and calculated measures.
Aggregate(«Set»[, «Numeric Expression»])	Returns the aggregate of the set according to the current member's default aggregation type.
Ancestor(«Member», «Level»I«Numeric-Expression»)	Returns an ancestor of the specified member. Where a level is specified, the member's ancestor is returned at that level. Where a numeric expression is given, an ancestor is returned that is the specified number of levels up the hierarchy.
Ancestors(«Member», «Level»INumeric-Expression)	Returns all the ancestors of the specified member at a particular level. Operates in the same way as the Ancestor() function, but returns a set rather than a member.
Ascendants(«Member»)	Returns all the ancestors of the specified member as a set, reaching the top of the hierarchy.
Avg(«Set»[, «Numeric Expression»])	Returns the mean average value for a measure or expression across a set.
Axis(«Numeric Expression»)	Represents a particular axis (see the upcoming section "MDX Axes" for more information).
BottomCount(«Set», «Count»[, «Numeric-Expression»])	Returns the bottom *n* items within a set based on the specified measure or numeric expression, where *n* is specified as the Count parameter. Similar to the TopCount function.
BottomPercent(«Set», «Percentage», «Numeric Expression»)	Returns the bottom *n* percent of items within a set based on the specified measure or numeric expression, where *n* is specified as the Percentage parameter.

Continued on next page

TABLE A.2 CONTINUED: MDX Functions

Function	Description
BottomSum(«Set», «Value», «Numeric Expression»)	Returns the largest set of items that cumulatively total at least *n* within a set (based on the specified measure or numeric expression), where *n* is specified as the sum parameter.
Call «UDF Name»	Calls an external user-defined function. This keyword is optional.
ClosingPeriod([«Level»[, «Member»]])	Returns the last descendant member matching the given level that is a child of the specified member. Thus, `ClosingPeriod(Quarter, [1999])` will return [1999].[Q4].
CoalesceEmpty(«Value Expression» [, «Value Expression»]...)	Coalesces an empty cell value to a number or string and returns the coalesced value.
Correlation(«Set», «Numeric Expression» [, «Numeric Expression»])	Returns the correlation of two numeric expressions across a set.
Count(«Set»[, ExcludeEmpty I IncludeEmpty])	Returns the number of items in the set, including duplicates and optionally empty cells.
Cousin(«Member1», «Member2»)	Returns the child member with the same ordinal index as «Member1» out of «Member2».Children.
Covariance(«Set», «Numeric Expression» [, «Numeric Expression»])	Returns the population covariance of two numeric expressions across a set, using the biased population formula.
CovarianceN(«Set», «Numeric Expression» [, «Numeric Expression»])	Returns the population covariance of two numeric expressions across a set, using the unbiased population formula.
Crossjoin(«Set1», «Set2»)	Returns a set of tuples, each containing every combination of one member from Set1 and one member from Set2. If you want to eliminate combinations with no data, use the NonEmpty-Crossjoin() function instead.
Descendants(«Member», «Level» I «Numeric-Expression»[, «Desc_flags»])	Returns a set containing all the descendants of a given member at a particular level (as specified by name or index). The flags for this function can be used to specify whether all levels between or after the member and the level are returned.
Dimensions(«Numeric Expression» I «String-Expression»)	Returns the dimension in the cube with index number or name provided as a parameter to the function.

Continued on next page

TABLE A.2 CONTINUED: MDX Functions

Function	Description
Distinct(«Set»)	Returns a set containing all unique tuples within that set. Thus, `Distinct({[Customer1], [Customer2], [Customer1])` returns {[Customer1], [Customer2]}.
DistinctCount(«Set»)	Returns the number of items in the set, excluding duplicates. Thus, `DistinctCount({[Customer1], [Customer2], [Customer1])` returns 2.
DrilldownLevel(«Set»[, «Level» | «Index»])	Drills down the members of a set to the next level down from the current level. If «Level» or «Index» are specified, drill down to below the specified level.
DrilldownLevelBottom(«Set», «Count» [, [«Level»][, «Numeric Expression»]])	Drills down the bottom *n* members (based on their values) of a set to the next level down from the current level, where *n* is specified in the «Count» parameter. If «Level» or «Index» are specified, drill down to below the specified level.
DrilldownLevelTop(«Set», «Count» [, [«Level»][, «Numeric Expression»]])	Drills down the top *n* members (based on their values) of a set to the next level down from the current level, where *n* is specified in the «Count» parameter. If «Level» or «Index» are specified, drill down to below the specified level.
DrilldownMember(«Set1», «Set2» [, RECURSIVE])	Drills down the members of Set1 that are present in Set2 to the next level. Where RECURSIVE is specified, repeat the process until the bottom level is reached.
DrilldownMemberBottom(«Set1», «Set2», «Count»[, «Numeric Expression»][, RECURSIVE]])	Drills down the bottom *n* members of Set1 that are present in Set2 to the next level. Where RECURSIVE is specified, repeat the process until the bottom level is reached.
DrilldownMemberTop(«Set1», «Set2», «Count»[, «Numeric Expression»][, RECURSIVE]])	Drills down the top *n* members of Set1 that are present in Set2 to the next level. Where RECURSIVE is specified, repeat the process until the bottom level is reached.
DrillupLevel(«Set»[, «Level»])	Drills up the members of a set until the set contains no members beyond the specified level.
DrillupMember(«Set1», «Set2»)	Drills up the members of Set1 that are present in Set2.
Except(«Set1», «Set2»[, ALL])	Returns the mathematical set difference (i.e., the exclusive OR, or XOR) of the sets specified, including duplicate intersections if the ALL parameter is specified.

TABLE A.2 CONTINUED: MDX Functions

Function	Description
Extract(«Set», «Dimension» [, «Dimension»...])	Returns a set containing each tuple that forms an element of the specified set that is a part of the specified dimension.
Filter(«Set», «Search Condition»)	Returns a set of all items for which the specified search condition returns TRUE.
Generate(«Set1», («Set2» [, ALL]) I («StringExpression»[, «Delimiter»]))	Generates a set based on a function (usually) contained in «Set2», applying the function to Set1. Thus, `Generate ({[Time].[1998], [Time].[1999]}, Head(Descendants(Time.CurrentMember, Month)))` returns the top month from each of 1998 and 1999. Where a string expression is provided in place of Set2, this expression is concatenated together for each element in Set1 (using «Delimiter» to separate the elements) to give a string as a return result.
Head(«Set»[, «Numeric Expression»])	Returns the first *n* items from the given set, where *n* is specified as the Count parameter and defaults to 1.
Hierarchize(«Set»[, POST])	Returns the current set in a hierarchical order, based on the individual members' natural ordering and levels.
Ilf(«Logical Expression», «Value Expression1», «Value Expression2»)	Depending on whether «Logical Expression» evaluates as TRUE or FALSE, returns the contents of «Value Expression1» or «Value Expression2», respectively. Equivalent to the Visual Basic Ilf() function. For example, `IIf([Measures].[Store Sales] > 50000, "On Target", "Below Target")` returns "On Target" where the current member's sales figures are greater than $50,000 and "Below Target" otherwise.
Intersect(«Set1», «Set2»[, ALL])	Returns the mathematical set intersection of the sets specified, including duplicate intersections if the ALL parameter is specified.
IsEmpty(«Value Expression»)	Returns a Boolean value indicating whether the expression contains an empty cell.
LastPeriods(«Index»[, «Member»])	Returns *n* siblings prior to and including the specified member at the same level as that member, where *n* is as specified in the «Index» parameter. If *n* is a negative number, returns siblings after and including the current member.
LinkMember(«Member», «Hierarchy»)	Identifies the equivalent member to the specified member within a different hierarchy.

Continued on next page

TABLE A.2 CONTINUED: MDX Functions

Function	Description
LinRegIntercept(«Set», «Numeric Expression»[, «Numeric Expression»])	Calculates the linear regression (i.e., the straight line on a plotted graph that best matches the trend within the data) for a series of points as a formula $y = ax+b$ and returns the value b.
LinRegPoint(«Numeric Expression», «Set», «Numeric Expression»[, «Numeric-Expression»])	Calculates the linear regression (i.e., the straight line on a plotted graph that best matches the trend within the data) for a series of points as a formula $y = ax+b$ and returns the value y.
LinRegR2(«Set», «Numeric Expression» [, «Numeric Expression»])	Calculates the linear regression (i.e., the straight line on a plotted graph that best matches the trend within the data) for a series of points as a formula $y = ax+b$ and returns the determination coefficient.
LinRegSlope(«Set», «Numeric Expression» [, «Numeric Expression»])	Calculates the linear regression (i.e., the straight line on a plotted graph that best matches the trend within the data) for a series of points as a formula $y = ax+b$ and returns the value a.
LinRegVariance(«Set», «Numeric Expression»[, «Numeric Expression»])	Calculates the linear regression (i.e., the straight line on a plotted graph that best matches the trend within the data) for a series of points as a formula $y = ax+b$ and returns the variance (match) to that line.
LookupCube(«Cube String», «MDX-Expression»)	Returns the value of an MDX expression calculated against a different cube from within the current database.
Max(«Set»[, «Numeric Expression»])	Returns the maximum value for a measure or expression across a set.
Median(«Set»[, «Numeric Expression»])	Returns the median average value for a measure or expression across a set. See also Avg().
Members(«String»)	Returns a set of members specified within the string.
MemberToStr(«Member»)	Converts the specified member to an equivalent string expression.
Min(«Set»[, «Numeric Expression»])	Returns the minimum value for a measure or expression across a set.
Mtd([«Member»])	Returns the "month-to-date" value for the given time-based member. Thus, `Avg(Mtd(),[Measures].[Store Sales])` returns the average sales across the month to date. Same as PeriodsToDate(Month, <<Member>>).

Continued on next page

TABLE A.2 CONTINUED: MDX Functions

Function	Description
NonEmptyCrossjoin(«Set1», «Set2»)	Returns a set of tuples, each containing every combination of one member from Set1 and one member from Set2, excluding any tuple *t* where IsEmpty(*t*) evaluates as TRUE. See also Crossjoin().
OpeningPeriod([«Level»[, «Member»]])	Returns the first descendant member matching the given level that is a sibling of the specified member. Thus, `Opening(Month, [1999])` returns [1999].[Q1].[January].
Order(«Set», «Expression» [,ASC | DESC | BASC | BDESC])	Orders a set based on the specified numeric or string expression. Depending on the flag specified, operates in ascending or descending order, keeping or breaking the set hierarchy.
ParallelPeriod([«Level»[, «Numeric-Expression»[, «Member»]]])	Returns a member from a parallel (usually time-based) period that is the cousin of the given member lagging by *n*, where *n* is the specified numeric expression. Thus, `ParallelPeriod(Year, 2, Time.[1999].June)` returns Time.[1997].June. This function is particularly suitable for comparing year-on-year performance, perhaps in a calculated measure.
PeriodsToDate([«Level»[, «Member»]])	Returns a set of periods (members) from a specified level starting with the first period and ending with a specified member.
Qtd([«Member»])	Returns the "quarter-to-date" value for the given time-based member. Same as PeriodsToDate(Quarter, <<Member>>).
Rank(«Tuple», «Set»)	Returns the location of the specified tuple within the given set as a numeric value starting from 1.
RollupChildren(«Member», «String-Expression»)	Returns a value based on the aggregation of the children of a given member, using the operator specified (+, -, *, /, %, or ~) to roll up the value of each child. Where ~ is specified, the child's value is ignored.
SetToArray(«Set»[, «Set»]...[, «Numeric-Expression»])	Converts the specified set or sets to an equivalent array, for use in an external library function.
SetToStr(«Set»)	Converts the specified set to an equivalent string expression.
Stddev(«Set»[, «Numeric Expression»])	Identical to the Stdev() function.

Continued on next page

TABLE A.2 CONTINUED: MDX Functions

Function	Description
StddevP(«Set»[, «Numeric Expression»])	Identical to the StdevP() function.
Stdev(«Set»[, «Numeric Expression»])	Returns the standard deviation of a numeric expression across a set, using the unbiased population formula.
StdevP(«Set»[, «Numeric Expression»])	Returns the standard deviation of a numeric expression across a set, using the biased population formula.
StripCalculatedMembers(«Set»)	Returns a set containing only "normal" (i.e., non-calculated) members.
StrToMember(«String Expression»)	Returns a member built from the corresponding string expression.
StrToSet(«String Expression»)	Returns a set built from the corresponding string expression.
StrToTuple(«String Expression»)	Returns a tuple built from the corresponding string expression.
StrToValue(«String Expression»)	Returns the numeric value corresponding to the string expression. Roughly equivalent to the Visual Basic Val() function.
Subset(«Set», «Start»[, «Count»])	Returns the subset of a set beginning with zero-based index «Start» and continuing for «Count» items. If «Count» is not specified, continues to the end of the set. This function is a set-based equivalent to the Visual Basic Mid() function. Thus, `Subset({[UK], [France], [Germany]}, 2)` returns {[France], [Germany]}.
Sum(«Set»[, «Numeric Expression»])	Returns the sum value for a measure or expression across a set.
Tail(«Set»[, «Count»])	Returns the last *n* items from the given set, where *n* is specified as the Count parameter and defaults to 1.
ToggleDrillState(«Set1», «Set2» [, RECURSIVE])	Drills down or up the members of Set1 that are present in Set2, depending on whether the appropriate members of Set1 already include descendants. Where RECURSIVE is specified, repeat the process until the bottom level is reached.
TopCount(«Set», «Count»[, «Numeric Expression»])	Returns the top *n* items within a set based on the specified measure or numeric expression, where *n* is specified as the Count parameter.

Continued on next page

TABLE A.2 CONTINUED: MDX Functions

Function	Description
TopPercent(«Set», «Percentage», «Numeric-Expression»)	Returns the top *n* percent of items within a set based on the specified measure or numeric expression, where *n* is specified as the Percentage parameter.
TopSum(«Set», «Value», «Numeric-Expression»)	Returns the smallest set of items that cumulatively total at least *n* within a set (based on the specified measure or numeric expression), where *n* is specified as the sum parameter.
TupleToStr(«Tuple»)	Converts the specified tuple to an equivalent string expression.
Union(«Set1», «Set2»[, ALL])	Returns the mathematical set union of the sets specified, including duplicates if the ALL parameter is specified. Thus, `Union({[Apples], [Pears]}, {[Bananas], [Apples]})` returns {[Apples], [Pears], [Bananas]}.
ValidMeasure(«Tuple»)	Returns a valid measure in a virtual cube by automatically forcing non-available dimensions to return their (All) member value.
Var(«Set»[, «Numeric Expression»])	Returns the sample variance of a numeric expression across a set, using the unbiased population formula.
Variance(«Set»[, «Numeric Expression»])	Identical to the Var() function.
VarianceP(«Set»[, «Numeric Expression»])	Identical to the VarP() function.
VarP(«Set»[, «Numeric Expression»])	Returns the sample variance of a numeric expression across a set, using the biased population formula.
VisualTotals(«Set», «Pattern»)	Returns a dynamically aggregated subtotal for the specified set, using the string expression in «Pattern» to determine the display name for the result.
Wtd([«Member»])	Returns the "week-to-date" value for the given time-based member. Same as PeriodsToDate(Wtd, <<Member>>).
Ytd([«Member»])	Returns the "year-to-date" value for the given time-based member. Thus, `Sum(YTD(),[Measures].[Store Sales])` returns the total sales for the year to date, including the current month. Equivalent to PeriodsToDate(Year, <<Member>>).

Property Reference

Strictly speaking, the properties in Table A.3 are also MDX functions, but they are used in the same way as Visual Basic properties, using an <entity>.<property> syntax, as in the following examples:

```
Products.Dairy.Cheese.Roquefort.UniqueName
Salesforce.Members
[1998].NextMember
```

Some of the properties seem to have little purpose in their own right. For example, the .Name property returns the name of the specified object. Why would you want the name, since you'd have already specified this in the first place? These properties gain their full power when used in combination with other properties. A realistic example of this property is, therefore, the following expression:

```
August.Level.Name
```

which returns the value "Month."

The following table lists the available properties, along with a brief description of their meaning.

NOTE   In this table, the "Operates On" column shows which type of object a property can be used for. D stands for dimension, H stands for hierarchy, L stands for level, M stands for member, S stands for set, and T stands for tuple.

TABLE A.3: MDX Member Properties

Property	Operates On	Description
AllMembers	D, L	Returns a set of all the members and calculated members contained within the specified dimension or level.
Children	M	Returns a set of all the child members for the specified member.
Count	D, L, S, T	Returns a count of the number of dimensions, levels, or items contained within a collection of the specified object.
Current	S	In iterating through a set, returns the current item.
CurrentMember	D	In iterating through a set of dimension members, returns the current member. Used heavily within calculated member statements.
DataMember	M	Returns the data member associated with a non-leaf dimension.
DefaultMember	D, H	Returns the default member for the specified dimension or hierarchy.

Continued on next page

TABLE A.3 CONTINUED: MDX Member Properties

Property	Operates On	Description
Dimension	M, L, H	Returns the dimension to which the specified object belongs.
FirstChild	M	Returns the "first" child (according to the designed order) of the specified member.
FirstSibling	M	Returns the "first" sibling member contained within the level of the specified member.
Hierarchy	M, L	Returns the hierarchy to which the specified member or level belongs.
Ignore	D	In iterating through a set of dimension members, this property forces the specified dimension to be ignored.
Item(«Expression »)	T, S	Returns the nth item of the set or tuple, where n is specified as a parameter to the property. Alternatively (in sets), returns the tuple specified as a string parameter.
Lag(«Numeric Expression»)	M	Returns the sibling n places before or after the specified member within the dimension, where n is specified within the numeric expression. The n value can be a positive or negative number.
LastChild	M	Returns the "last" child (according to the designed order) of the specified member.
LastSibling	M	Returns the "last" sibling member contained within the level of the specified member.
Lead(«Numeric Expression»)	M	Returns the sibling n places after the specified member within the dimension, where n is specified within the numeric expression.
Level	M	Returns the level into which the specified member falls.
Levels(«Expression»)	D	If the parameter expression is a numeric value, returns the level with the ordinal value (i.e., depth) specified. If the parameter expression is a string value, returns the level with the name specified.
Members	D, H, L	Returns the set of child members for the specified object.
Name	D, L, M, H	Returns the name of the specified object as a string.
NextMember	M	Returns the next sibling of the specified member, based on the ordering method specified as part of the dimension design.
Ordinal	L	Returns the index number representing the depth of the specified level, where 0 represents the (All) level.
Parent	M	Returns the parent member of the specified member.
PrevMember	M	Returns the previous sibling of the specified member, based on the ordering method specified as part of the dimension design.

Continued on next page

TABLE A.3 CONTINUED: MDX Member Properties

Property	Operates On	Description
Properties(«Expression»)	M	Returns the member property associated with the expression for the specified member.
Siblings	M	Returns a set containing all the siblings of the specified member (within its level), including the member itself.
UniqueName	D, L, M, H	Returns the single name that uniquely represents the specified object as a string.
Value	M	Returns the value of the specified member. This is the default property of a measure.

MDX Axes

Table A.4 shows how axes can be represented within an MDX query. You can always use the AXIS() numbering to refer to axes. But the first five axes also have special keywords associated with them. See Chapter 6 for examples of using the special keywords.

TABLE A.4: Special Keywords for Named Axes

Dimension	Keyword	Synonym
1	COLUMNS	AXIS(0)
2	ROWS	AXIS(1)
3	PAGES	AXIS(2)
4	SECTIONS	AXIS(3)
5	CHAPTERS	AXIS(4)
6	N/A	AXIS(5)
n	N/A	AXIS(n)

ADO/MD Object Model

One of the important object models for dealing with OLAP data is the ADO/Multi-dimensional (ADO/MD) object model. Figure B.1 shows the object hierarchy exposed by ADO/MD.

FIGURE B.1:

ADO/MD object hierarchy

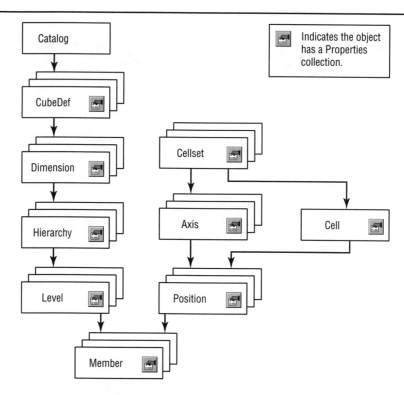

Table B.1 provides thumbnail descriptions for the ADO/MD objects. For more information on using these objects, refer to Chapter 7, "Building Analysis Services Applications with ADO/MD Part I: Cube Schema Objects" and Chapter 8, "Building OLAP Services Applications with ADO/MD Part II: Query Retrieval Objects."

TABLE B.1: ADO/MD Objects

Object	Description
Catalog	This object represents an individual OLAP database connection and can be used to connect to a particular provider. The Catalog object is the highest-level object in the library and provides access to an underlying collection, CubeDefs.
CubeDefs	A collection of CubeDef objects.
CubeDef	Represents an individual OLAP cube and the properties associated with it. Both real and virtual cubes are supported. Each CubeDef object contains a Dimensions collection.
Dimensions	A collection of Dimension objects.
Dimension	Represents a single dimension within a cube. All dimension types are supported, including time dimensions, virtual dimensions, and parent-child dimensions. The measures within a cube are also included as a "special" dimension. Each Dimension object contains a Hierarchies collection.
Hierarchies	A collection of Hierarchy objects.
Hierarchy	Represents a hierarchy within a cube. Hierarchies are used specifically within parent-child dimensions (new in SQL Server 2000) to present an arbitrary number of levels within a relationship. In other dimension types, only one Hierarchy exists within a Hierarchies collection. Each Hierarchy object contains a Levels collection.
Levels	A collection of Level objects.
Level	Represents a specific level within a dimension or hierarchy. Each Level object contains a Members collection.
Members	A collection of Member objects.
Member	Represents an individual point within the cube, which might be an aggregation of a number of underlying members or an individual row descriptor from the fact table itself. A member is the lowest denominator of information and contains no further collections.
Cellset	The multidimensional equivalent of an ADO Recordset, a Cellset contains a number of Cell objects stored across multiple axes. A Cellset can be used to retrieve the results of any MDX query.
Cell	Represents one discrete element of information, together with properties describing its format and other properties.
Axes	A collection of Axis objects.
Axis	Represents an individual axis within the returned cellset (such as columns or rows). Multiple dimensions or levels may be within one axis. Each Axis object contains a Positions collection.
Positions	A collection of Position objects.
Position	Represents a set of one or more members of different dimensions that define a particular point within a given axis.

DSO Object Model

Figure C.1 shows the object hierarchy exposed by DSO.

FIGURE C.1A:

DSO object hierarchy

Continued . . .

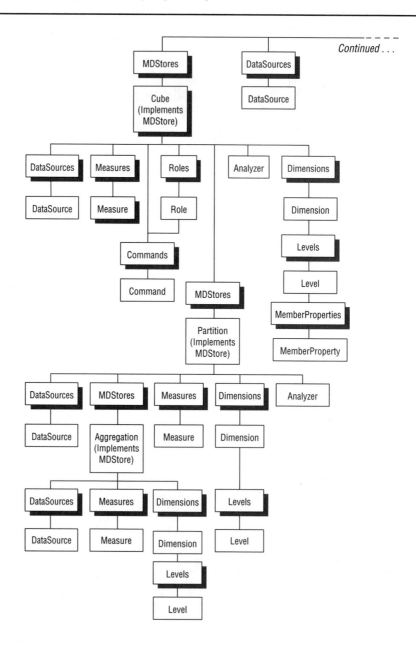

FIGURE C.1B:

DSO object hierarchy

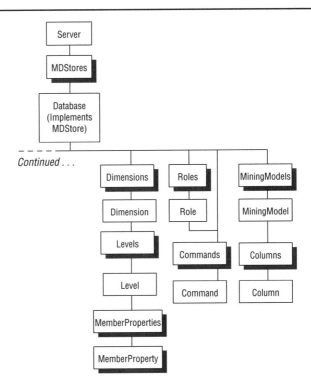

Table C.1 provides thumbnail descriptions for the DSO objects. For more information on using these objects, refer to Chapter 7, "Building Analysis Services Applications with ADO/MD Part I: Cube Schema Objects" and Chapter 10, "Managing an Analysis Services Environment Using DSO."

TABLE C.1: DSO Objects

Object	Description
Server	A single Analysis Services server.
MDStores	A collection of objects that implement the MDStore interface. Depending on the location in the object model, this can be a collection of Database, Cube, Partition, or Aggregation objects.
Database	An Analysis Services database.
Cube	A single OLAP cube.
Measures	A collection of Measure objects.
Measure	A measure within a cube.
DataSources	A collection of DataSource objects.

Continued on next page

TABLE C.1 CONTINUED: DSO Objects

Object	Description
DataSource	A source of data for Analysis Services.
Dimensions	A collection of Dimension objects.
Dimension	A single shared or private dimension.
Levels	A collection of Level objects.
Level	A level within a dimension.
MemberProperties	A collection of MemberProperty objects.
MemberProperty	A member property attached to a level.
Roles	A collection of Role objects.
Role	A security role for a cube.
Commands	A collection of Command objects.
Command	A calculated member or named set.
Analyzer	A representation of the algorithm used to choose aggregations to be precalculated.
Aggregation	A precalculated aggregation.
MiningModels	A collection of MiningModel objects.
MiningModel	A data mining model.
Columns	A collection of Column objects.
Column	An input or output column within a data mining model.

English Query Object Model

Figure D.1 shows the object hierarchy exposed by English Query.

FIGURE D.1:

English Query object
hierarchy

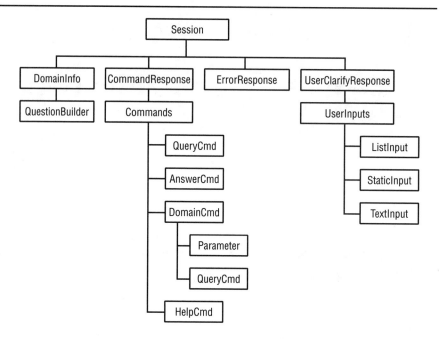

Table D.1 provides thumbnail descriptions for the English Query objects. For more information on using these objects, refer to Chapter 12, "Supporting Natural Language Queries with English Query."

TABLE D.1: English Query Objects

Object	Description
Session	An English Query application
DomainInfo	An English Query model of a particular domain of information
QuestionBuilder	The Question Builder interface
CommandResponse	One or more SQL or MDX commands to be executed
Commands	Collection of QueryCmd, AnswerCmd, DomainCmd, and HelpCmd objects
QueryCmd	A query to be executed against a database
AnswerCmd	The answer to a question that doesn't require database information
DomainCmd	A query translated into English Query syntax
HelpCmd	Help for an entity or relationship within an English Query application
Parameter	A value or field within a DomainCmd object

Continued on next page

TABLE D.1 CONTINUED: English Query Objects

Object	Description
ErrorResponse	An error returned by the English Query engine
UserClarifyResponse	One or more requests for clarification from the user
UserInputs	Collection of ListInput, StaticInput, and TextInput objects
ListInput	A list of choices for the user to select from
StaticInput	Static text to be displayed to the user
TextInput	Freeform text to be input by the user

INDEX

Note to the reader: Throughout this index **boldfaced** page numbers indicate primary discussions of a topic. *Italicized* page numbers indicate illustrations.

SYMBOLS

^ (caret), for private dimension, 328

A

Access database
    for Analysis Services Repository, 135
    for metadata, 32
Action Wizard, 121
actions, CREATE ACTION statement (MDX), **183**
Active Directory, registering Analysis Services server with, 135
ActiveConnection property
    for Catalog object, 196, 199
    for Cellset object, 197, 241, 242
ActiveX Control Interface Wizard, 214
ActiveX controls, 212
ActiveX Data Objects. *See* ADO (ActiveX Data Objects)
Add-Ins menu (Visual Basic), ➤ ActiveX Control Interface Wizard, 214
Add method of OlapCollection object, 306
AddCalculatedMembers function (MDX), 417
additive measures, 58
additive values, 18
AddNew method
    of DataSources collection, 314
    on MDStores collection, 311
    for measure, 331
    for member properties, 328–329
    of OlapCollection object, 306
administrator security, **129**
ADO (ActiveX Data Objects), 27, 33
    and Analysis Services, **188**
    Data Control, 81
ADO/MD (ActiveX Data Objects/Multidimensional), 33–35, 53, 188
    Dimension View control, **211–237**, *212*
        creating project, **214–215**

        design, **213–214**
        drilling down object model, **224–232**
        events and properties, **219–224**
        initialization, **215–219**
        using, **233–237**
    DSO (Decision Support Objects) vs., **189**, 303
    object model, **189–193**, *192*, *240*, *430*, **430–1**
    OLAP Workbench to display functionality, *249*, 249–267
    PivotTable Service, **193–194**
    query retrieval objects, **240–248**, 431
        Axis object, **246–247**
        Cell object, **245**
        Cellset object, **241–244**
        Member object, **248**
        Position object, **247**
    schema objects, **194–211**, 431
        Catalog object, **198–199**
        Connection object, **194–198**
        CubeDef object, **199–204**
        Dimension object, **204–206**
        Hierarchy object, **206–207**
        Level object, **207–209**
        Member object, **209–211**
age range, birth date vs., 46
Aggregate function (MDX), 417
Aggregate Function property of measure, 111
AggregateFunction property of DSO Measure object, 331
Aggregation object in DSO, 436
Aggregation Prefix property of cube, 110
Aggregation Usage property of dimensions, 112
aggregations, 58
    choosing options, 71
    exponential growth, **23–24**
    using DSO, **333–337**
ALIGNMENT property, 175
All Caption property of dimensions, 112
All Level property of dimensions, 112
All Member Formula property of dimensions, 112
AllMembers property, 425

B

C

D

J

K

L

N

Q

About the CD

This book's companion CD contains the following:

- All of the sample code and applications from the book, including the complete OLAP Workbench application from Chapter 8

- The data for the sample SQL Server databases used in the book examples, together with instructions for loading this data to your own SQL Server

- Instructions for creating the CallsCube OLAP cube used in the examples for Chapter 6

- Internet links to OLAP tool vendors and other useful web sites

- An evaluation version of ProClarity Corporation's ProClarity

- "The Cognos-Microsoft Solution," a white paper from Cognos

- An evaluation version of Hungry Dog Software's IntelliBrowser

To use the CD content, just insert it into your CD-ROM drive. The CD's installation program should launch automatically. If you've turned off AutoPlay, you can open the file readme.htm in the root directory of the CD to get started.